A Guide to Conquering the COMPASS Mathematics Placement Test

ANTHONY E. CLEMENT, PH. D.
Brooklyn College

STEPHEN MAJEWICZ, PH. D.
Kingsborough Community College

Custom Publishing

New York Boston San Francisco
London Toronto Sydney Tokyo Singapore Madrid
Mexico City Munich Paris Cape Town Hong Kong Montreal

Cover Art: *Roof*, by Barry Cronin.

Printed in the United States of America

10 9 8 7 6 5 4 3 2

2009360521

MP

**Pearson
Custom Publishing**
is a division of

www.pearsonhighered.com

ISBN 10: 0-558-37681-9
ISBN 13: 978-0-558-37681-9

Introduction

"A Guide to Conquering the COMPASS Mathematics Placement Test" is self-contained and covers topics (Prealgebra and Algebra) often encountered on the COMPASS Mathematics Placement Test. It is designed solely on preparing students to pass the COMPASS Mathematics Placement Test.

The text is written with the student in mind. Therefore, it offers an uncomplicated approach for ease of comprehension. It gives an account of the materials covered on the COMPASS test, which is then reinforced by lots of follow-up examples that illustrate the rules. The guide uses standard as well as alternative techniques that help students "get it". A skeleton of this text has been used by one of the authors' students with great success. Thus, this finished and more "polished" version would be of invaluable help for all students preparing to take the COMPASS Mathematics Placement Test. The text can be used for a fast paced Immersion Program as well as for an entire semester course.

Each chapter is divided into several sections. Each section contains numerous worked out examples, thus re-enforcing the material learned in that section. Sometimes the examples given stress different solutions, thus students can see different ways of looking at certain problems. At the end of each section, exercises are also given based on the topics covered. It is advised that all students take some time to go through each section to make sure that they understand the fundamentals.

In the multiple-choice questions, different answers, which have been carefully selected, are offered so that students can learn from them and avoid pitfalls on the actual test. The answers to all exercises and practice tests are given at the end of the book. One of the key principles to conquering the COMPASS Mathematics Placement Test is to practice questions repeatedly. The practice tests at the back of the book are "gems", uniquely developed after years continuous revision. They cover topics *often* encountered on the COMPASS test. These practice tests can be used as a *quick guide* in preparing for the actual test. We recommend that students redo these tests several times until they get every question correct. However, it should be noted that students should read the *entire textbook and do all exercises* before attempting to do these practice tests.

Table of Contents

Chapter 1:   Natural Numbers, Whole Numbers, and Integers

Section A.   Natural Numbers, Whole Numbers; Arithmetic of Whole Numbers

In this section, we discuss the arithmetic of whole numbers. We begin by reviewing some elementary facts about the number system.

The Natural Numbers (or Counting Numbers) are the numbers   1, 2, 3, ...

These are just the numbers which we use to count with. The three dots (ellipsis) after the comma indicates that this set of numbers continues without ever ending. Notice that the pattern which occurs in the set is 'add 1 to get the next element'. Hence, the next three numbers in the set will be 4, 5, and 6. Whenever you see the ellipsis, look for a pattern for which the numbers in the set satisfy.

The Whole Numbers are the numbers   0, 1, 2, 3, ...

The **digits** of a number are named in a certain way, from right to left. For example, in the number 718,294, there are 4 ones, 9 tens, 2 hundreds, 8 thousands, 1 ten thousands, and 7 hundred thousands. Notice that we can **expand** 718,294 as

$$700,000 + 10,000 + 8,000 + 200 + 90 + 4.$$

Example 1. Write the number 28,031 in words. Expand the number.

Solution: Twenty-eight thousand, thirty-one. The expansion of 28,031 is $20,000 + 8,000 + 30 + 1$.

Addition of Whole Numbers

The symbol that is used for addition is '+'. We read '$a + b$' as 'a plus b'.

Note: We will use the term "set up top and bottom" to mean align numbers in columns from the top to the bottom.

Rule for adding whole numbers: Set up top and bottom. Put ones under ones, tens under tens, hundreds under hundreds etc. From right to the left, add the numbers in each column, carrying "1" over to the next column on the left each time for every multiple of 10 and placing those less than 10 in their corresponding columns.

1

Example 2. Add.

1) $22 + 19$ 2) $187 + 814$ 3) $268 + 19 + 8,955$

Solution:

1)
$$\begin{array}{r} 22 \\ + 19 \\ \hline 41 \end{array}$$

2)
$$\begin{array}{r} 187 \\ + 814 \\ \hline 1,001 \end{array}$$

3)
$$\begin{array}{r} 268 \\ 19 \\ + 8,955 \\ \hline 9,242 \end{array}$$

The Commutative Property for Addition: $a + b = b + a$.

For example, $5 + 9 = 9 + 5$.

The Associative Property for Addition: $(a + b) + c = a + (b + c)$.

For example, $(8 + 2) + 7 = 8 + (2 + 7)$

Subtraction of Whole Numbers

The symbol that is used for subtraction is '$-$'. We read '$a - b$' as 'a minus b' or 'subtract b from a'. In this section it is important to note that we will be subtracting smaller valued whole numbers from larger valued whole numbers.

Rule for subtracting whole numbers: Set up top and bottom. Put ones under ones, tens under tens, hundreds under hundreds, etc. From right to the left, subtract the numbers in each column, borrowing "1" from the next column on the left each time we are subtracting a larger number from a smaller number.

Example 3. Subtract.

1) $653 - 405$ 2) $1,350 - 689$ 3) $4,003 - 1,754$

Solution:

1)
$$\begin{array}{r} 653 \\ - 405 \\ \hline 248 \end{array}$$

2)
$$\begin{array}{r} 1350 \\ - 689 \\ \hline 661 \end{array}$$

3)
$$\begin{array}{r} 4,003 \\ - 1,754 \\ \hline 2,249 \end{array}$$

Multiplication of Whole Numbers

There are various ways to write 'a multiplied by b', 'the product of a and b', or just simply 'a times b': $a \times b$, $a \cdot b$, ab, $a(b)$, $(a)b$, and $(a)(b)$. In each of these products, we call a and b the **factors** of the product.

Rule for multiplying whole numbers: To multiply two numbers, set up top and bottom. Put ones under ones, tens under tens, hundreds under hundreds, etc.

1) Take the bottom number, multiply the digit in its ones column by the top number, carrying "1" over to the next column on the left each time for every multiple of 10 and placing the results less than 10 in their corresponding columns.

2) Multiply the digit in the tens column of the bottom number by the top number, repeating the above procedure similar to that of the digit in its ones column. Put this second product shifted one place to the left, under the first product.

3) Repeat this procedure for the digit in the hundreds column, etc., each time shifting the products one place to the left.

4) Add the corresponding columns.

Example 4. Multiply.

1) 35×16 2) $182(9)$ 3) $6,031 \cdot 572$

Solution:

$$
\begin{array}{r}
35 \\
\times\ 16 \\
\hline
210 \\
+\ 35 \\
\hline
560
\end{array}
\qquad
\begin{array}{r}
182 \\
\times\ 9 \\
\hline
1,638
\end{array}
\qquad
\begin{array}{r}
6,031 \\
\times\ 572 \\
\hline
12062 \\
42217 \\
+\ 30155 \\
\hline
3449732 = 3,449,732
\end{array}
$$

Next we mention some properties of multiplication.

The Commutative Property for Multiplication: $a \times b = b \times a$

For example, $6 \times 14 = 14 \times 6$.

Associative Property for Multiplication: $(a \times b) \times c = a \times (b \times c)$

For example, $(9 \times 11) \times 2 = 9 \times (11 \times 2)$.

Distributive Property: $a(b + c) = ab + ac$

For example, $7(3 + 16) = 7(3) + 7(16)$.

Division of Whole Numbers

As with multiplication, we may write 'a divided by b' in various ways: $a \div b$, $\frac{a}{b}$, or $b\overline{)a}$. We call 'a' the dividend and 'b' the divisor. Recall that when you divide a whole number by a smaller whole number, you obtain a **quotient** and sometimes a **remainder** (R).

For example, when we divide 18 by 3, we obtain the quotient 6. When we divide 22 by 5, the quotient is 4 and the remainder is 2.

Rule for dividing whole numbers:

1) Put the divisor to the left and the dividend to the right of the division sign. Pair up the divisor and the dividend.

2) Find how many whole numbers you get when the dividend is divided by the divisor.

3) Take the product of that whole number (quotient) and the divisor.

4) Subtract this product from the paired part of the dividend. Carry down the digit on the immediate right of paired part of the dividend, and put it on the right of the subtracted result.

5) Take that resulting new number and find how many whole numbers you get when it is divided by the divisor.

6) Repeat the above procedure until you exhaust all the numbers in the dividend.

Example 5. Divide.

1) $5,544 \div 8$　　　　2) $7,106 \div 35$　　　　3) $\dfrac{38,159}{208}$

Solution:

1)
```
         693
    8) 5544
     - 48
       ────
        74
      - 72
       ────
        24
      - 24
       ────
         0
```

2)
```
          203 R 1
    35) 7106
      - 70
       ────
       106
     - 105
       ────
         1
```

3)
```
           183 R 95
    208) 38159
       - 208
        ─────
         1735
       - 1664
        ─────
          719
        - 624
         ────
           95
```

Exercises: Chapter 1, Section A

In Exercises 1 - 11, add.

1. $456 + 909$

2. $989 + 245$

3. $670 + 327$

4. $3,451 + 5698$

5. $6,712 + 4409$

6. $4,986 + 6,782$

7. $47,456 + 710,098$

8. $40,998 + 39,076$

9. $20,989 + 621,198$

10. $347 + 419 =$
(a) 765   (b) 746   (c) 756   (d) 766   (e) 767

11. $3,499 + 45,674 =$
(a) 48,074   (b) 49,173   (c) 48,173   (d) 48,073   (e) 48,003

In Exercises 12 - 22, subtract.

12. $405 - 29$

13. $608 - 535$

14. $925 - 326$

15. $5,114 - 4,445$

16. $3,211 - 3,099$

17. $2,008 - 1,917$

18. $34,011 - 8,045$

19. $80,009 - 20,933$

20. $51,101 - 49,033$

21. $437 - 259 =$
(a) 238   (b) 278   (c) 178   (d) 222   (e) 78

22. $39,207 - 23,492 =$
(a) 16,295   (b) 15,515   (c) 15,705   (d) 15,295   (e) 15,715

In Exercises 23 - 33, multiply.

23. 30×9

24. 93×24

25. 60×34

26. 341×406 27. 622×539 28. 953×275

29. $20,098 \times 609$ 30. $43,346 \times 123$ 31. $23,304 \times 2406$

32. $67 \times 25 =$
(a) $13,738$ (b) $1,575$ (c) $1,675$ (d) $1,625$ (e) 499

33. $392 \times 234 =$
(a) $91,728$ (b) $95,345$ (c) $90,728$ (d) $80,728$ (e) $91,628$

In Exercises 34 - 44, divide.

34. $56 \div 4$ 35. $819 \div 3$ 36. $2,045 \div 5$

37. $4,214 \div 14$ 38. $224,096 \div 32$ 39. $480,064 \div 16$

40. $9,048,143 \div 104$ 41. $642,144 \div 511$ 42. $450,314 \div 422$

43. $760,125 \div 25 =$
(a) 305 (b) $3,045$ (c) 350 (d) $30,405$ (e) 35

44. $616,080 \div 204 =$
(a) $3,020$ (b) 302 (c) $3,002$ (d) 320 (e) 32

6

Section B. Integers; Number Lines, Inequalities, and Absolute Value

__The Integers__ or __the Signed Numbers__ are the numbers ..., −2, −1, 0, +1, +2, +3,....

An integer is formed by taking a whole number and putting a **sign** (either a **negative sign** '−' or a **positive sign** '+') in front of it. Notice that the number 0 has no sign. If an integer has a '−' sign, we call it a **negative integer**. If an integer has a '+' sign, we call it a **positive integer**.

For example, −3, −11 and −7 **are** negative integers, whereas +1, +9 and +16 are positive integers. Whenever we have a positive integer, we may omit the '+' sign. For example, +5 = 5 and 9 = +9.

Integers arise in the real world. For example, a bank account with +$200 means that you have $200 in the bank, whereas an account with −$200 means that you owe $200 to the bank. Notice that $0 means that you have no money in the bank and you owe no money to the bank.

Another example of integers being used appears when talking about the weather. If you've taken a basic chemistry course, you know that the freezing temperature of water (in Celsius) is $0°C$. If you take the temperature of a liquid and its measurement is below the value zero, say $10°C$ below the zero, we say that the temperature is $10°C$ below zero and write this temperature as $−10°C$. On the other hand, if the temperature is above the value zero, say $35°C$ above the 0, we say that the temperature is $35°C$ above zero (or just $35°C$) and write this temperature as $35°C$.

Number Lines and Inequalities

We can visualize the integers using a number line. To do so, we draw a line (which we will draw horizontally) and label the integers on it as follows:

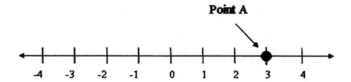

Each integer corresponds to a point on the line. We say that the integer is the **coordinate** of the point on the line which it corresponds to and we call the point the **graph** of the integer. For example, the point labelled A on the line above has coordinate 3 and point A is the graph of 3. Notice that the integers have been placed on the number line in increasing order from left to right (recall that a negative integer is always smaller than a positive integer). We call the number 0 the **origin**.

We can use the number line to compare the sizes of two numbers, say a and b. Since the number line is constructed in such a way that the numbers get larger from left to right, we can find the location of a and b on it and see which of the two is on the right-hand side of the other. The number on the right is always larger than the number on the left. When comparing two numbers, we use one of the **inequality symbols**, written as either > or <. The expression $a < b$ is read "a is **less than** b"

and the expression $a > b$ is read "a is **greater than** b". If the two numbers are equal, we use the **equality symbol** = and write $a = b$..

Example 1. Fill in the space with the inequality symbol < or >.
1) 7 __ −16   2) −17 __ −9   3) 3 __ −8

Solution: 1) 7 > −16   2) −17 < −9   3) 3 > −8

Two integers whose distances are the same from zero on the number line are called **additive inverses** of each other. For example, −5 and 5 are additive inverses of each other and −2 and 2 are additive inverses of each other.

Notice that when we put a negative sign in front of a negative integer, we get a positive integer. We will explain the rules for this later on. For example, −(−9) = 9 and −(−16) = 16.

Absolute Value

The **absolute value** of an integer n, written as $|n|$, is the distance between 0 to n on the number line. For example, $|-2| = 2$ because −2 is 2 units from 0 on the number line, and $|4| = 4$ because 4 is 4 units from 0 on the number line.

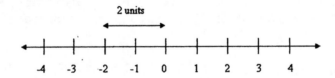

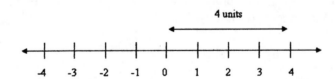

Rule for absolute value: The absolute value of a positive number is always the number, and the absolute value of a negative number is always the number excluding its negative sign.

Example 2. Find the absolute value.
1) |3| 2) |−5| 3) |0|

Solution: 1) |3| = 3   2) |−5| = 5   3) |0| = 0

8

Exercises: Chapter 1, Section B

In Exercises 1 - 8, place <, >, or = in the space provided to make the statement true.

1. 4 __ 7   2. 4 __ – 4   3. 9 __ 4 + 5   4. –12 __ 11

5. –6 __ –5   6. –31 __ –32   7. – 45 __ 14   8. – 156 __ –303

9. If $n < -54$, what number could n be?
(a) –53   (b) –25   (c) –60   (d) 54   (e) 60

10. If $n > -4$, what number could n be?
(a) 0   (b) –4   (c) –15   (d) –5   (e) –6

In Exercises 11 - 13, arrange the numbers from smallest to largest.

11. 5, 0, –3, 4, –5   12. 0, –4, 5, 3, 1, –2, 6   13. –2, 1, –1, 3, –3, 2, –5

In Exercises 14 - 17, find the additive inverse of each.

14. 45   15. –34   16. –12   17. –(–59)

In Exercises 18 - 20, evaluate.

18. |–94| 19. |–1| 20. |31|

In Exercises 21 - 24, place <, >, or = in the space provided to make the statement true.

21. |–3| __ |3| 22. |–3| __ |–4| 23. |10| __ |–9| 24. – |10| __ |–9|

9

Section C. Arithmetic of Integers

Addition of Integers of the Same Sign

Rule for adding two or more integers of the same sign:
1) Take the absolute values of the numbers.
2) Add the results together.
3) The sign of the answer is the same as the original signs of the numbers.

Note that the sum of two positive numbers is **always** positive, and the sum of two negative numbers is **always** negative.

Example 1. Add.
1) $(+5) + (+7)$ 2) $19 + 28$ 3) $(-6) + (-7)$ 4) $(-32) + (-405) + (-604)$

Solution: 1) $(+5) + (+7) = +12$ 2) $19 + 28 = 47$
        3) $(-6) + (-7) = -13$ 4) $(-32) + (-405) + (-604) = -1,041.$

Addition of Integers of Different Signs

Rule for adding two integers of different signs:
1) Take the absolute values of the numbers.
2) Subtract the smaller number from the **larger** number.
3) The sign of the answer is the same as the original sign of the **larger** number in (2).

Example 2. Add.
1) $-2 + 6$ 2) $-10 + 7$ 3) $(+23) + (-17)$ 4) $(-12) + 12$

Solution:
1) $|-2| = 2$ and $|6| = 6$. Now, $6 - 2 = 4$ and the original sign of the larger number, 6, is positive. Therefore, $-2 + 6 = 4$.

2) $|-10| = 10$ and $|7| = 7$. Now, $10 - 7 = 3$ and the original sign of the larger number, 10, is negative. Therefore, $-10 + 7 = -3$.

3) $|+23| = 23$ and $|-17| = 17$. Since $23 - 17 = 6$ and the original sign of the larger number, 23, is positive. Therefore, $(+23) + (-17) = +6$.

4) $|-12| = 12$ and $|12| = 12$. Now $12 - 12 = 0$, $(-12) + 12 = 0$. Notice that -12 and 12 are additive inverses of each other.

If you want to add more than two integers of different signs, the easiest way is to first collect the negative numbers together and the positive numbers together. This can be done by the Commutative

10

Property for Addition (this works for integers as well as for whole numbers). Next, add the negative numbers, add the positive numbers, then combine the two sums.

Example 3. Add: $-28 + 16 + 51 + (-43) + (+29)$

Solution: $-28 + 16 + 51 + (-43) + (+29) = \underbrace{-28 + (-43)}_{-71} + \underbrace{16 + 51 + 29}_{96} = 25$

Subtraction of Integers

Recall we write $a - b$ to mean subtract b from a.

Rule for subtraction of two integers:
1) Set up top and bottom. The number after "from" goes at the top and the number after "subtract" goes at the bottom.
2) Change the sign of the bottom and <u>add</u> that result to the top.

Note: $a - b = a + (-b)$ and $a - (-b) = a + b$.

Example 4. 1) Subtract: $3 - 14$ 2) Subtract: $-9 - 12$ 3) Subtract -19 from -13.

Solution: 1) $3 - 14 = 3 + (-14) = -11$ 2) $-9 - 12 = -9 + (-12) = -21$

$$
\begin{array}{llll}
3) & \begin{array}{r} -13 \\ -\ \underline{-19} \end{array} \text{ (top)} & \text{becomes} & \begin{array}{r} -13 \\ +\ \underline{19} \\ +6 \end{array} \text{ (top)} \\
& \quad\quad\quad \text{ (bottom)} & & \quad\quad\quad \text{ (bottom)}
\end{array}
$$

Therefore, if we subtract -19 from -13 the answer is 6.

Observe that we can interpret 1) as "subtract $+14$ from $+3$" and 2) as "subtract $+12$ from -9", then use the subtraction rule above.

Multiplication of Integers

It is *imperative* for students to learn the multiplication tables before attempting to learn the rules.

Rules for multiplication: The product of numbers of the same sign always gives a positive answer, and the product of numbers of different signs always gives a negative answer:

1) Positive × Positive = Positive   2) Negative × Negative = Positive
3) Positive × Negative = Negative   4) Negative × Positive = Negative

Example 5. Multiply.
1) $(-6)(+8)$ 2) $2(-9)$ 3) $(-7)(-5)$ 4) $(+9)(-3)(2)$

Solution: 1) $(-6)(+8) = -48$ 2) $2(-9) = -18$
            3) $(-7)(-5) = 35$ 4) $(+9)(-3)(2) = -54$

Division of Integers

Recall we write $a \div b$ to mean "a divided by b" (the number on the *left* is divided by the number on the *right*) as $\frac{a}{b}$ which we call "the quotient of a and b".

Rules for division: The quotient of numbers of the same sign always gives a positive answer, and the quotient of numbers of different signs always gives a negative answer:

1) Positive ÷ Positive = Positive   2) Negative ÷ Negative = Positive
3) Positive ÷ Negative = Negative   4) Negative ÷ Positive = Negative

Example 6. Divide.
1) $(-10) \div (-2)$ 2) $(-48) \div 8$ 3) $72 \div (-9)$
4) $\frac{-24}{+4}$ 5) $\frac{+74}{+2}$ 6) $\frac{-120}{-10}$

Solution: 1) $(-10) \div (-2) = 5$ 2) $(-48) \div 8 = -6$ 3) $72 \div (-9) = -8$

        4) $\frac{-24}{+4} = -6$ 5) $\frac{+74}{+2} = 37$ 6) $\frac{-120}{-10} = 12$

Exercises: Chapter 1, Section C

In Exercises 1 - 11, add.

1. $46 + 99$

2. $(-89) + (-45)$

3. $(-676) + (-357)$

4. $451 + 568$

5. $(-12) + 44$

6. $(-86) + 8$

7. $(-560) + 710$

8. $498 + (-376)$

9. $(-989) + 900$

10. $(-397) + (-919) =$
(a) -612 (b) -522 (c) $1,316$ (d) 522 (e) $-1,316$

11. $3,990 + (-4,574) =$
(a) 584 (b) -584 (c) $8,564$ (d) $-8,564$ (e) -524

In Exercises 12 - 22, subtract.

12. $45 - 56$

13. $68 - 55$

14. $-5 - 326$

15. $-114 - (-445)$

16. $211 - (-359)$

17. $768 - 917$

18. $-3,711 - 845$

19. $809 - 2,033$

20. $561 - 4,433$

21. $(-437) - (-259) =$
(a) 588 (b) 178 (c) -178 (d) 696 (e) -696

22. $7,307 - (-492) =$
(a) $-7,799$ (b) $6,815$ (c) $-6,815$ (d) $7,799$ (e) $15,715$

In Exercises 23 - 33, multiply.

23. 34×8

24. $5 \times (-45)$

25. $(-6)14$

26. $(-31)(-6)$ 27. -22×59 28. -93×25

29. $98 \times (-69)$ 30. $346 \times (-13)$ 31. $(-2,304)(-606)$

32. $-79 \times (-23) =$
(a) 1,817   (b) 1,697   (c) 1,675   (d) 1,871   (e) 237

33. $(32)(-24) =$
(a) 728   (b) −768   (c) 718   (d) 768   (e) 687

In Exercises 34 - 44, divide.

34. $65 \div 5$ 35. $-519 \div 3$ 36. $-210 \div (-15)$

37. $2,432 \div (-16)$ 38. $-4,500 \div 18$ 39. $-8,580 \div 132$

40. $15,038 \div (-146)$ 41. $(-29,125) \div (-233)$ 42. $450,314 \div 412$

43. $-12,250 \div 35 =$
(a) 35   (b) 30   (c) 350   (d) −350   (e) −35

44. $(-30,752) \div (-124) =$
(a) −24   (b) 24   (c) 248   (d) 25   (e) −248

Section D. Positive Exponents and the Order of Operations

Positive Exponents

If you want to write a product of a number by itself numerous times, a convenient way to do so is by using exponents. For example, the product $7 \times 7 \times 7 \times 7$ can be written as 7^4. We read this as '7 raised to the 4th power'. The number 7 is the **base** of the expression and 4 is called the **exponent**.

Rule: If a is any integer and n is a natural number, then $\underbrace{a \cdot a \cdot a \cdots a}_{n \text{ factors}} = a^n$.

If the exponent is 1, then $a^1 = a$.

Example 1. Evaluate.
1) 6^2 2) 2^4 3) 7^1 4) -3^3 5) $(-2)^3$

Solution: 1) $6^2 = 6 \times 6 = 36$ 2) $2^4 = 2 \times 2 \times 2 \times 2 = 16$ 3) $7^1 = 7$

4) $-(3^3) = -(27) = -27$ 5) $\underbrace{(-2)(-2)}_{4} (-2) = (4)(-2) = -8$

Order of Operations

Whenever you have to do a computation involving several arithmetic operations, there is a specific order that you need to follow in order to evaluate the expression. This order 1 through 4 below is known as the **order of operations**.

1. Start by doing any operations in **parenthesis**, beginning with the innermost and working outward.

2. Next work out any **exponentiation**.

3. Perform any **multiplications** and **divisions** from left to right (whichever ones come first).

4. Perform any **additions** and **subtractions** from left to right (whichever ones come first).

To help you remember this ordering, it is useful to remember the initials **PEMDAS**, where P is **parenthesis**, E is **exponentiation**, M is **multiplication**, D is **division**, A is **addition** and S is **subtraction**. A phrase that students sometimes remember with the same initials is

Please Excuse My Dear Aunt Sally.

Note the symbol " $\overleftrightarrow{}$ " at the top of MD and AS means that the order between multiplication and division is interchangeable and the order between addition and subtraction is interchangeable. For example, from left to right, if multiplication comes before division, do multiplication before division and if division comes before multiplication, do division before multiplication.

Example 2 . Evaluate.

1) $4(3) + 7$ 2) $4(3 + 7)$ 3) $5 - 6 \times 3$ 4) $(5 - 6) \times 3$

5) $(-6) + 12 \div 3$ 6) $(-6 + 12) \div 3$ 7) $(5 - 7)^2 + 16$ 8) $-23 - 4 + 18$

9) $-23 - (4 + 18)$ 10) $45 \div 9 \cdot 2 \div 10 \cdot 9$

11) $(-3 - 1)(-4 + 12) - 5 \times 6$ 12) $6^2 - (1 + 3)^2 \times 3 + 8$

13) $5 + 2\{3 - 7(10 - 12)\}$

Solution:

1) $\underbrace{4(3)}_{12} + 7 = 12 + 7 = 19$ 2) $4\underbrace{(3 + 7)}_{10} = 4(10) = 40$

3) $5 - \underbrace{6 \times 3}_{18} = 5 - 18 = -13$ 4) $\underbrace{(5 - 6)}_{-1} \times 3 = (-1) \times 3 = -3$

5) $(-6) + \underbrace{12 \div 3}_{4} = (-6) + 4 = -2$ 6) $\underbrace{(-6 + 12)}_{6} \div 3 = 6 \div 3 = 2$

7) $\underbrace{(5 - 7)^2}_{-2} + 16 = \underbrace{(-2)^2}_{4} + 16 = 4 + 16 = 20$

8) $\underbrace{-23 - 4}_{-27} + 18 = -27 + 18 = -9$

9) $-23 - \underbrace{(4 + 18)}_{22} = -23 - 22 = -45$

10) $\underbrace{45 \div 9}_{5} \cdot 2 \div 10 \cdot 9 = \underbrace{5 \cdot 2}_{10} \div 10 \cdot 9 = \underbrace{10 \div 10}_{1} \cdot 9 = 1 \cdot 9 = 9$

11) $\underbrace{(-3 - 1)}_{-4}\underbrace{(-4 + 12)}_{8} - 5 \times 6 = \underbrace{(-4)(8)}_{-32} - 5 \times 6 = -32 - \underbrace{5 \times 6}_{30} = -32 - 30 = -62$

12) $\underbrace{6^2}_{36} - \underbrace{(1 + 3)^2}_{4} \times 3 + 8 = 36 - \underbrace{4^2}_{16} \times 3 + 8 = 36 - \underbrace{16 \times 3}_{48} + 8 = \underbrace{36 - 48}_{-12} + 8 = -12 + 8 = -4$

13) $5 + 2\{3 - 7(10 - 12)\} = 5 + 2\{3 - 7(-2)\} = 5 + 2\{3 + 14\} = 5 + 2\{17\} = 5 + 34 = 39$

Exercises: Chapter 1, Section D

In Exercises 1 - 28, evaluate.

1. 8^2 2. 2^5 3. -6^3 4. $(-5)^3$

5. -1^3 6. $(-1)^6$ 7. $(-8)^3$ 8. $9(8) + 5$

9. $7 - 8 \times 5$ 10. $(-9) + 90 \div 30$ 11. $(-12 + 22) \div 5$

12. $(9 - 1)^2 + 106$ 13. $-163 - 9 + 45$ 14. $-97 - (14 + 18)$

15. $72 \div 8 \cdot 9 \div 3 \cdot 3$ 16. $(-13 - 11) + (-7 + 34) - 6 \times 8$ 17. $2^2 - (10 + 4)^2 \times 9 + 30$

18. $34 + 22\{6 - 16(12 - 35)\}$ 19. $(-2)(3) - 1(18 \div 9 - 10 \times 2) + 5$

20. $3^2 - 4(10 - 4) \times 9 + 30$ 21. $1 - (-1)^8$ 22. $\dfrac{-2 + 5(3 + 7)}{15 - 3^2}$

23. $(8 + 2)^2 \div 5 \times 100 \div 10 \times 10 + 4 - 8$ 24. $9^2 - 2(6 \div 3 - 80 \times 4) - 50$

25. $(7)(-2) + \dfrac{48 + 3(3 - 7)}{10 - 2^2} =$

(a) 4   (b) -6   (c) 20   (d) -8   (e) 6

26. $7^2 - 2(18 \div 3 - 11 \times 4) - 5 =$
(a) 120   (b) 49   (c) 24   (d) -32   (e) -49

27. $(8 + 2)^2 \div 10 \times 10 \times 10 \div 10 + 10 =$
(a) 110   (b) 1,010   (c) 1,100   (d) 100   (e) 10,010

28. $(2)^3 - 2(10 - 4) \times 3 - 3 =$
(a) -5   (b) 57   (c) 1   (d) -15   (e) -31

Section E. Factors and Multiples of Integers

Factoring Natural Numbers

Every natural number can be written as a product of natural numbers. For example, $10 = 10 \times 1$ and $10 = 5 \times 2$. Notice that 1, 2, 5, and 10 are exactly the numbers which divide into 10 without a remainder. We call these numbers the **factors** (or **divisors**) of 10, and we say that 10×1 and 5×2 are **factorizations** of 10. Similarly, the number 12 has factors 1, 2, 3, 4, 6, and 12. Furthermore, 12×1, 6×2, and 4×3 are factorizations of 12. The process of expressing a natural number as one of its factorizations is called **factoring**.

A natural number is called **composite** if it has factors other than 1 and itself. Otherwise, it is called **prime**. For example, 16 is composite since it has factors besides 1 and 16, namely 2, 4, and 8. On the other hand, 17 is a prime number since the only factors of 17 are 1 and 17. Prime numbers have only one factorization, whereas composite numbers have several.

Often it is the case that we want to factor a number into the product of its prime divisors. We do this by using a **factorization tree**. Every natural number has *exactly one* factorization into primes. It is called the **prime factorization** of the number.

Example 1. Find the prime factorization.
1) 12   2) 81   3) 220

Solution:

1)
```
       12
      /  \
     4  × 3
    / \
   2 × 2 × 3
```
$12 = 2^2 \times 3$

2)
```
        81
       /  \
      9  × 9
     / \  / \
    3×3 × 3×3
```
$81 = 3^4$

3)
```
         220
        /   \
      10  × 22
     / \   / \
    5×2 × 11×2
```
$220 = 5 \times 2^2 \times 11$

The Greatest Common Factor (GCF)

The **greatest common factor (GCF)** of two or more natural numbers is the largest number which is a factor of each of the given numbers.

For example, the factors of 15 are 1, 3, 5, and 15, and the factors of 20 are 1, 2, 4, 5, 10, and 20. The **common factors** are 1 and 5; since 5 is the larger number, it is the GCF of 15 and 20. The greatest common factor is also called the **greatest common divisor (GCD)**.

18

The method of finding a GCF described above requires us to write all the factors of each number and find the largest common one. Another way to find the GCF of two or more numbers is by factoring each number, then multiplying the common factors together.

Example 2. Find the GCF of   1) 8 and 28.   2) 42 and 24.   3) 17 and 29.

Solution:
1) $8 = 2 \times 2 \times 2$ and $28 = 7 \times 2 \times 2$. Notice that 2 is a factor of both numbers. Since it appears three times is 8 and twice in 28, it will appear twice in the GCF. Therefore, the GCF 8 and 28 is $2 \times 2 = 4$.

2) $42 = 7 \times 3 \times 2$ and $24 = 2 \times 2 \times 2 \times 3$. The numbers 2 and 3 are factors of both numbers. Since they each appear once in 42, they will each appear once in the GCF. Therefore, the GCF 42 and 24 is $2 \times 3 = 6$.

3) $17 = 17 \times 1$ and $29 = 29 \times 1$. The GCF is 1.

The Least Common Multiple (LCM)

If we multiply a natural number by any other natural number, we obtain a **multiple** of the given number. For example, the numbers 8, 16, 24, and 32 are multiples of 8 because $8 = 8 \times 1$, $16 = 8 \times 2$, $24 = 8 \times 3$, and $32 = 8 \times 4$. Finding more multiples of 8 is simple: just multiply 8 by 5, 6, 7, etc.

The **least common multiple (LCM)** of two or more natural numbers is the smallest number that is a multiple of both numbers.

For example, the LCM of 6 and 10 is 30 because the multiples of 6 are: $6, 12, 18, 24, \mathbf{30}, \ldots$, and the multiples of 10 are: $10, 20, \mathbf{30}, \ldots$. Also notice that 30 is the smallest number that both 6 and 10 divide into without a remainder. To explain this, we think of the multiples of 10: they are 10, 20, 30, etc. Now divide $10 \div 6$, $20 \div 6$, $30 \div 6$, etc. until you get an answer with no remainder. Notice that $30 \div 6$ works, so 30 is the LCM.

An alternative method of finding the LCM of two or more numbers is by finding their prime factorizations. That is, by factoring each number, then 'build' the LCM by multiplying some of the factors (as explained in the next example).

Example 3. Find the LCM of   1) 5 and 3.   2) 12 and 14.   3) 100 and 48.

Solution:
1) When the given numbers are prime, the LCM is just the product of them. In this case, the LCM is $5 \times 3 = 15$.

2) $12 = 2 \times 2 \times 3$ and $14 = 2 \times 7$. The LCM will contain all the factors 2, 3, and 7. However, since 2 appears twice as in 12 and once in 14, it will appear twice in the LCM (always put the largest amount of occurrences). Therefore, the LCM is $2 \times 2 \times 3 \times 7 = 84$.

3) $100 = 5 \times 5 \times 2 \times 2$ and $48 = 2 \times 2 \times 2 \times 2 \times 3$. The LCM will contain all the factors 5, 2, and 3. The factor 5 will occur twice, the factor 2 will occur four times (since 48 has four of them and 100 has only two of them), and the factor 3 will occur once. Therefore, the LCM is $5 \times 5 \times 2 \times 2 \times 2 \times 2 \times 3 = 1,200$.

Exercises: Chapter 1, Section E

In Exercises 1 - 12, list all the factors (divisors) of each number.

1. 46   2. 50   3. 102   4. 23   5. 18   6. 138

7. 67   8. 100   9. 133   10. 24   11. 99   12. 333

In Exercises 13 - 18, give the prime factorization of each number.

13. 60   14. 90   15. 78   16. 740   17. 296   18. 624

In Exercises 19 - 24, find the greatest common factor (GCF) of each pair of numbers.

19. 50, 24   20. 25, 60   21. 45, 25

22. 36, 72   23. 75, 125   24. 15, 25

In Exercises 25 - 30, find the least common multiple (LCM) of each pair of numbers.

25. 12, 20   26. 120, 100   27. 15, 300

28. 6, 72   29. 75, 150   30. 120, 420

Section F. Solving Word Problems

Certain **key words** and **key phrases** occur in word problems which tell us how to translate the problem into mathematics, and which operations to use.

Key Words and Key Phrases

I) **Addition:** plus, sum, added to, increased by, more than, total, altogether, in all
II) **Subtraction:** minus, subtracted from, less than, decreased by, difference, left over
III) **Multiplication:** times, product, multiplied by, of
IV) **Division:** quotient, divided by, over, to
V) **Equals:** is, equals

Translating Word Problems into Mathematical Expressions

In order to solve a word problem, we need to know how to translate it into mathematics.

Example 1. Write each statement as a mathematical expression.
1) The sum of 6 and 13.   2) subtract 12 from 28.   3) −7 plus −19.
4) The product of 7 and 16.   5) The quotient of 30 and 15.   6) 5 less than 33.
7) −11 decreased by twice 19.   8) 13 increased by 45 is 58.

Solution: 1) $6 + 13$ 2) $28 − 12$ (Notice that 28 comes **before** 12.)
3) $−7 + (−19)$ 4) $7(16)$
5) $30 ÷ 15$.   6) $33 − 5$ (Notice that 33 comes **before** 5.)
7) $−11 − 2(19)$ 8) $13 + 45 = 58$

Example 2. Write each mathematical expression into a statement.
1) $8 + 5$ 2) $9(−12)$ 3) $\dfrac{−36}{−4}$ 4) $14 − 2(−7)$

Solution: 1) The sum of 8 and 5.   2) The product of 9 and −12.
3) The quotient of −36 and −4.   4) 14 minus twice −7 or 14 decreased by twice −7

Word Problems

Example 3. Solve each word problem.

1) There are 12 eggs in a dozen. How many eggs are there in 6 dozen?

Solution: $6 × 12 = 72$, so there are 72 eggs.

22

2) Steve watched 3 hours of TV on Monday, 2 hours on Tuesday, and 4 hours on Wednesday. How many hours of TV did he watch altogether?

Solution: $3 + 2 + 4 = 9$, so he watched TV for 9 hours.

3) Fifty-four pieces of gum need to be divided into nine party bags so that each bag has the same amount of pieces. How many pieces should each bag contain?

Solution: $54 \div 9 = 6$, so each bag should get 6 pieces.

4) Annemarie has $800 on her debit card. On Saturday, she spends $275 on clothes, $18 on lunch, and $68 on a birthday gift for her nephew. How much money does she have left on her card?

Solution: She spends $275 + $18 + $68 = $361 altogether. Therefore, she has $800 − $361 = $439 left.

5) Anthony bought a book and two cups of coffee at his favorite bookstore. If he spent a total of $13 and each cup of coffee costs $2, how much did the book cost?

Solution: He spent $2 \times $2 = $4 on coffee. Therefore, the book costs $13 − $4 = $9.

6) On a cold winter day, the temperature at 6:00 AM was $8°F$. By 10:30 AM, the temperature increased to $25°F$. By how much did the temperature change?

Solution: The change in the temperature is $25°F − 8°F = 17°F$.

7) On Tuesday at 12:00 PM, Vinny's favorite stock was valued at $43. At the end of each hour, beginning at 12:00 PM and ending at 6 PM, he recorded the following changes in the value of the stock: −4, +1, +2, −1, −3, +2. What was the value of the stock at 6 PM that day?

Solution: The overall change in the value of the stock was $-4 + 1 + 2 - 1 - 3 + 2 = -3$. Therefore, the stock was valued at $43 − $3 = $40.

8) John has $230 and wants to purchase some shirts. If each shirt is on sale for $27, how many can he buy? How much money will he have left over?

Solution: Since $230 \div 27 = 8$ R 14, he can buy 8 shirts and will have $14 left.

9) Colleen is 5 ft. 8 in. tall and Trisha is 4 ft. 10 in. tall. What is the difference in their heights? (Note that 12 inches (in.) equals 1 foot (ft.).)

Solution: Let's convert each height into inches: Colleen is 5 ft. 8 in. = $(5 \times 12 + 8)$ in. = 68 in. tall and Trisha is 4 ft. 10 in. = $(4 \times 12 + 10)$ in. = 58 in. tall. The difference in their heights is:

$$68 \text{ in.} - 58 \text{ in.} = 10 \text{ in.}$$

Exercises: Chapter 1, Section F

In Exercises 1 - 28, solve each word problem.

1. A TV set sells for $1,250. The sales manager reduces the price by $260. The price is reduced further by $50. What is the final sale price of the TV set?

2. Susan planted 45 seedlings in the summer. During the winter only 37 survived. How many plants died?

3. Five out of 23 people invited to a party never arrived. However, 11 other people showed up uninvited. How many people attended the party?

4. It is 106 miles to Brooklyn, and Carol wants to drive there in a two days. If she travels 48 miles during the first day, how many miles should she travel during the second day?

5. It takes 12 oranges to make a cartoon of juice. How many oranges will it take to make 7 cartoons of juice?

6. Paula earned $68 in tips working as a waitress from three of her favorite customers. If two customers gave her $19 each, how much did she received from her third customer?

7. Peter worked 34 hours at $5 per hour. How much did he earn?

8. During one week, a clothing store sold 6 suits at $96 each and 3 coats at $120 each. How much was received from these sales?
(a) $576   (b) $360   (c) $936   (d) $576   (e) $216

9. Suzie can type 62 words per minute. How many minutes will it take her to type 12,710 words?
(a) 205   (b) 62   (c) 788,020   (d) 7,355   (e) 3,720

10. Paul bought a TV set for $700. He gave a deposit of $150 and he paid $200 when the TV set arrived. He paid the rest in 5 installments. How much was each installment?
(a) $350   (b) $70   (c) $500   (d) $550   (e) $140

11. Thomas is 6 ft. 2 in. and Bo is 5 ft. 7 in.. What is the difference in their heights?
(a) 5 in.   (b) 5 ft.   (c) 7 in.   (d) 55 in.   (e) 1ft. 5 in.

12. On a very cold winters day, the temperature at 1:00 PM was $3°F$. By 6:30 PM, the temperature was $-11°F$. By how much did the temperature change?
(a) $19°F$ (b) $9°F$ (c) $4°F$ (d) $13°F$ (e) $14°F$

13. It takes the planet Jupiter 4,329 days to travel once around the sun (a Jupiter year). If one earth year (yr.) is equal to 365 days, how many earth years is a Jupiter year?
(a) 11 yrs. 98 days   (b) 11 yrs. 4 days   (c) 1 yrs. 413 days   (d) 11 yrs. 314 days
(e) 11 yrs.

14. A plane flight from New York to Grenada takes 4 hours and 30 minutes. If the plane takes off at 1:45 PM, what time does it land?
(a) 5:15 PM   (b) 6:15 PM   (c) 2:45 PM   (d) 3:15 PM   (e) 6:30 PM

15. On Wednesday morning at 9:00 AM, Sal's favorite stock was valued at $98. At the end of each hour, beginning at 9:00 AM and ending at 2:00 PM, he recorded the following changes in the value of the stock: $-3, +5, +6, -3, -1$. What was the value of the stock at 2:00 PM that day?
(a) $2   (b) $102   (c) $4   (d) $109   (e) $116

16. Chris has $310 and wants to purchase some pants. If each pair of pants is on sale for $27, how many can he buy?
(a) 11   (b) 13   (c) 12   (d) 10   (e) 283

17. Diane spends $545 on shoes. If each pair of shoes costs $54, how much money does she have left over?
(a) $15   (b) $0   (c) $491   (d) $9   (e) $5

18. A boy bought 6 video games at $7 each. How much change did he receive from a $50 bill?
(a) $42   (b) $44   (c) $8   (d) $43   (e) $48

19. Julie has $9,016 in her checking account. She withdraws $97 from her account, then deposits a check in the account for $204. What is her new balance?
(a) $9,023   (b) $8,923   (c) $8,909   (d) $9,123   (e) $8,822

20. Jim purchases 4 dozen cigars. He gives each of his three friends 7 cigars, and he gives 8 to his brother. How many does he have for himself?
(a) 16   (b) 17   (c) 18   (d) 19   (e) 20

21. The perimeter of a rectangle is obtained by adding twice the length and twice the width. Find the perimeter of a rectangle whose length is 5 in. and width is 13 in.
(a) 18 in.   (b) 36 in.   (c) 23 in.   (d) 31 in.   (e) 26 in.

22. The area of a square is obtained by squaring the length of a side. Find the area of a square whose sides are 8 ft.
(a) 8 ft.^{2} (b) 16 ft.^{2} (c) 24 ft.^{2} (d) 64 ft.^{2} (e) 48 ft.^{2}

23. How many square inches are there in 2 square feet?
(a) 144   (b) 288   (c) 24   (d) 62   (e) 72

24. Tom purchases 16 feet of rope. He cuts it into 4 pieces. If each of the first 3 pieces are 50 inches long, how many inches is the fourth piece?
(a) 22   (b) 32   (c) 42   (d) 124   (e) 72

25. How many square feet are there in an area of 7 square yards?
(a) 21 ft.^{2} (b) 42 ft.^{2} (c) 63 ft.^{2} (d) 16 ft.^{2} (e) 68 ft.^{2}

26. How many 2 foot square tiles can fit in an area of 3 square yards?
(a) 12   (b) 7   (c) 14   (d) 8   (e) 6

27. How many 10 inch square blocks can be use to partition a wall that is 100 square feet?
(a) 100   (b) 1   (c) 10   (d) 144   (e) 1,440

28. How much does it cost to carpet a room that is 12 feet by 10 feet if carpeting cost $6 per square foot?
(a) $720   (b) $60   (c) $20   (d) $120   (e) $100

Chapter 2: Fractions

Section A. Proper Fractions, Improper Fractions, and Mixed Numbers

Suppose a round pizza pie is divided into 8 equally sized slices. If someone eats 2 of the slices, then we write $\frac{2}{8}$ to represent the amount of equally sized slices (2 slices) that were eaten from the whole pie (8 slices). We call $\frac{2}{8}$ a **fraction**.

$\frac{2}{8}$ of the pie is eaten.

In general, a **fraction** is used to represent the amount of equal parts of a whole (which is divided into equal parts). In the picture below, the square is divided into 4 equal parts. Three of the 4 parts are shaded in. Just as in the pizza example above, we can represent this as $\frac{3}{4}$.

$\frac{3}{4}$ of the circle is shaded.

We write a fraction as $\dfrac{\text{number of parts}}{\text{whole}}$. We call the top number of the fraction the **numerator** and the bottom number the **denominator**.

In the fraction $\frac{5}{14}$, for example, the numerator is 5 and the denominator is 14. It can be interpreted as saying '5 parts of a whole which has been divided into 14 equal parts'. For example, if $\frac{5}{14}$ of a cake has been eaten at a birthday party, it means that the whole cake has been divided into 14 equal slices, and 5 slices have been eaten.

Example 1. Write a fraction which describes the shaded part of each shape.

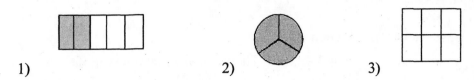

1)   2)   3)

Solution: 1) $\frac{2}{5}$ 2) $\frac{3}{3} = 1$ (The **whole** circle is shaded.)   3) $\frac{0}{6} = 0$ (**Zero** parts are shaded.)

When the numerator and denominator of a fraction are equal (and not zero), then the fraction is equal to 1. For example, if Joe paints $\frac{3}{3}$ of the ceiling in his kitchen, then he painted the **whole** ceiling. Similarly, if Ashley read $\frac{5}{5}$ of her book, then she read the **whole** book.

When a fraction has numerator zero (and the denominator is not), then it is equal to 0. For example, if Petey eats $\frac{0}{4}$ of his cat food, then he didn't eat anything; he has eaten 0 cat food.

Notice that a whole can always be divided into a positive number of equal parts (if the whole is divided into 1 part, it would be the whole itself). In other words, the denominator of a fraction can **never** be 0 because if it could, then this would mean that a whole can be divided into 0 equal parts, which doesn't make sense. For example, $\frac{4}{0}$ does not make sense. We say division by 0 is not defined. To indicate the denominator of a fraction $\frac{a}{b}$ is not equal to zero, we use the symbol $\neq$ (read "not equal to"), and write $b \neq 0$.

Example 2. A florist has a sale on roses. He sells one dozen red roses, 7 pink roses, and 3 yellow roses. What fraction of the roses he sold were red?

Solution: The 'parts' are the number of roses of each color that are sold, and the 'whole' is the total number of roses of all colors. He sells a total of $12 + 7 + 3 = 22$ roses. The fraction of red roses is $\frac{12}{22}$.

Example 3. The following table contains the number of exams a college student took during her Fall semester:

Course	Number of Exams
Calculus	4
Sociology	3
Chemistry	4
French	2

1) What fraction of the exams were taken in Chemistry?
2) What fraction of the exams were taken in Sociology and French?

Solution: The 'parts' in this example are the number of exams in each course, and the 'whole' is the total number of exams which is $4 + 3 + 4 + 2 = 13$.

1) Since 4 Chemistry exams were taken, the fraction is $\frac{4}{13}$.

2) The sum of the Sociology and French exams is $3 + 2 = 5$. Therefore, the fraction is $\frac{5}{13}$.

Various types of fractions can arise:

Proper Fractions are fractions whose numerators are smaller than their denominators. Examples are

$$\frac{2}{3}, \ \frac{5}{10}, \ \text{and} \ \frac{17}{24}.$$

Improper Fraction are fractions whose numerators are larger than or equal to their denominators. For example, the fraction $\frac{6}{5}$ may be viewed as follows:

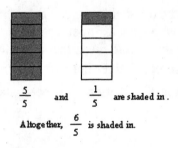

$\frac{5}{5}$ and $\frac{1}{5}$ are shaded in.

Altogether, $\frac{6}{5}$ is shaded in.

Other examples of improper fractions are $\frac{24}{8}$, $\frac{7}{2}$, and $\frac{32}{32}$.

Mixed Numbers are numbers formed by adding a whole number to a proper fraction. Examples of mixed numbers are $1 + \frac{1}{2} = 1\frac{1}{2}$ and $8 + \frac{5}{9} = 8\frac{5}{9}$. A picture of $1\frac{1}{2}$ is given in the next figure.

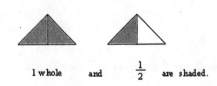

1 whole and $\frac{1}{2}$ are shaded.

Exercises: Chapter 2, Section A

In Exercises 1 - 8, divide, if possible.

1. $\dfrac{40}{5}$
2. $\dfrac{7}{7}$
3. $\dfrac{0}{9}$
4. $\dfrac{66}{3}$

5. $\dfrac{5}{0}$
6. $\dfrac{0}{1}$
7. $\dfrac{1}{0}$
8. $\dfrac{9}{9}$

In Exercises 9 - 16, identify each as either a proper fraction, an improper fraction, or a mixed number.

9. $\dfrac{2}{3}$
10. $\dfrac{2}{7}$
11. $\dfrac{8}{7}$
12. $1\dfrac{2}{3}$

13. $\dfrac{12}{3}$
14. $\dfrac{22}{3}$
15. $3\dfrac{5}{8}$
16. $\dfrac{11}{16}$

17. Derek had 7 base hits in 12 times at bat. What fraction describes Derek's base hits?
(a) $\dfrac{7}{12}$
(b) $\dfrac{7}{5}$
(c) $\dfrac{5}{12}$
(d) $\dfrac{7}{19}$
(e) $\dfrac{12}{7}$

18. There are 31 students in my Calculus 1 class, 15 of which are females. What fraction of the students are males?
(a) $\dfrac{15}{31}$
(b) $\dfrac{16}{31}$
(c) $\dfrac{15}{16}$
(d) $\dfrac{1}{31}$
(e) $\dfrac{31}{16}$

19. There are 23 women and 24 men working for a company. What fractional part of the employees consists of women only?
(a) $\dfrac{24}{23}$
(b) $\dfrac{1}{23}$
(c) $\dfrac{23}{24}$
(d) $\dfrac{23}{47}$
(e) $\dfrac{24}{47}$

20. There are 70 employees working for a company, 39 of which are women. What fractional part of employees consists of men only?
(a) $\dfrac{31}{70}$
(b) $\dfrac{39}{70}$
(c) $\dfrac{31}{39}$
(d) $\dfrac{35}{70}$
(e) $\dfrac{36}{70}$

Section B. Converting Mixed Numbers into Improper Fractions and Improper Fractions into Mixed Numbers

An improper fraction can be written as a mixed number. The next figure shows that $\frac{11}{4}$ is the same as 2 whole shaded rectangles, together with 3 shaded parts of a rectangle. This means that $\frac{11}{4} = 2 + \frac{3}{4} = 2\frac{3}{4}$.

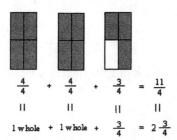

$$\frac{4}{4} \quad + \quad \frac{4}{4} \quad + \quad \frac{3}{4} \quad = \quad \frac{11}{4}$$

$$\| \qquad \qquad \| \qquad \qquad \| \qquad \qquad \|$$

$$1 \text{ whole} \quad + \quad 1 \text{ whole} \quad + \quad \frac{3}{4} \quad = \quad 2\frac{3}{4}$$

Rule for converting an improper fraction into a mixed number: Divide the numerator by the denominator. The quotient is the whole part of the mixed number, and the remainder (if any) is the numerator of the fractional part of the mixed number.

Note that the denominator of the fractional part of the mixed number is the same as the denominator of the improper fraction.

Example 1. Write each improper fraction as a mixed number.

1) $\frac{19}{3}$ 2) $\frac{32}{13}$ 3) $\frac{48}{5}$ 4) $\frac{100}{100}$

Solution: 1) $19 \div 3 = 6$ R 1, so $\frac{19}{3} = 6\frac{1}{3}$.   2) $32 \div 13 = 2$ R 6, so $\frac{32}{13} = 2\frac{6}{13}$.

             3) $48 \div 5 = 9$ R 3, so $\frac{48}{5} = 9\frac{3}{5}$.   4) $100 \div 100 = 1$, so $\frac{100}{100} = 1$.

A mixed number can be also be written as an improper fraction. The next figure shows that $3\frac{5}{8}$ is the same as 3 whole shaded circles, which is 24 shaded parts in all, together with 5 shaded parts of a circle. This means that $3\frac{5}{8} = \frac{24+5}{8} = \frac{29}{8}$.

$$1 \text{ whole} \quad + \quad 1 \text{ whole} \quad + \quad 1 \text{ whole} \quad + \quad \frac{5}{8} \quad = \quad 3\frac{5}{8}$$

$$\| \qquad \qquad \| \qquad \qquad \| \qquad \qquad \| \qquad \qquad \|$$

$$\frac{8}{8} \quad + \quad \frac{8}{8} \quad + \quad \frac{8}{8} \quad + \quad \frac{5}{8} \quad = \quad \frac{29}{8}$$

Rule for converting a mixed number into an improper fraction:
1) Multiply the denominator of the fraction part by the whole number.
2) Add the product to the numerator of the fraction part.

The result is the numerator of the improper fraction. The denominator of the improper fraction is the same as the denominator of the fractional part of the mixed number.

Example 2. Write each mixed number as an improper fraction.

1) $2\frac{1}{5}$ 2) $7\frac{3}{4}$ 3) $16\frac{5}{12}$ 4) $27\frac{2}{3}$

Solution:

1) $2\frac{1}{5} = \frac{5 \times 2 + 1}{5} = \frac{10 + 1}{5} = \frac{11}{5}$ 2) $7\frac{3}{4} = \frac{4 \times 7 + 3}{4} = \frac{28 + 3}{4} = \frac{31}{4}$

3) $16\frac{5}{12} = \frac{12 \times 16 + 5}{12} = \frac{192 + 5}{12} = \frac{197}{12}$ 4) $27\frac{2}{3} = \frac{3 \times 27 + 2}{3} = \frac{81 + 2}{3} = \frac{83}{3}$

Exercises: Chapter 2, Section B

In Exercises 1 - 9, write each improper fraction as a mixed number.

1. $\frac{45}{23}$ 2. $\frac{67}{10}$ 3. $\frac{59}{12}$ 4. $\frac{78}{7}$ 5. $\frac{49}{12}$

6. $\frac{213}{27}$ 7. $\frac{31}{8}$ 8. $\frac{94}{3}$ 9. $\frac{232}{17}$

In Exercises 10 - 17, write each mixed number as an improper fraction.

10. $6\frac{3}{5}$ 11. $9\frac{3}{4}$ 12. $13\frac{7}{12}$ 13. $24\frac{2}{3}$

14. $19\frac{8}{9}$ 15. $13\frac{11}{17}$ 16. $25\frac{21}{31}$ 17. $31\frac{7}{36}$

Section C. Equivalent Fractions; Reducing Fractions to Lowest Terms

Two fractions are called **equivalent** if they represent the same quantity. In the next figure, both rectangles have the same amount shaded in. Therefore, $\frac{1}{2}$ is equivalent to $\frac{2}{4}$.

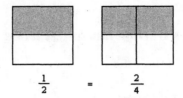

$$\frac{1}{2} \quad = \quad \frac{2}{4}$$

There are many fractions which are equivalent to each other. As the next figure shows, the fractions $\frac{1}{3}$, $\frac{2}{6}$, and $\frac{3}{9}$ are equivalent to one another.

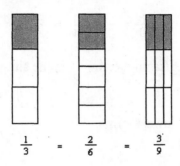

$$\frac{1}{3} \quad = \quad \frac{2}{6} \quad = \quad \frac{3}{9}$$

Even though the fractions $\frac{1}{3}$, $\frac{2}{6}$, and $\frac{3}{9}$ look different because they have different numerators and denominators, they are equal quantities. Therefore, we write $\frac{1}{3} = \frac{2}{6} = \frac{3}{9}$.

Rule for rewriting a fraction as an equivalent one: Multiply the numerator and denominator by a non-zero number.

We write this mathematically as: $\frac{a}{b} = \frac{a \times c}{b \times c}$

For example, $\frac{1}{3} = \frac{1 \times 2}{3 \times 2} = \frac{2}{6}$ and $\frac{1}{3} = \frac{1 \times 3}{3 \times 3} = \frac{3}{9}$.

Example 1. For each fraction, find an equivalent fraction whose denominator is 12.
1) $\frac{3}{4}$ 2) $\frac{1}{6}$ 3) $\frac{7}{3}$ 4) 5

Solution: 1) $\frac{3}{4} = \frac{3 \times 3}{4 \times 3} = \frac{9}{12}$ 2) $\frac{1}{6} = \frac{1 \times 2}{6 \times 2} = \frac{2}{12}$

35

3) $\dfrac{7}{3} = \dfrac{7 \times 4}{3 \times 4} = \dfrac{28}{12}$ 4) $5 = \dfrac{5}{1} = \dfrac{5 \times 12}{1 \times 12} = \dfrac{60}{12}$

When the numerator and denominator of a fraction has no common factors other than 1, we say that it is in **simplest form** or in **lowest terms**. For example, $\dfrac{6}{25}$ is in lowest terms because the only common factor of 6 and 25 is 1.

Rule for reducing (or simplifying) a fraction into lowest terms: Divide the numerator and denominator by the their GCF.

We write this mathematically as: $\dfrac{a}{b} = \dfrac{a \div c}{b \div c}$

For example, the fraction $\dfrac{16}{20}$ has numerator 16 and denominator 20. The GCF of 16 and 20 is 4, so we can reduce $\dfrac{16}{20}$ as follows:

$$\dfrac{16}{20} = \dfrac{16 \div 4}{20 \div 4} = \dfrac{4}{5}$$

Therefore, $\dfrac{16}{20}$ and $\dfrac{4}{5}$ are equivalent fractions, and $\dfrac{4}{5}$ is the simple form of $\dfrac{16}{20}$.

Example 2. Reduce each fraction to lowest terms.

1) $\dfrac{7}{21}$ 2) $\dfrac{8}{10}$ 3) $\dfrac{63}{27}$

Solution: 1) The GCF of 7 and 21 is 7. Therefore, $\dfrac{7}{21} = \dfrac{7 \div 7}{21 \div 7} = \dfrac{1}{3}$.

2) The GCF of 8 and 10 is 2. Therefore, $\dfrac{8}{10} = \dfrac{8 \div 2}{10 \div 2} = \dfrac{4}{5}$.

3) The GCF of 63 and 27 is 9, so $\dfrac{63}{27} = \dfrac{63 \div 9}{27 \div 9} = \dfrac{7}{3}$.

Another method of reducing a fraction to lowest terms is to factor the numerator and denominator, then cancel out any common factors.

Rule: $\dfrac{a \times c}{b \times c} = \dfrac{a}{b}$

To simplify the fraction $\dfrac{18}{24}$, for example, we factor 18 and 24 to obtain $\dfrac{18}{24} = \dfrac{3 \times 3 \times 2}{3 \times 2 \times 2 \times 2}$. Now we cancel out all common factors: $\dfrac{18}{24} = \dfrac{\overset{1}{\cancel{3}} \times 3 \times \overset{1}{\cancel{2}}}{\underset{1}{\cancel{3}} \times 2 \times \underset{1}{\cancel{2}} \times 2} = \dfrac{3}{2 \times 2} = \dfrac{3}{4}$

Observe that the GCF of 18 and 24 is 6, so $\dfrac{18}{24} = \dfrac{18 \div 6}{24 \div 6} = \dfrac{3}{4}$. Both methods give the same answer.

Example 3. Reduce each fraction to lowest terms by canceling common factors.

1) $\dfrac{8}{12}$ 2) $\dfrac{4}{30}$ 3) $\dfrac{25}{75}$

Solution: 1) $\dfrac{8}{12} = \dfrac{\cancel{2} \times \cancel{2} \times 2}{\cancel{2} \times \cancel{2} \times 3} = \dfrac{2}{3}$ 2) $\dfrac{4}{30} = \dfrac{\cancel{2} \times 2}{\cancel{2} \times 3 \times 5} = \dfrac{2}{15}$

3) $\dfrac{25}{75} = \dfrac{\cancel{5} \times 5}{\cancel{5} \times 5 \times 3} = \dfrac{1}{3}$

Notice that this canceling rule works as long as the numerator and denominator are **factored**. If we have addition or subtraction in the numerator or denominator, we **cannot** cancel.

Beware: 1) $\dfrac{a+c}{bc} \neq \dfrac{a}{b}$ 2) $\dfrac{ac}{b+c} \neq \dfrac{a}{b}$ 3) $\dfrac{a+c}{b+c} \neq \dfrac{a}{b}$

For example, $\dfrac{3+4}{5(4)} \neq \dfrac{3}{5}$ and $\dfrac{2+7}{9+7} \neq \dfrac{2}{9}$.

Exercises: Chapter 2, Section C

In Exercises 1 - 3, find an equivalent fraction whose denominator is 30.

1. $\frac{4}{5}$ 2. $\frac{2}{3}$ 3. $\frac{7}{15}$

In Exercises 4 - 7, find an equivalent fraction whose denominator is 24.

4. $\frac{1}{12}$ 5. $\frac{7}{8}$ 6. $\frac{3}{4}$ 7. $\frac{5}{6}$

In Exercises 8 - 23, reduce each fraction to lowest terms, if possible.

8. $\frac{22}{30}$ 9. $\frac{56}{98}$ 10. $\frac{28}{70}$ 11. $\frac{33}{55}$

12. $\frac{220}{330}$ 13. $\frac{14}{42}$ 14. $\frac{25}{56}$ 15 $\frac{70}{210}$

16. $\frac{12}{88}$ 17. $\frac{156}{198}$ 18. $\frac{225}{750}$ 19. $\frac{333}{993}$

20. $\frac{420}{810}$ 21. $\frac{55}{1050}$ 22. $\frac{25}{2000}$ 23. $\frac{170}{2010}$

Section D. Multiplication and Division of Fractions and Mixed Numbers

Rule for multiplying fractions:
1) Multiply the numerators together (numerator × numerator), then multiply the denominators together (denominator × denominator).
2) Simplify your answer.

For example, $\dfrac{2}{9} \times \dfrac{4}{5} = \dfrac{2 \times 4}{9 \times 5} = \dfrac{8}{45}$. Notice that $\dfrac{8}{45}$ cannot be simplified.

In some cases, you can simplify **before** multiplying. For example, $\dfrac{\overset{1}{\cancel{3}}}{\underset{5}{\cancel{20}}} \times \dfrac{\overset{2}{\cancel{8}}}{\underset{3}{\cancel{9}}} = \dfrac{2}{5 \times 3} = \dfrac{2}{15}$.

Example 1. Multiply and simplify.

1) $\dfrac{3}{7} \times \dfrac{4}{8}$ 2) $\dfrac{2}{7} \times \dfrac{1}{6}$ 3) $\dfrac{9}{10} \times \dfrac{7}{8}$ 4) $\dfrac{5}{12} \times \dfrac{4}{15}$ 5) $\dfrac{8}{21} \times 3$

Solution: 1) $\dfrac{3}{7} \times \dfrac{\overset{1}{\cancel{4}}}{\underset{2}{\cancel{8}}} = \dfrac{3 \times 1}{7 \times 2} = \dfrac{3}{14}$ 2) $\dfrac{\overset{1}{\cancel{2}}}{7} \times \dfrac{1}{\underset{3}{\cancel{6}}} = \dfrac{1}{21}$

3) $\dfrac{9}{10} \times \dfrac{7}{8} = \dfrac{9 \times 7}{10 \times 8} = \dfrac{63}{80}$ 4) $\dfrac{\overset{1}{\cancel{5}}}{\underset{3}{\cancel{12}}} \times \dfrac{\overset{1}{\cancel{4}}}{\underset{3}{\cancel{15}}} = \dfrac{1}{3 \times 3} = \dfrac{1}{9}$

5) $\dfrac{8}{21} \times 3 = \dfrac{8}{\underset{7}{\cancel{21}}} \times \dfrac{\overset{1}{\cancel{3}}}{1} = \dfrac{8}{7} = 1\dfrac{1}{7}$

Rule for dividing fractions: To divide two fractions, leave the first fraction alone (the fraction on the left), change the division symbol to multiplication, and 'flip'(invert) the second fraction (the fraction on the right). Multiply the resulting fractions.

Here's how division works: $\underbrace{\dfrac{2}{5} \div \dfrac{7}{8} = \dfrac{2}{5} \times \dfrac{8}{7}}_{\text{Flip over } \frac{7}{8}.} = \dfrac{2 \times 8}{5 \times 7} = \dfrac{16}{35}$

The number that you get by flipping over a fraction is called its **reciprocal**. For instance, the reciprocal of $\dfrac{7}{8}$ is $\dfrac{8}{7}$ and the reciprocal of $3 = \dfrac{3}{1}$ is $\dfrac{1}{3}$.

Example 2. Divide and simplify.

1) $\frac{2}{7} \div \frac{3}{4}$ 2) $\frac{8}{9} \div \frac{5}{18}$ 3) $28 \div \frac{7}{12}$ 4) $\frac{15}{22} \div 20$

Solution: 1) $\frac{2}{7} \div \frac{3}{4} = \frac{2}{7} \times \frac{4}{3} = \frac{2 \times 4}{7 \times 3} = \frac{8}{21}$ 2) $\frac{8}{9} \div \frac{5}{18} = \frac{8}{9} \times \frac{\overset{2}{\cancel{18}}}{5} = \frac{16}{5} = 3\frac{1}{5}$

3) $28 \div \frac{7}{12} = \frac{\overset{4}{\cancel{28}}}{1} \times \frac{12}{\underset{1}{\cancel{7}}} = \frac{48}{1} = 48$ 4) $\frac{15}{22} \div 20 = \frac{15}{22} \div \frac{20}{1} = \frac{\overset{3}{\cancel{15}}}{22} \times \frac{1}{\underset{4}{\cancel{20}}} = \frac{3}{88}$

Rule for multiplying and dividing mixed numbers: Convert the mixed numbers into improper fractions, then follow the rules for multiplying and dividing fractions.

Example 3. Multiply and simplify.

1) $\frac{5}{6} \times 2\frac{1}{3}$ 2) $9 \times 4\frac{5}{6}$ 3) $3\frac{1}{4} \times 7\frac{3}{5}$

Solution: 1) $\underbrace{\frac{5}{6} \times 2\frac{1}{3} = \frac{5}{6} \times \frac{7}{3}}_{2\frac{1}{3} = \frac{3\times2+1}{3} = \frac{7}{3}} = \frac{5 \times 7}{6 \times 3} = \underbrace{\frac{35}{18} = 1\frac{17}{18}}_{35 \div 18 = 1\ R\ 17}$

2) $\underbrace{9 \times 4\frac{5}{6} = \frac{9}{1} \times \frac{29}{6}}_{4\frac{5}{6} = \frac{6\times4+5}{6} = \frac{29}{6}} = \frac{3 \times 29}{1 \times 2} = \underbrace{\frac{87}{2} = 43\frac{1}{2}}_{87 \div 2 = 43\ R\ 1}$

3) $\underbrace{3\frac{1}{4} \times 7\frac{3}{5} = \frac{13}{4} \times \frac{38}{5}}_{3\frac{1}{4} = \frac{4\times3+1}{4} = \frac{13}{4}\text{ and } 7\frac{3}{5} = \frac{5\times7+3}{5} = \frac{38}{5}} = \frac{13 \times 19}{2 \times 5} = \underbrace{\frac{247}{10} = 24\frac{7}{10}}_{247 \div 10 = 24\ R\ 7}$

Example 4. Divide and simplify.

1) $12\frac{1}{6} \div 3\frac{11}{12}$ 2) $5 \div 3\frac{7}{10}$

Solution: 1) $\underbrace{12\frac{1}{6} \div 3\frac{11}{12} = \frac{73}{6} \div \frac{47}{12}}_{12\frac{1}{6} = \frac{6\times12+1}{6} = \frac{73}{6}\text{ and }3\frac{11}{12} = \frac{12\times3+11}{12} = \frac{47}{12}} = \underbrace{\frac{73}{6} \times \frac{\overset{2}{\cancel{12}}}{47}}_{1} = \frac{73 \times 2}{1 \times 47} = \underbrace{\frac{146}{47} = 3\frac{5}{47}}_{146 \div 47 = 3\ R\ 5}$

2) $\underbrace{5 \div 3\frac{7}{10} = \frac{5}{1} \div \frac{37}{10}}_{3\frac{7}{10} = \frac{10\times3+7}{10} = \frac{37}{10}} = \frac{5}{1} \times \frac{10}{37} = \frac{5 \times 10}{1 \times 37} = \underbrace{\frac{50}{37} = 1\frac{13}{37}}_{50 \div 37 = 1\ R\ 13}$

Exercises: Chapter 2, Section D

In Exercises 1 - 18, multiply and simplify.

1. $\dfrac{8}{9} \times \dfrac{15}{6}$

2. $\dfrac{12}{10} \times \dfrac{5}{4}$

3. $\dfrac{4}{9} \times \dfrac{5}{11}$

4. $\dfrac{5}{4} \times \dfrac{16}{9}$

5. $\dfrac{5}{6} \times 12$

6. $21 \times \dfrac{5}{28}$

7. $\dfrac{5}{12} \times \dfrac{1}{6}$

8. $18 \times \dfrac{7}{63}$

9. $\dfrac{5}{30} \times \dfrac{5}{12}$

10. $\dfrac{23}{25} \times \dfrac{35}{46}$

11. $18 \times \dfrac{3}{14}$

12. $\dfrac{42}{59} \times 4$

13. $\dfrac{8}{36} \times 4\dfrac{2}{3}$

14. $42 \times 4\dfrac{5}{7}$

15. $2\dfrac{3}{4} \times 18$

16. $2\dfrac{8}{36} \times 4\dfrac{2}{3}$

17. $8\dfrac{3}{9} \times 3\dfrac{6}{7}$

18. $5\dfrac{3}{4} \times 3\dfrac{2}{3}$

In Exercises 19 - 41, divide and simplify.

19. $\dfrac{7}{9} \div \dfrac{7}{12}$

20. $\dfrac{9}{10} \div \dfrac{3}{18}$

21. $60 \div \dfrac{7}{12}$

22. $\dfrac{49}{65} \div 98$

23. $\dfrac{8}{25} \div \dfrac{4}{5}$

24. $\dfrac{9}{2} \div \dfrac{3}{8}$

25. $6 \div \dfrac{1}{12}$

26. $\dfrac{34}{78} \div 128$

27. $\dfrac{15}{16} \div \dfrac{5}{6}$

28. $\dfrac{9}{18} \div \dfrac{3}{36}$

29. $680 \div \dfrac{4}{15}$

30. $\dfrac{17}{25} \div 56$

31. $\dfrac{13}{25} \div \dfrac{4}{5}$

32. $\dfrac{14}{44} \div \dfrac{45}{88}$

33. $34 \div \dfrac{7}{12}$

34. $\dfrac{34}{74} \div 18$

35. $2\dfrac{1}{6} \div 3\dfrac{5}{7}$

36. $15 \div 6\dfrac{7}{10}$

37. $4\dfrac{1}{6} \div 5\dfrac{9}{18}$

38. $\dfrac{4}{74} \div 17$

39. $1\dfrac{1}{8} \div 6\dfrac{5}{9}$

40. $14 \div 2\dfrac{7}{17}$

41. $8\dfrac{1}{6} \div 2\dfrac{6}{88}$

Section E. Addition and Subtraction of Fractions and Mixed Numbers

Adding and Subtracting Proper and Improper Fractions

Rule: To add (or subtract) two fractions, you must have common denominators.

When the denominators in a given problem are the same, you add (or subtract) their numerators and keep the same denominator. For example,

$$\frac{1}{7} + \frac{2}{7} = \frac{1+2}{7} = \frac{3}{7} \quad \text{and} \quad \frac{16}{3} - \frac{7}{3} = \frac{16-7}{3} = \frac{9}{3} = 3.$$

Example 1. Add or subtract and simplify.

1) $\frac{5}{11} + \frac{4}{11}$ 2) $\frac{10}{17} - \frac{8}{17}$ 3) $\frac{3}{8} + \frac{3}{8}$

4) $\frac{19}{20} - \frac{9}{20}$ 5) $\frac{10}{17} - \frac{8}{17}$ 6) $\frac{8}{5} + \frac{19}{5}$

Solution: 1) $\frac{5}{11} + \frac{4}{11} = \frac{5+4}{11} = \frac{9}{11}$ 2) $\frac{10}{17} - \frac{8}{17} = \frac{10-8}{17} = \frac{2}{17}$

3) $\frac{3}{8} + \frac{3}{8} = \frac{3+3}{8} = \frac{6}{8} = \frac{3}{4}$ 4) $\frac{19}{20} - \frac{9}{20} = \frac{19-9}{20} = \frac{10}{20} = \frac{1}{2}$

5) $\frac{10}{17} - \frac{8}{17} = \frac{10-8}{17} = \frac{2}{17}$ 6) $\frac{8}{5} + \frac{19}{5} = \frac{8+19}{5} = \frac{27}{5} = 5\frac{2}{5}$

Rule for adding or subtracting fractions when the denominators are not the same:
1) Find the least common multiple of the denominators. This is called the **least common denominator** (abbreviated as LCD).
2) Find an equivalent fraction for each of the given ones that have the LCD.
3) Add or subtract their numerators and keep the same denominator as before.
4) Simplify.

For example, $\underbrace{\frac{2}{3} + \frac{1}{5} = \left(\frac{5}{5}\right)\frac{2}{3} + \left(\frac{3}{3}\right)\frac{1}{5}}_{\text{The LCD is 15.}} = \frac{10}{15} + \frac{3}{15} = \frac{10+3}{15} = \frac{13}{15}$ and

$\underbrace{\frac{13}{4} - \frac{5}{6} = \left(\frac{3}{3}\right)\frac{13}{4} - \left(\frac{2}{2}\right)\frac{5}{6}}_{\text{The LCD is 12.}} = \frac{39}{12} - \frac{10}{12} = \frac{39-10}{12} = \frac{29}{12} = 2\frac{5}{12}.$

42

Example 2. Add or subtract and simplify.

1) $\frac{7}{9} + \frac{3}{4}$ 2) $\frac{5}{6} - \frac{1}{7}$ 3) $\frac{3}{4} + \frac{5}{8}$

4) $\frac{7}{10} - \frac{1}{6}$ 5) $\frac{19}{14} - \frac{8}{7}$ 6) $\frac{15}{8} + \frac{1}{6}$

Solution:

1) $\underbrace{\frac{7}{9} + \frac{3}{4} = \left(\frac{4}{4}\right)\frac{7}{9} + \left(\frac{9}{9}\right)\frac{3}{4}}_{\text{The LCD is 36.}} = \frac{28}{36} + \frac{27}{36} = \frac{28+27}{36} = \frac{55}{36} = 1\frac{19}{36}$

2) $\underbrace{\frac{5}{6} - \frac{1}{7} = \left(\frac{7}{7}\right)\frac{5}{6} - \left(\frac{6}{6}\right)\frac{1}{7}}_{\text{The LCD is 42.}} = \frac{35}{42} - \frac{6}{42} = \frac{35-6}{42} = \frac{29}{42}$

3) $\underbrace{\frac{3}{4} + \frac{5}{8} = \left(\frac{2}{2}\right)\frac{3}{4} + \frac{5}{8}}_{\text{The LCD is 8.}} = \frac{6}{8} + \frac{5}{8} = \frac{6+5}{8} = \frac{11}{8} = 1\frac{3}{8}$

4) $\underbrace{\frac{7}{10} - \frac{1}{6} = \left(\frac{3}{3}\right)\frac{7}{10} - \left(\frac{5}{5}\right)\frac{1}{6}}_{\text{The LCD is 30.}} = \frac{21}{30} - \frac{5}{30} = \frac{21-5}{30} = \frac{16}{30} = \frac{8}{15}$

5) $\underbrace{\frac{19}{14} - \frac{8}{7} = \frac{19}{14} - \left(\frac{2}{2}\right)\frac{8}{7}}_{\text{The LCD is 14.}} = \frac{19}{14} - \frac{16}{14} = \frac{19-16}{14} = \frac{3}{14}$

6) $\underbrace{\frac{15}{8} + \frac{1}{6} = \left(\frac{3}{3}\right)\frac{15}{8} + \left(\frac{4}{4}\right)\frac{1}{6}}_{\text{The LCD is 24.}} = \frac{45}{24} + \frac{4}{24} = \frac{45+4}{24} = \frac{49}{24} = 2\frac{1}{24}$

Note: Sometimes it is *not neccessary* to find the least common denominator (LCD) when adding or subtracting fractions. The following rule is *more general* and is more useful when adding or subtracting fractional expressions.

Alternative Rule for adding or subtracting fractions when the denominators are not the same:
1) Multiply both the numerator and the denominator of the fraction on the left by the denominator of the fraction on the right.
2) Multiply both the numerator and the denominator of the fraction on the right by the denominator of the fraction on the left.
3) Add or subtract the numerators and keep the same denominator.
4) Simplify.

43

Example 3: Add or subtract and simplify.

1) $\frac{7}{9} + \frac{3}{4}$ 2) $\frac{3}{4} + \frac{5}{8}$ 3) $\frac{7}{10} - \frac{4}{15}$

Solution: 1) $\frac{7}{9} + \frac{3}{4} = \left(\frac{4}{4}\right)\frac{7}{9} + \left(\frac{9}{9}\right)\frac{3}{4} = \frac{28}{36} + \frac{27}{36} = \frac{28+27}{36} = \frac{55}{36} = 1\frac{19}{36}$

2) $\frac{3}{4} + \frac{5}{8} = \left(\frac{8}{8}\right)\frac{3}{4} + \left(\frac{4}{4}\right)\frac{5}{8} = \frac{24}{32} + \frac{20}{32} = \frac{44}{32} = 1\frac{12}{32} = 1\frac{3}{8}$

3) $\frac{7}{10} - \frac{4}{15} = \left(\frac{15}{15}\right)\frac{7}{10} + \left(\frac{10}{10}\right)\frac{4}{15} = \frac{105}{150} - \frac{40}{150} = \frac{65}{150} = \frac{13}{30}$

Adding and Subtracting Mixed Numbers.

Rule for adding or subtracting mixed numbers: Convert each mixed number into an improper fraction and proceed as before.

For example, to add $6\frac{1}{2}$ and $5\frac{2}{3}$, we first change each number into an improper fraction:

$$6\frac{1}{2} = \frac{2 \times 6 + 1}{2} = \frac{13}{2} \quad \text{and} \quad 5\frac{2}{3} = \frac{3 \times 5 + 2}{2} = \frac{17}{3}$$

Now add the improper fractions together:

$$\frac{13}{2} + \frac{17}{3} = \left(\frac{3}{3}\right)\frac{13}{2} + \left(\frac{2}{2}\right)\frac{17}{3} = \frac{39}{6} + \frac{34}{6} = \frac{39+34}{6} = \frac{73}{6} = 12\frac{1}{6}$$

Therefore, $6\frac{1}{2} + 5\frac{2}{3} = 12\frac{1}{6}$.

Example 4. Add or subtract the mixed numbers and simplify.

1) $5\frac{1}{3} + 7\frac{1}{3}$ 2) $3\frac{7}{8} + 6\frac{3}{4}$ 3) $9\frac{9}{10} - 5\frac{7}{10}$

4) $17\frac{1}{4} - 10\frac{5}{6}$ 5) $32 + 24\frac{5}{14}$ 6) $17 - 12\frac{4}{5}$

Solution:

1) $5\frac{1}{3} + 7\frac{1}{3} = \frac{16}{3} + \frac{22}{3} = \frac{16+22}{3} = \frac{38}{3} = 12\frac{2}{3}$

2) $3\frac{7}{8} + 6\frac{3}{4} = \frac{31}{8} + \frac{27}{4} = \frac{31}{8} + \left(\frac{2}{2}\right)\frac{27}{4} = \frac{31}{8} + \frac{54}{8} = \frac{31+54}{8} = \frac{85}{8} = 10\frac{5}{8}$

3) $9\frac{9}{10} - 5\frac{7}{10} = \frac{99}{10} - \frac{77}{10} = \frac{99-77}{10} = \frac{22}{10} = \frac{11}{5} = 2\frac{1}{5}$

4) $17\frac{1}{4} - 10\frac{5}{6} = \frac{69}{4} - \frac{65}{6} = \left(\frac{3}{3}\right)\frac{69}{4} - \left(\frac{2}{2}\right)\frac{65}{6} = \frac{207}{12} - \frac{130}{12} = \frac{207-130}{12} = \frac{77}{12} = 6\frac{5}{12}$

5) To add a whole number to a mixed number, just add the whole numbers together and keep the fraction of the mixed number: $\underbrace{32 + 24\frac{5}{14} = 56\frac{5}{14}}_{32+24=56}$.

6) $17 - 12\frac{4}{5} = \frac{17}{1} - \frac{64}{5} = \left(\frac{5}{5}\right)\frac{17}{1} - \frac{64}{5} = \frac{85}{5} - \frac{64}{5} = \frac{85-64}{5} = \frac{21}{5} = 4\frac{1}{5}$

Exercises: Chapter 2, Section E

In Exercises 1 - 26, add and simplify.

1. $\frac{8}{9} + \frac{15}{6}$ 2. $\frac{12}{10} + \frac{5}{4}$ 3. $\frac{4}{9} + \frac{5}{11}$ 4. $\frac{1}{2} + \frac{10}{3}$

5. $\frac{5}{6} + 12$ 6. $21 + \frac{5}{28}$ 7. $\frac{5}{12} + \frac{1}{6}$ 8. $18 + \frac{7}{63}$

9. $\frac{1}{12} + \frac{3}{10}$ 10. $\frac{11}{26} + \frac{10}{13}$ 11. $18 + \frac{3}{14}$ 12. $\frac{42}{59} + 4$

13. $\frac{8}{36} + 4\frac{2}{3}$ 14. $42 + 4\frac{5}{7}$ 15. $2\frac{3}{4} + 18$ 16. $2\frac{8}{36} + 4\frac{2}{3}$

17. $8\frac{3}{9} + 3\frac{6}{7}$ 18. $5\frac{3}{4} + 3\frac{2}{3}$

19. $2\frac{1}{3} + \frac{1}{7} =$
(a) $\frac{2}{5}$ (b) $2\frac{10}{21}$ (c) $2\frac{1}{10}$ (d) $2\frac{1}{5}$ (e) $\frac{7}{10}$

20. $5\frac{3}{5} + 7 =$
(a) $12\frac{3}{5}$ (b) 3   (c) $2\frac{2}{5}$ (d) 12   (e) $13\frac{2}{5}$

21. $3\frac{2}{3} + \frac{8}{5} =$
(a) $4\frac{3}{5}$ (b) $\frac{1}{15}$ (c) $5\frac{4}{15}$ (d) 12   (e) $4\frac{1}{15}$

22. $1\frac{1}{2} + 1\frac{2}{9} =$
(a) $2\frac{1}{9}$ (b) $2\frac{13}{18}$ (c) $2\frac{1}{3}$ (d) $2\frac{3}{11}$ (e) 4

23. $1\frac{7}{9} + 2\frac{2}{3} =$
(a) 4   (b) $2\frac{7}{9}$ (c) $4\frac{1}{3}$ (d) $4\frac{4}{9}$ (e) 5

24. $6 + \frac{7}{3} =$

(a) $6\frac{4}{7}$ (b) $6\frac{1}{3}$ (c) $8\frac{1}{3}$ (d) $7\frac{1}{3}$ (e) $6\frac{3}{7}$

25. $1\frac{6}{7} + 11\frac{3}{4} =$

(a) $13\frac{17}{28}$ (b) $12\frac{9}{11}$ (c) $12\frac{9}{28}$ (d) $12\frac{9}{14}$ (e) 12

26. $9\frac{6}{7} + \frac{1}{2} =$

(a) $9\frac{8}{9}$ (b) $10\frac{5}{14}$ (c) 10 (d) $10\frac{1}{2}$ (e) $10\frac{8}{9}$

In Exercises 27 - 57, subtract and simplify.

27. $\frac{7}{9} - \frac{7}{12}$ 28. $\frac{9}{10} - \frac{3}{18}$ 29. $60 - \frac{7}{12}$ 30. $98 - \frac{15}{65}$

31. $\frac{4}{5} - \frac{8}{25}$ 32. $\frac{9}{2} - \frac{3}{8}$ 33. $6 - \frac{1}{12}$ 34. $128 - \frac{34}{78}$

35. $\frac{15}{16} - \frac{5}{6}$ 36. $\frac{9}{18} - \frac{9}{18}$ 37. $68 - \frac{4}{15}$ 38. $\frac{17}{25} - \frac{4}{15}$

39. $\frac{10}{17} - \frac{3}{34}$ 40. $\frac{14}{44} - \frac{4}{88}$ 41. $34 - 8\frac{7}{12}$ 42. $5\frac{34}{74} - 5$

43. $6\frac{1}{6} - 3\frac{15}{17}$ 44. $15 - 6\frac{7}{10}$ 45. $7\frac{1}{6} - 5\frac{9}{18}$ 46. $18\frac{4}{74} - 17$

47. $12\frac{1}{8} - 6\frac{5}{9}$ 48. $14 - 2\frac{7}{17}$ 49. $8\frac{1}{6} - 2\frac{6}{88}$

50. $2\frac{1}{3} - \frac{1}{7} =$

(a) $\frac{2}{5}$ (b) $2\frac{10}{21}$ (c) $2\frac{1}{10}$ (d) $2\frac{4}{21}$ (e) $\frac{7}{10}$

51. $5\frac{3}{5} - 3 =$

(a) $12\frac{3}{5}$ (b) 3 (c) $2\frac{3}{5}$ (d) 12 (e) $13\frac{2}{5}$

52. $3\frac{2}{3} - \frac{8}{5} =$
(a) $4\frac{3}{5}$ (b) $2\frac{1}{15}$ (c) $5\frac{4}{15}$ (d) 12   (e) $4\frac{1}{15}$

53. $1\frac{1}{2} - 1\frac{2}{9} =$
(a) $\frac{5}{18}$ (b) $2\frac{13}{18}$ (c) $2\frac{1}{3}$ (d) $2\frac{3}{11}$ (e) $\frac{1}{7}$

54. $5\frac{8}{9} - 2\frac{2}{3} =$
(a) 3   (b) $2\frac{2}{3}$ (c) $4\frac{1}{3}$ (d) $3\frac{2}{3}$ (e) $3\frac{2}{9}$

55. $6 - \frac{7}{3} =$
(a) $6\frac{2}{3}$ (b) $3\frac{1}{3}$ (c) $8\frac{1}{3}$ (d) $7\frac{1}{3}$ (e) $3\frac{2}{3}$

56. $11\frac{6}{7} - 1\frac{3}{4} =$
(a) $10\frac{3}{28}$ (b) $10\frac{9}{11}$ (c) $10\frac{9}{14}$ (d) 10   (e) $12\frac{3}{28}$

57. $9\frac{6}{7} - \frac{1}{2} =$
(a) $9\frac{8}{9}$ (b) $9\frac{5}{14}$ (c) 9   (d) $8\frac{6}{7}$ (e) $8\frac{8}{9}$

Section F. Comparing and Ordering Fractions; Order of Operations and Mixed Quotients

Given two fractions, we would like to know which one is larger. In this section, we learn how to determine this. We also learn how to arrange a given collection of fractions from smallest to largest and from largest to smallest.

Comparing Fractions

Rule for comparing two fractions: Find two fractions that are equivalent to the given ones and whose denominators are equal. The resulting fraction with the larger numerator is the larger fraction.

For example, let's compare the fractions $\frac{3}{4}$ and $\frac{1}{2}$. We begin by writing $\frac{1}{2}$ as $\frac{1 \times 2}{2 \times 2} = \frac{2}{4}$ (notice that $\frac{3}{4}$ already has denominator 4). Now we compare the fractions $\frac{3}{4}$ and $\frac{2}{4}$ by comparing their numerators. Since $3 > 2$, we have $\frac{3}{4} > \frac{2}{4}$. Therefore, $\frac{3}{4} > \frac{1}{2}$.

Example 1. Fill in the space with the inequality symbol $<$ or $>$.
1) $\frac{1}{6} \underline{\quad} \frac{2}{3}$ 2) $\frac{3}{4} \underline{\quad} \frac{4}{5}$ 3) $\frac{5}{12} \underline{\quad} \frac{7}{18}$ 4) $\frac{13}{20} \underline{\quad} \frac{17}{22}$

Solution:
1) The LCM of 6 and 3 is 6. The fraction $\frac{1}{6}$ already has this denominator, and the fraction $\frac{2}{3}$ is equivalent to $\frac{2 \times 2}{3 \times 2} = \frac{4}{6}$. Since $1 < 4$, we have $\frac{1}{6} < \frac{4}{6}$. Therefore, $\frac{1}{6} < \frac{2}{3}$.

2) The LCM of 4 and 5 is 20. Notice that $\frac{3}{4} = \frac{3 \times 5}{4 \times 5} = \frac{15}{20}$ and $\frac{4}{5} = \frac{4 \times 4}{5 \times 4} = \frac{16}{20}$. Since $\frac{15}{20} < \frac{16}{20}$, we have $\frac{3}{4} < \frac{4}{5}$.

3) The LCM of 12 and 18 is 36. Observe that $\frac{5}{12} = \frac{5 \times 3}{12 \times 3} = \frac{15}{36}$ and $\frac{7}{18} = \frac{7 \times 2}{18 \times 2} = \frac{14}{36}$. Since $\frac{15}{36} > \frac{14}{36}$, we have $\frac{5}{12} > \frac{7}{18}$.

4) The LCM of 20 and 22 is 220. Notice that $\frac{13}{20} = \frac{13 \times 11}{20 \times 11} = \frac{143}{220}$ and $\frac{17}{22} = \frac{17 \times 10}{22 \times 10} = \frac{170}{220}$. Since $\frac{143}{220} < \frac{170}{220}$, we have $\frac{13}{20} < \frac{17}{22}$.

Ordering Fractions

Example 2. Order the fractions $\frac{2}{3}$, $\frac{1}{18}$, $\frac{5}{6}$, and $\frac{7}{9}$ from smallest to largest.

Solution: The LCM of the denominators 3, 18, 6, and 9 is 18. Convert each fraction into an equivalent one with denominator of 18:

$$\frac{2}{3} = \frac{2 \times 6}{3 \times 6} = \frac{12}{18}, \quad \frac{1}{18} \text{ is ok}, \quad \frac{5}{6} = \frac{5 \times 3}{6 \times 3} = \frac{15}{18}, \quad \text{and} \quad \frac{7}{9} = \frac{7 \times 2}{9 \times 2} = \frac{14}{18}.$$

From smallest to largest, we have $\frac{1}{18}$, $\frac{2}{3}$, $\frac{7}{9}$, and $\frac{5}{6}$.

Example 3. Order the fractions $1\frac{3}{4}$, $3\frac{1}{5}$, $2\frac{7}{10}$, and $1\frac{1}{4}$ from largest to smallest.

Solution: When comparing mixed numbers, the one with the larger whole number is the larger mixed number. This means that $3\frac{1}{5}$ is larger than $2\frac{7}{10}$ because $3 > 2$. The mixed numbers $1\frac{3}{4}$ and $1\frac{1}{4}$ are both smaller than $2\frac{7}{10}$ since $2 > 1$. We need to compare $1\frac{3}{4}$ and $1\frac{1}{4}$ by comparing their fraction parts. Notice that $\frac{3}{4} > \frac{1}{4}$, so $1\frac{3}{4} > 1\frac{1}{4}$. From largest to smallest, we have $3\frac{1}{5}$, $2\frac{7}{10}$, $1\frac{3}{4}$, and $1\frac{1}{4}$.

Note: Sometimes it is *not neccessary* to find the least common denominator (LCD) when comparing or ordering fractions. The following rule is similar to the rule stated in Section E when adding or subracting fractions.

Alternative Rule for comparing fractions: Multiply both the numerator and the denominator of the fraction on the left by the denominator of the fraction on the right. Then multiply both the numerator and the denominator of the fraction on the right by the denominator of the fraction on the left. The fraction with the largest numerator is the largest fraction and the fraction with the smallest numerator is the smallest fraction.

In the case of comparing two or more fractions, we can compare two fractions at a time.

Example 4. Which is the largest fraction?
1) $\frac{2}{3}$, $\frac{1}{18}$ 2) $\frac{2}{3}$, $\frac{1}{18}$, $\frac{5}{6}$, and $\frac{7}{9}$

Solution:
1) The fractions $\frac{2}{3}$ and $\frac{1}{18}$ is equivalent to $\left(\frac{18}{18}\right)\frac{2}{3} = \frac{36}{54}$ and $\left(\frac{3}{3}\right)\frac{1}{18} = \frac{3}{54}$. Since $36 > 3$, we have $\frac{36}{54} > \frac{3}{54}$. Therefore, $\frac{2}{3} > \frac{1}{18}$.

2) We compare the first two fractions, then compare the largest of these to the third, and so on. First compare $\frac{2}{3}$ and $\frac{1}{18}$. We know that $\frac{2}{3} > \frac{1}{18}$ from Example 1.

Now take $\frac{2}{3}$ and compare it with $\frac{5}{6}$: $\left(\frac{6}{6}\right)\frac{2}{3} = \frac{12}{18}$ and $\left(\frac{3}{3}\right)\frac{5}{6} = \frac{15}{18}$

Since $15 > 12$, we have $\frac{15}{18} > \frac{12}{18}$. Therefore, $\frac{5}{6} > \frac{2}{3}$.

Next we compare $\frac{5}{6}$ with $\frac{7}{9}$: $\qquad \left(\frac{9}{9}\right)\frac{5}{6} = \frac{45}{54}$ and $\left(\frac{6}{6}\right)\frac{7}{9} = \frac{42}{54}$

Since $45 > 42$, we have $\frac{45}{54} > \frac{42}{54}$. And so, $\frac{45}{54} = \frac{5}{6}$ is the largest fraction.

Order of Operations

The order of operations with fractions and mixed numbers is the same as for integers; we use PE$\overleftrightarrow{MD}\overleftrightarrow{AS}$.

Example 5. Evaluate.

1) $\frac{4}{5} + 3 \times \frac{1}{12}$ $\qquad$ 2) $\left(\frac{4}{5} + 3\right) \times \frac{1}{12}$ $\qquad$ 3) $\frac{5}{6} - \frac{1}{30} + \frac{1}{3}$

4) $\frac{5}{6} - \left(\frac{1}{30} + \frac{1}{3}\right)$ $\qquad$ 5) $3 \div 2\frac{1}{7} - \frac{5}{7}$ $\qquad$ 6) $3 \div \left(2\frac{1}{7} - \frac{5}{7}\right)$

Solution:

1) $\frac{4}{5} + 3 \times \frac{1}{12} = \frac{4}{5} + \frac{3}{1} \times \frac{1}{12} = \frac{4}{5} + \frac{1}{4}$

$\qquad = \frac{4 \times 4}{5 \times 4} + \frac{1 \times 5}{4 \times 5} = \frac{16}{20} + \frac{5}{20} = \frac{21}{20} = 1\frac{1}{20}$

2) $\left(\frac{4}{5} + 3\right) \times \frac{1}{12} = \left(\frac{4}{5} + \frac{3}{1}\right) \times \frac{1}{12} = \left(\frac{4}{5} + \frac{3 \times 5}{1 \times 5}\right) \times \frac{1}{12}$

$\qquad = \left(\frac{4}{5} + \frac{15}{5}\right) \times \frac{1}{12} = \frac{19}{5} \times \frac{1}{12} = \frac{19}{60}$

3) $\frac{5}{6} - \frac{1}{30} + \frac{1}{3} = \frac{5 \times 5}{6 \times 5} - \frac{1}{30} + \frac{1 \times 10}{3 \times 10} = \frac{25}{30} - \frac{1}{30} + \frac{10}{30}$

$\qquad = \frac{25 - 1 + 10}{30} = \frac{34}{30} = 1\frac{4}{30} = 1\frac{2}{15}$

4) $\frac{5}{6} - \left(\frac{1}{30} + \frac{1}{3}\right) = \frac{5}{6} - \left(\frac{1}{30} + \frac{1 \times 10}{3 \times 10}\right) = \frac{5}{6} - \left(\frac{1}{30} + \frac{10}{30}\right)$

$\qquad = \frac{5}{6} - \frac{11}{30} = \frac{5 \times 5}{6 \times 5} - \frac{11}{30} = \frac{25}{30} - \frac{11}{30} = \frac{14}{30} = \frac{7}{15}$

51

5) $3 \div 2\frac{1}{7} - \frac{5}{7} = \frac{3}{1} \div \frac{15}{7} - \frac{5}{7} = \frac{3}{1} \times \frac{7}{15} - \frac{5}{7} = \frac{7}{5} - \frac{5}{7}$

$$= \frac{7 \times 7}{5 \times 7} - \frac{5 \times 5}{7 \times 5} = \frac{49}{35} - \frac{25}{35} = \frac{24}{35}$$

6) $3 \div \left(2\frac{1}{7} - \frac{5}{7}\right) = 3 \div \left(\frac{15}{7} - \frac{5}{7}\right) = 3 \div \frac{10}{7} = \frac{3}{1} \times \frac{7}{10} = \frac{21}{10} = 2\frac{1}{10}$

Mixed Quotients

A **mixed quotient** is a fraction whose numerator or denominator (or both) contains a fraction. Examples of mixed quotients are

$$\frac{\frac{2}{3} + \frac{1}{6}}{\frac{4}{9}}, \quad \frac{4 - \frac{1}{2}}{\frac{3}{4} + 2}, \quad \frac{1}{\frac{11}{12} - \frac{1}{8}}, \quad \text{and} \quad \frac{\frac{3}{10}}{\frac{6}{7}}.$$

To simplify a mixed quotient, first simplify the numerator and denominator of the given fraction. Then apply the following rule:

Rule: $\dfrac{\frac{a}{b}}{\frac{c}{d}} = \dfrac{a}{b} \div \dfrac{c}{d}$

Example 6. Simplify.

1) $\dfrac{\frac{2}{3} + \frac{1}{6}}{\frac{4}{9}}$ 2) $\dfrac{4 - \frac{1}{2}}{\frac{3}{4} + 2}$ 3) $\dfrac{1}{\frac{11}{12} - \frac{1}{8}}$

Solution:

1) First we add $\frac{2}{3} + \frac{1}{6}$:

$$\frac{2}{3} + \frac{1}{6} = \frac{2 \times 2}{3 \times 2} + \frac{1}{6} = \frac{4}{6} + \frac{1}{6} = \frac{5}{6}$$

Next we convert $\dfrac{\frac{2}{3} + \frac{1}{6}}{\frac{4}{9}} = \dfrac{\frac{5}{6}}{\frac{4}{9}}$ into a division problem by applying the rule, then simplify:

$$\frac{\frac{5}{6}}{\frac{4}{9}} = \frac{5}{6} \div \frac{4}{9} = \frac{5}{6} \times \frac{9}{4} = \frac{5 \times 3}{2 \times 4} = \frac{15}{8} = 1\frac{7}{8}$$

2) Work out the numerator:

$$4 - \frac{1}{2} = \frac{4 \times 2}{1 \times 2} - \frac{1}{2} = \frac{8}{2} - \frac{1}{2} = \frac{7}{2}$$

Next work out the denominator:

$$\frac{3}{4} + 2 = \frac{3}{4} + \frac{2 \times 4}{1 \times 4} = \frac{3}{4} + \frac{8}{4} = \frac{11}{4}$$

Now divide:

$$\frac{\frac{7}{2}}{\frac{11}{4}} = \frac{7}{2} \div \frac{11}{4} = \frac{7}{2} \times \frac{4}{11} = \frac{14}{11} = 1\frac{3}{11}.$$

3) First subtract the denominator (notice that the LCM of 12 and 8 is 24):

$$\frac{11}{12} - \frac{1}{8} = \frac{11 \times 2}{12 \times 2} - \frac{1 \times 3}{8 \times 3} = \frac{22}{24} - \frac{3}{24} = \frac{19}{24}$$

Now divide:

$$\frac{1}{\frac{19}{24}} = 1 \div \frac{19}{24} = 1 \times \frac{24}{19} = \frac{24}{19} = 1\frac{5}{19}$$

Exercises: Chapter 2, Section F

In Exercises 1 - 12, choose the smallest fraction.

1. $\frac{8}{9}, \frac{15}{9}$ 2. $\frac{1}{10}, \frac{5}{4}$ 3. $\frac{4}{9}, \frac{5}{11}$ 4. $\frac{5}{4}, \frac{3}{10}$

5. $\frac{5}{6}, \frac{7}{6}$ 6. $\frac{5}{4}, \frac{5}{28}$ 7. $\frac{5}{12}, \frac{1}{6}$ 8. $\frac{5}{3}, \frac{7}{63}$

9. $\frac{7}{8}, \frac{5}{12}$ 10. $\frac{23}{25}, \frac{9}{4}$ 11. $\frac{2}{3}, \frac{13}{14}$ 12. $\frac{63}{41}, \frac{9}{4}$

In Exercises 13 - 17, choose the largest fraction.

13. (a) $\frac{3}{4}$ (b) $\frac{2}{3}$ (c) $\frac{9}{4}$ (d) $\frac{2}{9}$ (e) $\frac{6}{7}$

14. (a) $\frac{5}{2}$ (b) $\frac{4}{5}$ (c) $\frac{9}{10}$ (d) $\frac{1}{9}$ (e) $\frac{8}{7}$

15. (a) $\frac{1}{2}$ (b) $\frac{1}{5}$ (c) $\frac{2}{7}$ (d) $\frac{4}{9}$ (e) $\frac{3}{4}$

16. (a) $\frac{2}{11}$ (b) $\frac{3}{13}$ (c) $\frac{5}{26}$ (d) $\frac{6}{7}$ (e) $\frac{5}{8}$

17. (a) $\frac{5}{4}$ (b) $\frac{3}{4}$ (c) $\frac{7}{10}$ (d) $\frac{4}{7}$ (e) $\frac{1}{2}$

In Exercises 18 - 32, evaluate.

18. $\frac{8}{9} + 9 \times \frac{7}{12}$ 19. $\left(\frac{6}{13} + 3\right) \times \frac{9}{16}$ 20. $\frac{11}{12} - \frac{1}{60} + \frac{1}{3}$

21. $\frac{6}{13} - \left(\frac{1}{30} + \frac{3}{10}\right)$ 22. $8 \div 5\frac{6}{7} - \frac{5}{8}$ 23. $7 \div \left(2\frac{7}{9} - 1\frac{5}{7}\right)$

24. $\frac{3}{4} + \left(\frac{3}{5} \div \frac{3}{10}\right) - \left(\frac{3}{35} \times \frac{5}{18}\right)$ 25. $\frac{5}{9} + 6 \times \frac{9}{16}$

26. $\frac{5}{6} - \left(\frac{3}{4} - \frac{1}{3}\right) + \left(\frac{2}{3} \div \frac{3}{5}\right) =$

(a) $1\frac{5}{12}$ (b) $2\frac{1}{15}$ (c) $\frac{11}{108}$ (d) $1\frac{5}{108}$ (e) $1\frac{57}{108}$

27. $5\frac{4}{5} + \left(\frac{1}{3} - \frac{3}{10}\right) =$

(a) $1\frac{5}{6}$ (b) $5\frac{5}{6}$ (c) $\frac{1}{30}$ (d) $1\frac{9}{10}$ (e) 4

28. $8 \div \left(3\frac{1}{5} + 1\frac{1}{6}\right) =$

(a) $1\frac{109}{131}$ (b) $\frac{131}{240}$ (c) $2\frac{109}{131}$ (d) $1\frac{131}{240}$ (e) 3

29. $\left(\frac{2}{3} - \frac{1}{8}\right) + \left(3\frac{1}{4} - 2\frac{2}{3}\right) =$

(a) $1\frac{1}{24}$ (b) $1\frac{1}{8}$ (c) $2\frac{5}{24}$ (d) $\frac{1}{24}$ (e) $2\frac{1}{12}$

30. $\frac{1}{4} + \left(\frac{2}{7} \times \frac{49}{8}\right) - \left(5\frac{1}{2} \div 3\frac{1}{3}\right) =$

(a) $\frac{1}{2}$ (b) $1\frac{1}{6}$ (c) $1\frac{7}{20}$ (d) $\frac{7}{20}$ (e) $1\frac{1}{20}$

31. $\frac{1}{2} - \left(\frac{2}{7} \div \frac{2}{3}\right) + \left(6\frac{1}{4} \times 1\frac{3}{5}\right) =$

(a) $10\frac{1}{14}$ (b) $\frac{1}{14}$ (c) $9\frac{4}{7}$ (d) $10\frac{13}{14}$ (e) $2\frac{1}{21}$

32. $4 \div 4\frac{3}{7} - \frac{1}{2} =$

(a) $\frac{17}{56}$ (b) $-\frac{1}{14}$ (c) $\frac{13}{14}$ (d) $\frac{3}{14}$ (e) $\frac{25}{62}$

In Exercises 33 - 37, simplify.

33. $\dfrac{\frac{3}{4} + \frac{4}{3}}{\frac{5}{24}} =$

(a) 10   (b) 5   (c) $1\frac{1}{12}$ (d) $2\frac{1}{12}$ (e) $\dfrac{125}{288}$

34. $\dfrac{2}{\frac{1}{2} - \frac{3}{10}} =$

(a) 10   (b) $\dfrac{2}{5}$ (c) $\dfrac{1}{5}$ (d) $\dfrac{1}{4}$ (e) $\dfrac{1}{20}$

35. $\dfrac{\frac{1}{4}}{2 - \frac{6}{7}} =$

(a) $1\frac{1}{7}$ (b) $\dfrac{7}{32}$ (c) $\dfrac{2}{7}$ (d) $2\frac{1}{14}$ (e) $\dfrac{1}{14}$

36. $\dfrac{3 - \frac{4}{9}}{\frac{9}{2} - 2} =$

(a) $\dfrac{1}{45}$ (b) 4   (c) $1\frac{1}{45}$ (d) $2\frac{1}{2}$ (e) $\dfrac{5}{9}$

37. $\dfrac{3 - \frac{4}{9}}{5} =$

(a) $2\frac{5}{9}$ (b) $\dfrac{23}{45}$ (c) $\dfrac{1}{9}$ (d) $\dfrac{1}{45}$ (e) $\dfrac{2}{5}$

Section G. Solving Word Problems

When solving word problems involving fractions or mixed numbers, the word 'of' often arises.

Rule: The word 'of' means multiply.

For example, $\frac{1}{2}$ of $\frac{2}{3}$ means $\frac{1}{2} \times \frac{2}{3} = \frac{1}{3}$ and $\frac{7}{12}$ of $\frac{9}{14}$ means $\frac{7}{12} \times \frac{9}{14} = \frac{3}{8}$.

Example 1. Solve each word problem.

1) If a $21\frac{3}{4}$ ounce soda bottle is $\frac{2}{5}$ full, how many ounces of soda does it contain?

Solution: We find $\frac{2}{5}$ of $21\frac{3}{4}$. To do so, we multiply $\frac{2}{5} \times 21\frac{3}{4}$.
$$\frac{2}{5} \times 21\frac{3}{4} = \frac{2}{5} \times \frac{87}{4} = \frac{87}{10} = 8\frac{7}{10}$$
It contains $8\frac{7}{10}$ ounces of soda.

2) Joe borrowed $450 from his friend. If he paid back $\frac{4}{9}$ of the amount, how much does he still owe?

Solution: Joe paid $200 back to his friend since
$$\frac{4}{9} \text{ of } 450 \text{ is } \frac{4}{9} \times 450 = \frac{4}{9} \times \frac{450}{1} = \frac{200}{1} = 200.$$
Therefore, he owes $450 − $200 = $250.

3) A painter purchased 10 gallons of paint. If he used $\frac{1}{5}$ of the paint on Monday and $\frac{3}{4}$ of the remaining paint on Tuesday, how much did he used altogether?

Solution: On Monday, he used 2 gallons:
$$\frac{1}{5} \text{ of } 10 \text{ is } \frac{1}{5} \times 10 = \frac{1}{5} \times \frac{10}{1} = \frac{2}{1} = 2$$
He is left with 10 gallons −2 gallons = 8 gallons. On Tuesday, he used 6 gallons because
$$\frac{3}{4} \text{ of } 8 \text{ is } \frac{3}{4} \times 8 = \frac{3}{4} \times \frac{8}{1} = \frac{6}{1} = 6.$$
Altogether, he used 2 gallons + 6 gallons = 8 gallons of paint.

4) A bag of mixed fruits and nuts contains $7\frac{5}{6}$ servings and each serving contains 42 calories of fat. How many calories of fat are in $\frac{2}{3}$ of a bag of mixed fruits and nuts?

Solution: In one bag, there are $7\frac{5}{6} \times 42 = \frac{47}{6} \times \frac{42}{1} = \frac{329}{1} = 329$ calories of fat. To find out the number of calories of fat in $\frac{2}{3}$ of a bag, we multiply

$$\frac{2}{3} \times \frac{329}{1} = \frac{658}{3} = 219\frac{1}{3}.$$

Therefore, there are $219\frac{1}{3}$ calories of fat in $\frac{2}{3}$ of a bag.

5) In a litter of kittens, three-fourths of the kittens are male and two-fifths of the kittens have blue eyes. What fraction of the litter contains blue-eyed female kittens?

Solution: If $\frac{3}{4}$ of the kittens are male, then $1 - \frac{3}{4} = \frac{4}{4} - \frac{3}{4} = \frac{4-3}{4} = \frac{1}{4}$ of the kittens are female. We need to find $\frac{2}{5}$ of $\frac{1}{4}$: $\frac{2}{5} \times \frac{1}{4} = \frac{1}{10}$. Therefore, $\frac{1}{10}$ of the kittens are blue-eyed females.

6) How many pieces of a 18 foot long rope can be made if it is cut into $2\frac{1}{3}$ foot pieces? How much excess rope will be left over?

Solution: We want to divide an 18 foot rope into $2\frac{1}{3}$ foot pieces:

$$18 \div 2\frac{1}{3} = \frac{18}{1} \div \frac{7}{3} = \frac{18}{1} \times \frac{3}{7} = \frac{18 \times 3}{7} = \frac{54}{7} = 7\frac{5}{7}$$

Therefore, the rope can be cut into 7 pieces, each $2\frac{1}{3}$ feet long, and there will be a $\frac{5}{7}$ foot piece remaining.

7) A jar of instant coffee contains $26\frac{7}{12}$ ounces of coffee. How many cups of coffee containing $1\frac{5}{6}$ ounces of coffee can be made?

Solution: $26\frac{7}{12} \div 1\frac{5}{6} = \frac{319}{12} \div \frac{11}{6} = \frac{319}{12} \times \frac{6}{11} = \frac{319 \times 1}{2 \times 11} = \frac{319}{22} = 14\frac{11}{22} = 14\frac{1}{2}$.
Therefore, $14\frac{1}{2}$ cups can be made.

8) Danielle and Marcos share a steak for dinner. Danielle ate $\frac{1}{5}$ of the steak and Marcos ate $\frac{7}{10}$ of the steak. What fraction of the steak has been eaten?

Solution: To find the fraction of the steak that was eaten, add the fractions:

$$\frac{1}{5} + \frac{7}{10} = \left(\frac{2}{2}\right)\frac{1}{5} + \frac{7}{10} = \frac{2}{10} + \frac{7}{10} = \frac{2+7}{10} = \frac{9}{10}$$

9) Steve, Avi, and Tom go to dinner. Steve paid $\frac{1}{3}$ of the bill and Avi paid $\frac{1}{4}$ of the bill. What fraction of the bill did Tom pay?

Solution: Together, Steve and Avi paid

$$\frac{1}{3} + \frac{1}{4} = \left(\frac{4}{4}\right)\frac{1}{3} + \left(\frac{3}{3}\right)\frac{1}{4} = \frac{4}{12} + \frac{3}{12} = \frac{4+3}{12} = \frac{7}{12}$$

of the bill. Therefore, Tom paid

$$1 - \frac{7}{12} = \frac{12}{12} - \frac{7}{12} = \frac{12-7}{12} = \frac{5}{12}$$

of the bill.

10) A carpenter earns \$45 an hour. He worked $6\frac{1}{2}$ hours on Monday, $5\frac{3}{4}$ hours on Wednesday, and $7\frac{3}{4}$ hours on Friday. How much did he earned for the three days?

Solution: The total number of hours that the carpenter worked is:

$$6\frac{1}{2} + 5\frac{3}{4} + 7\frac{3}{4} = \frac{13}{2} + \frac{23}{4} + \frac{31}{4} = \left(\frac{2}{2}\right)\frac{13}{2} + \frac{23}{4} + \frac{31}{4}$$
$$= \frac{26}{4} + \frac{23}{4} + \frac{31}{4} = \frac{80}{4} = 20 \text{ hours}$$

Therefore, the carpenter earned $\$45 \times 20 = \$900$.

Exercises: Chapter 2, Section G

In Exercises 1 - 14, solve each word problem.

1. A bottle of contains antibiotic capsules. Each capsule contains $\frac{3}{4}$ grams of antibiotic. How many grams of antibiotics are contained in a bottle of 300 capsules?

2. Each vitamin pill contains $\frac{2}{9}$ of the daily requirements of vitamin B. What part of the daily requirement will 4 pills contain?

3. In a shipment of 350 light bulbs, $\frac{3}{14}$ were defective. Find the number of good light bulbs.

4. If $\frac{5}{9}$ of Tom's $4,500 tuition bill was paid by his father, how much did Tom pay by himself?

5. A plumber has a piece of pipe $2\frac{1}{2}$ feet long. He needs $\frac{1}{5}$ of the pipe to repair a sink. What length must he cut off from the piece of pipe to do the repair?
   (a) $\frac{5}{2}$ ft.   (b) $\frac{1}{5}$ ft.   (c) $\frac{1}{2}$ ft.   (d) $\frac{2}{7}$ ft.   (e) 5 ft.

6. Steven's sister ate $\frac{2}{7}$ of his candy. If there were 56 pieces of candy in all, how many pieces did his sister eat?
   (a) 40   (b) 12   (c) 196   (d) 16   (e) 56

7. Carl and his brother Max are mowing their lawn together. If Carl has mowed $\frac{2}{5}$ of the lawn and Max has mowed another $\frac{1}{4}$ of the lawn, how much of the lawn has not been mowed?
   (a) $\frac{1}{10}$ (b) $\frac{9}{20}$ (c) $\frac{9}{10}$ (d) $\frac{3}{10}$ (e) $\frac{7}{20}$

8. At 8:00 AM, Joe mowed $\frac{2}{5}$ of his lawn. Later that morning, his brother Sam mowed $\frac{1}{4}$ of the lawn that Joe didn't mow. How much of the lawn has not been mowed?
   (a) $\frac{3}{10}$ (b) $\frac{7}{20}$ (c) $\frac{9}{20}$ (d) $\frac{1}{10}$ (e) $\frac{9}{10}$

9. Paul borrowed $5,000 from his sister Diane. If he paid back $\frac{2}{5}$ of the amount, how much does he still owe Diane?
   (a) $3,000   (b) $2,000   (c) $1,000   (d) $200   (e) $300

10. At a church, $\frac{3}{4}$ of the congregation is composed of adults and the rest are youths. Two-thirds of the youths in the congregation are female. What fraction of the congregation are female youths?

(a) $\frac{1}{2}$ (b) $\frac{1}{6}$ (c) $\frac{5}{12}$ (d) $\frac{1}{12}$ (e) $\frac{2}{3}$

11. An interior designer ordered cloth materials for 12 windows. Each window has 3 drapery panels. How many yards of material should the designer order if each panel requires $2\frac{2}{3}$ yards of material?

(a) 36 yds.   (b) 96 yds.   (c) $13\frac{1}{2}$ yds.   (d) 32 yds.   (e) 8 yds.

12. Frances spends $\frac{1}{4}$ of his money and loses $\frac{2}{3}$ of the remainder. If he has 10¢ left, how much money did he start with?

(a) 10¢   (b) 20¢   (c) 50¢   (d) 80¢   (e) 40¢

13. What is the cost of $3\frac{3}{4}$ pounds of cheese if the cost is \$4 per pound?

(a) \$15   (b) \$12   (c) \$14   (d) \$11   (e) \$16

14. Patricia is 14 years old, Laurel's age is $\frac{3}{7}$ of Patricia 's age, Bob's age is $2\frac{2}{3}$ of Laurel's age, and Christian's age is $2\frac{1}{2}$ of Bob's age. How old is Christian?

(a) 4   (b) 3   (c) 40   (d) 20   (e) 10

Chapter 3:   Decimals

Section A.   Decimals and Decimal Fractions

A fraction whose denominator is 10, 100, 1,000, etc. (the denominator is a power of 10) is called a **decimal fraction**. Examples of decimal fractions are

$$\frac{3}{10}, \ \frac{97}{100}, \ \text{and} \ \frac{78,500}{10,000}.$$

We write decimal fractions in **decimal notation** as follows:

$$\frac{3}{10} = .3 \text{ or } 0.3, \quad \text{and} \quad \frac{97}{100} = .97 \text{ or } 0.97.$$

The 'dot' is called the **decimal point**. We read .3 as 'point three' and .97 as 'point ninety-seven. Note that 0.3 is read as 'zero point three' and 0.97 as 'zero point ninety-seven'. Decimal fractions can be always be written in decimal notation. We call a fraction written in decimal notation a **decimal number (or just decimal)**, and say that it is in a **decimal form**.

Rule for writing a decimal fraction as a decimal number: The number of zeros in the denominator of a decimal fraction tells you how many 'decimal places' (digits) are after the decimal point in the decimal number:

For example, the denominator of the fraction $\frac{5}{10}$ has one zero. This means that there is one decimal place (1 digit) after the decimal point of the decimal number: $\frac{5}{10} = 0.5$.

Similarly, the denominator of the fraction $\frac{17}{100}$ has two zeros. This means that there are two decimal places (2 digits) after the decimal point of the decimal number: $\frac{17}{100} = 0.17$. Notice that $\frac{356}{10,000}$ has four zeros in the denominator, but only three digits in the numerator. There should be 4 decimal places (4 digits) after the decimal point of the decimal number. In this case, we put a zero before 356. This zero is called a **leading zero**. This makes sense because 0356 = 356. Therefore,

$$\underbrace{\frac{0356}{10,000} = 0.0356}.$$

Four decimal places are needed.

A mixed number can be converted into decimal form in a similar way. The resulting decimal number will have a **whole number part** (which is the same as the whole number part of the mixed number) and a **decimal part**. For example:

$$\underbrace{13\frac{52}{100} = 13.52}_{\frac{52}{100}=.52} \quad \text{and} \quad \underbrace{410\frac{8}{1,000} = 410.008}_{\frac{8}{1,000}=.008}$$

To convert an a decimal fraction that is also an improper fraction into a decimal, first turn it into a mixed number, then proceed as before. For example,

$$\frac{49}{10} = \underbrace{4\frac{9}{10} = 4.9}_{\frac{9}{10}=.9} \quad \text{and} \quad \frac{856}{100} = 8\underbrace{\frac{56}{100} = 8.56.}_{\frac{56}{100}=.56}$$

Example 1. Convert each fraction to decimal notation.

1) $\frac{4}{10}$ 2) $\frac{6}{100}$ 3) $\frac{15}{100,000}$ 4) $3\frac{1}{1,000}$ 5) $25\frac{713}{10,000}$

Solution: 1) 0.4   2) 0.06   3) 0.00015   4) 3.001   5) 25.0713

Rule for writing a decimal number as a decimal fraction: The number of digits after the decimal point tells you how many zeros come after the one in the denominator.

For example, the decimal 0.9 has one digit, 9, after the decimal point. Therefore, $0.9 = \frac{9}{10}$ (the denominator has one 0 after the 1).

Similarly, 0.518 has three digits (5, 1, and 8) after the decimal point. Therefore, $0.518 = \frac{518}{1,000}$ (the denominator has three 0's after the 1). When the decimal number has a whole number part other than zero, simply put it on the left of the decimal fraction. For example,

$$\underbrace{7.21 = 7\frac{21}{100}}_{.21=\frac{21}{100}} \quad \text{and} \quad \underbrace{1,215.002 = 1,215\frac{2}{1,000}}_{.002=\frac{2}{1,000}}.$$

Example 2. Convert each decimal number to a decimal fraction.

1) 0.44   2) 0.0093   3) 6.901   4) 1.00001

Solution: 1) $\frac{44}{100}$ 2) $\frac{93}{10,000}$ 3) $6\frac{901}{1,000}$ 4) $1\frac{1}{100,000}$

Sometimes we will need to add zeros to a decimal number:

Rule for adding zeros to decimal numbers: Zeros can always be added at the end of a decimal number without changing its value. These additional zeros are called **trailing zeros**.

For example, 0.3, 0.30, 0.300, and 0.3000 are equal to each other because their decimal fractions are equivalent to each other:

$$0.3 = \frac{3}{10}, \quad 0.30 = \frac{30}{100}, \quad 0.300 = \frac{300}{1,000}, \quad \text{and } 0.3000 = \frac{3,000}{10,000}.$$

Example 3. Write each decimal without trailing zeros.
1) 0.8100   2) 14.4030   3) 389.0050000   4) 7.00000

Solution: 1) 0.81   2) 14.403   3) 389.005   4) 7

A decimal number has the same **word name** as its corresponding decimal fraction. For example, $0.1 = \frac{1}{10}$ is **one tenth**, $0.15 = \frac{15}{100}$ is **fifteen hundredths**, and $0.0793 = \frac{793}{10,000}$ is **seven hundred ninety-three ten thousandths**. The word name for $507.02 = 507\frac{2}{100}$ is **five hundred seven and two hundredths**. Notice that the word 'and' joins the word name 507 and the word name .02.

Example 4. Write the word name for each decimal.
1) 0.64   2) 0.053   3) 27.90405

Solution: 1) Sixty-four hundredths
          2) Fifty-three thousandths
          3) Twenty-seven and ninety thousand, four hundred five hundred thousandths

Recall that each digit of a whole number has a name which designates its position in the number. The number 5,172, for example, has 5 in the thousands place, 1 in the hundreds place, 7 in the tens place, and 2 in the ones place. Notice:

$$5,172 = 5,000 + 100 + 70 + 2$$
$$= \underbrace{5 \times 1,000}_{\text{five thousands}} + \underbrace{1 \times 100}_{\text{one hundred}} + \underbrace{7 \times 10}_{\text{seven tens}} + \underbrace{2 \times 1}_{\text{two ones}}$$

For decimal forms, we have a similar naming system. The decimal 0.13592 has 1 in the **tenths** place, 3 in the **hundredths** place, 5 in the **thousandths** place, 9 in the **ten thousandths** place, and 2 in the **hundredth thousandths** place. Observe that $0.13592 = \frac{13,592}{100,000}$ and we can expand this fraction:

$$\frac{13,592}{100,000} = \frac{10,000}{100,000} + \frac{3,000}{100,000} + \frac{500}{100,000} + \frac{90}{100,000} + \frac{2}{100,000}$$
$$= \frac{1}{10} + \frac{3}{100} + \frac{5}{1,000} + \frac{9}{10,000} + \frac{2}{100,000}$$
$$= \underbrace{1\left(\frac{1}{10}\right)}_{\text{one tenth}} + \underbrace{3\left(\frac{1}{100}\right)}_{\text{three hundredths}} + \underbrace{5\left(\frac{1}{1,000}\right)}_{\text{five thousandths}} + \underbrace{9\left(\frac{1}{10,000}\right)}_{\text{nine ten thousandths}} + \underbrace{2\left(\frac{1}{100,000}\right)}_{\text{two hundred thousandths}}$$

In decimal form, this becomes:

$$0.13592 = 0.10000 + 0.03000 + 0.00500 + 0.00090 + 0.00002$$
$$= 0.1 + 0.03 + 0.005 + 0.0009 + 0.00002$$
$$= \underbrace{0.1}_{\text{one tenth}} + \underbrace{3(0.01)}_{\text{three hundredths}} + \underbrace{5(0.001)}_{\text{five thousandths}} + \underbrace{9(0.0001)}_{\text{nine ten thousandths}} + \underbrace{2(0.00001)}_{\text{two hundred thousandths}}$$

Similarly, $3,205.087$ can be expanded in decimal form as:

$$3,205.087 = 3,000 + 200 + 5 + 0.08 + 0.007$$
$$= 3(1,000) + 2(100) + 5(1) + 8(0.01) + 7(0.001)$$

There are 3 thousands, 2 hundreds, 0 tens, 5 ones, 0 tenths, 8 hundredths, and 7 thousandths.

Example 5. Expand in decimal form.
1) 52.16   2) 8.202   3) 400.3109

Solution: 1) $5(10) + 2(1) + 1(0.1) + 6(0.01)$
2) $8(1) + 2(0.1) + 2(0.001)$
3) $4(100) + 3(0.1) + 1(0.01) + 9(0.0001)$

Exercises: Chapter 3, Section A

In Exercises 1 - 12, convert each decimal fraction to decimal number.

1. $\dfrac{9}{10}$ 2. $\dfrac{2}{100}$ 3. $\dfrac{13}{100,000}$ 4. $5\dfrac{7}{1,000}$ 5. $25\dfrac{313}{10,000}$

6. $\dfrac{315}{10}$ 7. $\dfrac{456}{100}$ 8. $\dfrac{2,345}{100,000}$ 9. $\dfrac{10,489}{1,000}$ 10. $\dfrac{7,143}{10,000}$

11. $5\dfrac{23}{1,000} =$
(a) 0.523   (b) 523.001   (c) 5.023   (d) 5.0023   (e) 5.23

12. $\dfrac{1,301}{10,000} =$
(a) 130.1   (b) 0.01301   (c) 13.01   (d) 0.1301   (e) 1.301

In Exercises 13 - 22, convert each decimal number to a decimal fraction.

13. 0.39   14. 9.003   15. 23.9931   16. 0.20001

17. 0.0206   18. 458.0081   19. 0.0003   20. 0.474

21. 6.0003 =
(a) $\dfrac{63}{1,000}$ (b) $6\dfrac{3}{10,000}$ (c) $6\dfrac{3}{100,000}$ (d) $\dfrac{60,003}{1,000}$ (e) $6\dfrac{30}{10,000}$

22. 0.507 =
(a) $\dfrac{507}{1,000}$ (b) $\dfrac{57}{100}$ (c) $\dfrac{57}{10,000}$ (d) $\dfrac{507}{10,000}$ (e) $5\dfrac{7}{1,000}$

In Exercises 23 - 30, write each decimal without trailing zeros.

23. 0.43100   24. 395.0030   25. 9.30500   26. 45.00000

27. 1.3700   28. 5.20300   29. 0.30520   30. 5.02000

In Exercises 31 - 38, write the word name for each decimal.

31. 0.31   32. 395.2   33. 9.285   34. 4.45092

35. 0.07   36. 1.0002   37. 0.366   38. 0.2

Section B. Comparing, Ordering, and Rounding Decimals

Comparing Decimals

If we are given two decimal numbers, we might want to compare their values and decide which one is the larger (or smaller) one. To do this, we follow the next rule:

Rule for comparing two decimals:
1) Compare their whole number parts. If one is larger than the other, then the decimal number with the larger whole number part is the larger number.
2) If their whole number parts are equal, compare the digits in their tenths place. If one is larger than the other, then the decimal number with the larger tenths digit is the larger number.
3) If their tenths digit is equal, compare the digits in their hundredths place. Again, if one is larger than the other, then the decimal number with the larger hundredths digit is the larger number. And so on.

Example 1. Fill in the blank with < or >.
1) 5.1 __ 3.6   2) 275.13 __ 276.13   3) 0.325 __ 0.375
4) 0.65 __ 0.652   5) 19.0781 __ 19.0781001

Solution:
1) 5.1 > 3.6 because 5 > 3.

2) 275.13 < 276.13 since 275 < 276.

3) 0.325 and 0.375 have the same whole number part (0) and the same tenths digit (3). The hundredths place of 0.375 (which is 7) is larger than the hundredths place of 0.325 (which is 2). Therefore, 0.325 < 0.375.

4) The whole number parts, the tenths digits, and the hundredths digits of 0.65 and 0.652 are equal. We need to compare the thousandths digit. Since 0.65 doesn't have a thousandths digit, we add on a trailing zero. This turns 0.65 into 0.650, and 0.650 < 0.652 because 0 is smaller than 2 in the thousands place.

5) All of the digits of 19.0781 and 19.0781001 are equal up to the ten thousandths place. We need to add three trailing zeros to 19.0781 because the number 19.0781001 has zeros in the hundred thousandths and millionths place. Therefore,

$$\underbrace{19.0781000}_{19.0781} \ < \ 19.0781001$$

because 0 is smaller than 1 in the millionths place.

Ordering Decimals

Example 2. Order the decimals 0.34, 1.9, 0.108, and 0.6 from smallest to largest.

Solution: Notice that 0.108 has the most number of digits to the right of the decimal point (3). We add on trailing zeros to the other decimals so that they all have three digits to the right of the decimal point: 0.340, 1.900, 0.108, and 0.600. Now we compare them by following the rule and write in order from smallest to largest: 0.108, 0.3400, 0.600, 1.900. Therefore, the order is 0.108, 0.34, 0.6, 1.9.

Example 3. Order the decimals 4.601, 4.6102, 4.60012, and 0.46001 from largest to smallest.

Solution: Each decimal requires 5 digits to the right of the decimal point. Adding on trailing zeros where needed, we have: 4.60100, 4.61020, 4.60012, and 0.46001. By the rule for comparing decimals, we have (from largest to smallest): 4.61020, 4.60100, 4.60012, and 0.46001. Therefore, the order is 4.6102, 4.601, 4.60012, 0.46001.

Rounding Decimals

We can 'cut down' the number of digits proceding the decimal place of a decimal by using **decimal approximation**. One method of approximating a decimal is called **rounding off**.

Rule for rounding off a decimal: Look at the digit to the right of the **round off digit**. If it is less than 5, you delete everything after the round off digit. If it is 5 or more, you increase the round off digit by 1, and then delete everything after it.

Example 4. Round off to the nearest tenth.
1) 8.72   2) 31.693   3) 6.249093

Solution:
1) 8.72 has a 2 in the digit to the right of the round off digit (which is 7), and 2 is less than 5. Therefore, everything after the 7 is deleted, so 8.72 rounds off to 8.7.

2) 31.693 has a 9 in the digit to the right of the round off digit, and 9 is more than 5. Therefore, we increase the round off digit (6) by 1, then delete everything after the 'new digit' in the tenths place, 7. Therefore, 31.693 rounds off to 31.7.

3) Since 4 is less than 5, you delete everything after the round off digit 2. Therefore, 6.249093 rounds off to 6.2.

Example 5. Round off to the nearest ten thousandth.
1) 0.60451   2) 2.21345   3) 15.00997

Solution:
1) 0.60451 has a 1 in the digit to the right of the round off digit, and 1 is less than 5. Therefore, everything after the 5 is deleted, so 0.60451 rounds off to 0.6045.

2) 2.21345 has a 5 in the digit to the right of the round off digit. Therefore, we increase the round off digit (4) by 1, then delete everything after the 'new digit' in the ten thousandths place, 5. Therefore, 2.21345 rounds off to 2.2135.

3) 15.00997 has a 7 in the digit to the right of the round off digit. Therefore, we increase the round off digit (9) by 1, which requires a 'carry over' of 1 into the thousandths place; since the thousandths place has a 9, this requires a further 'carry over' of 1 into the hundredths place; then delete everything after the 'new digit' 1 in the hundredths place and add trailing zeros up to the ten thousandths place. Thus, 15.00997 rounds off to 15.0100.

Exercises: Chapter 3, Section B

In Exercises 1 - 6, fill in the blank with < or >.

1. 0.1 __ 0.6   2. 21.13 __ 22.13   3. 0.375 __ 0.325

4. 3.63 __ 4.52   5. 1.112781 __ 1.11201   6. 0.6110 __ 0.61101

In Exercises 7 - 9, order the decimals from largest to smallest.

7. 12.209, 12.098, 12.099, 12.0999   8. 109.9, 112.12, 112.099, 109.099

9. 45.56, 45.9, 45.65, 45.056

In Exercises 10 - 14, round off to the nearest hundredth.

10. 2.94105   11. 3.7603   12. 10.1853   13. 23.9861   14. 0.0137

In Exercises 15 - 20, round off to the nearest thousandth.

15. 3.24109   16. 24.60802   17. 60.101808   18. 7.90555

19. 9.222777   20. 0.1498125

Section C.   Addition and Subtraction of Decimals

Rule for adding and subtracting decimals:
1) Put the decimal point under the decimal point, the ones under the ones, the tens(ths) under the tens(ths), the hundreds(ths) under the hundreds(ths), etc.
2) Add (subtract) the numbers and keep the place of the decimal point.

Example 1. Perform the indicated operation.
1) $0.09 + 2.1$ 2) $17.016 + 809.49$ 3) $2.08 - 1.99$ 4) $70.41 - 36.879$

Solution:

1)
$$\begin{array}{r} 0.09 \\ +\ 2.10 \\ \hline 2.19 \end{array}$$

2)
$$\begin{array}{r} 17.016 \\ +\ 809.492 \\ \hline 826.508 \end{array}$$

3)
$$\begin{array}{r} 2.08 \\ -\ 1.99 \\ \hline 0.09 \end{array}$$

4)
$$\begin{array}{r} 70.410 \\ -\ 36.879 \\ \hline 33.531 \end{array}$$

Example 2. Subtract 19.6 from 57.23.

Solution:
$$\begin{array}{r} 57.23 \\ -\ 19.60 \\ \hline 37.63 \end{array}$$

Example 3. Find the sum of 2.8, 79.59, and 306.003.

Solution:
$$\begin{array}{r} 2.800 \\ 79.590 \\ +\ 306.003 \\ \hline 388.393 \end{array}$$

Exercises: Chapter 3, Section C

In Exercises 1 - 8, add.

1. $23.98 + 3.2409$

2. $9.207 + 3.24$

3. $0.375 + 0.909$

4. $234.7 + 5.75 + 0.1109$

5. $100.047 + 36.814$

6. $7.02233 + 0.008$

7. $2,056.41 + 30.009$

8. $9.091 + 9.9 + 0.099$

In Exercises 9 - 18, subtract.

9. $29.08 - 9.19$

10. $22 - 5.24$

11. $45.075 - 36.083$

12. $7.001 - 1.0129$

13. $199.047 - 14$

14. $2.233 - 0.344$

15. $2,236.091 - 2,130.8$

16. $17.1 - 4.001$

17. Subtract 45.015 from 54.1.
(a) 9.085   (b) 9.301   (c) 9.01   (d) 0.085   (e) 9

18. Subtract 8.09 from 50.142.
(a) 42.52   (b) 42   (c) 42.052   (d) 42.25   (e) 42.0052

Section D. Multiplication and Division of Decimals

Multiplying Decimals

Rule for multiplying decimals:
1) Multiply the numbers without worrying about the decimal point.
2) Count the number of digits after the decimal point in the numbers that you are multiplying; take the "total".
3) The final answer should have the "total" number of digits after the decimal point.

Example 1. Multiply.
1) 0.65×177 2) 0.02×1.2 3) 5.03×0.38 4) 0.064×8.3

Solution:

$$
\begin{array}{r}
1) \quad 177 \\
\times\ .65 \\
\hline
885 \\
+\ 1062 \\
\hline
115.05
\end{array}
\qquad
\begin{array}{r}
2) \quad 0.02 \\
\times\ 1.2 \\
\hline
04 \\
+\ 02 \\
\hline
0.024
\end{array}
\qquad
\begin{array}{r}
3) \quad 5.03 \\
\times\ 0.38 \\
\hline
4024 \\
+\ 1509 \\
\hline
1.9114
\end{array}
\qquad
\begin{array}{r}
4) \quad 0.064 \\
\times\ 8.3 \\
\hline
0192 \\
+\ 0512 \\
\hline
0.5312
\end{array}
$$

Multiplying a Decimal by a Power of 10

To multiply a decimal by whole-number power of 10, move the decimal point to the right by that whole-number power.

Example 2. Multiply.
1) 3.93×10 2) 4.945×100 3) $1.45 \times 1,000$

Solution:
1) $10 = 10^1$ has power 1, so move the decimal point one place to the right:
$$3.93 \times 10 = 39.3$$

2) Since $100 = 10^2$, 10 has power 2. Move the decimal point two places to the right:
$$4.945 \times 100 = 494.5$$

3) Observe that $1,000 = 10^3$, and 10 has power 3. Move the decimal point three places to the right:
$$1.45 \times 1,000 = 1,450$$

Dividing Decimals

Rule for dividing decimals:
The procedure for dividing decimals is similar to that of division of whole numbers, **except for**:
(1) the positions of the **decimal points**;
(2) the **remainder** (we treat the remainder differently).

(a) When the **divisor is a whole number** and the **dividend is a decimal**, we place the decimal point in the quotient above the decimal point in the dividend, then we divide as though the dividend were a whole number.

Example 3. Divide: $84.48 \div 24$

Solution:

$$
\begin{array}{r}
3.52 \\
24)\overline{84.48} \\
-72 \\
\hline
124 \\
-120 \\
\hline
48 \\
-48 \\
\hline
0
\end{array}
$$

Notice that the remainder is zero. Sometimes the remainder may not be zero. In those cases (once we carry down all the numbers in the dividend), we **add on trailing zeros** to the right of the dividend and then proceed until we get our answer to our desired number of decimal places.

Example 4. Divide: $850.9 \div 24$ (Round off your answer to the nearest hundredth.)

Solution: Since we want the answer rounded off to the nearest hundredth, we will need to preceed until we get the thousandth digit in the quotient.

$$
\begin{array}{r}
35.454 \\
24)\overline{850.900} \\
-72 \\
\hline
130 \\
-120 \\
\hline
109 \\
-96 \\
\hline
130 \\
-120 \\
\hline
100 \\
-96 \\
\hline
4
\end{array}
$$

Since $4 < 5$, the answer rounded off to the nearest hundredth is 35.45.

Example 5. Divide: $2.5 \div 99$ (Round off your answer to the nearest thousandth.)

Solution: Since we want the answer rounded off the nearest thousandth, we will need to preceed until we get the ten thousandth digit in the quotient.

$$
\begin{array}{r}
0.0252 \\
99) \overline{2.5000} \\
-198 \\
\hline
520 \\
-495 \\
\hline
250 \\
-198 \\
\hline
52
\end{array}
$$

Since $2 < 5$, the answer rounded off to the nearest thousandth is 0.025.

(b) When the **divisor is a decimal**, and the **dividend is any number** (a whole number or a decimal), **make the divisor a whole number by multiplying it by an appropriate whole-number power of 10, and then multiply the dividend by that same whole-number power of 10**. Then apply part (a) if necessary.

This makes sense because if we write $a \div b$ as $\frac{a}{b}$, then we can multiply a and b by any number and obtain an equivalent fraction. When we multiply a and b by a certain whole-number power of 10, the decimal point in a and b moves to the right and the resulting denominator will be a whole number.

For example, $\quad \dfrac{17}{9.3} = \underbrace{\dfrac{17.0 \times 10}{9.3 \times 10}}_{\text{Multiplying 9.3 by 10 results in 93.}} = \dfrac{170}{93}$, and $\quad \dfrac{2.815}{12.01} = \underbrace{\dfrac{2.815 \times 100}{12.01 \times 100}}_{\text{Multiplying 12.01 by 100 results in 1,201.}} = \dfrac{281.5}{1,201}$.

Example 6. Divide: $3.15 \div 0.35$

Solution: $3.15 \div 0.35 = \dfrac{3.15}{0.35} = \dfrac{3.15 \times 100}{0.35 \times 100} = \dfrac{315}{35} = 9$

Example 7. Divide: $658 \div 0.047$

Solution: $658 \div 0.047 = \dfrac{658}{0.047} = \dfrac{658 \times 1,000}{0.047 \times 1,000} = \dfrac{658,000}{47} = 14,000$

Example 8. Divide: $10.08 \div 9.6$

Solution: $10.08 \div 9.6 = \dfrac{10.08}{9.6} = \dfrac{10.08 \times 10}{9.6 \times 10} = \dfrac{100.8}{96}$.

Now we have $100.8 \div 96$. We apply procedure (a):

```
        1.05
  96) 100.80
     −96
     ────
      480
     −480
     ────
        0
```

Dividing a Decimal by a Power of 10

To divide a decimal by whole-number power of 10, move the decimal point to the left by that whole-number power.

Example 9. Divide.
1) $5.11 \div 10$ 2) $348.6 \div 100$ 3) $56.5 \div 1,000$

Solution:
1) $10 = 10^1$ has power 1, so move the decimal point one place to the left:
$$5.11 \div 10 = 0.511$$

2) Observe that $100 = 10^2$; 10 has power 2. Move the decimal point two places to the left:
$$348.6 \div 100 = 3.486$$

3) Since $1,000 = 10^3$; 10 has power 3. Move the decimal point three places to the left:
$$56.5 \div 1,000 = 0.0565$$

Exercises: Chapter 3, Section D

In Exercises 1 - 8, multiply.

1. 23.98×3.09 2. 0.027×3.2 3. 0.375×0.909 4. 24.7×5.001

5. 100.047×36.11 6. 7.02×0.008 7. 205.41×0.009 8. 9.091×0.099

In Exercises 9 - 17, multiply by the given power of 10.

9. 3.486×10 10. 0.5312×100 11. $12.17 \times 1,000$ 12. 0.00711×100

13. 0.223×10^4 14. 0.12×10^1 15. 1.07×10^3 16. 34.7×10^5

17. $4.08 \times 10^4 =$
(a) $408,000$ (b) 408 (c) $4,080$ (d) $40,800$ (e) 40.8

In Exercises 18 - 25, divide completely (until you get remainder zero).

18. $68.94 \div 3$ 19. $91.77 \div 4.2$ 20. $288.12 \div 24$ 21. $6.12 \div 0.17$

22. $4.725 \div 1.89$ 23. $7.02 \div 0.008$ 24. $9.471 \div 0.41$ 25. $3.0525 \div 0.33$

In Exercises 26 - 34, divide by the given power of 10.

26. $3.486 \div 10$ 27. $531.2 \div 100$ 28. $12.17 \div 1,000$ 29. $0.711 \div 100$

30. $0.2 \div 10^4$ 31. $0.92 \div 10^1$ 32. $107 \div 10^3$ 33. $561,434.7 \div 10^5$

34. $408 \div 10^4 =$
(a) $4,080,000$ (b) 0.408 (c) 4.08 (d) 0.0408 (e) 0.004080

In Exercises 35 - 42, divide and round off to the nearest hundredth.

35. $29.08 \div 0.19$ 36. $22 \div 5.24$ 37. $45.075 \div 4.25$ 38. $7.001 \div 1.11$

39. $199.047 \div 14$ 40. $2.233 \div 0.344$ 41. $22.091 \div 30.8$ 42. $1.1 \div 4.12$

In Exercises 43 - 50, divide and round off to the nearest thousandth.

43. $7.08 \div 6.3$ 44. $31 \div 6.16$ 45. $43.195 \div 7.5$ 46. $9.8 \div 6.088$

47. $207 \div 3.61$ 48. $6.235 \div 0.04$ 49. $188.223 \div 19$ 50. $764.19 \div 802.19$

Section E. Converting Fractions to Decimals and Decimals to Fractions

Converting Fractions to Decimals

Rule for converting fractions to decimals: Divide the numerator of the fraction by the denominator, then round off the answer (the quotient) to a desired number of decimal places.

Example 1. Write each fraction as a decimal.

1) $\frac{1}{2}$ 2) $\frac{5}{8}$ 3) $\frac{13}{6}$ 4) $\frac{25}{99}$

Solution: 1) $\frac{1}{2} = 0.5$

```
     0.5
2) 1.0
   - 10
   ____
     0
```

2) $\frac{5}{8} = 0.625$

```
      0.625
8) 5.000
   - 48
   ____
     20
   - 16
   ____
     40
   - 40
   ____
      0
```

3) $\frac{13}{6} = 2.1\overline{6}$

```
      2.166...
6) 13.000
   - 12
   ____
     10
    - 6
   ____
     40
   - 36
   ____
     40
      ⋮
```

4) $\frac{25}{99} = 0.\overline{25}$

```
       0.2525...
99) 25.00000...
    - 198
    _____
      520
    - 495
    _____
      250
    - 198
    _____
      520
    - 495
    _____
       25
        ⋮
```

Notice that in 3) and 4), the quotient continues on forever in a repeating pattern. This kind of decimal is called a **non-terminating, repeating decimal** (as seen in Chapter 4), and the symbol used for the repeating numbers is a "bar" above the repeating numbers.

Example 2. Write each fraction as a decimal. Round off each decimal to the nearest thousandth.

1) $\frac{5}{8}$ 2) $\frac{2}{7}$

Solution: 1)
```
          0.625
     8) 5.0000
      -  48
          20
       -  16
          40
       -  40
           0
```
2)
```
          0.2857
     7) 2.00000
      -  14
          60
       -  56
          40
       -  35
          50
       -  49
           1
```

1) $\frac{5}{8} = 0.625$ 2) $\frac{2}{7} = 0.286$

Converting Decimals to Fractions

As we've seen, there are decimals which terminate, and decimals which are non-terminating, but have a repeating pattern. Next we discuss how to convert a terminating decimal into a fraction. The method for converting a non-terminating, repeating is more difficult and will not be studied here.

Rule: To convert a terminating decimal into a fraction, write the decimal as a decimal fraction and reduce it if possible. This means:
1. Write the whole number (the digits to the left of the decimal point).
2. Then write the decimal part (the digits to the right of the decimal point) divided by the number that has a "1" followed by the same number of zeros as the number of digits in the decimal part.
3. Add the results found in Steps 1. and 2.

For example, $5.193 = 5 + \frac{193}{1,000} = 5\frac{193}{1,000}$. Notice that we put 3 zeros after the 1 in the denominator because there are three digits in 193 (this is Step 2 of the rule).

Example 3. Write each decimal as a fraction.
1) 0.345   2) 30.13

Solution:
1) The whole number of 0.345 is 0. By Step 2., we divide the decimal part, 345, by 1,000 (3 zeros are added after the 1 because there are three digits in 345) and get $\frac{347}{1,000}$. Adding 0 and $\frac{347}{1,000}$ gives $\frac{347}{1,000}$. Therefore, $0.345 = \frac{347}{1,000}$.

2) The whole number of 30.13 is 30. By Step 2., we divide the decimal part, 13, by 100 (2 zeros are added after the 1 because there are two digits in 13) and we get $\frac{13}{100}$. Adding 30 and $\frac{13}{100}$ gives $30\frac{13}{100}$. Therefore, $30.13 = 30\frac{13}{100}$.

Example 4. Convert each decimal to a fraction or to mixed number in lowest terms.

1) 0.2   2) 0.47   3) 17.001   4) 9.0008

Solution: 1) $\dfrac{2}{10} = \dfrac{1}{5}$ 2) $\dfrac{47}{100}$ 3) $17\dfrac{1}{1,000}$ 4) $\underbrace{9\dfrac{8}{10,000} = 9\dfrac{1}{1,250}}_{10,000 \div 8 = 1,250}$

Exercises: Chapter 3, Section E

In Exercises 1 - 12, write each fraction as a decimal. If a repeating decimal is obtained, write the answer using the bar notation.

1. $\frac{8}{5}$ 2. $\frac{5}{22}$ 3. $\frac{2}{3}$ 4. $\frac{4}{5}$ 5. $\frac{9}{11}$

6. $\frac{1}{4}$ 7. $\frac{2}{9}$ 8. $\frac{5}{12}$ 9. $\frac{7}{16}$ 10. $\frac{8}{25}$

11. $\frac{3}{81}$ =
(a) $0.3\overline{7}$ (b) $0.\overline{3}$ (c) $0.\overline{037}$ (d) $0.3\overline{77}$ (e) $0.\overline{37}$

12. $\frac{6}{7}$ =
(a) 0.857142 (b) $0.857\overline{142}$ (c) 0.86 (d) $0.\overline{857142}$ (e) $8.\overline{57142}$

In Exercises 13 - 18, write each fraction as a decimal (round off to the nearest hundredth).

13. $\frac{7}{34}$ 14. $\frac{23}{24}$ 15. $\frac{492}{19}$ 16. $\frac{6}{16}$ 17. $\frac{916}{69}$

18. $\frac{4}{61}$ =
(a) 0.1 (b) 0.07 (c) 0.06 (d) 0.05 (e) 0.065

In Exercises 19 - 24, write each fraction as a decimal (round off to the nearest thousandth).

19. $\frac{5}{13}$ 20. $\frac{6}{35}$ 21. $\frac{512}{17}$ 22. $\frac{3}{14}$ 23. $\frac{916}{67}$

24. $\frac{8}{89}$ =
(a) 0.0898 (b) 0.0899 (c) 0.89 (d) 0.08 (e) 0.090

Section F. Solving Word Problems

A variety of word problems can be given with decimals in them. Below will give some examples to illustrate this.

Example 1. Solve each word problem.

1) Find the cost of 8 shirts if each cost $9.56.

Solution: Since one shirt costs $9.56, 8 shirts will cost 8 times as much. Therefore, the total cost is $8 \times \$9.56 = \$76.48$.

2) Philip pays $28.68 for a tank of gas. If gas sells for $2.39 per gallon, how many gallons does he buy?

Solution: We divide the total cost, $28.68, by the cost per gallon, $2.39:
$$28.68 \div 2.39 = 2868 \div 239 = 12$$
Philips buys 12 gallons of gas.

3) A business person buys a carton of 22 boxes of cereal for $55.88. If each box sells for $4.25. What is the profit?

Solution: We use the formula: Profit = total sales − total costs. First we find the total sales by multiplying the number of boxes sold, 22, by the cost of each box, $4.25 (1 box cost $4.25, so 22 boxes would cost 22 times as much):
$$4.25 \times 22 = 93.5$$
This means that the total sales is $93.50. The total cost to the business person is $55.88. Therefore,

$$\text{Profit} = \text{total sales} - \text{total costs}$$
$$= \$93.50 - \$55.88 = \$37.62.$$

4) Charles went grocery shopping last week. He bought 20 ounces (oz.) of cheese, $2\frac{1}{4}$ pounds (lbs.) of beef, and 3.25 lbs. of sugar. How many pounds of groceries did Charles buy?

Solution: First convert all items into either decimals or fractions, and make all units the same. We change the decimal 3.25 into a fraction since the other two items are given as fractions:
$$3.25 = 3\frac{1}{4}$$

Next, we convert 20 oz. into pounds. Since 1 pound = 16 ounces, we divide 20 by 16 to find the number of pounds in 20 ounces:

$$20 \div 16 = 1\frac{4}{16} = 1\frac{1}{4}$$

And so, 20 oz. $= 1\frac{1}{4}$ lbs. Now we add (note that the answer is in pounds):

$$\underbrace{1\frac{1}{4}}_{\text{cheese}} + \underbrace{2\frac{1}{4}}_{\text{beef}} + \underbrace{3\frac{1}{4}}_{\text{sugar}} = \frac{5}{4} + \frac{9}{4} + \frac{13}{4} = \frac{27}{4} = 6\frac{3}{4}$$

Therefore, Charles bought $6\frac{3}{4}$ pounds of groceries.

5) A printing company charges 10¢ per copy for the first 5 copies, 8¢ per copy for the next 25 copies, and 5¢ for each additional copy.
(a) What is the cost, in dollars, of making 38 copies?
(b) If the a person made 12 copies, how much copies were made at 8¢ per copy?

Solution:
(a) For the first 5 copies, the cost is $5 \times 10 = 50$¢. The cost for the next 25 copies is $25 \times 8 = 200$¢ $= \$2.00$. The cost of the remaining 8 copies is $8 \times 5 = 40$¢. Therefore, the total cost is

$$50\text{¢} + \$2.00 + 40\text{¢} = \$0.50 + \$2.00 + \$0.40 = \$2.90.$$

(b) Since the first five copies were made at 10¢ per copy, we have $12 - 5 = 7$ which falls into the 8¢ per copy category. Therefore, 7 copies were made at 8¢.

Exercises: Chapter 3, Section F

In Exercises 1 - 8, solve each problem.

1. Find the cost of 7 apples at $0.82 each.
(a) $14.00   (b) $22.00   (c) $574.00   (d) $57.40   (e) $5.74

2. Pepe paid $61.50 for movie tickets for his friends. If the movie tickets sell for $12.30 per ticket, how many tickets did he buy?
(a) 4   (b) 7   (c) 5   (d) 6   (e) 756

3. A supermaket manager buys a carton of 24 boxes of milk for $49.20. He sells each box for $2.89. What is his profit?
(a) $20.16   (b) $69.36   (c) $8.30   (d) $46.31   (e) $25.20

4. Lucy went shopping for beauty supplies last week. She bought 24 ounces of soap, $2\frac{3}{4}$ pounds of cocoa butter cream, and 2.25 ounces of anti-perspirant. How many ounces of beauty supplies did Lucy buy?
(a) 26.25 oz.   (b) 70.25 oz.   (c) 44 oz.   (d) 6 oz.   (e) 756 oz.

5. A box of nails weighs 456 ounces (oz). If each nail weighs 0.6 oz., how many nails are in the box?
(a) 600   (b) 700   (c) 500   (d) 660   (e) 760

6. A stockbroker bought saving bonds at $32.50 each. If he spent $812.50, how many bonds did he purchase?
(a) 40   (b) 350   (c) 50   (d) 25   (e) 26

7. Mr. Smith owns a house valued at $310,000.00. For every $1,000.00 of assessed value, he must pay $70.50 in taxes. How much does he pay in taxes?
(a) $21.00   (b) $23,561.00   (c) $21,855.00   (d) $4,600.00   (e) $25,000.00

8. A man bought 7 mangoes at $1.29 each. How much change did he received from a ten dollar bill?
(a) $0.97   (b) $0.36   (c) $0.30   (d) $8.71   (e) $0.20

In Exercises, 9 - 10, the following applies: A printing company charges 12¢ per copy for the first 9 copies, 10¢ per copy for the next 15 copies, and 7¢ for each additional copy.

9. What is the cost, in dollars, of making 42 copies?
(a) $3.84   (b) $3.96   (c) $2.65   (d) $2.71   (e) $1.26

10. If a person made 25 copies, how many copies were made at 7¢ per copy?
(a) 24   (b) 6   (c) 17   (d) 1   (e) 2

Section G. Powers of Ten and Scientific Notation

Positive Powers of Ten

In Chapter 1 (Section D), we've learned how to compute with exponents. As a quick reminder, $5^2 = 5 \times 5 = 25$, $(-3)^4 = \underbrace{(-3)(-3)}_{9}\underbrace{(-3)(-3)}_{9} = 81$, and $10^3 = 10 \times 10 \times 10 = 1,000$.

In general, if a represents any integer and n represents any natural number, then

$$\underbrace{a \times a \times \cdots \times a}_{n \text{ times}} = a^n.$$

We call a the **base** and n the **exponent**, and we read the expression a^n as 'a raised to the nth power'. Calculating powers of 10 can easily be done.

Rule for positive powers of 10: $10^n = 1\,\underbrace{00 \cdots 000}_{n \text{ zeros}}$

For example, $10^1 = 10$, $10^2 = \underbrace{100}_{2 \text{ zeros}}$, $10^3 = \underbrace{1,000}_{3 \text{ zeros}}$, and so on.

Rule for a number times a positive power of 10: When a number is multiplied by 10^n, we move the decimal point n places to the right of it, adding in any trailing zeros, if necessary.

For example, $362 \times 1,000 = 362.000 \times 1,000 = 362,000$ and
$15.2813 \times 10^2 = 15.2813 \times 100 = 1528.13$.

Example 1. Evaluate.
1) 32×100 2) $681 \times 1,000$ 3) 5×10^7
4) $56 \times 10,0000$ 5) 0.03975×100 6) 0.284×10^2

Solution: 1) $32 \times 100 = 3,200$
         2) $681 \times 1,000 = 681,000$
         3) $5.0000000 \times 10^7 = 50,000,000$
         4) $56 \times 10,000 = 56.0000 \times 10,000 = 560,000$
         5) $0.03975 \times 100 = 3.975$
         6) $0.284 \times 10^2 = 28.4$

Negative Powers of Ten

A decimal fraction can be expressed as a **negative power** of 10 as follows:

$$0.1 = \frac{1}{10} = 10^{-1}, \quad 0.01 = \frac{1}{100} = 10^{-2}, \quad 0.001 = \frac{1}{1,000} = 10^{-3}, \quad \text{etc.}$$

Rule for negative powers of 10: $10^{-n} = \frac{1}{10^n} = 0.\underbrace{00\cdots0}_{n-1 \text{ zeros}} 1.$

Example 2. Represent as a negative power of 10.

1) $\dfrac{1}{100,000}$ 2) 0.0001 3) 0.000000001

Solution: 1) 10^{-5} 2) 10^{-4} 3) 10^{-9}

Rule for a number times a negative power of 10: When a number is multiplied by 10^{-n}, We move the decimal point n places to the left of it, adding in any leading zeros if necessary.

For example,

$362 \times 10^{-2} = 362.\times10^{-2} = 3.62$ and $6.801 \times 10^{-5} = 00006.801 \times 10^{-5} = 0.00006801.$

Example 3. Evaluate.

1) 362.15×10^{-1} 2) 13.046×10^{-5} 3) 901×10^{-2} 4) 0.7639×10^{-3}

Solution: 1) $362.15 \times 10^{-1} = 36.215$
2) $13.046 \times 10^{-5} = 00013.0046 \times 10^{-5} = 0.00013046$
3) $901 \times 10^{-2} = 901.\times10^{-2} = 9.01$
4) $0.7639 \times 10^{-3} = 000.7639 \times 10^{-3} = 0.0007639$

The Zero Power of 10

By definition, $10^0 = 1$. If you multiply a number by 10^0, the answer is just the number. For example,

$$4 \times 10^0 = 4, \quad 61.93 \times 10^0 = 61.93, \quad \text{and} \quad 5,012.008 \times 10^0 = 5,012.008.$$

Example 4. Evaluate.

1) 7.25×10^0 2) 83×10^0 3) 0.0012×10^0

Solution: 1) 7.25 2) 83 3) 0.0012

Arithmetic Operations With Powers of 10

When you multiply or divide powers of 10, the answer is also a power of 10 whose power can easily be computed. Next we state the rules for performing these operations. In Chapter 10, we explain why these rules work. For now, just practice using them.

Rule for multiplying powers of 10: If m and n represent any two integers, then $10^m \times 10^n = 10^{m+n}$.

For example,

$$10^3 \times 10^5 = 10^{3+5} = 10^8, \quad 10^{-6} \times 10^{-1} = 10^{-6+(-1)} = 10^{-7}, \quad \text{and} \quad 10^{-13} \times 10^3 = 10^{-13+3} = 10^{-10}.$$

Example 5. Write each product as a power of 10.
1) $10^2 \times 10^4$ 2) $10^8 \times 10^0$ 3) $10^{-5} \times 10^2$
4) $10^{16} \times 10^{-9}$ 5) $10^{-2} \times 10^{-2}$ 6) $10^{-12} \times 10^{-15}$

Solution: 1) $10^{2+4} = 10^6$ 2) $10^{8+0} = 10^8$ 3) $10^{-5+2} = 10^{-3}$
               4) $10^{16+(-9)} = 10^7$ 5) $10^{-2+(-2)} = 10^{-4}$ 6) $10^{-12+(-15)} = 10^{-27}$

Rule for dividing powers of 10: If m and n represent any two integers, then $\dfrac{10^m}{10^n} = 10^{m-n}$. This can also be written as $10^m \div 10^n = 10^{m-n}$.

For example,

$$\frac{10^{17}}{10^{14}} = 10^{17-14} = 10^3, \quad 10^{-8} \div 10^3 = 10^{-8-3} = 10^{-11}, \quad \text{and} \quad \frac{10^1}{10^{-12}} = 10^{1-(-12)} = 10^{13}.$$

Example 6. Write each quotient as a power of 10.
1) $\dfrac{10^5}{10^{16}}$ 2) $10^{-3} \div 10^7$ 3) $\dfrac{10^4}{10^{-11}}$

4) $10^{-8} \div 10^0$ 5) $\dfrac{10^{-1}}{10^{-19}}$ 6) $10^{26} \div 10^5$

Solution: 1) $10^{5-16} = 10^{-11}$ 2) $10^{-3-7} = 10^{-10}$ 3) $10^{4-(-11)} = 10^{15}$
               4) $10^{-8-0} = 10^{-8}$ 5) $10^{-1-(-19)} = 10^{18}$ 6) $10^{26-5} = 10^{21}$

Scientific Notation

A number n, which is written as a product of a number m between 1 and 10 (this number may equal 1, but never equals 10) and a number of the form 10^p, where p is some integer, is said to be in **scientific notation**. For instance,

$$24 = 2.4 \times 10^1, \quad 0.0007016 = 7.016 \times 10^{-4}, \text{ and } 8.0003 = 8.0003 \times 10^0$$

are written in scientific notation. Next we learn how to write a (positive terminating) decimal in scientific notation.

Rules for converting a decimal into scientific notation: Suppose that n is a (positive terminating) decimal.

Rule 1. If n is less than 1, then you move the decimal point of your number to the **right** until it is to the right of the first **nonzero** digit. If this digit, together with all other digits to the right of the moved decimal, is called m, and if you moved your decimal point p places to the right, then $n = m \times 10^{-p}$.

For example, using our rule $0.215 = 2.15 \times 10^{-1}$ and $0.00895 = 8.95 \times 10^{-3}$.

Rule 2. If n is between 1 and 10, then we write it as $n = n \times 10^0$.

For example, $7 = 7 \times 10^0$ and $4.211 = 4.211 \times 10^0$.

Rule 3. If n is greater than 10, then you move the decimal point of your number to the **left** until it is to the right of the first digit. If this digit, together with all other digits to the right of the moved decimal, is called m, and if you moved your decimal point p places to the left, then $n = m \times 10^p$.

For example, using our rule $19.671 = 1.9671 \times 10^1$ and $5,000,000 = 5000000. = 5 \times 10^6$. Note that the scientific notation for 10 is just $10 = 1 \times 10^1$.

Example 7. Write each number in scientific notation.
1) 0.5   2) 8   3) 283.471   4) 0.000411
5) 14,733   6) 0.0038921   7) 3.427   8) 571,123.166

Solution:
1) Use Rule 1: $0.5 = 5 \times 10^{-1}$
2) Use Rule 2: $8 = 8 \times 10^0$
3) Use Rule 3: $283.471 = 2.83471 \times 10^2$
4) Use Rule 1: $0.000411 = 4.11 \times 10^{-4}$
5) Use Rule 3: $14,733 = 14,733. = 1.4733 \times 10^4$
6) Use Rule 1: $0.0038921 = 3.8921 \times 10^{-3}$
7) Use Rule 2: $3.427 = 3.427 \times 10^0$
8) Use Rule 3: $571,123.166 = 5.71123166 \times 10^5$

Next we will multiply and divide numbers that are written in scientific notation. To do this, we apply the rules for multiplying and dividing powers of 10.

Example 8. Perform the indicated operation. Write each answer in scientific notation.

1) $(1.5 \times 10^2) \times (4 \times 10^2)$ 2) $(7 \times 10^{-3})(9 \times 10^{-1})$ 3) $\dfrac{2.5 \times 10^{-1}}{2.5 \times 10^6}$

4) $\dfrac{8 \times 10^9}{4 \times 10^{-3}}$ 5) $0.0000032 \times 1,900,000$ 6) $\dfrac{600,000}{0.15}$

Solution:

1) $\underbrace{(1.5 \times 10^2) \times (4 \times 10^2) = (1.5 \times 4) \times 10^{2+2}}_{\text{Multiply 1.5 and 4, then add the powers of 10.}} = 6 \times 10^4$

2) $\underbrace{(7 \times 10^{-3})(9 \times 10^{-1}) = (7 \times 9)(10^{-3+(-1)})}_{\text{Multiply 7 and 9, then add the powers of 10.}} = \underbrace{63 \times 10^{-4} = (6.3 \times 10^1) \times 10^{-4}}_{\text{Convert 63 to scientific notation.}}$

$$= 6.3 \times 10^{1+(-4)} = 6.3 \times 10^{-3}$$

3) $\underbrace{\dfrac{2.5 \times 10^{-1}}{2.5 \times 10^6} = \dfrac{2.5}{2.5} \times 10^{-1-6} = 1 \times 10^{-7}}_{\text{Divide 2.5 by 2.5, then subtract the powers of 10.}}$

4) $\underbrace{\dfrac{8 \times 10^9}{4 \times 10^{-3}} = \dfrac{8}{4} \times 10^{9-(-3)} = 2 \times 10^{12}}_{\text{Divide 8 by 4, then subtract the powers of 10.}}$

5) $0.0000032 \times 19,000 = (3.2 \times 10^{-6}) \times (1.9 \times 10^4) = (3.2 \times 1.9) \times 10^{-6+4}$

$$= 6.08 \times 10^{-2}$$

6) $\dfrac{600,000}{0.15} = \dfrac{6 \times 10^5}{1.5 \times 10^{-1}} = \dfrac{6}{1.5} \times 10^{5-(-1)} = 4 \times 10^6$

Exercises: Chapter 3, Section G

In Exercises 1 - 15, write each number in scientific notation.

1. 0.3

2. 0.00734

3. 0.0007229

4. 0.01000101

5. 8

6. 7.612

7. 50

8. 23

9. 94.16

10. 452.935

11. 1,726

12. $496.08 =$
(a) 4.9608×10^{-2}
(b) 4.9608×10^2
(c) 4.9608×10^3
(d) 49.608×10^2
(e) 49.608×10^{-2}

13. $0.000341 =$
(a) 341×10^{-4}
(b) 3.41×10^4
(c) 3.41×10^{-4}
(d) 3.41×10^{-3}
(e) 3.41×10^{-6}

14. $20,157 =$
(a) 2.0157×10^{-4}
(b) 2.0157×10^3
(c) 2.157×10^{-5}
(d) 2.0157×10^4
(e) 2.0157×10^{-6}

15. $5,909.9 =$
(a) 5.9099×10^{-3}
(b) 5.9099×10^3
(c) 5.91×10^3
(d) 59×10^{-3}
(e) 59×10^4

In Exercises 16 - 27, write each number as a terminating decimal.

16. 4×10^1

17. 9.1×10^2

18. 7.56×10^1

19. 1.1053×10^3

20. 5.62093×10^4

21. 4.0×10^5

22. 2.00×10^8

23. 2.61694×10^7

24. 6.0195×10^1

25. 8×10^{-1}

26. 7.3615×10^{-3}

27. 4.112×10^{-4}

In Exercises 28 - 54, write the answer in scientific notation.

28. $(2 \times 10^1)(3 \times 10^2)$ 29. $(2.5 \times 10^4)(5 \times 10^3)$ 30. $(3 \times 10^3)(4.1 \times 10^5)$

31. $(1 \times 10^{-5})(2 \times 10^{-1})$ 32. $(9 \times 10^{-5})(8 \times 10^6)$ 33. $(7 \times 10^{-6})(9 \times 10^2)$

34. $(8 \times 10^7)(8 \times 10^{-3}) =$
(a) 6.4×10^{-1} (b) 6.4×10^1 (c) 6.4×10^3 (d) 6.4×10^5 (e) 6.4×10^2

35. $(9 \times 10^{-4})(2 \times 10^{-2}) =$
(a) 1.8×10^{-7} (b) 1.8×10^{-6} (c) 1.8×10^{-5} (d) 9.2×10^{-6} (e) 1.8×10^6

36. $(3 \times 10^5)(9 \times 10^3) =$
(a) 27×10^{15} (b) 2.7×10^{-9} (c) 2.7×10^9 (d) 2.7×10^{-6} (e) 2.7×10^{-8}

37. $(7 \times 10^{-9})(8 \times 10^9) =$
(a) 5.6×10^{-1} (b) 5.6×10^1 (c) 5.6×10^0 (d) 5.6×10^{-2} (e) 5.6×10^2

38. $\dfrac{4 \times 10^5}{2 \times 10^3}$ 39. $\dfrac{9 \times 10^7}{3 \times 10^{13}}$ 40. $\dfrac{612 \times 10^{-5}}{17 \times 10^3}$

41. $\dfrac{120 \times 10^9}{2 \times 10^{-4}}$ 42. $\dfrac{450 \times 10^{-12}}{50 \times 10^{-3}}$ 43. $\dfrac{65 \times 10^{-4}}{5 \times 10^{-8}}$

44. $\dfrac{121 \times 10^{-8}}{11 \times 10^2} =$
(a) 1.1×10^{-6} (b) 1.1×10^9 (c) 1.1×10^{-8} (d) 1.1×10^{-7} (e) 1.1×10^{-9}

45. $\dfrac{144 \times 10^{-2}}{6 \times 10^{-7}} =$
(a) 2.4×10^{-9} (b) 2.4×10^9 (c) 2.4×10^6 (d) 2.4×10^{-7} (e) 2.4×10^{-6}

46. $\dfrac{240 \times 10^8}{1 \times 10^{-13}} =$
(a) 2.4×10^{23} (b) 2.4×10^{-23} (c) 2.4×10^5 (d) 2.4×10^{-5} (e) 2.4×10^{-6}

47. $0.0067 \times 6,000$ 48. 0.00112×300 49. 0.0002×30

50. $0.0000032 \times 21,000 =$
a) 6.72×10^{-4} (b) 6.72×10^{-2} (c) 6.72×10^{4} (d) 6.72×10^{3} (e) 6.72×10^{-3}

51. $\dfrac{8,080}{0.202}$ 52. $\dfrac{2,300}{0.08}$ 53. $\dfrac{56,000}{0.112}$

54. $\dfrac{300,000}{0.15} =$
(a) 2×10^{6} (b) 2×10^{9} (c) 2×10^{4} (d) 2×10^{-9} (e) 2×10^{-6}

Chapter 4:   The Real Numbers; Square Roots

Section A.   The Real Numbers

Recall that a natural number is any number from the set $\{1, 2, 3, ...\}$, and a whole number is a number from the set $\{0, 1, 2, 3, ...\}$. The integers, or signed numbers, are the numbers in the set

$$... ,\ -2,\ -1,\ 0,\ +1,\ +2,\ +3,\ ....$$

Notice that every natural number is a whole number, and every whole number is an integer.

The next set of numbers to study is the set of rational numbers.

The Rational Numbers are the fractions whose numerator and denominator are integers, but the denominator is not zero.

Examples of rational numbers are

$$\frac{1}{2},\ \frac{3}{-5},\ \frac{-9}{-18},\ \frac{0}{7},\ \frac{-5,001}{173},\ \text{and } \frac{16}{1}.$$

Notice that $\frac{1}{0}$, $\frac{-8}{0}$, and $\frac{15}{0}$ are not rational numbers since they have zero as the denominator. Such expressions are undefined.

Every integer is a rational number. For instance, $3 = \frac{3}{1}$ and $-24 = \frac{-24}{1}$. As we know, there is more than one way to write an integer in fractional form:

$$3 = \frac{3}{1} = \frac{6}{2} = \frac{9}{3} = \frac{12}{4} = \cdots \quad \text{and} \quad -24 = \frac{-24}{1} = \frac{-48}{2} = \frac{24}{-1} = \frac{48}{-2} = \cdots.$$

Rational numbers can be expressed as decimals by dividing the numerator by the denominator. For example,

$$\frac{1}{2} = 0.5, \quad \frac{3}{-4} = -0.75, \quad \text{and} \quad \frac{17}{3} = 5.66... = 5.\overline{6}.$$

The decimals 0.5 and -0.75 are called **terminating decimals** because they 'end'. Here are more terminating decimals:

$$0.4,\ \ 3.19,\ \ 0.6552,\ \ \text{and}\ \ 2,012.9945.$$

The decimal $5.\overline{6}$ is a **non-terminating, repeating decimal** since the 6's continue repeatedly without ending.

Other examples of non-terminating, repeating decimals are

$$0.\overline{32} = 0.323232\ldots, \quad 5.18\overline{04} = 5.18040404\ldots, \quad \text{and} \quad 10.750\overline{012} = 10.750012012012\ldots.$$

It turns out that every rational number can be expressed as a decimal which is either **terminating** or a **non-terminating, repeating**. Furthermore, a decimal which is either **terminating** or a **non-terminating, repeating** comes from dividing two integers; that is, every such decimal can be expressed as a rational number.

There is another kind of decimal which does not come from dividing two integers. This type of decimal is **non-terminating and non-repeating**, and is called an irrational number.

<u>**The Irrational Numbers**</u> are the decimals that are non-terminating and non-repeating.

Next we mention some examples of irrational numbers.

1) The number π (pronounced as 'pi') is irrational. It represents the circumference (or length) of a circle divided by its diameter and is approximately equal to either 3.14 or $\frac{22}{7}$.

2) The number $5.72772777277772\ldots$ is irrational. It is non-terminating because there will always be 7's and 2's in its decimal if you continued the pattern. It is also non-repeating because the pattern which arises is 'increase the number of 7's by one once you past 2.' There will never be a repeating part of the decimal since there will always be an additional 7 added as you continue the pattern.

3) There is a number n for which $n^2 = 2$. The number n, which is approximately 1.414, is irrational. It comes from taking the **square root** of 2 (we will learn about this in the next section).

The collection of all rational numbers and irrational numbers is called the set of **real numbers**.

Example 1. State the name(s) of each number; natural, whole, integer, rational, irrational.

1) $\frac{3}{5}$ 2) 6   3) -0.32 4) $19.515115111\ldots$

5) $102.\overline{95}$ 6) 33.00 7) $-\pi$ 8) $14\frac{8}{9}$

Solution: 1) rational   2) natural, whole, integer, and rational.
            3) rational   4) irrational
            5) rational   6) natural, whole, integer, and rational
            7) irrational   8) rational

Exercises: Chapter 4, Section A

In Exercises 1 - 12, place a check mark in the correct columns. Exercise 1. has been done for you.

	Number	Natural Number	Integer	Rational Number	Irrational Number
1.	7	✓	✓	✓	
2.	$-\dfrac{2}{9}$				
3.	+15				
4.	−2				
5.	$-9.13\overline{6}$				
6.	π				
7.	3.8802				
8.	$\dfrac{15}{423}$				
9.	18.131331333…				
10.	18.131331333				
11.	−23.0				
12.	$42\dfrac{11}{16}$				

In Exercises 13 - 27, express each fraction as either a terminating or non-terminating, repeating decimal.

13. $\dfrac{1}{4}$ 14. $\dfrac{2}{5}$ 15. $\dfrac{3}{2}$ 16. $\dfrac{3}{4}$ 17. $\dfrac{1}{8}$

18. $\dfrac{7}{8}$ 19. $-\dfrac{1}{10}$ 20. $-\dfrac{9}{10}$ 21. $\dfrac{17}{3}$ 22. $\dfrac{22}{3}$

23. $-\dfrac{1}{9}$ 24. $-\dfrac{5}{9}$ 25. $\dfrac{18}{5}$ 26. $\dfrac{16}{5}$ 27. $\dfrac{16}{99}$

Section B. Introduction to Square Roots

Notice that $4^2 = 16$ and $(-4)^2 = 16$. We say that 4 and -4 are **square roots** of 16 because squaring both 4 and -4 gives 16. Similarly, the square root of 81 are 9 and -9 since $9^2 = 81$ and $(-9)^2 = 81$. Notice that the square root of 0 is only 0 because $0^2 = 0$, and the square of no other number is 0.

As we will see shortly, every positive number has two square roots, a positive one and a negative one. The positive square root of a positive number n is called the **principal square root** of n, and is written using the **radical symbol** as $\sqrt{n}$ (we call n, the **radicand**).

For example, $\sqrt{16} = 4$ and $\sqrt{81} = 9$. The negative square root of n is written as $-\sqrt{n}$. Thus, $-\sqrt{16} = -4$ and $-\sqrt{81} = -9$. We also use the radical symbol when $n = 0$: $\sqrt{0} = 0$.

Example 1. Evaluate.

1) $\sqrt{4}$ 2) $\sqrt{49}$ 3) $-\sqrt{64}$ 4) $-\sqrt{9}$ 5) $\sqrt{0.25}$ 6) $\sqrt{\dfrac{36}{121}}$

Solution:

1) $2^2 = 4$, so $\sqrt{4} = 2$.   2) $7^2 = 49$, so $\sqrt{49} = 7$.

3) $(-8)^2 = 64$, so $-\sqrt{64} = -8$.   4) $(-3)^2 = 9$, so $-\sqrt{9} = -3$.

5) $(0.5)^2 = 0.25$, so $\sqrt{0.25} = 0.5$.   6) $\left(\dfrac{6}{11}\right)^2 = \dfrac{36}{121}$, so $\sqrt{\dfrac{36}{121}} = \dfrac{6}{11}$.

Whenever you square a number, the answer must be **non-negative** (meaning that it is positive or zero). Therefore, the square root of a negative number doesn't make sense. For example,

$$\sqrt{-1}, \quad \sqrt{-36}, \quad \text{and} \quad \sqrt{-1}$$

do not exist.

A **perfect square** is an integer which is the square of another integer. Examples of perfect squares are

$$\underbrace{1}_{1^2}, \quad \underbrace{4}_{2^2}, \quad \underbrace{9}_{3^2}, \quad \text{etc.}$$

Next, we provide a list with some principal square roots of perfect squares.

$\sqrt{1} = 1$	$\sqrt{16} = 4$	$\sqrt{49} = 7$	$\sqrt{100} = 10$
$\sqrt{4} = 2$	$\sqrt{25} = 5$	$\sqrt{64} = 8$	$\sqrt{121} = 11$
$\sqrt{9} = 3$	$\sqrt{36} = 6$	$\sqrt{81} = 9$	$\sqrt{144} = 12$

The list above only includes the (principal) square roots of perfect squares. However, every positive number has a principal square root. For example, let's try to calculate $\sqrt{3}$. Notice that

$$(1.7)^2 = 2.89 \quad \text{and} \quad (1.8)^2 = 3.24.$$

This means that $\sqrt{3}$ is between 1.7 and 1.8, but closer to 1.7 because

$$\underbrace{3 - 2.89}_{0.11} \text{ is smaller than } \underbrace{3.24 - 3}_{0.24}.$$

Now observe that

$$(1.73)^2 = 2.9929 \text{ and } (1.74)^2 = 3.0276,$$

so $\sqrt{3}$ is between 1.73 and 1.74, but closer to 1.73. Let's try one more time:

$$(1.732)^2 = 2.999824 \text{ and } (1.733)^2 = 3.003289$$

And so, $\sqrt{3}$ is between 1.732 and 1.733, but closer to 1.732. This process of 'zeroing in' on the value of $\sqrt{3}$ will lead us closer to the value of $\sqrt{3}$. However, we can never get the exact value of $\sqrt{3}$ because $\sqrt{3}$ is a non-terminating, non-repeating decimal; that is, $\sqrt{3}$ is an irrational number. Notice that $\sqrt{3}$ can be rounded off to the nearest tenth as 1.7 and to the nearest hundredth as 1.73.

Property: $\sqrt{n}$ is an irrational number whenever n is a positive integer which is *not* a perfect square.

Example 2. State whether each number is rational or irrational. If it is irrational, find two consecutive integers for which it is between.

1) $\sqrt{25}$ 2) $\sqrt{225}$ 3) $\sqrt{18}$ 4) $\sqrt{105}$

Solution: 1) $\sqrt{25} = 5$ is rational.

           2) $\sqrt{225} = 15$ is rational

           3) $\sqrt{18}$ is irrational. It is between 4 and 5 since $4^2 = 16$, $5^2 = 25$, and 18 is between 16 and 25.

           4) $\sqrt{105}$ is irrational. It is between 10 and 11 because $10^2 = 100$, $11^2 = 121$, and 105 is between 100 and 121.

Exercises: Chapter 4, Section B

In Exercises 1 - 16, evaluate (if possible).

1. $\sqrt{81}$

2. $-\sqrt{81}$

3. $\sqrt{-81}$

4. $\sqrt{16}$

5. $-\sqrt{16}$

6. $\sqrt{-16}$

7. $\sqrt{\frac{1}{9}}$

8. $\sqrt{\frac{25}{81}}$

9. $-\sqrt{\frac{64}{25}}$

10. $\sqrt{-\frac{64}{25}}$

11. $\sqrt{\frac{100}{121}}$

12. $-\sqrt{-\frac{1}{36}}$

13. $\sqrt{0.04}$

14. $\sqrt{1.44}$

15. $-\sqrt{0.25}$

16. $\sqrt{0.0169}$

In Exercises 17 - 24, determine whether or not the number is rational or irrational.

17. $\sqrt{15}$

18. $\sqrt{49}$

19. $-\sqrt{64}$

20. $\sqrt{27}$

21. $\sqrt{196}$

22. $\sqrt{190}$

23. $\sqrt{205}$

24. $-\sqrt{361}$

In Exercises 25 - 31, choose the correct answer.

25. Which two integers is $\sqrt{44}$ between?
(a) 4 and 5 (b) 5 and 6 (c) 6 and 7 (d) 7 and 8 (e) 8 and 9

26. Which two integers is $\sqrt{110}$ between?
(a) 8 and 9 (b) 9 and 10 (c) 10 and 11 (d) 11 and 12 (e) 12 and 13

27. Which two integers is $\sqrt{985}$ between?
(a) 30 and 31 (b) 31 and 32 (c) 32 and 33 (d) 33 and 34 (e) 34 and 35

28. Which two integers is $-\sqrt{5,137}$ between?
(a) −71 and −72 (b) −70 and −71 (c) −73 and −74 (d) −69 and −70
(e) −68 and −69

29. Which integer is closest to $\sqrt{186}$?
(a) 13   (b) 14   (c) 15   (d) 16   (e) 17

30. Which integer is closest to $\sqrt{7,019}$?
(a) 81   (b) 82   (c) 83   (d) 84   (e) 85

31. Which integer is closest to $\sqrt{39,112}$?
(a) 196   (b) 197   (c) 198   (d) 199   (e) 200

Section C. Simplifying Square Roots

Properties of Square Roots

Property 1. If a is any real number, then $\sqrt{a^2} = |a|$.

For example, if $a = 7$, then $\sqrt{7^2} = |7| = 7$. If $a = -7$, then $\sqrt{(-7)^2} = |-7| = 7$. Note that if a is a **non-negative number**, then this property simplifies to $\sqrt{a^2} = a$.

Example 1. Simplify using Property 1.
1) $\sqrt{5^2}$ 2) $\sqrt{37^2}$ 3) $\sqrt{(-19)^2}$

Solution: 1) $\sqrt{5^2} = 5$ 2) $\sqrt{37^2} = 37$ 3) $\sqrt{(-19)^2} = |-19| = 19$

Property 2. If a and b are non-negative numbers, then $\sqrt{a} \times \sqrt{b} = \sqrt{a \times b}$.

For example, $\sqrt{13} \times \sqrt{13} = \sqrt{13 \times 13} = \sqrt{169} = 13$ and $\sqrt{9 \times 16} = \sqrt{9} \times \sqrt{16} = 3 \times 4 = 12$.

Example 2. Simplify using Property 2.
1) $\sqrt{8} \times \sqrt{8}$ 2) $\sqrt{36 \times 25}$ 3) $\sqrt{(144)(121)}$ 4) $\left(7\sqrt{6}\right)\left(3\sqrt{6}\right)$

Solution:
1) $\sqrt{8} \times \sqrt{8} = \sqrt{8 \times 8} = \sqrt{64} = 8$
2) $\sqrt{(36)(25)} = \sqrt{36} \times \sqrt{25} = 6 \times 5 = 30$
3) $\sqrt{(144)(121)} = \sqrt{144} \times \sqrt{121} = 12 \times 11 = 132$
4) $\left(7\sqrt{6}\right)\left(3\sqrt{6}\right) = \underbrace{(7 \times 3) \times \sqrt{6 \times 6}}_{\text{Multiply 7×3 and } \sqrt{6} \times \sqrt{6}.} = 21 \times \sqrt{36} = 21 \times 6 = 126$

Property 3. If a is a non-negative number and b is a positive number, then $\sqrt{\dfrac{a}{b}} = \dfrac{\sqrt{a}}{\sqrt{b}}$.

For example, $\sqrt{\dfrac{81}{4}} = \dfrac{\sqrt{81}}{\sqrt{4}} = \dfrac{9}{2}$ and $\dfrac{\sqrt{2,000}}{\sqrt{500}} = \sqrt{\dfrac{2,000}{500}} = \sqrt{4} = 2$.

Example 3. Simplify using Property 3.
1) $\sqrt{\dfrac{169}{4}}$ 2) $\sqrt{\dfrac{162}{18}}$ 3) $\dfrac{\sqrt{2}}{\sqrt{98}}$

Solution:

1) $\sqrt{\dfrac{169}{4}} = \dfrac{\sqrt{169}}{\sqrt{4}} = \dfrac{13}{2}$

2) $\underbrace{\sqrt{\dfrac{162}{18}} = \sqrt{9}}_{\text{Simplify the fraction.}} = 3$

3) $\dfrac{\sqrt{2}}{\sqrt{98}} = \underbrace{\sqrt{\dfrac{2}{98}} = \sqrt{\dfrac{1}{49}}}_{\text{Simplify the fraction.}} = \dfrac{\sqrt{1}}{\sqrt{49}} = \dfrac{1}{7}$

Property 4. If a is a non-negative number, then $\left(\sqrt{a}\,\right)^2 = a$.

For example, $\left(\sqrt{14}\,\right)^2 = 14$ and $\left(\sqrt{2,015.76}\,\right)^2 = 2,015.76$

Example 4. Simplify using Property 4.

1) $\left(\sqrt{29}\,\right)^2$ 2) $\left(\sqrt{100}\,\right)^2$ 3) $\left(5\sqrt{3}\,\right)^2$ 4) $\left(8\sqrt{2}\,\right)^2$

Solution: 1) $\left(\sqrt{29}\,\right)^2 = 29$

           2) $\left(\sqrt{100}\,\right)^2 = 100$

           3) $\left(5\sqrt{3}\,\right)^2 = \underbrace{\left(5\sqrt{3}\,\right)\left(5\sqrt{3}\,\right) = 5^2 \times \left(\sqrt{3}\,\right)^2}_{\text{Multiply the 5's and multiply the }\sqrt{3}\text{'s.}} = 25 \times 3 = 75$

           4) $\left(8\sqrt{2}\,\right)^2 = \underbrace{\left(8\sqrt{2}\,\right)\left(8\sqrt{2}\,\right) = 8^2 \times \left(\sqrt{2}\,\right)^2}_{\text{Multiply the 8's and multiply the }\sqrt{2}\text{'s.}} = 64 \times 2 = 128$

Here are some additional examples:

Example 5. Evaluate each expression and simplify.

1) $\sqrt{25} - \sqrt{16}$ 2) $\sqrt{25 - 16}$ 3) $\left(\sqrt{25}\,\right)\left(\sqrt{16}\,\right)$ 4) $\sqrt{25^2 \times 16}$

5) $\sqrt{64} + \sqrt{36}$ 6) $\sqrt{64 + 36}$ 7) $\sqrt{64 \times 36}$ 8) $64 \times \sqrt{36^2}$

9) $\dfrac{\sqrt{25-9}}{\sqrt{25 \times 9}}$ 10) $\dfrac{\left(\sqrt{1} + \sqrt{49}\,\right)^2}{\left(\sqrt{49}\,\right)^2}$

Solution:

1) $\sqrt{25} - \sqrt{16} = 5 - 4 = 1$ 2) $\sqrt{25 - 16} = \sqrt{9} = 3$

3) $\left(\sqrt{25}\,\right)\left(\sqrt{16}\,\right) = (5)(4) = 20$ 4) $\sqrt{25^2 \times 16} = \sqrt{25^2} \times \sqrt{16} = 25 \times 4 = 100$

5) $\sqrt{64} + \sqrt{36} = 8 + 6 = 14$ 6) $\sqrt{64 + 36} = \sqrt{100} = 10$

7) $\sqrt{64 \times 36} = \sqrt{64} \times \sqrt{36} = 8 \times 6 = 48$ 8) $64 \times \sqrt{36^2} = 64 \times 36 = 2,304$

9) $\dfrac{\sqrt{25-9}}{\sqrt{25 \times 9}} = \dfrac{\sqrt{16}}{\sqrt{25} \times \sqrt{9}} = \dfrac{4}{5 \times 3} = \dfrac{4}{15}$ 10) $\dfrac{\left(\sqrt{1} + \sqrt{49}\,\right)^2}{\left(\sqrt{49}\,\right)^2} = \dfrac{(1 + 7)^2}{49} = \dfrac{64}{49} = 1\dfrac{15}{49}$

Next, we will simplify square roots whose radicand is not a perfect square. Let's simplify $\sqrt{24}$. First, we need to factor the number 24 so that one of the factors is a perfect square. Notice that $24 = 4 \times 6$, and 4 is a perfect square. Next, we apply Property 2 from the previous section and simplify:

$$\sqrt{24} = \sqrt{4 \times 6} = \sqrt{4} \times \sqrt{6} = 2 \times \sqrt{6} = 2\sqrt{6}$$

Example 6. Simplify.

1) $\sqrt{18}$ 2) $\sqrt{27}$ 3) $-\sqrt{50}$ 4) $-\sqrt{98}$

5) $\sqrt{32}$ 6) $7\sqrt{20}$ 7) $-8\sqrt{300}$ 8) $19\sqrt{16}$

Solution:

1) $\sqrt{18} = \sqrt{9 \times 2} = \sqrt{9} \times \sqrt{2} = 3\sqrt{2}$

2) $\sqrt{27} = \sqrt{9 \times 3} = \sqrt{9} \times \sqrt{3} = 3\sqrt{3}$

3) $-\sqrt{50} = -\sqrt{25 \times 2} = -\sqrt{25} \times \sqrt{2} = -5\sqrt{2}$

4) $-\sqrt{98} = -\sqrt{49 \times 2} = -\sqrt{49} \times \sqrt{2} = -7\sqrt{2}$

5) $\sqrt{32} = \sqrt{16 \times 2} = \sqrt{16} \times \sqrt{2} = 4\sqrt{2}$

6) $7\sqrt{20} = 7 \times \sqrt{4 \times 5} = 7 \times \sqrt{4} \times \sqrt{5} = 7 \times 2 \times \sqrt{5} = 14\sqrt{5}$

7) $-8\sqrt{300} = -8 \times \sqrt{100 \times 3} = -8 \times \sqrt{100} \times \sqrt{3} = -8 \times 10 \times \sqrt{3} = -80\sqrt{3}$

8) $19\sqrt{16} = 19 \times 4 = 76$

Exercises: Chapter 4, Section C

In Exercises 1 - 27, choose the correct answer.

1. $\sqrt{12} \cdot \sqrt{12} =$
(a) 12   (b) 6   (c) 144   (d) 14   (e) 16

2. $\sqrt{18^2} =$
(a) 324   (b) 6   (c) 18   (d) 22   (e) 14

3. $\sqrt{(-36)^2} =$
(a) −36   (b) 36   (c) 6   (d) 18   (e) undefined

3. $\sqrt{49 \times 36} =$
(a) 40   (b) 1,764   (c) 882   (d) 44   (e) 42

4. $\sqrt{(81)(169)} =$
(a) 127   (b) 117   (c) 22   (d) 107   (e) 217

5. $\left(4\sqrt{2}\right)\left(7\sqrt{2}\right) =$
(a) $28\sqrt{2}$ (b) 112   (c) 28   (d) 56   (e) $56\sqrt{2}$

6. $\left(9\sqrt{7}\right)\left(5\sqrt{7}\right) =$
(a) $45\sqrt{7}$ (b) 295   (c) 215   (d) 305   (e) 315

7. $\sqrt{\dfrac{64}{121}} =$

(a) $\dfrac{8}{121}$ (b) $\dfrac{8}{11}$ (c) $\dfrac{4}{11}$ (d) $\sqrt{\dfrac{8}{11}}$ (e) $\dfrac{11}{8}$

8. $\sqrt{\dfrac{500}{5}} =$
(a) 20   (b) $\dfrac{\sqrt{500}}{5}$ (c) 25   (d) 10   (e) $\dfrac{1}{10}$

9. $\dfrac{\sqrt{15}}{\sqrt{540}} =$

(a) 6 (b) $\dfrac{1}{6}$ (c) $\dfrac{1}{36}$ (d) 36 (e) $\dfrac{1}{\sqrt{6}}$

10. $\left(\sqrt{64}\right)^2 =$

(a) 8 (b) 16 (c) 32 (d) 64 (e) 4,096

11. $\left(4\sqrt{6}\right)^2 =$

(a) 66 (b) $16\sqrt{6}$ (c) 144 (d) 48 (e) 96

12. $\left(-3\sqrt{10}\right)^2 =$

(a) $9\sqrt{10}$ (b) $-9\sqrt{10}$ (c) 90 (d) 900 (e) undefined

13. $\sqrt{81} - \sqrt{64} =$

(a) $\sqrt{17}$ (b) 1 (c) –1 (d) 3 (e) 4

14. $\sqrt{169 - 144} =$

(a) $\sqrt{15}$ (b) 25 (c) 5 (d) 1 (e) undefined

15. $\sqrt{16 - 25} =$

(a) –3 (b) 3 (c) $-\sqrt{3}$ (d) –1 (e) undefined

16. $\sqrt{6^2 \times 9} =$

(a) 12 (b) 18 (c) 324 (d) 54 (e) 15

17. $\sqrt{100} + \sqrt{4} =$

(a) $\sqrt{104}$ (b) 12 (c) 16 (d) 14 (e) 11

18. $\sqrt{5^2 - 3^2} =$

(a) $\sqrt{2}$ (b) 2 (c) 4 (d) 16 (e) undefined

19. $\sqrt{144 \times 5^2} =$

(a) 6 (b) 60 (c) 300 (d) 600 (e) 30

20. $4 \times \sqrt{8^2} =$

(a) 32 (b) 16 (c) 64 (d) 8 (e) 48

21. $\dfrac{\sqrt{25}}{\sqrt{25-9}} =$

(a) $\dfrac{5}{4}$ (b) $\dfrac{5}{3}$ (c) $\dfrac{1}{4}$ (d) $\dfrac{5}{2}$ (e) undefined

22. $\dfrac{\sqrt{100-64}}{\sqrt{100}-\sqrt{64}} =$

(a) 18   (b) $\dfrac{1}{3}$ (c) 9   (d) 3   (e) undefined

23. $\dfrac{\left(\sqrt{4}\right)^2 + 12^2}{\left(\sqrt{4}+12\right)^2} =$

(a) $\dfrac{49}{37}$ (b) $\dfrac{37}{49}$ (c) 1   (d) $\dfrac{37}{59}$ (e) $\dfrac{37}{64}$

24. $\sqrt{24} =$
(a) $6\sqrt{2}$ (b) $2\sqrt{2}$ (c) $2\sqrt{6}$ (d) $12\sqrt{2}$ (e) $4\sqrt{6}$

25. $\sqrt{98} =$
(a) $7\sqrt{7}$ (b) $2\sqrt{7}$ (c) $4\sqrt{7}$ (d) 14   (e) $7\sqrt{2}$

25. $-\sqrt{600} =$
(a) $-6\sqrt{10}$ (b) $-10\sqrt{6}$ (c) $-100\sqrt{6}$ (d) $-10\sqrt{60}$ (e) undefined

26. $8\sqrt{132} =$
(a) $16\sqrt{33}$ (b) $33\sqrt{16}$ (c) $10\sqrt{33}$ (d) $17\sqrt{33}$ (e) $32\sqrt{33}$

27. $-19\sqrt{112} =$
(a) $72\sqrt{7}$ (b) $-72\sqrt{7}$ (c) $-133\sqrt{4}$ (d) $-7\sqrt{72}$ (e) undefined

Section D. Addition and Subtraction of Square Roots

If two or more square roots have the same radicand, then we call them **like roots**. For example, $2\sqrt{5}$ and $8\sqrt{5}$ are like roots, and $-6\sqrt{13}$, $-18\sqrt{13}$, and $7\sqrt{13}$ are like roots. The numbers outside of the radical symbol are called the **coefficients**. The coefficient of $2\sqrt{5}$ is 2, and the coefficient of $-6\sqrt{13}$ is -6.

Like roots can be added or subtracted to form a single root.

Rule for combining like roots: Combine the coefficients, then multiply it by the original square root.

For example,

$$\underbrace{2\sqrt{5} + 8\sqrt{5} = 10\sqrt{5}}_{\text{Add 2+8, then multiply by } \sqrt{5}.} \quad \text{and} \quad \underbrace{-6\sqrt{13} - 18\sqrt{13} + 7\sqrt{13} = -17\sqrt{13}}_{\text{Combine } -6-18+7, \text{ then multiply by } \sqrt{13}.}.$$

Observe that $7\sqrt{3} + \sqrt{6}$ cannot be combined into a single square root since $7\sqrt{3}$ and $\sqrt{6}$ are not like roots. Similarly, $\sqrt{5} - 10 + 3\sqrt{7}$ cannot be combined because $\sqrt{5}$, 10, and $3\sqrt{7}$ are not like roots. However, $9\sqrt{15} + 17 - 13\sqrt{15}$ can be combined to give $-4\sqrt{15} + 17$ (just combine $9\sqrt{15} - 13\sqrt{15}$, and leave $+17$ as it is).

Sometimes we can simplify the given square roots and produce like roots. For example,

$$\underbrace{9\sqrt{3} - 14\sqrt{75} = 9\sqrt{3} - 14\left(5\sqrt{3}\right)}_{\substack{\text{These aren't like roots.} \\ \text{Simplify } \sqrt{75} = \sqrt{25} \times \sqrt{3} = 5\sqrt{3}.}} = \underbrace{9\sqrt{3} - 70\sqrt{3}}_{\text{These are like roots!}} = -61\sqrt{3}.$$

Example 1. Combine and simplify.
1) $3\sqrt{7} + 9\sqrt{7}$ 2) $3\sqrt{11} - 7\sqrt{11}$ 3) $6\sqrt{7} + 13\sqrt{7} - 20\sqrt{7}$
4) $5\sqrt{2} + 9\sqrt{8}$ 5) $12\sqrt{5} - 14\sqrt{25} + 3\sqrt{45}$ 6) $3\sqrt{50} - \frac{1}{2}\sqrt{288} + \sqrt{18}$

Solution:
1) $3\sqrt{7} + 9\sqrt{7} = (3+9)\sqrt{7} = 12\sqrt{7}$
2) $3\sqrt{11} - 7\sqrt{11} = (3-7)\sqrt{11} = -4\sqrt{11}$
3) $6\sqrt{7} + 13\sqrt{7} - 20\sqrt{7} = (6+13-20)\sqrt{7} = -1\sqrt{7} = -\sqrt{7}$
4) $\underbrace{5\sqrt{2} + 9\sqrt{8} = 5\sqrt{2} + 9\left(2\sqrt{2}\right)}_{\sqrt{8} = \sqrt{4} \times \sqrt{2} = 2\sqrt{2}} = 5\sqrt{2} + 18\sqrt{2} = (5+18)\sqrt{2} = 23\sqrt{2}$

5) $\underbrace{12\sqrt{5} - 14\sqrt{25} + 3\sqrt{45}}_{\sqrt{25}=5 \text{ and } \sqrt{45}=\sqrt{9}\times\sqrt{5}=3\sqrt{5}.} = 12\sqrt{5} - 14(5) + 3\left(3\sqrt{5}\right) = 12\sqrt{5} - 70 + 9\sqrt{5} = 21\sqrt{5} - 70$

6) $\underbrace{3\sqrt{50} - \frac{1}{2}\sqrt{288} + \sqrt{18}}_{\sqrt{50}=\sqrt{25}\times\sqrt{2}=5\sqrt{2},\ \sqrt{288}=\sqrt{144}\times\sqrt{2}=12\sqrt{2},\ \text{and } \sqrt{18}=\sqrt{9}\times\sqrt{2}=3\sqrt{2}.} = 3\left(5\sqrt{2}\right) - \frac{1}{2}(12\sqrt{2}) + 3\sqrt{2} = 15\sqrt{2} - 6\sqrt{2} + 3\sqrt{2} = 12\sqrt{2}$

Exercises: Chapter 4, Section D

In Exercises 1 - 6, combine.

1. $8\sqrt{5} + 3\sqrt{5}$

2. $9\sqrt{6} + 7\sqrt{6}$

3. $4\sqrt{10} - 11\sqrt{10}$

4. $6\sqrt{5} + 9\sqrt{5} - 14\sqrt{5}$

5. $9\sqrt{2} - 17\sqrt{2} - 2\sqrt{2}$

6. $5\sqrt{15} - 2\sqrt{15} - 8\sqrt{15}$

In Exercises 7 - 16, choose the correct answer.

7. $\sqrt{27} + \sqrt{3} =$
(a) $\sqrt{30}$ (b) $5\sqrt{3}$ (c) $4\sqrt{3}$ (d) 6 (e) $2\sqrt{3}$

8. $6\sqrt{8} + \sqrt{2} =$
(a) $6\sqrt{10}$ (b) $12\sqrt{2}$ (c) $9\sqrt{2}$ (d) $13\sqrt{2}$ (e) $11\sqrt{2}$

9. $4\sqrt{2} - 5\sqrt{72} =$
(a) $-26\sqrt{2}$ (b) $-\sqrt{70}$ (c) $-5\sqrt{2}$ (d) $26\sqrt{2}$ (e) $4\sqrt{2} - 10\sqrt{6}$

10. $-7\sqrt{12} + 10\sqrt{3} =$
(a) -6 (b) $-4\sqrt{3}$ (c) $4\sqrt{3}$ (d) $3\sqrt{15}$ (e) $3\sqrt{3}$

11. $-8\sqrt{18} - 2\sqrt{8} =$
(a) $-26\sqrt{2}$ (b) $28\sqrt{2}$ (c) $-20\sqrt{2}$ (d) $12\sqrt{2}$ (e) $-28\sqrt{2}$

12. $3\sqrt{24} + 7\sqrt{54}$
(a) $27\sqrt{2}$ (b) $18\sqrt{3}$ (c) $10\sqrt{78}$ (d) $27\sqrt{6}$ (e) $17\sqrt{6}$

13. $12\sqrt{5} - \sqrt{20} + 17\sqrt{5} =$
(a) $25\sqrt{5}$ (b) $26\sqrt{5}$ (c) $28\sqrt{5}$ (d) $22\sqrt{5}$ (e) $27\sqrt{5}$

14. $-14\sqrt{7} - \sqrt{49} + 5\sqrt{28} =$
(a) $-11\sqrt{7}$ (b) $-4\sqrt{7} - 7$ (c) $-7\sqrt{7}$ (d) $4\sqrt{7} - 7$ (e) -4

15. $-\sqrt{3} + 2\sqrt{40} + 9\sqrt{243} =$
(a) $80\sqrt{3} + 4\sqrt{10}$
(b) $10\sqrt{280}$
(c) $-80\sqrt{3} + 4\sqrt{10}$
(d) $17\sqrt{3} + 4\sqrt{10}$
(e) $80\sqrt{3} + 8\sqrt{10}$

16. $6\sqrt{4} - 4\sqrt{7} + 8\sqrt{63} + 2\sqrt{121} =$
(a) $54\sqrt{7}$
(b) $34 + 14\sqrt{5}$
(c) $32\sqrt{7} + 22$
(d) $34 + 20\sqrt{7}$
(e) $34 + 28\sqrt{7}$

Chapter 5: Ratios and Proportions

Section A. Ratios

As described in the begining of Chapter 2, suppose a round pizza pie is divided into 8 equally sized slices. If someone eats 2 of the slices, then we write $\frac{2}{8}$ to represent the amount of equally sized slices (2 slices) that were eaten from the whole pie (8 slices). The fraction can be read as "the ratio of 2 to 8".

A **ratio** is a comparison of two quantities by their indicated quotient. In other words, a ratio of one number to another non-zero number is the first number (on the left) divided by the second number (on the right).

The ratio of a to b can be expressed as follows:

$$\frac{a}{b}, \quad a \div b, \quad \text{or} \quad a : b$$

Observe the fractions $\frac{2}{8}$ and $\frac{6}{24}$ represent equal number; that is, by comparing the fractions $\frac{2}{8}$ and $\frac{6}{24}$, we see that $\left(\frac{3}{3}\right)\frac{2}{8} = \frac{6}{24}$. Thus $\frac{2}{8}$ and $\frac{6}{24}$ are equal ratios.

To find the ratio of two quantities, we must express both quantities in the same unit of measure before finding their quotient. For example, to compare a nickel with a dime, first convert the dime to 2 nickels and then find the ratio, which is $\frac{1}{2}$ or 1 : 2. Thus, a dime is worth twice as much as a nickel. Note that the resulting ratio has no unit of measure.

A ratio is said to be in **simplest form** (lowest terms) when both terms of the ratio are whole numbers and there is no whole number other than 1 that are factors of both terms. Therefore, in order to express a ratio in simplest form, we divide both terms by the GCF.

For example, to express the ratio 24 : 36 in simplest form, we divide both terms by the GCF of 24 and 36, which is 12. Therefore, 24 : 36 is the same as 2 : 3.

Example 1. Find the ratio of 3 dimes to 5 quarters.

Solution: Observe that 3 dimes = $3 \times 10 = 30$¢ and 5 quarters = 5×25¢ = 125¢. Therefore the ratio of 3 dimes to 5 quarters is $\frac{30}{125} = \frac{6}{25}$, which is can also be written as 6 : 25 or 6 to 25.

Example 2. Bob spends $400 a month for food and $1,200 a month for rent. Find the ratio of monthly cost of food to the monthly cost of rent. Express the ratio in different forms.

Solution: $\frac{400}{1,200} = \frac{1}{3}$ or $400 : 1,200 = 1 : 3$ or 400 to $1,200$, which simplifies as 1 to 3

Example 3. It costs Jill $310 for bus fares and $550 for books this semester.
(a) What is the ratio (expressed as a fraction) of the cost of books to the total cost of bus fares and books?
(b) What is the ratio (expressed as a fraction) of the cost of bus fares to the total cost of bus fares and books?

Solution:
(a) The total cost is $310 + $550 = $860, and the cost of books is $550. Therefore, the required ratio is $\frac{550}{860} = \frac{55}{86}$.
(b) Since the cost of bus fares is $310, the required ratio is $\frac{310}{860} = \frac{31}{86}$.

A comparison of more than two quantites can be expressed as a **continued ratio**. For example, suppose a room has length 20 feet, width 15 feet, and height 10 feet. The ratio of the length to the width is $20 : 15$, and the ratio of the width to the height is $15 : 10$. We can write these two ratios in an abbreviated form as the continued ratio $20 : 15 : 10$. In simplified form, the ratio of the measures of length, width, and height of the room is $4 : 3 : 2$, in simplest form.

Example 4. A piece of rope 60 inches long is cut into 3 pieces such that the lengths of the pieces are in the ratios $3 : 4 : 5$. Find the length of the three pieces.

Solution: We take the sum of the numbers in the ratio:

$$3 + 4 + 5 = 12$$

The 3 in the ratio $3 : 4 : 5$ represents $\frac{3}{12}$ of "the total length of rope". Since the entire length of the rope is 60 inches, we have

$$\frac{3}{12} \times 60 = \frac{3}{12} \times \frac{60}{1} = 15.$$

Therefore, the first piece is 15 inches.

The 4 in the ratio $3 : 4 : 5$ represents $\frac{4}{12}$ of "the total length of rope". We have

$$\frac{4}{12} \times 60 = \frac{4}{12} \times \frac{60}{1} = 20.$$

Therefore, the second piece is 20 inches.

The 5 in the ratio $3 : 4 : 5$ represents $\frac{5}{12}$ of "the total length of rope". We have

$$\frac{5}{12} \times 60 = \frac{4}{12} \times \frac{60}{1} = 25.$$

The third piece is 25 inches. Observe that

$$15 \text{ inches} + 20 \text{ inches} + 25 \text{ inches} = 60 \text{ inches}.$$

Exercises: Chapter 5, Section A

In Exercises 1 - 17, find the ratio and express it as fraction in simpliest form (lowest terms).

1. 12 to 36

2. 40 to 80

3. 56 to 16

4. 25 to 10

5. 14 to 14

6. 34 to 71

7. 40 seconds to 5 minutes

8. 3 hours to 80 minutes

9. 6 inches to 4 feet

10. 4 inches to 36 inches

11. 70 minutes to 7 hours

12. 50 minutes to 400 seconds

13. 24 feet to 24 inches

14. 30 hours to 60 minutes

15. 100 feet to 20 inches

16. 25 feet to 100 inches
(a) $\frac{1}{3}$　　(b) $\frac{3}{1}$　　(c) $\frac{1}{4}$　　(d) $\frac{4}{1}$　　(e) $\frac{15}{1}$

17. 500 minutes to 500 seconds
(a) $\frac{6}{1}$　　(b) $\frac{1}{6}$　　(c) $\frac{1}{1}$　　(d) $\frac{5}{6}$　　(e) $\frac{6}{5}$

In Exercises 18 - 19, a mixture contains 50 milliliters of water and 40 milliliters sulphuric acid.

18. The ratio of sulphuric acid to water is:
(a) $\frac{4}{5}$　　(b) $\frac{5}{9}$　　(c) $\frac{4}{9}$　　(d) $\frac{9}{4}$　　(e) $\frac{9}{5}$

19. The ratio of water to sulphuric acid is:
(a) $\frac{9}{5}$　　(b) $\frac{5}{9}$　　(c) $\frac{5}{4}$　　(d) $\frac{9}{4}$　　(e) $\frac{4}{9}$

20. A piece of rope 240 inches long is cut into 3 pieces such that the lengths of the pieces are in the ratios 4 : 5 : 6. The length of the three pieces, in inches, are:
(a) 6, 48, 40　　(b) 4, 5, 6　　(c) 960, 1,200, 1,440　　(d) 40, 50, 60　　(e) 64, 80, 96

Section B. Rates

In Section A, you learned how to use a ratio to compare two quantities that are measured in the same unit. It is also possible to compare two quantities of different units. When a ratio is used to compare two different quantities, we call it a **rate**. Rates are often seen as comparisons of a quantity to a single unit of another quantity.

For example, suppose a man drives 60 miles in 3 hours. The ratio is

$$\frac{60 \text{ miles}}{3 \text{ hours}} = \frac{20 \text{ miles}}{1 \text{ hour}} = 20 \text{ miles per hour.}$$

We say that he travels at a **rate** of 20 miles per hour.

Example 1. A student drives 260 miles on 13 gallons of gas. What is the rate in miles per gallon?

Solution: $\dfrac{260 \text{ miles}}{13 \text{ gallons}} = \dfrac{20}{1} = 20$ miles per gallon.

Example 2. A baker makes 6 pies in 4 hours. What is the rate in pies per hour?

Solution: $\dfrac{6 \text{ pies}}{4 \text{ hours}} = \dfrac{3 \text{ pies}}{2 \text{ hours}} = 1\frac{1}{2}$ pies per hour.

Example 3. A fruit vender sells 5 apples for $3. What is the cost per apple in cents?

Solution: First convert $3 into cents:

$$\$3 = 3 \times 100\cent = 300\cent$$

Therefore, $\dfrac{300\cent}{5 \text{ apples}} = \dfrac{60\cent}{1 \text{ apple}} = 60\cent$ per apple.

Example 4: Peter travels 500 miles in 80 hours and Sandy travels $512\frac{1}{2}$ miles in 82 hours. Is Peter's rate of speed greater than, less than, or equal to Sandy's? (Note: miles per hour is abbreviated as mph and for emphasis in other cases as mi/hr.)

Solution: Peter's rate of speed is

$$\frac{500 \text{ miles}}{80 \text{ hours}} = \frac{25 \text{ miles}}{4 \text{ hours}} = 6\frac{1}{4} \text{ mph.}$$

Sandy's rate of speed is

$$\frac{512\frac{1}{2} \text{ miles}}{82 \text{ hours}} = \frac{\frac{1025}{2} \text{ miles}}{82 \text{ hours}} = \left(\frac{1025}{2} \div 82\right) \text{ mph}$$

$$= \left(\frac{1025}{2} \times \frac{1}{82}\right) \text{ mph} = \frac{25}{4} \text{ mph} = 6\frac{1}{4} \text{ mph}.$$

Therefore, their rates of speed are equal.

Example 5. Suppose that a pears cost $c\cent$.
(a) How much does 1 pear cost (in cents)?
(b) What is the cost, in cents, of x pears?

Solution:
(a) We want to find the cost of 1 pear. We set up a rate of cost per pear (notice that the denominator contains the number of pears):

$$\frac{c\cent}{a \text{ pears}} = \frac{\frac{c}{a}\cent}{1 \text{ pear}}.$$

Therefore, 1 pear costs $\frac{c}{a}\cent$.

(b) Since we know the cost of 1 pear, we can find the cost of x pears by multiplying the cost by x:

$$\left(\frac{c}{a}\cent\right)(x) = \frac{c}{a}x\cent$$

Therefore, x pears cost $\frac{c}{a}x\cent$.

Exercises: Chapter 5, Section B

In Exercises 1 - 6, find the rate.

1. 12 feet to 2 seconds   2. $400 to 80 hours   3. 300 kilowatts to 25 hours

4. 250 miles to 10 hours   5. $140 to 28 gallons   6. $505 to 10 square feet

In Exercises 7 - 16, solve each problem.

7. Stan runs 4 miles in 20 minutes. How many miles per hour is he moving?

8. A fruit vender sells 9 oranges for $4.50. What is the cost per orange in cents?

9. John travels 500 miles in 80 hours and Anthony travels 509 miles in 87 hours. Who is traveling at a higher rate of speed?

10. Sue drives 143 miles in 5.5 hours. The number of miles per hour Sue drives is:
(a) 2.6   (b) 28   (c) 26   (d) 24   (e) 260

11. A satellite travels 672,000 miles (mi.) per day. How far does it travels per hour?
(a) 280 mi.   (b) 14,000 mi.   (c) 2,800 mi.   (d) 28,000 mi.   (e) 28 mi.

12. If x mangoes cost $\$y$, then the cost (in dollars) of 1 mango is:
(a) x (b) y (c) $\frac{y}{x}$ (d) $\frac{x}{y}$ (e) xy

13. A man worked for 7 hours and earned $88.40. What was his hourly wage?
(a) $24   (b) $618.80   (c) $12   (d) $11.20   (e) $12.63

14. If a map has a scale, where 1 inch represents 45 miles, how many miles would $3\frac{1}{4}$ inches represent?
(a) $146\frac{1}{4}$ mi.   (b) $13\frac{11}{13}$ mi.   (c) $\frac{11}{13}$ mi.   (d) 135 mi.   (e) 13 mi.

15. If x oranges cost y¢, then what is the general formula for the cost, in cents, of z oranges?
(a) $\frac{y}{xz}$ (b) $\frac{y}{z}x$ (c) $\frac{y}{x}z$ (d) $\frac{x}{y}z$ (e) xyz

16. A supermarket bought 300 jars of honey for $950 and sold them for a total of $1175. What was the supermarket's profit per jar?
(a) $1.33   (b) 50¢   (c) $3.92   (d) 75¢   (e) $3.17

For Exercises 17 - 20, a science department at Brooklyn College has the policy requiring that for every 120 students there are 10 instructors, and for every 35 students there are 7 tutors.

17. How many students per instructor does the department have?
(a) 12   (b) 5   (c) 10   (d) 1,200   (e) 350

18. How many students per tutor does the department have?
(a) 10   (b) 1,200   (c) 5   (d) 350   (e) 260

19. How many instructors are needed to satisfy the policy if there are 480 students in the department?
(a) 12   (b) 4   (c) 20   (d) 40   (e) 4,800

20. How many tutors are needed to satisfy the policy if there are 175 students in the department?
(a) 350   (b) 5   (c) 1,225   (d) 1,200   (e) 35

Section C. Proportions

A **proportion** is an equation that states that two ratios or rates are equal. For example, the ratios $\frac{6}{8}$ and $\frac{3}{4}$ are equal since $\frac{6}{8} = \frac{6 \div 2}{8 \div 2} = \frac{3}{4}$. Therefore, the equation $\frac{6}{8} = \frac{3}{4}$ is a proportion, and we say that $\frac{6}{8}$ and $\frac{3}{4}$ are **proportional** to each other.

Similarly, the equations

$$\frac{72 \text{ miles}}{54 \text{ hours}} = \frac{4 \text{ miles}}{3 \text{ hours}} \quad \text{and} \quad \frac{54 \text{ hours}}{72 \text{ miles}} = \frac{3 \text{ hours}}{4 \text{ miles}}$$

are proportions. Observe that the units of the numerators are the same and the units of the denominators are the same.

Rule: In a proportion (fraction = fraction), the following are always true:
   a) The ratios are equal.
   b) If the proportion contains units, then the units of the numerators are the same and the units of the denominators are the same.
   c) One ratio can be obtained from the other by multiplying both its numerator and denominator by the same non-zero number.
   d) The **cross products** are equal.

By the cross product we mean multiply the denominator of one fraction by the numerator of the other fraction:

$$\frac{a}{b} = \frac{c}{d} \quad \text{gives us} \quad ad = bc$$

We also call this **cross multiplying**.

Example 1. Determine whether or not $\dfrac{126 \text{ miles}}{147 \text{ hours}} = \dfrac{6 \text{ miles}}{7 \text{ hours}}$ is a true proportion.

Solution: $\dfrac{126 \text{ miles}}{147 \text{ hours}} = \dfrac{6 \text{ miles}}{7 \text{ hours}}$ is a proportion because:

a) The ratios are equal: $\dfrac{126}{147} = \dfrac{126 \div 21}{147 \div 21} = \dfrac{6}{7}$

b) The units of the numerators (miles) are the same and the units of the denominator (hours) are the same.

c) $\dfrac{126}{147}$ is obtained by mutiplying the numerator and denominator of $\dfrac{6}{7}$ by 21:

$$\frac{6}{7} = \frac{6 \times 21}{7 \times 21} = \frac{126}{147}$$

d) The cross products in $\frac{126}{147} = \frac{6}{7}$ are equal: $\underbrace{126 \times 7}_{882} = \underbrace{147 \times 6}_{882}$.

Exercises: Chapter 5, Section C

In Exercises 1 - 14, determine whether each proportion is true

1. $\dfrac{5}{8} = \dfrac{45}{72}$ 2. $\dfrac{72}{81} = \dfrac{8}{9}$ 3. $\dfrac{49}{36} = \dfrac{7}{6}$ 4. $\dfrac{3}{9} = \dfrac{1}{3}$

5. $\dfrac{6}{8} = \dfrac{3}{4}$ 6. $\dfrac{2}{2} = \dfrac{1}{4}$ 7. $\dfrac{8}{12} = \dfrac{24}{36}$ 8. $\dfrac{5}{15} = \dfrac{1}{5}$

9. $\dfrac{66 \text{ hits}}{14 \text{ walks}} = \dfrac{11 \text{ hits}}{7 \text{ walks}}$ 10. $\dfrac{11 \text{ miles}}{121 \text{ hours}} = \dfrac{1 \text{ miles}}{21 \text{ hours}}$ 11. $\dfrac{\$160}{7 \text{ hours}} = \dfrac{\$6}{7 \text{ hours}}$

12. $\dfrac{34 \text{ hits}}{17 \text{ balls}} = \dfrac{6 \text{ hits}}{7 \text{ balls}}$ 13. $\dfrac{240 \text{ miles}}{13 \text{ hours}} = \dfrac{23 \text{ miles}}{1 \text{ hour}}$ 14. $\dfrac{\$90}{6 \text{ hours}} = \dfrac{\$15}{1 \text{ hour}}$

In Exercises 15 - 16, determine which proportion is true.

15. (a) $\dfrac{1}{8} = \dfrac{1}{4}$ (b) $\dfrac{11}{8} = \dfrac{7}{4}$ (c) $\dfrac{6}{8} = \dfrac{13}{4}$ (d) $\dfrac{44}{22} = \dfrac{2}{11}$ (e) $\dfrac{32}{18} = \dfrac{3}{7}$

16. (a) $\dfrac{21}{7} = \dfrac{2}{1}$ (b) $\dfrac{77}{11} = \dfrac{1}{7}$ (c) $\dfrac{56}{48} = \dfrac{7}{6}$ (d) $\dfrac{10}{22} = \dfrac{5}{101}$ (e) $\dfrac{32}{18} = \dfrac{0}{9}$

Section D. Solving $ax = b$

A **variable** is a letter that represents a real number. If we do not know the value of a number, we may represent it by letters such as x, y, z and n. Note that the variable x means $1 \cdot x$ (1 times x). When we write a product, say $6 \cdot x$, we simply write $6x$. Thus, $7 \cdot y = 7y$ and $(-3)(t) = -3t$.

An **algebraic expression** (or **expression**) is a real number, a variable, or a combination of numbers and variables. For example,

$$8, \quad y, \quad 12t, \quad 3x - 1, \quad \text{and} \quad -\frac{2}{5}x + 4.5$$

are algebraic expressions.

In the product $2x$, 2 and x are called the **factors** of the product. Note that $x(2) = 2(x)$; that is, $x2 = 2x$ since multiplication is commutative (recall that $xy = yx$ for any real numbers x and y). Similarly, the factors of $5y$ are 5 and y.

Rule for evaluating algebraic expressions: Replace (substitute) the variable by the given value, then simplify.

Example 1. Evaluate $5x$ when $x = 6$.

Solution: $5(6) = 30$, so $5x$ equals 30 when $x = 6$.

Example 2. Evaluate $56x$, when $x = -3$.

Solution: $56(-3) = -168$, so $56x$ equals -168 when $x = -3$.

An **equation** is a mathematical sentence showing two expressions are equal. For example, $4x = 8$ is an equation.

A **solution** to an equation is a value of the variable that makes the equation true. The solution to the equation $4x = 8$, for example, is 2 because

$$4(2) \overset{\checkmark}{=} 8.$$

The process of finding a solution to an equation is called **solving an equation** for the variable.

Example 3. Is 7 a solution to the equation $6x = 42$?

Solution: Yes: $6(7) \overset{\checkmark}{=} 42$.

Example 4. Is 7 a solution to the equation $8x = 72$?

123

Solution: No: $8(7) \neq 72$.

Next we learn how to solve an equation of the form $ax = b$, where a and b are real numbers and x is a variable.

The Division Principle: If both sides of the equation $ax = b$ are divided by the same non-zero number a, the results on both sides are equal in value.

For example, to solve the equation $3x = 81$, we divide both sides of the equation by 3:

$$\frac{\cancel{3}x}{\cancel{3}} = \frac{81}{3}$$

Notice that $\frac{3x}{3} = \frac{3}{3}x = 1x = x$. Therefore,

$$\frac{\cancel{3}x}{\cancel{3}} = \frac{81}{3}$$
$$x = 27$$

The solution is $x = 27$. We can check the answer by replacing x in the equation by 27:

$$3(27) \overset{\checkmark}{=} 81$$

Example 5. Solve each equation and check your answer.
1) $5x = 45$ 2) $3x = 50$ 3) $-23x = 46$ 4) $-4x = -56$ 5) $-45x = 5$

Solution:
1) Divide both sides of the equation by 5:

$$\frac{\cancel{5}x}{\cancel{5}} = \frac{45}{5}$$
$$x = 9$$

Check: $5(9) \overset{\checkmark}{=} 45$

2) Divide both sides of the equation by 3:

$$\frac{\cancel{3}x}{\cancel{3}} = \frac{50}{3}$$
$$x = \frac{50}{3} = 16\frac{2}{3}$$

Check: $\underbrace{3\left(16\frac{2}{3}\right) = 3\left(\frac{50}{3}\right)}_{\text{Write } 16\frac{2}{3} \text{ as an improper fraction}} = \frac{3}{1}\left(\frac{50}{3}\right) \overset{\checkmark}{=} 50$

3) Divide both sides of the equation by –23:

$$\frac{-23x}{-23} = \frac{46}{-23}$$

$$x = -2$$

Check: $-23(-2) \overset{\checkmark}{=} 46.$

4) Divide both sides of the equation by –4:

$$\frac{-4x}{-4} = \frac{-56}{-4}$$

$$x = 14$$

Check: $-4(14) \overset{\checkmark}{=} -56$

5) Divide both sides of the equation by –45:

$$\frac{-45x}{-45} = \frac{5}{-45}$$

$$x = -\frac{1}{9}$$

Check: $-45(-\frac{1}{9}) = \frac{-45}{1}(-\frac{1}{9}) \overset{\checkmark}{=} 5$

Exercises: Chapter 5, Section D

In Exercises 1 - 12, solve and check.

1. $8x = 96$ 2. $9x = 45$ 3. $-3x = 67$ 4. $4x = -32$

5. $-32x = -256$ 6. $8p = 44$ 7. $87 = -3y$ 8. $89 = -34a$

9. $-238x = 96$ 10. $72 = -36y$ 11. $-5x = 55$ 12. $-19x = -76$

In Exercises 13 - 15, find x.

13. $49x = -7$
(a) -7 (b) 7 (c) $-\frac{1}{7}$ (d) $\frac{1}{7}$ (e) 0

14. $-35x = 70$
(a) 2 (b) -2 (c) $\frac{1}{2}$ (d) $-\frac{1}{2}$ (e) 10

15. $35x = 56$
(a) 2 (b) 1 (c) $1\frac{3}{5}$ (d) $\frac{1}{2}$ (e) $1\frac{3}{8}$

Section E. Solving Proportions

Given a proportion, sometimes it is neccessary to find one of the four numbers in the proportion. We call the number we want to find the **unknown** and represent it as a variable.

Rule for solving a proportion: Take the cross product of the proportion, then solve the resulting equation.

Example 1. Solve for x: $\dfrac{4x}{21} = \dfrac{8}{3}$

Solution: First cross multiply and obtain

$$(4x)(3) = (21)(8)$$
$$12x = 168$$

Now divide by 12 and solve for x:

$$\frac{\cancel{12}x}{\cancel{12}} = \frac{168}{12}$$

$$x = 14$$

Example 2. Solve for p: $\dfrac{-112}{28} = \dfrac{4}{3p}$

Solution: $(-112)(3p) = (28)(4)$ (by cross multiplying)
$$-336p = 112$$

$$\frac{-\cancel{336}p}{-\cancel{336}} = \frac{112}{-336}$$ (Divide by -336 and solve for p.)

$$p = -\frac{1}{3}$$

Example 3: Solve and check: $\dfrac{3x}{72} = \dfrac{7}{3}$

Solution: $(3x)(3) = (72)(7)$ (by cross multiplying)
$$9x = 504$$

$$\frac{\cancel{9}x}{\cancel{9}} = \frac{504}{9}$$ (Divide by 9 and solve for x.)

$$x = 56$$

Exercises: Chapter 5, Section E

In Exercises 1 - 22, solve and check.

1. $\dfrac{x}{8} = \dfrac{45}{72}$ 2. $\dfrac{y}{81} = \dfrac{8}{9}$ 3. $\dfrac{49}{x} = \dfrac{7}{6}$ 4. $\dfrac{3}{9} = \dfrac{1}{z}$

5. $\dfrac{6}{8} = \dfrac{x}{4}$ 6. $\dfrac{2}{2} = \dfrac{1}{x}$ 7. $\dfrac{x}{8} = \dfrac{3}{4}$ 8. $\dfrac{5}{x} = \dfrac{1}{5}$

9. $\dfrac{x}{14} = \dfrac{11}{7}$ 10. $\dfrac{11 \text{ miles}}{121 \text{ hours}} = \dfrac{1 \text{ miles}}{x \text{ hours}}$ 11. $\dfrac{\$160}{7 \text{ hours}} = \dfrac{\$x}{7 \text{ hours}}$

12. $\dfrac{34 \text{ hits}}{17 \text{ balls}} = \dfrac{6 \text{ hits}}{x \text{ balls}}$ 13. $\dfrac{1}{8} = \dfrac{x}{4}$ 14. $\dfrac{14}{8} = \dfrac{7}{x}$ 15. $\dfrac{6}{x} = \dfrac{13}{4}$

16. $\dfrac{44}{x} = \dfrac{2}{11}$ 17. $\dfrac{32}{18} = \dfrac{x}{7}$ 18. $\dfrac{21}{7} = \dfrac{x}{1}$ 19. $\dfrac{\$77}{11 \text{ hours}} = \dfrac{\$x}{7 \text{ hours}}$

20. $\dfrac{56}{48} = \dfrac{x}{6}$ 21. $\dfrac{10}{22} = \dfrac{x}{101}$ 22. $\dfrac{x}{18} = \dfrac{0}{9}$

Section F. Translating and Solving Proportion Word Problems

Recall that in the proportion $\frac{a}{b} = \frac{c}{d}$, a and c should have the same units, and b and d should have the same units (see Section C). The proportion $\frac{a}{b} = \frac{c}{d}$ or $a : b = c : d$ is read as "a is to b as c is to d".

Example 1. Write a proportion to express the phrase: "If 3 inches of rain had fallen in 10 hours, then 6 inches of rain would have fallen in 20 hours."

Solution: Set up the proportion: 3 inches is to 10 hours as 6 inches is to 20 hours:

$$\frac{3 \text{ inches}}{10 \text{ hours}} = \frac{6 \text{ inches}}{20 \text{ hours}}$$

There is a "ring" to it: "inches over hours equal inches over hours".

Another way we can interpret the expression above is as follows: 10 hours is to 3 inches as 20 hours is to 6 inches:

$$\frac{10 \text{ hours}}{3 \text{ inches}} = \frac{20 \text{ hours}}{6 \text{ inches}}$$

There is a "ring" to it: "hours over inches equal hours over inches".

Example 2. If the ratio of 5 to x is 40 to 8, find x.

Solution: Set up the proportion and solve: $\frac{5}{x} = \frac{40}{8}$

$$(5)(8) = (x)(40) \qquad \text{(by cross multiplying)}$$
$$40 = 40x$$

$$\frac{4\!\!\!/0}{4\!\!\!/0} = \frac{4\!\!\!/0x}{4\!\!\!/0} \qquad \text{(Divide by 40 and solve for } x\text{.)}$$

$$1 = x$$

Example 3. John must solve 38 math problems on a test. He solves 5 problems every $7\frac{1}{2}$ minutes. At this rate, how long will it take him to solve all 38 problems?

Solution: We set up the proportion and solve:

$$\frac{5 \text{ problems}}{7\frac{1}{2} \text{ minutes}} = \frac{38 \text{ problems}}{x \text{ minutes}}$$

$$(5)(x) = \left(7\frac{1}{2}\right)(38) \qquad \text{(by cross multiplying)}$$

$$5x = \left(\frac{15}{2}\right)\left(\frac{38}{1}\right) \qquad \text{(Change } 7\frac{1}{2} \text{ and 38 into improper fractions.)}$$

$$5x = 285$$

$$\frac{5x}{5} = \frac{285}{5} \qquad \text{(Divide by 5 and solve for } x.)$$

$$x = 57$$

It will take John 57 minutes to solve all 38 problems.

Example 4. Susan's doctor prescribes 12 milligrams (mg.) of antibiotics to be taken every four hours (hrs.) for her flu. The medicine given in liquid form contains 8 mg. of antibiotics for every 10 milliliters (ml.) of solution.

(a) How many milliliters should Susan take every four hours?
(b) How many milliliters should Susan have taken in 24 hours?

Solution:
(a) We are given that there is 8 mg. of antibiotics for every 10 ml. of solution. We need to find out how many milliliters are in 12 mg. To find this, we solve a proportion:

$$\frac{8 \text{ mg.}}{10 \text{ ml.}} = \frac{12 \text{ mg.}}{x \text{ ml.}}$$

$$(8)(x) = (10)(12) \qquad \text{(by cross multiplying)}$$
$$8x = 120$$

$$\frac{8x}{8} = \frac{120}{8} \qquad \text{(Divide by 8 and solve for } x.)$$

$$x = 15$$

Therefore, there are 12 mg. of antibiotics in 15 ml. of solution. Since Susan's doctor precribes 12 mg. of antbiotics to be taken every four hours, she should take 15 ml. of solution every four hours.

(b) We know from (a) that Susan takes 15 ml. of antibiotic every four hours. If she follows the prescription, how many milliliters should Susan have taken in 24 hours? We set up the proportion and solve:

$$\frac{15 \text{ ml.}}{4 \text{ hrs.}} = \frac{x \text{ ml.}}{24 \text{ hrs.}}$$

$$(15)(24) = (4)(x) \qquad \text{(by cross multiplying)}$$

$$360 = 4x$$

$$\frac{360}{4} = \frac{4x}{4} \qquad \text{(Divide by 4 and solve for } x.)$$

$$90 = x$$

Susan should have taken 90 ml. in 24 hrs.

Example 5. In a security company, 3 out of every 8 employees drink coffee. If the company has 360 employees, what is the number of employees who *do not* drink coffee?

Solution: We set up the proportion:

$$\frac{3 \text{ drink coffee}}{8 \text{ employees}} = \frac{x \text{ drink coffee}}{360 \text{ employees}}$$

$$(3)(360) = (8)(x) \qquad \text{(by cross multiplying)}$$

$$1,080 = 8x$$

$$\frac{1,080}{8} = \frac{8x}{8} \qquad \text{(Divide by 8 and solve for } x.)$$

$$135 = x$$

Therefore, 135 employees drink coffee. Be careful! We want the number of employees who *do not* drink coffee. Since there are a total of 360 employees in the company, the number of employees do not drink cofee is $360 - 135 = 225$.

Example 6. Bob burns p calories (cal.) for every q miles that he runs. How many calories (written as a formula) would Bob burn if he runs r miles?

Solution: We set up the proportion:

$$\frac{p \text{ cal.}}{q \text{ mi.}} = \frac{x \text{ cal.}}{r \text{ mi.}} \qquad \text{(where } x \text{ is the unkown)}$$

$$(p)(r) = (q)(x) \qquad \text{(by cross multiplying)}$$
$$pr = qx$$

$$\frac{pr}{q} = \frac{qx}{q} \qquad \text{(Divide by } q \text{ and solve for } x.)$$

$$\frac{pr}{q} = x$$

Bob would burn $\frac{pr}{q}$ calories in r miles.

Exercises: Chapter 5, Section F

In Exercises 1 - 21, solve each problem.

1. If 250 grams of ice cream contains 30 grams of fat, how many grams of fat are there in 600 grams of ice cream?

2. A college has a faculty to student ratio of 2 to 13. If the college has 7,800 students, how many faculty members does the college have?

3. If 3 shirts cost $87, how much does it cost to buy 7 shirts?

4. Colleen must solve 78 math problems on a test. She solves 10 problems every 14 minutes. At this rate, how long will it take her to solve all 78 problems?

5. Peter burns k calories for every l miles that he runs. How much calories (written as a formula) would Peter burn if he runs m miles?

6. Anthony is traveling to Grenada. He can exchange 3 US dollars for 8.10 EC dollars. How many EC dollars will he receive for 93 US dollars?

7. If two cups of cereal contains 58 grams of sugar, how many grams of sugar does 5 cups of cereal contain?

8. In a bread recipe, the ratio of milk to flour is $\frac{4}{3}$. If 12 cups of milk are used, how many cups of flour are used?

9. A man brought a new car. In the first 9 months he drove it 12,000 miles. At this rate, how many miles will he drive it at the end of one year?

10. In a metal alloy, the ratio of copper to zinc is 3 : 7. If there are 330 pounds of copper, how many pounds of zinc is there?

11. In an insurance company, 4 out of every 7 employees drinks black tea. If 440 empolyees drink black tea, the number of employees in the company is:
(a) 251   (b) 700   (c) 770   (d) 330   (e) 440

12. In security company 4 out of every 11 employees drink coffee. If the company has 396 employees, the number of employees who *do not* drink coffee is:
(a) 99   (b) 396   (c) 144   (d) 252   (e) 56

13. A researcher needs 6 pounds (lbs.) of corn to feed 40 rats. If the rat population grows to 55, how much corn is needed to feed the rats?
(a) $8\frac{1}{4}$ lbs.   (b) 8 lbs.   (c) $366\frac{2}{3}$ lbs.   (d) $4\frac{1}{3}$ lbs.   (e) 7 lbs.

14. If paper cost 22¢ per sheet, how many sheets can be purchased for $33?
(a) $1\frac{1}{2}$ (b) 120   (c) 12   (d) 150   (e) 10

15. The length and width of a 9 inch by 5 inch picture are enlarged proportionally. If the length is enlarged to 14 inches, what is the enlarged width?
(a) 7 in.   (b) $7\frac{7}{9}$ in.   (c) 10 in.   (d) 11 in.   (e) $25\frac{1}{2}$ in.

16. If 2 peppers sell for $0.39, how many peppers can be bought for $19.89?
(a) 51   (b) 4   (c) 102   (d) 11   (e) 12

17. The ratio 45 to y is 7 to 2. Find y.
(a) 6   (b) $7\frac{7}{9}$ (c) 9   (d) 11   (e) $12\frac{6}{7}$

18. How many gallons of paint is needed to paint a wall 1,400 square feet if 1 gallon covers 400 square feet?
(a) 3.5   (b) 3   (c) 560,000   (d) 700   (e) 1,000

19. Steve paid $10.18 for two frozen yogurts. How much would it cost him if he purchased 6 frozen yogurts?
(a) $61.08   (b) $30.54   (c) $3.39   (d) $16.18   (e) $31.00

20. Frank purchases 17 shares of a stock for $114.75. How much will 31 shares of that stock cost?
(a) $229.25   (b) $324.00   (c) $209.25   (d) $62.93   (e) $228.75

21. A cricket team won 3 times as many games as it lost. How many games did it lose if it played a total of 40 games?
(a) 3   (b) 120   (c) 12   (d) 11   (e) 10

Chapter 6:   Percentages

Section A.   Understanding Percents

Percents are very useful in conveying information. How often do we hear statements such as: there is a 50 percent sale, or there is an 80 percent chance of rain. The word **percent** means *per hundred*. The symbol % indicates percent.

For example, we write 5% as $\frac{5}{100}$ in fractional form or 5% as .05 in terms of a decimal number. In the Chapter 2, fractions were used to represent parts of a whole, and in Chapter 3, decimals were used to represent parts of a whole. Now, we see that percent can be used to describe parts of a whole, with the whole being 100.

In general, we have $n\% = \frac{n}{100}$. This means that $n\%$ of a quantity is $\frac{n}{100}$ of the quantity. Therefore, $1\% = \frac{1}{100}$ is one hundredth of a whole and $100\% = \frac{100}{100} = 1$ represents the entire quantity. Note that 300% represents $\frac{300}{100} = 3$ times the given quantity.

Example 1. State using percents: 97 out of 100 cars made have air-conditioning.

Solution: $\frac{97}{100} = 97\%$, so 97% of cars made have air-conditioning.

Example 2. A private school enrolled 100 students last year. This year's enrollment is 127. Write this year's enrollment as a percent of last year's.

Solution: $\dfrac{\text{this year's enrollment}}{\text{last year's enrollment}} = \frac{127}{100} = 127\%$, so this year's enrollment is 127% of last year's.

Example 3. In a mixture of water and chlorine, what percent of the mixture is chlorine if 70% is water?

Solution: We know that 100% represents the entire mixture. If 70% of the mixture is water, then $100\% - 70\% = 30\%$ of the mixture is chlorine.

Example 4. A bottle contains 100 ml. of hydrochloric acid. If 2.5 ml. of the hydrochloric acid is used for an experiment,
(a) What percent of acid is used?
(b) What percent is not used?

Solution:

(a) 2.5 ml. out of 100 ml. is used. Therefore, $\frac{2.5}{100}$ = 2.5% of acid is used.

(b) Since 100% represents the entire mixture, if 2.5% of acid is used, then 100% − 2.5% = 97.5% is not used.

Example 5. Express each as a percent:

1) $\frac{4}{100}$ 2) 5.5 hundredths   3) 0.08   4) $7\frac{3}{4}$ out of a hundred

Solution: 1) $\frac{4}{100}$ = 4%   2) 5.5 hundredths = $\frac{5.5}{100}$ = 5.5%

3) 0.08 = $\frac{8}{100}$ = 8%   4) $7\frac{3}{4}$ out of a hundred = $\frac{7\frac{3}{4}}{100}$ = $7\frac{3}{4}$%

Exercises: Chapter 6, Section A

In Exercises 1 - 5, write each statement using percents.

1. 30 out of 100 cars made are red.

2. 41 out of 100 students scored a *B* on their test.

3. 7 out of 100 games played are won.

4. 84 out of 100 students handed in their quiz.

5. 21 out of 100 stocks decreased in value yesterday.

In Exercises 6 - 10, solve.

6. A maritime college enrolled 100 cadets last year. This year's enrollment is 90. Write this year's enrollment as a percent of last year's.

7. A chemist has a bottle containing 100 ml. of benzene. If he uses 0.7 ml. of the benzene for an experiment,
a) what percent of benzene is used?
b) what percent of benzene is not used?

8. 40 out of 100 kittens are in a basket. What percent of kittens are in the basket?

9. 11 out of 100 people in the park smoke. What percentage of people in the park smoke?

10. 69 out of 100 students received financial aid. What percent do not received financial aid?

In Exercises 11 - 14, express each as a percent.

11. $\dfrac{3}{100}$ 12. 23 hundredths   13. 0.45   14. 35 out of a hundred

In Exercises 15 - 17, choose the correct answer.

15. Which of the following is equivalent to 39%?
(a) 0.039   (b) 0.39   (c) 390   (d) 39   (e) 3.9

16. Which of the following is not equivalent to 4%?
(a) 0.04   (b) 4 out of a hundred   (c) 40 hundredths   (d) $\frac{4}{100}$
(e) 4 hundredths

17. What percent of the population are women if 47% are men?
(a) 3%   (b) 47%   (c) 53%   (d) 43%   (e) 13%

Section B. Converting Percents, Decimals, and Fractions from One Form into Another

Rule for converting a percent to an equivalent decimal:
1. Remove the percent sign.
2. Multiply the number by 0.01 (this moves the decimal point **two places to the left**).

Note: Multiplying by 0.01 is equivalent to dividing by 100. Also remember that there is always an imaginary decimal point at the end of every whole number.

Example 1. Write each percent as a decimal.
1) 23%   2) 313%   3) 21.5%   4) 0.07%

Solution: 1) $23\% = 23 \times 0.01 = 0.23$ 2) $313\% = 313 \times 0.01 = 3.13$

3) $21.5\% = 21.5 \times 0.01 = 0.215$ 4) $0.07\% = 0.07 \times 0.01 = 0.0007$

Rule to convert a decimal to an equivalent percent:
1. Multiply the decimal by 100 (this moves the decimal point **two places to the right**).
2. Write the % sign at the end of the number.

Example 2. Write each decimal as a percent.
1) 0.045   2) 12.6   3) 0.3   4) 7.0

Solution: 1) $0.045 \times 100 = 4.5\%$ 2) $12.6 \times 100 = 1,260\%$

3) $0.3 \times 100 = 30\%$ 4) $7.0 \times 100 = 700\%$

Rule to convert a fraction to an equivalent decimal: Divide the numerator by the denominator. The resulting quotient can be rounded to a desired number of decimal places.

Example 3. Write each fraction as a decimal (for Examples 2 and 3, round off to 3 decimal places).
1) $\frac{4}{5}$ 2) $\frac{5}{8}$ 3) $\frac{2}{7}$

Solution:

1)
$$
\begin{array}{r}
0.8 \\
5{\overline{\smash{\big)}\,4.0}} \\
\underline{-40} \\
0
\end{array}
$$

2)
$$
\begin{array}{r}
0.625 \\
8{\overline{\smash{\big)}\,50.000}} \\
\underline{-48} \\
20 \\
\underline{-16} \\
40 \\
\underline{-40} \\
0
\end{array}
$$

3)
$$
\begin{array}{r}
0.2857 \\
7{\overline{\smash{\big)}\,20.0000}} \\
\underline{-14} \\
60 \\
\underline{-56} \\
40 \\
\underline{-35} \\
50 \\
\underline{-49} \\
1
\end{array}
$$

1) $\frac{4}{5} = 0.8$ 2) $\frac{5}{8} = 0.625$ 3) $\frac{2}{7} = 0.286$

Rule for converting a decimal to an equivalent fraction:
1. Write the whole number (the digits to the left of the decimal point).
2. Then write the decimal part (the digits to the right of the decimal point) divided by the number that has a 1 followed by the same number of zeros as the number of digits in the decimal part.
3. Add the results found in Steps 1. and 2.

For example, $5.193 = 5 + \frac{193}{1,000} = 5\frac{193}{1,000}$. Notice that we put 3 zeros after the 1 in the denominator because there are three digits in 193 (this is Step 2 in the rule).

Note: To convert a *whole number percent* to a fraction, just divide the whole number by 100. For example,

$$3\% = \frac{3}{100} \quad \text{and} \quad 75\% = \frac{75}{100} = \frac{3}{4}.$$

Example 4. Write each decimal as a fraction.
1) 0.345   2) 30.13

Solution:
1) The whole number of 0.345 is 0. By Step 2., we divide the decimal part, 345, by 1,000 (3 zeros are added after the 1 because there are three digits in 345) and get $\frac{347}{1,000}$. Adding 0 and $\frac{347}{1,000}$ gives $\frac{347}{1,000}$. Therefore, $0.345 = \frac{347}{1,000}$.

2) The whole number of 30.13 is 30. By Step 2., we divide the decimal part, 13, by 100 (2 zeros are added after the 1 because there are two digits in 13) and get $\frac{13}{100}$. Adding 30 and $\frac{13}{100}$ gives $30\frac{13}{100}$. Therefore, $30.13 = 30\frac{13}{100}$.

Rule for converting a percent to an equivalent fraction: Convert the percent to an equivalent decimal, then convert the decimal to an equivalent fraction.

Example 5. Write each percent as a fraction.

1) 24.67%   2) $\frac{1}{2}$%   3) 34%

Solution:

1) First convert 24.67% to a decimal:

$$24.67 \times 0.01 = 0.2467$$

Now convert 0.2467 to a fraction:

$$0.2467 = 0 + \frac{2,467}{10,000} = \frac{2,467}{10,000}$$

Note that 4 zeros are added after the 1 in the denominator because there are four digits in 2467. Therefore, $24.67\% = \frac{2,467}{10,000}$.

2) First convert $\frac{1}{2}$% to a decimal by writing $\frac{1}{2}$ as a decimal (keeping the % sign!), then convert the percent to a decimal by removing the percent sign and multiply by 0.01:

$$\frac{1}{2}\% = 0.5\% = 0.5 \times 0.01 = 0.005$$

Now convert 0.005 to a fraction:

$$0.005 = 0 + \frac{5}{1,000} = \frac{5}{1,000} = \frac{1}{200}$$

Note that 3 zeros are added after the 1 in the denominator because there are three digits in 005. Therefore, $\frac{1}{2}\% = \frac{1}{200}$.

3) $34\% = \frac{34}{100} = \frac{17}{50}$

Rule for converting a fraction to an equivalent percent:
1. Convert the fraction to an equivalent decimal.
2. Then convert the decimal to an equivalent percent.

Example 6. Write $\frac{3}{5}$ as a percent.

Solution: First convert $\frac{3}{5}$ to a decimal:

$$\begin{array}{r} 0.6 \\ 5)\overline{3.0} \\ -30 \\ \hline 0 \end{array}$$

And so, $\frac{3}{5} = 0.6$. Now convert 0.6 to a percent by multiplying by it by 100:

$$0.6 = 0.60 \times 100 = 60\%$$

Therefore, $\frac{3}{5} = 60\%$.

Example 7. Write $\frac{8}{9}$ as a percent (round off to two decimal places).

Solution: First convert $\frac{8}{9}$ to a decimal:

$$
\begin{array}{r}
0.888\cdots \\
9)\overline{8.000} \\
-72 \\
\hline
80 \\
-72 \\
\hline
80 \\
-72 \\
\hline
\vdots
\end{array}
$$

Therefore, $\frac{8}{9} = 0.888\cdots = 0.\overline{8}$, which rounds off to 0.8889. Now convert 0.8889 to a percent by multiplying by it by 100:

$$0.8889 = 0.8889 \times 100 = 88.89\%$$

And so, $\frac{8}{9} = 88.89\%$.

Exercises: Chapter 6, Section B

In Exercises 1 - 7, write each percent as a decimal.

1. 3.5% 2. 122% 3. 1% 4. 0.22% 5. $\frac{1}{5}\%$ 6. 30%

7. If 0.289% interest is given on a savings account, then the interest written as a decimal is:
(a) 28.9 (b) 0.289 (c) 2.89 (d) 0.00289 (e) 0.0289

In Exercises 8 - 15, write each decimal as a percent.

8. 0.98 9. 0.2 10. 12.98 11. 0.008 12. 1.1 13. 3.09

14. If 0.78 of a pie is eaten, then the percent eaten is:
(a) 0.22% (b) 78% (c) 7.8% (d) 780% (e) 22%

15. If 0.4 of toys made are red, then the percent of red toys made is:
(a) 0.4% (b) 0.6% (c) 4% (d) 40% (e) 60%

In Exercises 16 - 22, write each percent as a fraction reduced to lowest terms.

16. 23% 17. 120% 18. 2% 19. 60% 20. $\frac{3}{8}\%$ 21. $\frac{7}{5}\%$

22. 45.7% written as a fraction is:
(a) $\frac{457}{100}$ (b) $\frac{457}{10}$ (c) $\frac{457}{1,000}$ (d) $\frac{457}{100}$ (e) $\frac{457}{1}$

In Exercises 23 - 29, write each fraction as a percent.

23. $\frac{1}{5}$ 24. $\frac{45}{50}$ 25. $\frac{7}{10}$ 26. $\frac{1}{4}$

27. $\frac{2}{3}$ (to two decimal places)   28. $\frac{6}{11}$ (to two decimal places)

29. What is $\frac{7}{25}$ written as a percent?

(a) 7%   (b) $\frac{7}{25}$%   (c) 25%   (d) 0.25%   (e) 28%

In Exercises 30 - 35, write each fraction as a decimal.

30. $\frac{1}{50}$ 31. $\frac{1}{100}$ 32. $\frac{2}{5}$ 33. $\frac{3}{4}$

34. $\frac{8}{15}$ (to two decimal places)

35. What is $\frac{4}{25}$ written as a decimal?

(a) 0.16   (b) 0.06   (c) 0.25   (d) 0.8   (e) 0.48

In Exercises 36 - 42, write each decimal as a fraction reduced to lowest terms.

36. 0.34   37. 1.48   38. 0.04   39. 0.205

40. 0.11   41. 0.099

42. What is 0.035 written as a fraction reduced to lowest terms?

(a) $\frac{7}{200}$ (b) $\frac{1}{3,500}$ (c) $\frac{1}{350}$ (d) $\frac{1,000}{35}$ (e) $\frac{3,500}{1}$

Section C. Solving Basic Percent Problems

We begin by giving some guidelines for solving basic percent problems.

1. a) The word "of" is written as "×" (times).
   b) The word "is" is witten as "=" (equals).
   c) The words "what" or "find" is written as "x" or "n" (the unknown).

2. **Basic Percent Statements**.

i) 'What is *a*% of *b*?'   and   'Find *a*% of *b*.'

Example 1. What is 20% of 100?

Solution: What is   20% of   100?
   $\updownarrow$ $\updownarrow$ $\updownarrow$
   x $= 20\%$ $\times$ 100

$$x = 0.20 \times 100 \quad (\text{note: } 20\% = 0.20)$$

$$x = 20$$

Example 2. Find 60% of 0.015.

Solution: Find   60%   of   0.015.
   $\updownarrow$ $\updownarrow$
   x $= 60\%$ $\times$ 0.015

$$x = 0.60 \times 0.015 \quad (\text{note: } 60\% = 0.60)$$

$$x = 0.009$$

ii) 'What percent of *a* is *b*?'

Example 3. What percent of 80 is 45?

Solution: What percent of   80 is   45?
      $\updownarrow$ $\updownarrow$ $\updownarrow$
      $x\%$ $\times$ 80 $=$ 45

$$x\% = \frac{45}{80} \qquad (\text{Solve for } x\%.)$$

$$x\% = 0.5625$$

The % sign after x means we need to write 0.5625 as a percent: $0.5625 = 56.25\%$. Therefore, we get $x = 56.25\%$.

iii) '*b* is what percent of *a*?'

Example 4. 38 is what percent of 5?

Solution:

38	is	what percent of	5?
↕		↕	↕
38	=	$x\%$	$\times$ 5

$$\frac{38}{5} = x\% \quad \text{(Solve for } x\%.)$$

$$7.6 = x\% \quad \text{(The \% sign after } x \text{ means we need to write 7.6 as a percent.)}$$
$$760\% = x$$

iv) '*a* is *b*% of what number?'

Example 5. 48 is 60% of what number?

Solution:

48	is	60%	of	what number?
↕		↕		↕
48	=	60%	$\times$	n

$$48 = 0.60n \quad \text{(Change the percent to a decimal.)}$$

$$\frac{48}{0.60} = n \quad \text{(Solve for } n.)$$

$$\frac{480}{6} = n \quad \text{(Multiply both the numerator and the denominator by 10.)}$$

$$80 = n$$

v) 'What is *a*% of *b*% of *n*?'

Example 6. What is 50% of 40% of 90?

Solution: 50% of 40% of 90 = 50% of (40% of 90) = 50% of (0.40 × 90)
= 50% of 36 = 0.50 × 36 = 18

A different approach to solving *i*) through *iv*) is to use:

$$vi) \quad \frac{part}{whole} = \frac{part\ (x\%)}{whole\ (100\%)}$$

Note: The word "part" is equivalent to the number with the word "is", and the word "whole" is equivalent to the number with the word "of".

Example 7: What is 20% of 150?

Solution: 20% is written over 100%; that is, 20% is part of the whole 100%. Note that 150 is with the word "of "; it is the whole and is written as the denominator.

Set up the proportion: $\dfrac{part}{whole} = \dfrac{part\ (x\%)}{whole\ (100\%)}$

$$\frac{part}{150} = \frac{20}{100} \qquad \text{(We need to the find the ``}part\text{''.)}$$

$$\frac{n}{150} = \frac{20}{100} \qquad \text{(Let }n\text{ be the ``}part\text{''.)}$$

$$(n)(100) = 20(150) \qquad \text{(after cross multiplying)}$$
$$100n = 3,000$$

$$n = \frac{3,000}{100} = 30$$

Example 8: 48 is 60% of what number?

Solution: Let *n* be the number we are looking for. Notice that 48 is with the word "is" and it is part of the whole number *n*, and 60% is part of the whole 100%.

Set up the proportion: $\dfrac{part}{whole} = \dfrac{part\ (x\%)}{whole\ (100\%)}$

$$\frac{48}{n} = \frac{60}{100} \qquad \text{(We need to the find the ``}whole\text{'', }n.\text{)}$$

$$(48)(100) = (n)(60) \qquad \text{(after cross multiplying)}$$
$$4,800 = 60n$$

$$n = \frac{4,800}{60} = 80$$

Exercises: Chapter 6, Section C

In Exercises 1 - 17, solve each problem.

1. What percent of 450 is 90?

2. What is 35% of 80?

3. 70 is what percent of 25?

4. 54 is 90 percent of what number?

5. 20% of what number is 20?

6. 18 is what percent of 19?

7. 30% of what number is 6?

8. What is 0.4% of 8?

9. What is 5.5% of 50?

10. What is 20% of 20% of 30?

11. What is 50% of 50% of 10?

12. 80% of a number is 350. Find the number.

13. What percent of 80 is 14?
(a) 17.5%   (b) 1.75%   (c) 175%   (d) 11.2%   (e) 0.175%

14. 30.5% of what number is 24.4?
(a) 60   (b) 80   (c) 72   (d) 27   (e) 73.2

15. 54 is 45% of what number?
(a) 24.3   (b) 60   (c) 120   (d) 80   (e) 115

16. What percent of 12 is 24?
(a) 50%   (b) 0.5%   (c) 200%   (d) 20%   (e) 6%

17. What is 10% of 20% of 30?
(a) 1   (b) 0.6   (c) 60   (d) 6   (e) 9

Section D.   Solving Word Problems involving Percent

Word problems involving percent are not always stated in a manner which is easily translated. In such cases, it is helplful to restate the problems into basic percent forms as illustrated in Section C. Note that, when appropriate, we can use *any* of the techniques that we have learnt from Section B as well.

Example 1. Tom did 16 math problems for homework. If he got 5 wrong, what percent of the problems did he got wrong?

Solution: We want to find the percent of the problems Tom got wrong out of 16. Since he got 5 problems wrong, we need to answer:

$$\text{What percent of } 16 \text{ is } 5?$$
$$x\% \quad \times \quad 16 \quad = \quad 5$$

$$x\% = \frac{5}{16} \quad \text{(Solve for } x\%.)$$

$$x\% = 0.3125$$
$$x = 31.25\%$$

Therefore, Tom got 31.25% of the problems wrong.

Example 2. In a Spanish class there are 15 boys, which represents 75% of the students in the class. How many girls are in the class?

Solution: 15 is 75% of what number? (find total number of students in the class)

$$15 = 75\% \times n$$

$$15 = 0.75n \quad \text{(Change \% to decimal.)}$$

$$\frac{15}{0.75} = n \quad \text{(Solve for } n.)$$

$$\frac{1500}{75} = n \quad \text{(Multilply both the numerator and the denominator by 100.)}$$

$$20 = n \quad \text{(the total number of students in the class)}$$

Therefore, the number of girls in the class is $20 - 15 = 5$.

Example 3. John took a math test containing 30 prealgebra questions and 40 algebra questions. He got 90% of the prealgebra questions correct and 20% of the algebra questions correct. What percent did John got correct out of the total 70 questions on the math test?

Solution: What is 90% of 30? (This is the number of prealgebra question John got correct.)

$$90\% \text{ of } 30 = 0.90 \times 30 = 27$$

What is 20% of 40? (This is the number of algebra question John got correct.)

$$20\% \text{ of } 40 = 0.20 \times 40 = 8$$

Therefore, John got $27 + 8 = 35$ questions correct out of 70 questions.

Now, we need to find what percent of 70 is 35:

$$x\% \times 70 = 35 \quad \text{(Solve for } x\%.)$$

$$x\% = \frac{35}{70} = 0.5$$

$$x = 50\%$$

Therefore, John got 50% of the questions correct out of the total 70 questions.

Example 4. A college consists of $20,000$ students. The students can be put into four categories; those who have black hair, those have blond hair, those who have brunette hair, and those who have no hair (bald). 50% of the students have black hair, 20% of the students are blond, and the number of students who are brunettes is half the number of students who are blond. How many students have no hair (bald)?

Solution: What is 50% of $20,000$? (This is the number of students who have black hair.)

$$50\% \times 20,000 = 0.50 \times 20,000 = 10,000$$

There are $10,000$ who have black hair.

What is 20% of $20,000$? (This is the number of students who have blond hair.)

$$20\% \times 20,000 = 0.20 \times 20,000 = 4,000$$

There are $4,000$ students who are blond.

Since $4,000$ students are blond and the number of students who are brunette is half of those who are blond, $\frac{1}{2} \times 4,000 = 2,000$ are brunettes. The number of students who have black, blond, and brunette hair is

$$10,000 + 4,000 + 2,000 = 16,000.$$

Therefore, the number students with no hair: $20,000 - 16,000 = 4,000$.

Note: In Example 4, a quick breakdown: 50% black hair, 20% blond, 10% brunette, so 20% bald. Therefore, 20% of 20,000 is $0.2 \times 20,000 = 4,000$ bald.

There are problems involving percent increase or percent decrease. In order to find percent increase or decrease, the following steps are used:

Percent Increase

a) New amount − original amount = amount of increase
b) **Percent** increase × **original** amount = **amount** of increase

Percent Decrease

a) Original amount − New amount = amount of decrease
b) **Percent** decrease × **original** amount = **amount** of decrease

Rule: Whether we have percent increase or decrease, we have the general formula:

$$\textbf{Percent} \times \textbf{Original} = \textbf{Amount}$$

Example 5. Peter's base salary for the week is $500. In addition, he receives a commission of 8% of his sales. His total earning this week is $650. What is Peter's total sales for the week?

Solution: Notice: New amount − original amount = amount of increase

becomes

Total earnings − base salary = commission

Therefore, Peter's commission is $650 − $500 = $150. Let x be Peter's total sales for the week. We want to find x:

Commission = commission rate × total sales

$$150 = 8\% \text{ of } x$$
$$150 = 0.08 \times x$$

$$\frac{150}{0.08} = x$$

$$1,875 = x$$

Peter's total sales for the week is $1,875.

Example 6. Philip earns $40,000 a year. If he receives a 5% increase, what is his new salary?

Solution: New amount − original amount = amount of increase

becomes

New amount = original amount + amount of increase

New salary = original salary + amount of increase
$$\updownarrow \qquad\qquad \updownarrow$$
$$= 40,000 \quad + \quad 5\% \text{ of } 40,000$$
$$\updownarrow$$
$$= 40,000 \quad + \quad 0.05 \times 40,000$$
$$= 40,000 \quad + \quad 2,000$$
$$= 42,000$$

Therefore, his new salary is $42,000.

Example 7. A coat sells for $300 plus an 8% sales tax. What is the total price?

Solution: We will use the equation: New amount = original amount + amount of increase

First let's find the amount of increase from the tax. Let x be the tax. Then

$$x = 8\% \text{ of } 300 = 0.08 \times 300 = 24.$$

The tax is $24. Therefore, the total price of the coat is $\underbrace{\$300 + \$24}_{\text{original + increase}} = \underbrace{\$324.}_{\text{new}}$

Example 8. A sweater that is selling for $24.50 is reduced by 30%. What is the new price of the sweater?

Solution: Original amount − new amount = amount of decrease

becomes

New amount = original amount − amount of decrease

First let's find the amount the sweater is reduced by. Let x be the amount of reduction. Then

$$x = 30\% \text{ of } 24.50 = 0.30 \times 24.50 = 7.35.$$

The sweater is reduced by $7.35, and the new price of the sweater is $24.50 − $7.35 = $17.15.

Example 9. A certain school's enrollment decreased 5% this year over last year's enrollment. If the school now has 3, 800 students enrolled, how many students were enrolled last year?

Solution: Let x represent the number of students enrolled last year, which represents 100%. Since enrollment decreased by 5%, this year's enrollment of 3, 800 students represents 95% of last years enrollment, x. To find x, we solve a proportion:

$$\underbrace{\frac{\text{number of students}}{\%}}_{\text{last year}} = \underbrace{\frac{\text{number of students}}{\%}}_{\text{this year}}$$

$$\frac{x}{100} = \frac{3,800}{95}$$

$$(x)(95) = (100)(3,800)$$

$$95x = 380,000$$

$$x = \frac{380,000}{95} = 4,000$$

There was an enrollment of 4, 000 students last year.

Example 10. An electronic store is having a sale on cameras. The sales price of a camera is $250 after 20% of the original price is deducted. What was the original price of the camera?

Solution: Since the sales price represented a 20% discount, the sales price was 80% of the original price. Let x be the original price. Then:

$$\text{Percent} \times \text{Original} = \text{Amount}$$

$$80\% \times x = 250$$

$$0.8x = 250$$

$$x = \frac{150}{0.8} = \frac{250 \times 10}{0.8 \times 10} = \frac{2,500}{8} = 312.5$$

Therefore, the original price of the camera was $312.50.

Alternatively, notice we could have set this up as a proportion as we did before: $\frac{\$}{\%} = \frac{\$}{\%}$

Let x represent the original amount. We **always** let 100% represent the original amount. As before, $250 is 80% of the original price. We have

$$\frac{x}{100} = \frac{250}{80}.$$

Solving for x gives $x = \dfrac{(250)(100)}{80} = \$312.50$.

Example 11. What is the interest paid on a $2,000 bank loan at a simple interest rate of $8\frac{1}{2}\%$ per year for 24 months?

Solution: We use the formula $I = P \times R \times T$, where I is the interest paid, P is the principal (the loan amount), R is the interest rate, and T is the time period of the loan.

We are given that $P = \$2000$, $R = 8\frac{1}{2}\% = 8.5\% = 0.085$, and $T = 24$ months $= 2$ years (we convert 24 months to years because the rate is per year).

$$I = P \times R \times T$$
$$= 2000 \times 0.085 \times 2$$
$$= 340$$

Therefore, the interest for 24 months is $340.

Example 12: Distilled water is poured into a beaker containing 30 ml. of hydrochloric acid to form an acid-water solution. How much water must be added to form a solution that is 40% acid?

Solution: Let x represent the total amount of acid-water solution. We know 30 ml. represents 40% acid in the acid-water solution.

$$40\% \text{ of } x = 30$$

$$0.40 \times x = 30$$

$$x = \dfrac{30}{0.40} = 75$$

And so, 75 ml. is the total amount of the acid-water solution. Therefore, 75 ml. $-$ 30 ml. $=$ 45 ml. of water must be added.

Exercises: Chapter 6, Section D

In Exercises 1 - 25, solve.

1. Mark did 20 math problems for homework. If he got 7 problems wrong, what percent of problems did he got wrong?

2. In a large history class, there are 52 boys, which represents 65% of the students in the class. How many girls are in the class?

3. Neil took a math test containing 20 prealgebra questions and 30 algebra questions. He got 80% of the prealgebra questions correct and 50% of the algebra questions correct. What percent did Neil get correct out of the total 50 questions on the math test?

4. A college consists of 12,000 students. The students can be put into four categories: those who have black hair, those have blond hair, those who have brunette hair, and those who have no hair (bald). If 40% of the students have black hair, 10% of the students are blond, and the number of students who are brunettes is half the number of students who are blond. How many students have no hair (bald)?

5. Sam's base salary for the week is $600. In addition, he receives a commission of 9% of his sales. His total earning this week is $825. What is Sam's total sales for the week?

6. A salesman earns a commission of $3,000 for selling $35,000 worth of computers. What is his commission rate?

7. Simon earns $35,000 a year. If he receives a 6% increase, what is his new salary?
(a) 2,100   (b) 21,000   (c) 32,900   (d) 37,100   (e) 40,833

8. A boat sells for $50,000 plus a 7% sales tax. What is the total price?
(a) 53,500   (b) 3,500   (c) 46,500   (d) 49,300   (e) 57,000

9. A college enrollment decreased 15% this year over last year's enrollment. If the college now has 5,950 students enrolled, how many students were enrolled last year?
(a) 4,900   (b) 7,000   (c) 6,843   (d) 7,450   (e) 5,950

10. Distilled water is pured into a beaker containing 60 milliliters of ammonia to form an alkaline-water solution. How much water must be added to form a solution that is 30% alkaline?
(a) 30 ml.   (b) 60 ml.   (c) 140 ml.   (d) 40 ml.   (e) 20 ml.

11. A suit selling for $125.50 is reduced by 40%. What is the new price of the suit?
(a) $175.50   (b) $120.30   (c) $156.89   (d) $130.70   (e) $75.30

12. A dress costs $35. After a discount of 20%, the new price of the dress is
(a) $28   (b) $7   (c) $30   (d) $20   (e) $6.50

13. The price of a book increase from $25 to $28. The increase is what percent of the original price?
(a) 10.7%   (b) 3%   (c) 12%   (d) 300%   (e) 30%

14. The price of a bed was $1,000 on Monday. On Wednesday, the price increased by 4%. On Friday, the price decreased by 4%. What is the cost of the bed on Friday?
(a) $1,000   (b) $998.40   (c) $958.40   (d) $1,041.60   (e) $0

15. A pair of pants $3\frac{1}{5}$ feet long shrunk to 3 feet when it was put into a dryer. What percent of the original length pants was lost after drying?
(a) 6.25%   (b) 144%   (c) 45%   (d) 16.4%   (e) 9%

16. Patrick won $3,000 from lottery tickets. He bought a computer for $945, then he gave his bother one-fifth of the remaining money. What percent of the entire lottery winnings did Patrick give to his brother?
(a) 20%   (b) 13.7%   (c) 35%   (d) 11%   (e) 68.5%

17. In a zoo, 6 monkeys have browns spots on their back. This is exactly 3% of the total number of monkeys in the zoo. How many monkeys are in the zoo?
(a) 100   (b) 200   (c) 2,000   (d) 180   (e) 1,800

18. At a bookstore, the sales price of a book was $56. This price represented a 30% discount. What was the original price of the book?
(a) $75   (b) $72.80   (c) $80   (d) $70   (e) $74

19. What is the interest paid on a $5,000 bank loan at a simple interest rate of $9\frac{1}{2}$% per year for 6 months?
(a) $237.50   (b) $475   (c) $2,850   (d) $23,750   (e) $700

20. What is the interest paid on a $6,000 bank loan at a simple interest rate of $7\frac{1}{2}$% per year for 3 years?
(a) $135,000   (b) $13,500   (c) $3,000   (d) $1,350   (e) $9,000

21. The price of a washing machine is $3,000. This represents 120% of the original price. If x represents the original price of the machine, which equation can be used to find x?
(a) $1.2x = 3000$ (b) $12x = 3000$ (c) $1.2 = 3000x$ (d) $120x = 3000$ (e) $0.2x = 3000$

22. The price of a bed is $400. This represents a 25% increase. What is the original price of the bed?
(a) $380   (b) $370   (c) $300   (d) $312   (e) $320

23. An alloy contains 40% copper. How much copper is there in 30 tons of alloy?
(a) 12 tons   (b) 120 tons   (c) 3 tons   (d) 15 tons   (e) 20 tons

24. 35% of 80.5 equals 25% of what number?
(a) 80.5   (b) 112.7   (c) 12.7   (d) 40.25   (e) 70

25. An air-conditioner sells for $500 plus an 12% sales tax. What is the total price of the air-conditioner?
(a) $550   (b) $600   (c) $300   (d) $560   (e) $56

Chapter 7:   Averages: Mean, Median, and Mode

Section A.   Understanding Mean, Median, and Mode

The word "average" has many different meanings. How often are we bombarded with data and hear phrases like "the average grade", "the average person", "the average size of SUV's" or "in an average person's lifetime"? These averages are not necessarily found by using the same methods.

Two important aspects of data are its center and its spread. The mean, median, and mode are measures of central tendency that describes where the data are centered. These terms will be defined below.

The **mean** (also called the **arithmetic mean** or **average**) of a set of items is the sum of the items divided by the number of items:

$$\text{Average} = \frac{\text{sum of items}}{\text{number of items}}$$

Example 1. Find the average of each set of numbers.
1) 4, 12, 50, 30, 14   2) 16, 12, 0, 20   3) 34.09, 55.2, 46.9, 32.03, 45.1, 70

Solution: 1) Average = $\frac{4 + 12 + 50 + 30 + 14}{5} = \frac{110}{5} = 22$.

2) Average = $\frac{16 + 12 + 0 + 20}{4} = \frac{48}{4} = 12$.

Be careful! Even though the number 0 has no value, it is one of the items in the average.

3) Average = $\frac{34.09 + 55.2 + 46.9 + 32.03 + 45.1 + 70}{6} = \frac{283.32}{6} = 47.22$.

Example 2. John got the following scores on his math tests: 90, 81, and 75. What was John's mean test score?

Solution: Average = $\frac{90 + 81 + 75}{3} = \frac{246}{3} = 82$.

The **median** of a set of items can be found in the following way:

(1) Arrange the items in order from least to greatest.
(2) (i) If the number of items is an odd number, then the median is the middle number.
    (ii) If the number of items is an even number, then the median is the average of the two
        middle numbers.

Example 3. Find the median of each set of numbers.

1) 32, 19, 8, 7, 81, 5, 44, 78, 23   2) 8, 0, 5, 9, 3, 6, 22, 12

3) 1, 3, 4, 6, 3, 2, 6, 77, 9 , 1

Solution:

1) First we arrange the numbers from smallest to largest:

$$\underbrace{5, 7, 8, 19,}_{4 \text{ numbers}} 23, \underbrace{32, 44, 78, 81}_{4 \text{ numbers}}$$

Notice that we have 9 numbers and since 9 is an odd number, there is a single middle number. To find the middle number, we group equal numbers from each side of the row of numbers until we end up with the middle number. The median is 23.

2) First we arrange the numbers from smallest to largest:

$$\underbrace{0, 3, 5,}_{3 \text{ numbers}} 6, 8, \underbrace{9, 12, 22}_{3 \text{ numbers}}$$

We have 8 numbers and since 8 is an even number, there are two middle numbers. To find them, we group equal numbers from each side of the row of numbers until we end up with the two middle numbers. Now we take the average of these two numbers: $\frac{6+8}{2} = \frac{14}{2} = 7$. The median 7.

3) Arrange the numbers from smallest to largest:

$$\underbrace{1, 1, 2,}_{3 \text{ numbers}} 3, 3, 4, \underbrace{6, 6, 9, 77}_{3 \text{ numbers}}$$

We have 10 numbers and since 10 is an even number, there are two middle numbers. To find them, group equal numbers from each side of the row of numbers untill we end up with the two middle numbers. Now we take the average of these two numbers: $\frac{3+4}{2} = \frac{7}{2} = 3\frac{1}{2}$. The median is $3\frac{1}{2}$.

The **mode** of a set of items is the number or numbers of items that appear most often. If two items appear most often, then we say that the set has two modes (bimodal). If three items appear most often we say that the set has three modes (trimodal). If no item appears more than once, we say that there is no mode.

Example 4. Find the mode (if any) of each set of numbers.

1) 8, 9, 2, 8, 3, 4, 8   2) 7, 2, 4, 9, 8, 6, 2, 9, 45, 2, 5, 9, 2, 9

3) 2, 8, 5, 4, 9, 6, 7, 0, 23

Solution: 1) The mode is 8 since it appears 3 times in the set.

2) The numbers 2 and 9 are modes; they both appear 4 times in the set.

3) There is no mode because no number appears more than once in the set.

Exercises: Chapter 7, Section A

In Exercises 1 - 8, find the average (mean) of the given sets of numbers.

1. 3, 45, 10, 50, 23

2. 4, 9, 12, 54, 26, 42

3. 32, 98, 44, 22

4. 49, 33, 43, 26, 76, 56, 102

5. 12, 34, 66.8, 12.6, 16
(a) 28.4   (b) 30   (c) 28.28   (d) 2.88   (e) 29

6. 41.7, 3.04, 62.4, 11.76, 230.3
(a) 58.4   (b) 69   (c) 67.12   (d) 69.84   (e) 70

7. 30.04, 30, 54.6, 110.8
(a) 56.36   (b) 56   (c) 36.56   (d) 45   (e) 56.9

8. 0.03, 5, 14, 9, 100.7, 2.67
(a) 7.17   (b) 21.29   (c) 21   (d) 21.9   (e) 12

In Exercises 9 - 16, find the median of the given sets of numbers.

9. 3, 45, 10, 50, 23

10. 4, 9, 12, 54, 26, 42

11. 32, 98, 44, 22

12. 49, 33, 43, 26, 76, 56, 102

13. 12, 34, 66.8, 12.6, 16
(a) 12.3   (b) 34   (c) 16   (d) 66.8   (e) 25

14. 41.7, 3.04, 62.4, 11.76, 230.3
(a) 41.7   (b) 6   (c) 62.4   (d) 3.04   (e) 7

15. 30.04, 30, 54.6, 110.8
(a) 30   (b) 42.32   (c) 30.04   (d) 40   (e) 42

16. 0.03, 5, 14, 9, 100.7, 6.01
(a) 9.95   (b) 29   (c) 24   (d) 2.09   (e) 7.505

In Exercises 17 - 24, find the mode (if any) of the given sets of numbers.

17. 3, 4, 1, 5, 0, 2, 3   18. 4, 1, 5, 4, 2, 2

19. 32, 98, 44, 22   20. 49, 33, 43, 26, 76, 56, 43

21. 12, 34, 12, 6, 1, 6, 3, 3, 6
(a) 12   (b) 6   (c) 3   (d) 2   (e) 1

22. 4, 1, 7, 3, 6, 1, 2 , 3
(a) 7   (b) 2 and 6   (c) 1 and 3   (d) 2   (e) 4

23. 3, 0, 3, 0, 5, 4, 6, 1, 8, 0, 1
(a) 3   (b) 6   (c) 1   (d) 4   (e) 0

24. 4, 5, 1, 4, 9, 1, 7, 6, 1
(a) 4   (b) 9   (c) 1   (d) 7   (e) 12

Section B. Solving Mean, Median, and Mode Word Problems

In this section, we provide some examples of how mean, median and mode are expressed in word problems. The first set of problems deal with **average speed**. The formula that is used is:

$$\text{Average speed} = \frac{\text{total distance}}{\text{total time elapsed}}$$

Example 1. A driver drove 205 miles in 5 hours. What was the average number of miles per hour?

Solution: $\text{Average speed} = \dfrac{\text{total distance}}{\text{total time elapsed}} = \dfrac{205 \text{ miles}}{5 \text{ hours}} = 41$ miles per hour.

Example 2. A train travels 230 miles in x hours and then 60 miles in y hours, what is an expression for the train's average rate (speed), in miles per hour, for the entire distance traveled?

Solution: First we find the total distance: 230 miles + 60 miles = 290 miles. Next we the total time elapsed: $(x + y)$ hours. Now we divide:

$$\text{Average speed} = \frac{290 \text{ miles}}{(x + y) \text{ hours}} = \frac{290}{x + y} \text{ miles per hour.}$$

Example 3. The local Q train travels 60 miles per hour for 4 hours. How many miles did it travel?

Solution: $\text{Average speed} = \dfrac{\text{total distance}}{\text{total time elapsed}}$. After cross multiplying, we obtain

$$\text{total distance} = \text{Average speed} \times \text{total time elapsed}$$

$$= \frac{60 \text{ miles}}{1 \text{ hour}} \times 4 \text{ hours} = \frac{60 \text{ miles}}{1 \text{ hour}} \times \frac{4 \text{ hours}}{1}$$

$$= 240 \text{ miles.}$$

Example 4. Tim drove from New York to Florida. He drove for 15 hours (hrs.) at an average speed 56 miles per hour (mi./hr.) and the next for 8 hrs. at 58 mi./ hr. What was Tim's average speed during the entire trip?

Solution: We need to find the total distance traveled during the entire trip. For the first 15 hours, he traveled

$$\frac{56 \text{ mi.}}{1 \text{ hr.}} \times 15 \text{ hrs.} = 840 \text{ mi.}$$

For the next 9 hours, he traveled

$$\frac{52 \text{ mi.}}{1 \text{ hr.}} \times 9 \text{ hrs.} = 684 \text{ mi.}$$

So the total miles traveled is 840 mi. +684 mi.= 1,308 mi. The total hours elapsed during the trip is 15 hrs. +9 hrs. = 24 hrs. Therefore, the average speed is

$$\frac{\text{total distance}}{\text{total time elapsed}} = \frac{1,308 \text{ mi.}}{24 \text{ hrs.}} = 54\frac{1}{2} \text{ mi./hr.}$$

The next examples deal with mean, median, and mode.

Example 5. The average test score for 3 tests was 76. What was the sum of the test scores?

Solution: Average $= \dfrac{\text{sum of scores}}{\text{number of scores}}$. After cross multiplying, we obtain

$$\text{sum of scores} = \text{average} \times \text{number of scores}$$
$$= 76 \times 3 = 228.$$

Example 6. David took 4 exams in Calculus 1. If he received scores 70, 84, and 81 on the first 3 exams, what score must he had earned on the fourth exam to have an average of 80?

Solution: We collect what is given in the problem: the average is 80 and number scores is 4. Since
$$\text{sum of scores} = \text{average} \times \text{number of scores}$$
(see the previous example), we know that the sum of the scores is $80 \times 4 = 320$. Observe that this sum includes the missing score (the fourth score we want to find).

We know the sum of 3 scores equals $70 + 84 + 81 = 235$. Since the sum of all the scores is 320,.the fourth score is $320 - 235 = 85$. Therefore, David must get 85 on the fourth test to have an average of 80.

Example 7. Tommy's average score on 4 tests is 82. Tommy took two more tests and got scores 78 and 80. What is Tommy's new average?

Solution: For the first 4 tests, we have
$$\text{sum of scores} = \text{average} \times \text{number of scores}$$
$$= 82 \times 4 = 328.$$

Now, Tommy took two more tests and got scores 78 and 80. Their total is $78 + 80 = 158$. Therefore,

Tommy's new average is

$$\frac{\text{sum of scores}}{\text{number of scores}} = \frac{158 + 328}{2 + 4} = \frac{486}{6} = 81.$$

Example 8. Cathy's average score on 6 tests is 76. Her lowest score is 66, and the professor will drop that score. What is Cathy's new average?

Solution: The sum of her scores is: average × number of scores = $76 \times 6 = 456$
Since the professor will drop score 66, we subtract 66 from the original sum, 456, and divide this new sum by 1 less than 6 (original number of scores). Therefore, Cathy's new average is:

$$\frac{\text{sum of scores}}{\text{number of scores}} = \frac{456 - 66}{6 - 1} = \frac{390}{5} = 78.$$

Example 9. Harold got the following scores on 5 quizzes: 90, 80, 80, 60, and 50.
(a) Find the mean, median, and mode.
(b) If Harold took another quiz and he got 5, what is the new mean, median, and mode?
(c) Which (mean, median, or mode) is affected the most by this score in part (b)?

Solution:

(a) mean $= \dfrac{\text{sum of scores}}{\text{number of scores}} = \dfrac{90 + 80 + 80 + 60 + 50.}{5} = \dfrac{360}{5} = 72.$

To find the median, we rearrange the scores from least to greatest:

$$\underbrace{50, \ 60,}_{\text{2 numbers}} \ 80, \ \underbrace{80, \ 90}_{\text{2 numbers}}.$$

The middle score, 80, is the median .The mode is the score that occurs most often, which is that 80 (it occurs twice).

(b) If Harold took another quiz, then the new mean is

$$\frac{5 + \text{ sum of scores}}{1 + \text{ number of scores}} = \frac{5 + 360}{1 + 5} = \frac{365}{6} = 60.8.$$

To find the new median, we rearrange the new scores from least to greatest:

$$5, \ \underbrace{50 \ ,60,}_{\text{2 numbers}} 80, \ \underbrace{80, \ 90}_{\text{2 numbers}}.$$

The new median is $\dfrac{60 + 80}{2} = \dfrac{140}{2} = 70.$ The new mode is 80.

(c) Observe:

$$\text{old mean} - \text{new mean} = 72 - 60.8 = 11.2$$
$$\text{old median} - \text{new median} = 80 - 70 = 10$$
$$\text{old mode} - \text{new mode} = 80 - 80 = 0 \quad \text{(the mode didn't change)}$$

We see that the mean is affected the most by this very low score.

Exercises: Chapter 7, Section B

In Exercises 1 - 8, solve.

1. A bus driver drove 432 miles in 8 hours. What was the average number of miles per hour?
   (a) 48   (b) 34   (c) 8   (d) 54   (e) 62

2. A rocket travels 742 miles per hour for 7 hours. How many miles did it travel?
   (a) 106   (b) 4   (c) 5,194   (d) 504   (e) 45

3. A car travels x miles in 7 hours and then y miles in 5 hours. What is an expression for the car's average rate (speed), in miles per hour, for the entire distance traveled?
   (a) $\dfrac{12}{x+y}$ (b) $\dfrac{35}{x+y}$ (c) $x+y$ (d) $x-y$ (e) $\dfrac{x+y}{12}$

4. The average test score for 5 tests was 77. What was the sum of the test scores?
   (a) 15.4   (b) 100   (c) 77   (d) 385   (e) 36

5. Billy drove for 9 hours at an average speed 42 miles per hour, then another 6 hours at 50 miles per hour. What was Billy's average speed during the entire trip?
   (a) 45.2   (b) 43   (c) 36   (d) 6   (e) 45

6. Paul took five COMPASS practice tests. If he received scores 80, 86, 77, and 68 on the first four tests, what score must he had earned on the fifth test to have an average of 78?
   (a) 80   (b) 79   (c) 76   (d) 86   (e) 87

7. Jason's average score on 4 tests is 81. He took two more tests and got scores 75 and 93. What is Jason's new average?
   (a) 84   (b) 91   (c) 82   (d) 78   (e) 42

8. Collin's average score on 5 tests is 80. His lowest score is 60, and the professor will drop that score. What is Collin's new average?
   (a) 85   (b) 90   (c) 88   (d) 98   (e) 68

In Excercise 9 - 12, the following applies: Hall got these scores on 6 quizzes: 92, 87, 53, 74, 87, and 90.

9. What is the mean score?
(a) 75   (b) 92   (c) 83   (d) 79   (e) 80.5

10. What is the median score?
(a) 90   (b) 87   (c) 53   (d) 92   (e) 83

11. What is the mode?
(a) 92   (b) 90   (c) 87   (d) 53   (e) 74

12. If Hall took another quiz and he got 0, which of the following is affected the most?
(a) mean   (b) median   (c) mode   (d) all   (e) none

In Exercises 13 - 20, solve.

13. A truck driver drove 585 miles in 9 hours. What was his average speed (in miles per hour)?
(a) 58   (b) 40   (c) 80   (d) 65   (e) 60

14. A satellite travels 642 miles per hour for 3 hours. How many miles did it travel?
(a) 1,926   (b) 214   (c) 4,194   (d) 2,504   (e) 405

15. A car travels 4 miles in a hours and then b miles in 9 hours, what is an expression for the train's average rate (speed), in miles per hour, for the entire distance traveled?
(a) $\dfrac{4+a}{b+9}$ (b) $\dfrac{4+b}{a+9}$ (c) $4+b$ (d) $\dfrac{13}{a+b}$ (e) $\dfrac{a+9}{b+4}$

16. The average test score for 3 tests was 86. What was the sum of the test scores?
(a) 172   (b) 100   (c) 27   (d) 258   (e) 26

17. Peter drove for 3 hours at an average speed of 48 miles per hour and for the next 5 hours at an average speed of 54 miles per hour. What was Peter's average speed, in miles per hour, during the entire trip?
(a) 42   (b) 403   (c) 12.75   (d) 50   (e) 51.75

18. Elsa took four GED practice tests. If she received scores 74, 90, and 91 on the first 3 tests, what score must she had earned on the fourth test to have an average of 88?
(a) 83   (b) 97   (c) 74   (d) 89   (e) 80

167

19. Jack's average score on four tests is 91. He took two more tests and got scores 81 and 95. What is Jack's new average?
(a) 89   (b) 90   (c) 86   (d) 71   (e) 92

20. Karen's average score on 5 tests is 84. Her lowest score is 58, and the professor will drop that score. What is Karen's new average?
(a) 82   (b) 90   (c) 90.5   (d) 96   (e) 92

In Excercises 21 - 24, the following applies: Jill got these scores on 5 quizzes: 63, 77, 50, 83, and 81.

21. What is the mean score?
(a) 75   (b) 92   (c) 83   (d) 79   (e) 70.8

22. What is the median score?
(a) 77   (b) 83   (c) 69   (d) 70   (e) 70.8

23. What is the mode?
(a) 50   (b) none   (c) 63   (d) 81   (e) 77

24. If Jill took another quiz and she scored 99, which is affected most?
(a) mode   (b) median   (c) mean   (d) all   (e) none

168

Chapter 8: Introduction to Algebra

Section A. Variables and Algebraic Expressions; Evaluating Algebraic Expressions

Variables and Algebraic Expressions

Mathematical expressions which contain one or more unknown quantities use alphabetical letters such as x, y, and z to represent them. We call these unknown quantities **variables**.

For example, in the expression $5x + 3$, the letter x is a variable; it represents a real number. Note that $5x$ means '5 times x'. The expressions that are being added together, $5x$ and 3, are called the **terms** of $5x + 3$, and the number 5 is called the **coefficient** of the product $5x$. Since 3 is not multiplied by a variable, we call it a **constant** because its value never changes; it **always** equals 3 (whereas the term $5x$ varies for different values of x). The coefficient of a constant term is the term itself. For example, the coefficient of 3 is 3.

The variables of the expression $6x - 2y + xy - 14$ are x and y. When two variables are next to one another with no symbol between them, such as in xy, it means 'x times y'. The terms of $6x - 2y + xy - 14$ are $6x$, $-2y$, xy, and -14. Notice that we put the negative sign with $2y$ and 14 because

$$6x - 2y + xy - 14 = 6x + (-2y) + xy + (-14).$$

The coefficient of $6x$ is 6, the coefficient of $-2y$ is -2, and the coefficient of $xy = 1 \cdot xy$ is 1. The term -14 is a constant.

An **algebraic expression** (or **expression**) is a real number, a variable, or a combination of numbers and variables. For example,

$$7, \quad y, \quad -12t, \quad 6x^2 + 3x - 1, \quad \text{and} \quad \sqrt{3} - \frac{2}{5}x - 15.602x^3$$

are algebraic expressions.

Example 1. Name the term of each expression and state its coefficient.
1) $8x$ 2) $6y + 9 - 3y^2$ 3) $4a - ab + 16b$

Solution: 1) $8x$ has coefficient 8.
          2) $6y$ has coefficient 6, 9 has coefficient 9, and $-3y^2$ has coefficient -3.
          3) $4a$ has coefficient 4, $-ab = -1 \cdot ab$ has coefficient -1, and $16b$ has coefficient 16.

Evaluating Algebraic Expressions

An algebraic expression such $5x + 3$ can be evaluated for a specified numerical value of x. For example,

$$\text{if } x = 0, \text{then } 5(0) + 3 = 0 + 3 = 3;$$

$$\text{if } x = -6, \text{ then } 5(-6) + 3 = -30 + 3 = -27;$$

$$\text{if } x = 0.14, \text{ then } 5(0.14) + 3 = 0.7 + 3 = 3.7;$$

$$\text{if } x = \frac{3}{10}, \text{ then } 5\left(\frac{3}{10}\right) + 3 = \frac{5}{1}\left(\frac{3}{10}\right) + 3 = \frac{3}{2} + 3 = \frac{3}{2} + \frac{6}{2} = \frac{9}{2} = 4\frac{1}{2}.$$

As you can see, the expression $5x + 3$ has no numerical value until we replace x by a number. If an expression has two or more variables, you can evaluate it in the same way. The expression $-3y + 4z^2$, for instance, has the following values:

$$\text{if } y = 1 \text{ and } z = 2, \text{then } -3(1) + 4(2)^2 = -3 + 4(4) = -3 + 16 = 13;$$

$$\text{if } y = -5 \text{ and } z = -6, \text{then } -3(-5) + 4(-6)^2 = 15 + 4(36) = 15 + 144 = 159;$$

$$\text{if } y = \frac{1}{6} \text{ and } z = 0, \text{then } -3\left(\frac{1}{6}\right) + 4(0)^2 = \frac{-3}{1}\left(\frac{1}{6}\right) + 4(0) = -\frac{1}{2} + 0 = -\frac{1}{2}.$$

Rules for evaluating an expression:
1) Put parentheses around each variable in the expression.
2) Replace each variable by its given numerical value.
3) Compute the answer using the order of operations.

Example 2. Evaluate the expression $9x^2 + 4x - 1$ for each given value of x.
1) $x = 0$ 2) $x = 3$ 3) $x = -5$ 4) $x = \frac{2}{9}$

Solution:
1) $9(0)^2 + 4(0) - 1 = 9(0) + 0 - 1 = 0 + 0 - 1 = -1$
2) $9(3)^2 + 4(3) - 1 = 9(9) + 12 - 1 = 81 + 12 - 1 = 92$
3) $9(-5)^2 + 4(-5) - 1 = 9(25) + (-20) - 1 = 225 - 20 - 1 = 204$
4) $9\left(\frac{2}{9}\right)^2 + 4\left(\frac{2}{9}\right) - 1 = \frac{9}{1}\left(\frac{4}{81}\right) + \frac{4}{1}\left(\frac{2}{9}\right) - 1 = \frac{4}{9} + \frac{8}{9} - \frac{1}{1}\left(\frac{9}{9}\right)$

$$= \frac{4}{9} + \frac{8}{9} - \frac{9}{9} = \frac{3}{9} = \frac{1}{3}$$

Example 3. Evaluate each expression if $x = 5$, $y = -2$, and $z = 1$.
1) $x + y + 2z$ 2) $3x - 5y$ 3) $(9z - 2x)(y + 2x)$ 4) $-4xz + 2yz - z^2 + 2$

Solution: 1) $5 + (-2) + 2(1) = 3 + 2 = 5$
             2) $3(5) - 5(-2) = 15 + 10 = 25$

3) $(9(1) - 2(5))((-2) + 2(5)) = (9 - 10)(-2 + 10) = (-1)(8) = -8$

4) $-4(5)(1) + 2(-2)(1) - (1)^2 + 2 = -20 + (-4) - 1 + 2 = -20 + (-4) - 1 + 2 = -23$

Example 4. If $t = -6$, find the value of each expression.

1) $3t^2$ 2) $-3t^2$ 3) $(3t)^2$ 4) $(-3t)^2$ 5) $-(3t)^2$

Solution: 1) $3(-6)^2 = 3(36) = 108$ 2) $-3(-6)^2 = -3(36) = -108$

3) $(3(-6))^2 = (-18)^2 = 324$ 4) $(-3(-6))^2 = (18)^2 = 324$

5) $-(3(-6))^2 = -(-18)^2 = -324$

Formulas

In the applications of mathematics, many quantities are related to each other. A **formula** is a mathematical expression used to express the relationship among quantities. We use variables to represent these quantities in the formula.

For example, the **area (A) of a rectangle** is related to its length (l) and width (w) by the formula $A = l \times w$.

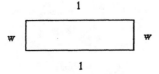

Example 5. Find the area of a rectangle (in square inches (in^2.)) whose length is 8 in. and width is 5 in.

Solution:

We substitute $l = 8$ in. and $w = 5$ in. in the formula:

$$A = l \times w = 8 \text{ in.} \times 5 \text{ in.} = 40 \text{ in.}^2$$

Example 6. The **perimeter (P) of a rectangle** is related to its length (l) and width (w) by the formula $P = 2l + 2w$. Find the perimeter of a rectangle whose length is 15 in. and width is 6 in.

Solution: Substitute $l = 15$ in. and $w = 6$ in. in the formula:

$$P = 2l + 2w = 2(15 \text{ in.}) + 2(6 \text{ in.}) = 30 \text{ in.} + 12 \text{ in.} = 42 \text{ in.}$$

Example 7. The **area** (A) **of a circle** is related to its radius (r) by the formula $A = \pi r^2$, where π is approximately equal to 3.14. Find the area of a circle whose radius is 5 cm.

Solution:

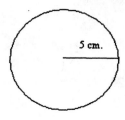

Substitute $\pi = 3.14$ and $r = 5$ cm. in the formula:
$$A = \pi r^2 = 3.14(5 \text{ cm.})^2 = 3.14(25 \text{ cm.}^2) = 78.5 \text{ cm.}^2$$

Example 8. The **circumference** (C) **of a circle** is related to its radius (r) by the formula $C = 2\pi r$. Find the circumference and area of each circle. Leave your answer in terms of π.

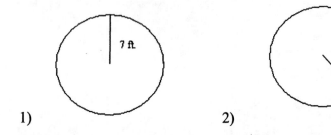

1)   2)

Solution:
1) The radius of the circle is $r = 7$ ft. The circumference is $C = 2\pi r = 2\pi\left(7 \text{ ft.}\right) = 14\pi$ ft. and the area is $A = \pi r^2 = \pi(7 \text{ ft.})^2 = 49\pi \text{ ft.}^2$.
2) The radius of the circle is $r = 14$ cm. The circumference is $C = 2\pi r = 2\pi(14 \text{ cm.}) = 28\pi$ cm. and the area is $A = \pi r^2 = \pi(14 \text{ cm.})^2 = 196\pi \text{ cm.}^2$.

Example 9. The **area** (A) **of a triangle** is related to its base b and height h by the formula $A = \frac{1}{2}bh^2$. Find the area of a triangle whose height is 7 cm. and base is 26 cm.

Solution: First let's get a picture:

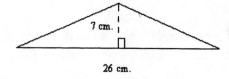

26 cm.

Substitute $h = 7$ cm. and $b = 26$ cm. in the formula:

$$A = \tfrac{1}{2}(26 \text{ cm.})(7 \text{ cm.}) = \tfrac{1}{2}\left(182 \text{ cm.}^2\right) = 91 \text{ cm.}^2$$

Exercises: Chapter 8, Section A

In Exercises 1 - 8, find the value of the given expression when $x = 3$ and $y = -2$.

1. $7x - 3y$

2. $5x^2$

3. $4y + 6x$

4. $(2x)^2$

5. $8y^2 - (8x)^2$

6. $-(7x + y)$

7. $-7x + y$

8. $2xy^2 + 12x$

In Exercises 9 - 20, find the value of the given expression when $x = 4$, $y = -3$, and $z = 0$.

9. $3x - 2y + z$

10. $5z + y - 4x$

11. $2x^2 + y + 3z$

12. $-x + 3y^2 - z$

13. $3xy + 2yz - 7xz$

14. $-9xz - yx + 8yz$

15. $x^2 + 3x - 12$

16. $y^2 - 4y + 9$

17. $z^2 + z + 18$

18. $2 + 3x - 9z^2$

19. $(x + y)^2 - 5xz$

20. $12 - (x - y)^2$

In Exercises 21 - 26, find the value of the given expression when $a = -5$ and $b = 2$.

21. $9a + 2b =$
(a) 41   (b) −41   (c) 49   (d) 8   (e) −19

22. $b^2 - 3a^2 =$
(a) −71   (b) 25   (c) 71   (d) 13   (e) 75

23. $2a^2 + 3b - 7 =$
(a) 51   (b) −51   (c) 99   (d) 49   (e) 25

24. $(-4b)^2 + 3a + 6b =$
(a) −7   (b) 13   (c) −61   (d) 61   (e) 91

25. $14 - a + (a - b)^2 =$
(a) 58   (b) 28   (c) −38   (d) −28   (e) 68

26. $a^3 + b^3 - 2ab =$
(a) 153   (b) 97   (c) −97   (d) −137   (e) −139

In Exercises 27 - 29, choose the correct answer.

27. If $y = 7x + 4x^2 - 12$, what is the value of y when $x = 3$?
(a) 153   (b) 45   (c) 55   (d) 37   (e) 28

28. If $s = -16t^2 + 32t + 64$, find the value of s when $t = 2$.
(a) 128   (b) 1,152   (c) 192   (d) 64   (e) 292

29. Find the value of $8m^2 - mn - 13n^2$ when $m = 3$ and $n = -4$.
(a) −114   (b) 114   (c) −148   (d) −124   (e) 68

In Exercises 30 - 32, use the formula $C = \frac{5}{9}(F - 32)$ to convert degrees Fahrenheit into degrees Celsius.

30. 32° Fahrenheit equals
(a) 14° Celsius   (b) 0° Celsius   (c) 36° Celsius   (d) 18° Celsius
(e) $\frac{5}{9}$° Celsius

31. 302° Fahrenheit equals
(a) 140° Celsius   (b) 35° Celsius   (c) 160° Celsius   (d) 150° Celsius
(e) 1,500° Celsius

32. −13° Fahrenheit equals
(a) 25° Celsius   (b) 19° Celsius   (c) −19° Celsius   (d) −25° Celsius
(e) −15° Celsius

In Exercises 33 - 36, choose the correct answer.

33. Find the perimeter, in inches, of a rectangle whose length is 6 inches and whose width is 8 inches.
(a) 18 in.   (b) 12 in.   (c) 16 in.   (d) 24 in.   (e) 28 in.

34. The area (A) of a trapezoid whose bases are b_1 and b_2 and whose height is h is given by the formula $A = \frac{h}{2}(b_1 + b_2)$. Find the area of a trapezoid whose bases measure 3 yards and 19 yards, and whose height is 10 yards.

(a) 34 yd.^{2} (b) 110 yd.^{2} (c) 100 yd.^{2} (d) 98 yd.^{2} (e) 120 yd.^{2}

35. Find the area of a triangle whose base is 8 inches and whose height is 4 inches.

(a) 160 in.^{2} (b) 32 in.^{2} (c) 16 in.^{2} (d) 6 in.^{2} (e) 18 in.^{2}

36. The volume (V) of a cube, each of whose edges measure s units, is given by the formula $V = s^3$. Find the volume, in cubic feet, of a cube whose edges are 4 feet each.

(a) 12 ft.^{3} (b) 62 ft.^{3} (c) 74 ft.^{3} (d) 64 ft.^{3} (e) 48 ft.^{3}

Section B. Multiplying Algebraic Expressions and Combining Like Terms

Multiplying Algebraic Expressions

Suppose we want to multiply the expressions 7 and $3x$. Since $3x$ is a product, we can multiply these simply by multiplying the coefficients 7 and 3, then multiply by x:

$$7(3x) = 7 \cdot 3 \cdot x = 21x$$

We can disregard the parenthesis because of the **Associative Property of Multiplication**:

If a, b, and c are any real numbers, then

$$a \cdot (b \cdot c) = (a \cdot b) \cdot c = a \cdot b \cdot c.$$

To multiply the expressions $5y$ and $-12z$, we follow the same procedure; multiply 5 and -12, then multiply by y and z:

$$5y(-12z) = 5 \cdot (-12) \cdot y \cdot z = -60yz$$

Once again, this can be done because $5y$ and $-12z$ are products. We can 'move' the -12 to the left of y because of the **Commutative Property of Multiplication**:

If a and b are any real numbers, then

$$a \cdot b = b \cdot a.$$

Next let's multiply $4x$ and $9x$. We proceed by multiplying 4 and 9, then multiplying x and x:

$$4x(9x) = 4 \cdot 9 \cdot x \cdot x = 36x^2$$

In the single term variable x^2, x is called the **base** and 2 is called the **exponent**.

Notice that when we multiply x^3 and x^4, the product will be x^7 because

$$x^3 \cdot x^4 = \underbrace{x \cdot x \cdot x}_{x^3} \cdot \underbrace{x \cdot x \cdot x \cdot x}_{x^4} = x^7.$$

In other words, we **add up** the exponents and keep the same base.

Rule for multiplying single term expressions: Multiply the coefficients together, then multiply the variables. If the bases are the same in both expressions, and add up the exponents and keep the same base.

Example 1. Multiply.

1) $8(6y)$

2) $-2m(7n)$

3) $5a(6a)$

4) $0.02x^6(0.3x^2)$

5) $(-3x)(-4x^3)$

6) $(-8)(-mn)$

7) $9t\left(\dfrac{4}{3}\right)$

8) $\dfrac{8}{15}\left(\dfrac{5}{6}z^4\right)$

177

Solution:
1) $8(6y) = 8 \cdot 6 \cdot y = 48y$

2) $-2m(7n) = (-2) \cdot 7 \cdot m \cdot n = -14mn$

3) $5a(6a) = 5 \cdot 6 \cdot a^2 = 30a^2$

4) $0.02x^6(0.3x^2) = 0.02 \cdot 0.3 \cdot x^{6+2} = 0.006x^8$

5) $(-3x)(-4x^3) = (-3) \cdot (-4) \cdot x^{1+3} = 12x^4$

6) $(-8)(-mn) = (-8) \cdot (-1)mn = 8mn$

7) $9t\left(\dfrac{4}{3}\right) = \dfrac{9}{1} \cdot \dfrac{4}{3} \cdot t = 12t$

8) $\dfrac{8}{15}\left(\dfrac{5}{6}z^4\right) = \dfrac{8}{15} \cdot \dfrac{5}{6} \cdot z^4 = \dfrac{4}{9}z^4$

Suppose we want to multiply 6 and $x + 3$. Unlike before, the expression $x + 3$ has **two** terms. Whenever we multiply a single term expression by a multiple term expression, we use the **Distributive Property**:

If a, b, and c are any real numbers, then

$$a(b + c) = ab + ac \quad \text{and} \quad a(b - c) = ab - ac.$$

For example,

$$6(x + 3) = 6(x) + 6(3) = 6x + 18 \quad \text{and} \quad 4a(2a - 7) = 4a(2a) - 4a(7) = 8a^2 - 28a.$$

When we multiply by a **negative term**, the signs of the terms in the answer are different from those that were originally in the parenthesis (rule for multiplication of numbers of the same/different signs):

$$-10(5y - 14) = -10(5y) - (-10)(14)$$
$$= -50y + 140$$

As you can see, the terms $-50y$ and $+140$ differ from the ones in the original parenthesis ($+5y$ and -14).

The same method applies when the expression in parenthesis contains more than two terms. For instance,

$$3(9x^2 - 12x + 6) = 3(9x^2) + 3(-12x) + 3(6) = 27x^2 - 36x + 18 \quad \text{and}$$

$$-5t(-10t^3 + t - 14) = -5t(-10t^3) + (-5t)(t) + (-5t)(-14) = 50t^4 - 5t^2 + 70t.$$

Example 2. Multiply.

1) $4(7a - 6)$

2) $5(3x^2 + 7)$

3) $2y(6y^2 + y - 2)$

4) $-3x^2(4x^2 - 7x - 12)$

5) $-(-8p + 7q)$

Solution:

1) $4(7a - 6) = 4(7a) + 4(-6) = 28a - 24$

2) $5(3x^2 + 7) = 5(3x^2) + 5(7) = 15x^2 + 35$

3) $2y(6y^2 + y - 2) = 2y(6y^2) + 2y(y) + 2y(-2) = 12y^3 + 2y^2 - 4y$

4) $-3x^2(4x^2 - 7x - 12) = -3x^2(4x^2) - 3x^2(-7x) - 3x^2(-12) = -12x^4 + 21x^3 + 36x^2$

5) $\underbrace{-(-8p + 7q) = -1(-8p + 7q)}_{-x=-1 \cdot x} = -1(-8p) + (-1)(7q) = 8p - 7q$

Combining Like Terms

Two or more terms are called **like terms** if they have the same **variable parts** (that is, they have the same bases and the bases have the same exponents). The following pairs of terms are like terms:

1) $\underbrace{3x \text{ and } 4x}$

Both variable parts are x.

2) $\underbrace{-8a^2 \text{ and } 14a^2}$

Both variable parts are a^2.

3) $\underbrace{9s^3t^4 \text{ and } 0.014t^4s^3}$

s^3t^4 and t^4s^3 are the same.

Examples of terms that are not like terms are:

1) $\underbrace{4x \text{ and } 5x^2}$

x and x^2 have different exponents.

2) $\underbrace{-3a^2y \text{ and } 12a^2y^2}$

The y-variable has different exponents.

3) $\underbrace{0.4r^3s^2 \text{ and } 0.86r^3t^2}$

s and t aren't in both terms.

If two or more terms are like terms, they can be combined into a single term.

Rule for combining like terms: Combine the coefficients of the terms, and keep the same variable part.

For example,

$$5x + 18x = (5 + 18)x = 23x \quad \text{and} \quad -26m^2n + 14m^2n = (-26 + 14)m^2n = -12m^2n.$$

Notice that $5s^2t^2 - 14st$ cannot be combined into a single term since $5s^2t^2$ and $14st$ are not like terms. Also observe, that in using the rule to combine $5x + 18x$, in the step $5x + 18x = (5 + 18)x$, the distributive law holds in the reverse direction.

Example 3. Combine like terms.
1) $6a + 5a$
2) $-8xy + 3xy$
3) $-7x^2y^3 - 11x^2y^3$
4) $-15st^2 + (-st^2)$
5) $9a^2 - 7a^2 + 13a^2$
6) $-12x^3y - (-2x^3y) + 6x^3y + 8x^3y$

Solution:

1) $6a + 5a = (6 + 5)a = 11a$
2) $-8xy + 3xy = (-8 + 3)xy = -5xy$
3) $-7x^2y^3 - 11x^2y^3 = (-7 - 11)x^2y^3 = -18x^2y^3$
4) $-15st^2 + (-st^2) = -15st^2 - 1st^2 = (-15 - 1)st^2 = -16st^2$
5) $9a^2 - 7a^2 + 13a^2 = (9 - 7 + 13)a^2 = 15a^2$
6) $-12x^3y - (-2x^3y) + 6x^3y + 8x^3y = -12x^3y + 2x^3y + 6x^3y + 8x^3y$
$$= (-12 + 2 + 6 + 8)x^3y = 4x^3y$$

Simplifying Algebraic Expressions

Next, we simplify algebraic expressions which involve multiplication and combining like terms.

Example 4. Simplify.

1) $2(2x + 1) - 7$ 2) $2(x - 5) + 4(6x - 3)$ 3) $a(10 + 3a) - 4a(6 - 7a)$
4) $-3x(8x + 3y) + 12y(2x - 3y)$ 5) $8k^2(7k^2 + k + 2) - 3k(-6k + 11) + 5k^4 - 3k$

Solution:

1) $2(2x + 1) - 7 = 4x + 2 - 7 = 4x - 5$

2) $2(x - 5) + 4(6x - 3) = 2x - 10 + 24x - 12 = 26x - 22$

3) $a(10 + 3a) - 4a(6 - 7a) = 10a + 3a^2 - 24a + 28a^2 = -14a + 31a^2$

4) $-3x(8x + 3y) + 12y(2x - 3y) = -24x^2 - 9xy + 24yx - 36y^2 = -24x^2 + 15xy - 36y^2$

5) $8k^2(7k^2 + k + 2) - 3k(-6k + 11) + 5k^4 - 3k = 56k^4 + 8k^3 + 16k^2 + 18k^2 - 33k + 5k^4 - 3k$
$$= 61k^4 + 8k^3 + 34k^2 - 36k$$

Exercises: Chapter 8, Section B

In Exercises 1 - 8, multiply.

1. $3x(-4x)$ 2. $(-6s)(-14t)$ 3. $-10m^2(2m^3)$ 4. $(12y)(-y^3)$

5. $8(15x)$ 6. $(19a^3)(13b^2)$ 7. $-t(-t)$ 8. $(23jk)(-3j^2k)$

In Exercises 9 - 12, multiply.

9. $7(x^2 + 3x - 9) =$
(a) $7x^2 + 3x - 9$ (b) $7x^2 + 21x + 63$ (c) $7x^2 + 10x - 2$
(d) $7x^2 + 21x - 63$ (e) $7x^2 + 21x - 16$

10. $-6y^2(5y^2 - 3y + 11) =$
(a) $-30y^4 - 18y^3 - 66y^2$ (b) $-30y^4 + 18y^3 - 66y^2$ (c) $-30y^4 + 18y^2 - 66y$
(d) $30y^4 + 18y^3 - 66y^2$ (e) $-30y^4 + 18y^2 + 66y$

11. $5y^3(-9y^2 + 7) =$
(a) $-45y^5 + 35y^4$ (b) $45y^5 + 35y^4$ (c) $-45y^5 + 35y^3$
(d) $-45y^6 + 35y^3$ (e) $-10y^8$

12. $-4x(9x^2 + 2x - 8) =$
(a) $-36x^3 - 8x^2 + 32x$ (b) $-36x^3 - 8x^2 - 32x$ (c) $-36x^4 + 8x^3 - 32x^2$
(d) $-36x^2 - 8x + 32$ (e) $36x^3 + 8x^2 - 32x$

In Exercises 13 - 16, combine.

13. $(3a + 2) + (7a - 11) =$
(a) $10a - 9$ (b) $10a + 9$ (c) a (d) $10a + 13$ (e) 1

14. $(-x + 2y) + (3x - 7y) =$
(a) $2x - 9y$ (b) $2x + 5y$ (c) $2x - 5y$ (d) $4x - 5y$ (e) $-2x + 5y$

15. $(16a^2 - 3a + 15) + (-a^2 + 8a - 29) =$
(a) $15a^2 + 5a - 14$ (b) $16a^2 + 5a + 14$ (c) $15a^2 + 11a - 14$
(d) $15a^2 + 5a + 14$ (e) $6a^3$

16. $(-5x^2 + 18xy) + (7y^2 - 16yx) =$
(a) $-5x^2 - 2xy - 7y^2$ (b) $-5x^2 - 2xy + 7y^2$ (c) $2x^2y^2 + 2xy$
(d) $-5x^2 + 2xy + 7y^2$ (e) $2x^2 - 2xy$

In Exercises 17 - 24, simplify.

17. $4(2m - 11n) + (-5m + n) =$
(a) $3m - 10n$ (b) $13m - 43n$ (c) $3m - 43n$ (d) $3m - 43$
(e) $-3m + 43n$

18. $(9x^2 + 3x - 1) + 2(x^2 + 6) =$
(a) $9x^2 + 3x + 11$ (b) $11x^2 + 3x + 5$ (c) $11x^2 + 3x + 11$
(d) $9x^2 + 5x + 11$ (e) $11x^2 + 15x - 1$

19. $5s(6s + 10t) + 3t(s - 12t) =$
(a) $30s^2 + 47st - 36t^2$ (b) $30s^2 + 53st + 36t^2$ (c) $30s^2 + 53st - 36t^2$
(d) $30s^2 - 2st - 36t^2$ (e) $11s^2 + 18st - 9t^2$

20. $(6ab - 14a^2) - (3a^2 + ab) =$
(a) $-17a^2 + 6ab$ (b) $-17a^2 + 5ab$ (c) $-12a^3b$ (d) $7ab - 17a^2$
(e) $-11a^2 + 5ab$

21. $(3x^2 - 11xy + 4y^2) - (-3x^2 + 5xy - y^2) =$
(a) $-16xy + 5y^2$ (b) $6x^2 + 16xy + 5y^2$ (c) $6x^2 - 6xy + 3y^2$
(d) $6x^2 - 16xy + 5y^2$ (e) $6x^4 - 16x^2y^2 + 5y^4$

22. $-(-x + 7) + 8(2 + 3x) =$
(a) $25x - 9$ (b) $23x + 9$ (c) $25x + 23$ (d) $17x + 17$ (e) $25x + 9$

23. $9(4 - 12xy + y^2) - 6(-y^2 + 3) =$
(a) $3y^2 - 108xy + 54$ (b) $15y^2 - 98xy + 54$ (c) $15y^2 - 108xy + 16$
(d) $15y^2 - 108xy + 54$ (e) $-15y^2 + 108xy - 54$

24. $(5uv + 9v) - 6u(-3u + v) =$
(a) $18u^2 - uv + 9v$ (b) $-uv + 9v - 18u^2$ (c) $uv + 9v + 18u^2$
(d) $18u^2 + 11uv + 9v$ (e) $-18u^2 + uv + 9v$

Section C. Solving Linear Equations

An **equation** is a statement showing two expressions are equal. For example, $x + 4 = 5$ and $2a - 9 = 5a + 3$ are equations. A number which can replace the variable to make the equation a true statement is called a **solution** or **root** of the equation. The solution to $x + 4 = 5$ is $x = 1$, since replacing x by 1 in the equation gives us $1 + 4 \overset{\checkmark}{=} 5$. Similarly, $a = -4$ is a solution to $2a - 9 = 5a + 3$ because:

$$2(-4) - 9 \overset{?}{=} 5(-4) + 3$$
$$-8 - 9 \overset{?}{=} -20 + 3$$
$$-17 \overset{\checkmark}{=} -17$$

To obtain a solution to an equation, we need to get the variable on one side of the equation by itself. Some rules that we may use to do this are:

Rule 1: You can add or subtract equal expressions on both sides of an equation.
Rule 2: You can multiply or divide equal (non-zero) expressions on both sides of an equation.

Performing any one of these operations results in an equation which has the same solution as the original (the equations are **equivalent**).

Our main concern for the moment is to learn how solve linear equations. A **linear equation (in one variable)** is an equation which is equivalent to the equation $ax + b = 0$, where a and b are real numbers and $a \neq 0$. Some examples of linear equations are

$$3x - 1 = 4, \quad 5y + 6 = -9y + 13, \quad 4 - 3(7t + 1) = 5t, \quad \text{and} \quad \tfrac{13x}{7} + 5 = 0.092.$$

We begin by solving linear equations that require a single step.

Example 1. Solve each equation.
1) $x + 5 = 7$ 2) $x - 2.25 = -16.08$ 3) $2y = 6$
4) $\frac{4}{3}t = -6$ 5) $-\frac{x}{7} = -12.36$

Solution:
1) Add -5 on both sides of the equation:

$$\begin{array}{rl} x + 5 &= 7 \\ -5 & -5 \\ \hline x &= 2 \end{array}$$

184

2) Add 2.25 on both sides of the equation:

$$x - 2.25 = -16.08$$
$$\underline{+2.25 \quad +2.25}$$
$$x \qquad = -13.83$$

3) Divide both sides of the equation by 2:

$$\frac{2y}{2} = \frac{6}{2}$$
$$y = 3$$

4) Multiply both sides of the equation by the reciprocal of $\frac{4}{3}$, which is $\frac{3}{4}$:

$$\frac{4}{3}t = -6$$

$$\frac{3}{4}\left(\frac{4}{3}t\right) = \frac{3}{4}\left(\frac{-6}{1}\right)$$

$$t = \frac{-18}{4} = -\frac{9}{2} = -4\frac{1}{2}$$

5) Multiply both sides of the equation by $-\frac{7}{1}$:

$$-\frac{x}{7} = -12.36$$

$$-\frac{7}{1}\left(-\frac{x}{7}\right) = -12.36\left(\frac{-7}{1}\right)$$

$$x = 86.52$$

Next, we solve equations that require multiple steps.

Example 2. Find the root of each equation.

1) $7y + 6 = 20$ 2) $9a - 2 = 5a + 18$ 3) $1 + 8(x - 2) = 3 - 4(2x + 1)$

4) $\frac{1}{2}m + 3 = \frac{5}{6}m$ 5) $-\frac{2}{3}t + \frac{5}{8} = \frac{3}{4}t - \frac{1}{24}$

Solution:

1) Add −6 on both sides of the equation, then divide both sides by 7:

$$7y + 6 = 20$$
$$\underline{\quad -6 \quad -6}$$
$$\frac{7y}{7} \quad = \frac{14}{7}$$

$$y = 2$$

185

2) First, collect the terms containing the variable on one side of the equation.

$$9a - 2 = 5a + 18$$
$$\underline{-5a \qquad\quad -5a}$$
$$4a - 2 = \qquad 18$$
$$\underline{\quad +2 \qquad\qquad +2}$$
$$\frac{4a}{4} = \frac{20}{4}$$

$$a = 5$$

3) Remove the parenthesis by distributing. Afterwards, combine any like terms and proceed as before.

$$1 + 8(x - 2) = 3 - 4(2x + 1)$$
$$1 + 8x - 16 = 3 - 8x - 4$$
$$-15 + 8x = -1 - 8x$$
$$\underline{\quad + 8x \qquad\quad + 8x}$$
$$-15 + 16x = -1$$
$$\underline{+15 \qquad\qquad + 15}$$
$$\frac{16x}{16} = \frac{14}{16}$$

$$x = \frac{7}{8}$$

4) When dealing with a linear equation which contains fractions, one approach in solving the equation is to eliminate the fractions. To do this, you multiply both sides of the equation by the LCM of the denominators. This is called **clearing the fractions**. Notice that the LCM of 2 and 6 is 6.

$$\frac{1}{2}m + 3 = \frac{5}{6}m$$

$$\frac{6}{1}\left(\frac{1}{2}m + 3\right) = \frac{6}{1}\left(\frac{5}{6}m\right)$$

$$\frac{6}{1}\left(\frac{1}{2}m\right) + \frac{6}{1}(3) = \frac{6}{1}\left(\frac{5}{6}m\right)$$

$$3m + 18 = 5m$$
$$\underline{-3m \qquad\quad - 3m}$$
$$\frac{18}{2} = \frac{2m}{2}$$
$$9 = m$$

5) The LCM of 3, 8, 4, and 24 is 24.

$$-\frac{2}{3}t + \frac{5}{8} = \frac{3}{4}t - \frac{1}{24}$$

$$\frac{24}{1}\left(-\frac{2}{3}t+\frac{5}{8}\right)=\frac{24}{1}\left(\frac{3}{4}t-\frac{1}{24}\right)$$

$$\frac{24}{1}\left(-\frac{2}{3}t\right)+\frac{24}{1}\left(\frac{5}{8}\right)=\frac{24}{1}\left(\frac{3}{4}t\right)-\frac{24}{1}\left(\frac{1}{24}\right)$$

$$
\begin{aligned}
-16t+15 &= 18t-1 \\
+16t & +16t \\
\hline
15 &= 34t-1 \\
+1 & +1 \\
\hline
\frac{16}{34} &= \frac{34t}{34}
\end{aligned}
$$

$$\frac{8}{17}=t$$

Example 3. Solve for x.

1) $9-x=14$ 2) $1.2=0.6x-0.03$ 3) $8x=9.5x+1.5$ 4) $4\frac{2}{3}+\frac{1}{6}x=19\frac{1}{3}$

Solution:

1)
$$
\begin{aligned}
9-x &= 14 \\
-9 & -9 \\
\hline
-x &= 5 \\
x &= -5
\end{aligned}
$$

2)
$$
\begin{aligned}
1.2 &= 0.6x-0.03 \\
+0.03 & +0.03 \\
\hline
\frac{1.23}{0.6} &= \frac{0.6x}{0.6} \\
2.05 &= x
\end{aligned}
$$

3)
$$
\begin{aligned}
8x &= 9.5x+1.5 \\
-9.5x & -9.5x \\
\hline
\frac{-1.5x}{-1.5} &= \frac{1.5}{-1.5} \\
x &= -1
\end{aligned}
$$

4) First change the mixed numbers into improper fractions. Then clear the fractions.

$$\frac{14}{3}+\frac{1}{6}x=\frac{58}{3}$$

$$6\left(\frac{14}{3}+\frac{1}{6}x\right)=6\left(\frac{58}{3}\right)$$

$$6\left(\frac{14}{3}\right)+6\left(\frac{1}{6}x\right)=6\left(\frac{58}{3}\right)$$

$$
\begin{aligned}
28+x &= 116 \\
-28 & -28 \\
\hline
x &= 88
\end{aligned}
$$

Next, we solve some equations that are **not linear**, but use the same methods as before.

Example 4. Determine the root of each equation.

1) $\frac{2}{3x}=\frac{5}{6}$ 2) $\frac{9}{14t}=\frac{3t}{7t}$ 3) $\frac{-4}{15}=\frac{11}{10x}$ 4) $\frac{2}{x+5}=\frac{4}{x+7}$

Solution: To solve each equation, we first multiply both sides of the equation by the LCM of the denominators.

1) The LCM of $3x$ and 6 is $6x$: $\left(\frac{6x}{1}\right)\frac{2}{3x} = \left(\frac{6x}{1}\right)\frac{5}{6}$

$$\frac{4}{5} = \frac{\cancel{5}x}{\cancel{5}}$$

$$\frac{4}{5} = x$$

2) The LCM of $14t$ and $7t$ is $14t$. Clear the fractions: $\left(\frac{14t}{1}\right)\frac{9}{14t} = \left(\frac{14t}{1}\right)\frac{3t}{7t}$

$$\frac{9}{6} = \frac{\cancel{6}t}{\cancel{6}}$$

$$\frac{3}{2} = t$$

3) The LCM of 15 and $10x$ is $30x$. Clear the fractions: $\left(\frac{30x}{1}\right)\frac{-4}{15} = \left(\frac{30x}{1}\right)\frac{11}{10x}$

$$\frac{-8}{33} = \frac{3\cancel{3}x}{3\cancel{3}}$$

$$-\frac{8}{33} = x$$

4) Cross multiply and solve.

$$\frac{2}{x+5} = \frac{4}{x+7}$$

$$4(x+5) = 2(x+7)$$
$$4x + 20 = 2x + 14$$
$$\underline{-2x \qquad\quad -2x}$$
$$\underline{2x + 20 = \qquad 14}$$
$$\underline{-20 \qquad\quad -20}$$
$$\frac{\cancel{2}x}{\cancel{2}} = \frac{-6}{2}$$

$$x = -3$$

Here's an example of an equation in two variables.

Example 5. If $x^2 - kx = 12$, find the value of k when $x = 4$.

188

Solution:

$$4^2 - k(4) = 12$$
$$16 - 4k = 12$$
$$-16 \qquad -16$$
$$\frac{-4k}{-4} = \frac{-4}{-4}$$

$$k = 1$$

The next examples deal with different types of algebraic operations.

Example 6. Define an operation $*$ by $a * b = 2a + b$.
1) Find $5 * (-4)$.　　　2) Find the value of x if $x * 3 = 6$.

Solution:
1) Look at the right side of the equation: $2a + b$. Setting $a = 5$ and $b = -4$, we obtain
$$5 * (-4) = 2(5) + (-4) = 10 - 4 = 6.$$
2) Notice that $x * 3 = 6$ is the same as $2x + 3 = 6$. We need to solve this equation:

$$2x + 3 = 6$$
$$-3 \quad -3$$
$$\frac{2x}{2} = \frac{3}{2}$$

$$x = \frac{3}{2} = 1\frac{1}{2}$$

Example 7. Define an operation $\circ$ by $a \circ b = 3 - 4ab$.
1) Find $1 \circ 6$.　　　2) Find the value of x if $3 \circ x = 4$.

Solution: 1) Look at the right side of the equation: $3 - 4ab$. Setting $a = 1$ and $b = 6$, we obtain
$$1 \circ 6 = 3 - 4(1)(6) = 3 - 24 = -21.$$
2) Notice that $3 \circ x = 4$ is the same as $3 - 12x = 4$. We need to solve this equation:

$$3 - 12x = 4$$
$$-3 \qquad -3$$
$$\frac{-12x}{-12} = \frac{1}{-12}$$

$$x = \frac{1}{-12}$$

Exercises: Chapter 8, Section C

In Exercises 1 - 9, find the value of x which makes the equation true.

1. $x + 7 = 13$
   (a) $x = 20$ (b) $x = 6$ (c) $x = 9$ (d) $x = -6$ (e) $x = \frac{13}{7}$

2. $12x = 132$
   (a) $x = 14$ (b) $x = 120$ (c) $x = \frac{1}{11}$ (d) $x = 11$ (e) $x = 18$

3. $x - 3.6 = 14.97$
   (a) $x = 18.57$ (b) $x = 11.37$ (c) $x = 18.03$ (d) $x = 41.5$ (e) $x = 18.27$

4. $3x + 11 = -19$
   (a) $x = -33$ (b) $x = -27$ (c) $x = -10$ (d) $x = 10$ (e) $x = -12$

5. $5.25x = 0.945$
   (a) $x = 1.8$ (b) $x = 4.96$ (c) $x = 0.16$ (d) $x = -4.305$ (e) $x = 0.18$

6. $-\frac{3}{8} + x = 2\frac{7}{8}$
   (a) $x = 2\frac{5}{8}$ (b) $x = 3\frac{1}{4}$ (c) $x = 3\frac{1}{8}$ (d) $x = 1\frac{1}{4}$ (e) $x = 4\frac{1}{8}$

7. $\frac{1}{16}x = -1\frac{3}{8}$
   (a) $x = 22$ (b) $x = -1\frac{7}{16}$ (c) $x = -\frac{1}{22}$ (d) $x = -22$ (e) $x = \frac{7}{16}$

8. $\frac{x}{3} - \frac{x}{7} = 2$
   (a) $x = 1.5$ (b) $x = 10.5$ (c) $x = 4.2$ (d) $x = 14.2$ (e) $x = 10.2$

9. If $-x + 6 = 18$, then what is x?
   (a) -12 (b) 12 (c) -3 (d) 3 (e) $\frac{1}{12}$

In Exercises 10 - 23, choose the correct answer.

10. If $\frac{x}{7} = -14$, then what is x?

(a) –2   (b) 2   (c) 98   (d) –98   (e) –7

11. If $\frac{2}{5}y + 6 = 11$, then what is y?

(a) $42\frac{1}{2}$ (b) 2   (c) $12\frac{1}{2}$ (d) $21\frac{1}{2}$ (e) $-2\frac{1}{5}$

12. If $19m - 10.1 = -10.062$, then what is m?

(a) –0.002   (b) –0.02   (c) 0.002   (d) 500   (e) 0.2

13. If $\frac{5}{12} = \frac{x}{36}$, then what is x?

(a) 15   (b) 8   (c) $\frac{1}{15}$ (d) 12   (e) 29

14. What is the root of the equation $6t + 3(t - 4) = 16$?

(a) $\frac{9}{28}$ (b) $\frac{20}{9}$ (c) $\frac{4}{9}$ (d) $\frac{9}{2}$ (e) $\frac{28}{9}$

15. What is the root of the equation $-5.05 + 3(y - 0.1) = 4.25$?

(a) 0.32   (b) 32   (c) 3.2   (d) 3   (e) 2.32

16. Find the root of the equation $\frac{6}{7} + \frac{3}{14} = b - 3\frac{2}{7}$.

(a) $4\frac{5}{14}$ (b) $2\frac{3}{14}$ (c) $-3\frac{9}{14}$ (d) $\frac{14}{61}$ (e) $6\frac{4}{5}$

17. Find the root of the equation $\frac{1}{5k} + \frac{3}{10k} = 4$.

(a) $\frac{5}{8}$ (b) $\frac{1}{4}$ (c) $\frac{1}{8}$ (d) 8   (e) $\frac{5}{4}$

18. If $\frac{3}{p} - 8 = \frac{5}{p}$, then $p =$

(a) $\frac{1}{2}$ (b) $\frac{1}{4}$ (c) –1   (d) 8   (e) $-\frac{1}{4}$

19. If $3.04x = 6.08$, then $x =$
(a) $\frac{1}{2}$ (b) 2 (c) 3.04 (d) 0 (e) -3.04

20. If $\frac{3}{8a} = \frac{7a}{24a}$, then $a =$

(a) $\frac{7}{9}$ (b) $\frac{9}{7}$ (c) 7 (d) $\frac{1}{7}$ (e) $\frac{1}{9}$

21. If $x^2 + kx = 24$, find the value of k when $x = 2$.
(a) -10 (b) 10 (c) 14 (d) 12 (e) -12

22. If $5kx - 6x = 19$, find the value of k when $x = -6$.
(a) $1\frac{13}{17}$ (b) $-1\frac{5}{6}$ (c) $\frac{17}{30}$ (d) $-\frac{17}{30}$ (e) $1\frac{1}{30}$

23. If $\frac{4x}{2x+5} = 7k$, find the value of k when $x = 3$.

(a) $\frac{12}{77}$ (b) $6\frac{5}{12}$ (c) $\frac{6}{35}$ (d) $\frac{4}{29}$ (e) $-6\frac{1}{11}$

In Exercises 24 - 26, the operation $*$ is defined by $a * b = 4a - 2b$.

24. Find $3 * (-1)$.
(a) 10 (b) 8 (c) -14 (d) 14 (e) -10

25. Find the value of x if $x * 2 = 20$.
(a) 8 (b) 6 (c) 4 (d) 12 (e) -10

26. Find the value of t if $t * \frac{1}{6} = -\frac{1}{3}$.
(a) $-\frac{1}{3}$ (b) $\frac{1}{3}$ (c) 3 (d) -3 (e) 0

In Exercises 27 - 30, the operation $\#$ is defined by $x\#y = -y + 8x$.

27. Find $(-2)\#6$.
(a) -20 (b) -22 (c) 22 (d) 50 (e) -10

28. Find the value of m if $m\#3 = -19$.

(a) $\frac{1}{3}$ (b) $\frac{1}{2}$ (c) -2 (d) 43   (e) $1\frac{1}{3}$

29. Find the value of t if $7\#t = 2$.

(a) -58 (b) 58   (c) -54 (d) 54   (e) $\frac{9}{8}$

30. Find the value of k if $k\#(-16) = k$.

(a) $\frac{9}{16}$ (b) $\frac{16}{7}$ (c) $-\frac{16}{7}$ (d) 0   (e) -64

Section D. Solving Word Problems

In Chapter 1, we mentioned some **key words** and **key phrases** which often occur in word problems. They tell us how to translate the problem into mathematics.

Key Words and Key Phrases

I) **Addition:**   plus, sum, added to, increased by, more than, total, altogether, in all
II) **Subtraction:**   minus, subtracted from, less than, decreased by, difference, left over
III) **Multiplication:** times, product, multiplied by, of
IV) **Division:**   quotient, divided by, to, over, ratio
V) **Equals:**   is, equals

Translating Statements into Mathematical Expressions

In order to solve a word problem, we need to know how to translate the problem into mathematics. We will often need to use a letter to represent some unknown quantity. Such a letter is called a **variable**.

Example 1. Write each verbal statement as a mathematical expression, where the variable x represents the number.

1) The sum of x and 13.   2) x subtracted from 28.   3) 5 less than x.
4) The product of 7 and x.   5) 20% of 60   6) The ratio 4 to 5.
7) 13 increased by x is 19.   8) The quotient of x and 15 or $\frac{x}{15}$
9) 11 decreased by twice the number.   10) x is the square of 8, divided by -4.

Solution: 1) $x + 13$ 2) $28 - x$ 3) $x - 5$ 4) $7x$
   5) $\frac{20}{100} \times 60$ 6) $4 : 5$ or $\frac{4}{5}$ 7) $13 + x = 19$ 8) $x \div 15$
   9) $2x - 11$ 10) $x = \frac{8^2}{-4}$

Translating Mathematical Expressions into Statements

Example 2. Write each mathematical expression into a statement.
1) $x + 5$ 2) $8y$ 3) $\frac{t}{3}$ 4) $y - 2x$

Solution: 1) The sum of x and 5.   2) The product of 8 and y.
   3) The quotient of t and 3.   4) y minus twice x (or $2x$ less than y).

Some Types of Word Problems

Number Problems

Example 3. Two more than a number equals 13 less than twice the number. Find the number.

Solution: Let x be the number.

$$
\begin{array}{rcl}
2 + x & = & 2x - 13 \\
-x & & -x \\
\hline
2 & = & x - 13 \\
+13 & & +13 \\
\hline
15 & = & x
\end{array}
$$

The number is 15.

Example 4. The larger of two numbers is 5 less than twice the smaller. Four times the smaller exceeds the larger by 23. Find the numbers.

Solution: We break up the problem in two parts. In the first sentence, we are given information about the **larger number in terms of the smaller number**. If we let x be the smaller number, then we can find an expression for the larger in terms of x: the larger number is $2x - 5$.

The second sentence tells us how to set up an equation. The word "exceeds" means "more than". We interpret the phrase "exceeds .... by ...." using mathematical symbols as follows:

$$
\underbrace{\text{exceeds}}_{=} \; .... \; \underbrace{\text{by}}_{+} \; ....
$$

The second sentence translates to:

$$
\underbrace{\text{Four times the smaller}}_{4x} \; \underbrace{\text{exceeds}}_{=} \; \underbrace{\text{the larger}}_{2x-5} \; \underbrace{\text{by}}_{+} \; \underbrace{23}_{23} \; .
$$

We solve for x:

$$
\begin{array}{rcl}
4x & = & 2x - 5 + 23 \\
4x & = & 2x + 18 \\
-2x & & -2x \\
\hline
\dfrac{2x}{2} & = & \dfrac{18}{2} \\
x & = & 9
\end{array}
$$

Therefore, the smaller is 9. The larger is $2x - 5 = 2(9) - 5 = 18 - 5 = 13$

The next two examples deal with consecutive integers. **Consecutive integers** are integers that follow a specific sequence in which any integer in the sequence is 1 more than the previous integer. For example, the numbers 7, 8, and 9 are consecutive integers.

   Consecutive even (odd) integers are even (odd) integers that follow a specific sequence in which any integer in the sequence is 2 more than the previous one. For example, 14, 16, and 18 are consecutive even integers, and -9, -7, -5, and -3 are consecutive odd integers.

Example 5. The sum of three consecutive integers is 66. Find the integers.

Solution: Let x be the first integer. Then the second integer is $x + 1$ and the third integer is $x + 2$. Since their sum is 66, we have:

$$(x) + (x + 1) + (x + 2) = 66$$
$$3x + 3 = 66$$
$$\underline{ -3 \quad -3}$$
$$3x \quad = 63$$
$$\frac{3x}{3} = \frac{63}{3}$$
$$x = 21$$

Therefore, the integers are

$$\underbrace{21}_{x}, \quad \underbrace{22}_{x+1=21+1}, \quad \text{and} \quad \underbrace{23}_{x+2=21+2}.$$

Observe that $21 + 22 + 23 = 66$.

Example 6. Find 3 consecutive odd integers whose sum is 213. Find the integers.

Solution: Let x be the first odd integer. Then the second odd integer is $x + 2$ and the third odd integer is $x + 4$.
Since their sum is 213, we have

$$(x) + (x + 2) + (x + 4) = 213$$
$$3x + 6 = 213$$
$$\underline{ -6 \quad -6}$$
$$\frac{3x}{3} = \frac{207}{3}$$
$$x = 69$$

Therefore, the odd integers are

$$\underbrace{69}_{x}, \quad \underbrace{71}_{x+2=69+2}, \quad \text{and} \quad \underbrace{73}_{x+4=69+4}.$$

Observe that $69 + 71 + 73 = 213$.

Age Problems

Example 7. Steve is twice as old as Michael. Four years ago, Steve was 19 years older than Michael was then. How old is Steve and Michael now?

Solution: We divide the problem into pieces so that we can solve it. The first sentence gives us information about **Steve's age in terms in terms of Michael's age.** Let x be Michael's present age. Then Steve's present age is $2x$

The second sentence may be misleading. If Steve was 19 years older than Michael four years ago, then today (now), Steve is STILL 19 years older. Steve will **always** be 19 years older than Michael; in particular,

$$\underbrace{\text{Steve's present age}}_{2x} \quad \underbrace{\text{is}}_{=} \quad \underbrace{\text{Michael's present age}}_{x} \quad \underbrace{\text{plus 19}}_{+19}.$$

We need to solve the equation:

$$\begin{array}{r} 2x = x + 19 \\ -x \quad -x \\ \hline x = \quad 19 \end{array}$$

Thus, Michael is 19 years old and Steve is $2(19) = 38$ years old.

Ratio Problems

Example 8. The ratio 65 to x is 13 to 8. Find x.

Solution: Set up a proportion:
$$\frac{65}{x} = \frac{13}{8}$$

$$(65)(8) = x(13) \quad \text{(by cross multiplying)}$$
$$520 = 13x$$

$$\frac{520}{13} = x$$

$$40 = x$$

Example 9. Nigel reads x pages per day, and Cheryl reads 20 more pages than Nigel per day. If Nigel reads a book in exactly 6 days and Cheryl reads the same book in exactly 2 days, how many pages are in the book?

Solution: We set up a proportion by using the information given.
Nigel reads x pages per day and he reads a book in 6 days. Therefore, Nigel reads $6x$ pages in 6 days (the whole book).
The ratio is $6x$ **pages** : 1 **book** or $\frac{6x}{1}$.

Cheryl reads $20 + x$ pages per day and she reads the same book in 2 days. Therefore, Cheryl reads $2(20 + x)$ pages in 2 days (the whole book).

The ratio is $2(20 + x)$ **pages** : 1 **book** or $\dfrac{2(20 + x)}{1}$.

Since they both read the same book, and the book has the same number of pages, we have $\dfrac{6x}{1} = \dfrac{2(20 + x)}{1}$. Therefore, $6x = 2(20 + x)$. Now we solve for x.

$$6x = 2(20 + x)$$
$$6x = 40 + 2x$$
$$\underline{-2x \qquad\quad -2x}$$
$$\frac{\cancel{4}x}{\cancel{4}} = \frac{40}{4}$$

$$x = 10$$

Therefore, since (using Nigel's information) there are $6x$ pages in the book, it contains $6(10) = 60$ pages.

Observe that we could have used Cheryl's information as well: There are $2(20 + x)$ pages in the book, so it contains $2(20 + 10) = 2(30) = 60$ pages.

Example 10. John must solve 52 math problems on a test. He solves 5 problems every 8 minutes. At this rate, how long will it take him to solve all 52 problems?

Solution: We set up a proportion: $\dfrac{5 \text{ problems}}{8 \text{ minutes}} = \dfrac{52 \text{ problems}}{x \text{ minutes}}$

$$(5)(x) = (8)(52) \qquad \text{(by cross multiplying)}$$
$$5x = 416$$
$$\frac{\cancel{5}x}{\cancel{5}} = \frac{416}{5}$$

$$x = 83\frac{1}{5} = 83\underbrace{\frac{1 \times 12}{5 \times 12}}_{\text{Convert } \frac{1}{5} \text{ minute to seconds.}} = 83\frac{12}{60}$$

It will take John 83 minutes and 12 seconds to solve all 52 problems.

Example 11. Two numbers have ratio 3 : 4. If their sum is 245, find the numbers.

Solution: First, take the sum of the numbers in the ratio: $3 + 4 = 7$.
This means that 3 in the ratio 3 : 4 represents $\frac{3}{7}$ of "the sum of numbers". Since the sum is 245, we have

$$\frac{3}{7} \times 245 = 105.$$

Similarly, the 4 in the ratio 3 : 4 represents $\frac{4}{7}$ of "the sum of numbers":

$$\frac{4}{7} \times 245 = 140$$

Therefore, the two numbers are 105 and 140. Observe that $105 + 140 = 245$.

Geometry Problems

Example 12. The perimeter (P) of a square whose sides have length s is given by the formula $P = 4s$. Find the length of a side of a square whose perimeter is 36 inches.

Solution:

We are given $P = 36$ inches and we want to find s. Using the formula $P = 4s$, we obtain:

$$\frac{36 \text{ inches}}{4} = \frac{\cancel{4}s}{\cancel{4}}$$

$$9 \text{ inches} = s$$

The length of a side is 9 inches.

Example 13. Find the width of a rectangle whose perimeter is 28 inches and whose length is 10 inches.

Solution:

We are given $P = 28$ inches and $l = 10$ inches. We want to find w. Using the formula $P = 2l + 2w$, we have:

$$28 \text{ inches} = 2(10 \text{ inches}) + 2w$$
$$28 \text{ inches} = 20 \text{ inches} + 2w$$
$$\underline{-20 \text{ inches} \quad -20 \text{ inches}}$$
$$\frac{8 \text{ inches}}{2} = \frac{\cancel{2}w}{\cancel{2}}$$
$$4 \text{ inches} = w$$

The width of the rectangle is 4 inches.

Example 14. If the area of a triangle is 108 in.^{2}, find the base if the height is $h = 16$ in.

Solution: The area of a triangle is $A = \frac{1}{2}bh$. We are given that $A = 108$ in.^{2} and $h = 16$ in. Put these values into the formula and solve for b:

$$108 \text{ in.}^2 = \frac{1}{2}(b)(16 \text{ in.})$$

$$108 \text{ in.}^2 = \left(8 \text{ in.}\right) b \qquad \text{(Divide by 8 in.)}$$

$$\frac{108 \text{ in.}^2}{8 \text{ in.}} = b$$

$$13\frac{1}{2} \text{ in.} = b$$

And so, the base is $13\frac{1}{2}$ in.

Example 15. If the area of a circle is 530.66 cm.^{2}, what is the radius of the circle? (Use $\pi = 3.14$).

Solution: The area of a circle is $A = \pi r^2$. We are given that $A = 530.66$ cm.^{2}:

$$530.66 \text{ cm.}^2 = 3.14 r^2 \qquad \text{(Divide both sides by 3.14.)}$$

$$\frac{530.66 \text{ cm.}^2}{3.14} = \frac{3.14 r^2}{3.14}$$

$$169 \text{ cm.}^2 = r^2$$
$$13 \text{ cm.} = r$$

The radius is 13 cm.

Example 16. The length of a rectangle is 1 inch more than twice its width. If the perimeter of the rectangle is 74 inches, what is its width?

Solution: Let w be the width. The first sentence tells us that the length is $2w + 1$.

$$P = 2l + 2w$$

$$74 = 2(2w + 1) + 2w$$
$$74 = 4w + 2 + 2w$$

$$74 = 6w + 2$$
$$\underline{-2 \qquad\quad -2}$$
$$\frac{72}{6} = \frac{6w}{6}$$
$$12 = w$$

The width is 12 inches.

Motion Problems

Example 17. A train travels 190 miles (mi.) in x hours (hr.) and then 68 miles in y hours, what is an expression for the train's average rate (speed), in miles per hour, for the entire distance traveled?

Solution: The average speed (r) is the total distance traveled (d) divided by the total time elapsed (t):

$$\text{Average speed} = \frac{\text{total distance}}{\text{total time elapsed}} \quad \text{or} \quad r = \frac{d}{t}$$

First we sum up the distances traveled: 230 mi. +60 mi. = 258 mi. Next we sum up the times elapsed: x hr. $+y$ hr. $= (x + y)$ hr.
Now use the formula:

$$\text{Average speed} = \frac{\text{total distance}}{\text{total time elapsed}} = \frac{258 \text{ mi.}}{(x + y) \text{ hr.}} = \frac{258}{x + y} \text{ mi./hr.}$$

Example 18. An express bus travels for 5 hours at a speed of 65 miles per hour and x miles per hour for 4 hours. The average speed for the entire journey is 63 miles per hour. Find x.

Solution: We know that average speed $= \dfrac{\text{total distance}}{\text{total time elapsed}}$. First we find the total distance traveled. In the first 5 hours, the distance traveled is:

$$5 \text{ hr.}\left(\frac{65 \text{ mi.}}{1 \text{ hr.}} \right) = 325 \text{ mi.}$$

For the next 4 hours, the distance traveled is:

$$4 \text{ hr.}\left(\frac{x \text{ mi.}}{1 \text{ hr.}} \right) = 4x \text{ mi.}$$

The total distance traveled during the entire journey is $325 + 4x$.
Next we find the total time elapsed for the entire journey:

$$5 \text{ hrs.} + 4 \text{ hrs.} = 9 \text{ hrs.}$$

We are given that the average speed for the entire journey is 63 miles per hour. Use the formula:

$$\text{Average speed} = \frac{\text{total distance}}{\text{total time elapsed}}$$

201

$$\frac{63 \text{ mi.}}{1 \text{ hr.}} = \frac{(325 + 4x) \text{ mi.}}{9 \text{ hrs.}}$$

$$1(325 + 4x) = 63(9) \quad \text{(after cross multiplying)}$$
$$325 + 4x = 567$$
$$\underline{-325 \qquad -325}$$
$$\frac{4x}{4} = \frac{242}{4} = 60\frac{1}{2}$$

The bus traveled $60\frac{1}{2}$ miles per hour for the last 4 hours.

Mixture Problems

Example 19. Distilled water is poured into a beaker containing 45 ml. of hydrochloric acid to form an acid-water solution. How much water must be added to form a solution that is 60% acid?

Solution: Let x represent the total amount of acid-water solution. We know 45 ml. represents 60% acid in the acid-water solution.

$$60\% \text{ of } x = 45$$
$$0.60 \times x = 45$$

$$x = \frac{45}{0.60} = 75$$

And so, 75 ml. is the total amount of the acid-water solution. Therefore, 75 ml. − 45 ml. = 30 ml. of water must be added.

See Chapter 6, Section D for more mixture probems.

Commision Problems

Example 20. Peter's base salary for the week is $\$1,000$. In addition, he receives a commission of 8% of his sales. His total earning this week is $\$1,250$. What is Peter's total sales for the week?

Solution: Notice: New amount − original amount = amount of increase

becomes

Total earnings − base salary = commission

Therefore, Peter's commission is $\$1,250 − \$1,000 = \$250$. Let x be Peter's total sales for the week. We want to find x:

Commission = commission rate × total sales

$$250 = 8\% \text{ of } x$$
$$250 = 0.08 \times x$$

$$\frac{250}{0.08} = x$$

$$x = 3,125$$

Peter's total sales for the week is $3,125.

See Chapter 6, Section D for more commision probems.

Exercises: Chapter 8 Section D

In Exercises 1 - 18, solve.

1. A cricket team won 4 times as many games as it lost. How many games did it lose if it played a total of 120 games?
(a) 30   (b) 120   (c) 12   (d) 24   (e) 40

For Exercises 2 - 3, Tim reads x pages per day and Don reads 12 more pages than Tim per day. Suppose Tim reads a book in exactly 4 days and Don reads the same book in exactly 3 days.

2. What equation can be used to find the number of pages read by each?
(a) $3x = 4(x + 12)$ (b) $4x = 3(x + 12)$ (c) $2x = 3(x + 12)$ (d) $x + 12 = 4x$
(e) $x = 3(x + 12)$

3. What is the number of pages in the book?
(a) 10   (b) 360   (c) 36   (d) 24   (e) 48

4. If x is to 18 as 3 is to 72, find x.
(a) 4   (b) $\frac{3}{4}$ (c) 6   (d) $\frac{1}{4}$ (e) 3

5. The degrees of the angles of a triangle are in ratio 6 : 5 : 7. Find the degree measure of each angle.
(a) 6°, 5°, 7°   (b) 30°, 60°, 90°   (c) 66°, 55°, 77°   (d) 90°, 10°, 80°
(e) 60°, 50°, 70°

6. Two numbers have the ratio 16 : 5. If their sum is 105, find the numbers.
(a) 95, 10   (b) 60, 45   (c) 36, 69   (d) 80, 25   (e) 48, 97

7. The sum of Kelly's age and Tina's age is 52 years. Kelly's age 6 years from now will be 8 less than twice Tina's age now. How old is Tina now?
(a) 22   (b) 36   (c) 28   (d) 20   (e) 18

8. Jason is three times as old as Lauren. Ten years from now, he will be twice as old as she will be then. How old is Jason now?
(a) 24   (b) 6   (c) 30   (d) 22   (e) 19

9. The sum of two consecutive integers is 29. Find the integers.
(a) 22, 7   (b) 24, 5   (c) 14, 15   (d) 20, 9   (e) 18, 11

10 Find 3 consecutive even integers whose sum is –36.
(a) –14, –12, – 10   (b) –16, –12, –10   (c) –14, –13, – 12
(d) 10, 12, 14   (e) –16, –14, –12

11. Two more than twice a number equals 16 less than three times the number. Find the number.
(a) 18   (b) 16   (c) 40   (d) 13   (e) 19

12. A train travels x miles in 7 hours and then y miles in 9 hours. What is an expression for the train's average speed, in miles per hour, for the entire distance traveled?
(a) $\dfrac{x+9}{7+y}$ (b) $\dfrac{x+y}{16}$ (c) $\dfrac{16}{x+y}$ (d) $\dfrac{x+7}{y+9}$ (e) $\dfrac{y+9}{x+7}$

13. David took four exams in Calculus 1. If he received scores 84, 88, and 77 on the first three exams, what score must he had earned on the fourth exam to have an average of 82?
(a) 81   (b) 79   (c) 86   (d) 77   (e) 89

14. Distilled water is poured into a beaker containing 20 ml. of hydrochloric acid to form an acid-water solution. How much water must be added to form a solution that is 40% acid?
(a) 30 ml.   (b) 40 ml.   (c) 50 ml.   (d) 70 ml.   (e) 89 ml.

15. Sam's base salary for the week is $400. In addition, he receives a commission of 8% of his sales. His total earning this week is $560. What is Sam's total sales for the week?
(a) $2,000   (b) $2,500   (c) $1,600   (d) $160   (e) $1,500

16. The length of a rectangle is 5 inches more than three times its width. If the perimeter of the rectangle is 106 inches, what is the width (in inches)?
(a) 25   (b) 12   (c) 10   (d) 27   (e) 40

17. The area of a triangle is 96 square yards. Find the base of the triangle if its height is 6 yards.
(a) 32 yards   (b) 16 yards   (c) 14 yards   (d) 20 yards   (e) 36 yards

18. The area of a circle is 153.86 square miles. Find the radius of the circle. (Use $\pi = 3.14$.)
(a) 49 miles   (b) 13 miles   (c) 7 miles   (d) 25 miles   (e) $\sqrt{51}$ miles

For Exercises 19 - 20, a square has perimeter 144 inches.

19. The length of a side of the square is:
(a) 32 in.   (b) 16 in.   (c) 14 in.   (d) 20 in.   (e) 36 in.

20. The area of the square is:
(a) 1,296 in.^{2} (b) 144 in.^{2} (c) 49 in.^{2} (d) 400 in.^{2} (e) 36 in.^{2}

Chapter 9: Integer Exponents

Section A. Properties of Integer Exponents

Recall that if a is any real number and n is a natural number, then $\underbrace{a \cdot a \cdot a \cdots a}_{n \text{ factors}} = a^n$. We call a the

base and n the exponent. The expression a^n is called an **exponential expression**. For example,

$$\underbrace{5 \times 5 \times 5 = 5^3}_{\text{base=5, exponent=3}}, \quad \underbrace{y \cdot y \cdot y \cdot y = y^4}_{\text{base=}y\text{, exponent=4}}, \quad \text{and} \quad \underbrace{(3x)(3x) = (3x)^2}_{\text{base=}3x\text{, exponent=2}}$$

are exponential expressions.

Note that $a^1 = a$. For example, $5^1 = 5$ and $(-4.16)^1 = -1(4.16) = -4.16$.

Example 1. Evaluate.

1) $(0.13)^2$ 2) $(7.0)^3$ 3) -4^4 4) $(-4)^4$ 5) $\left(\frac{2}{5}\right)^3$ 6) π^1

Solution: 1) $(0.13)^2 = (0.13)(0.13) = 0.0169$ 2) $(7.0)^3 = 7^3 = 7 \times 7 \times 7 = 343$

          3) $-4^4 = -1(4^4) = -1(4)(4)(4)(4) = -256$ 4) $(-4)^4 = (-4)(-4)(-4)(-4) = 256$

          5) $\left(\frac{2}{5}\right)^3 = \left(\frac{2}{5}\right)\left(\frac{2}{5}\right)\left(\frac{2}{5}\right) = \frac{8}{125}$ 6) $\pi^1 = \pi$

Properties of Integer Exponents

Property 1. When you multiply exponential expressions with the same base, keep the same base and add up the exponents:

$$a^m \cdot a^n = a^{m+n}$$

First, we illustrate cases when m and n are natural numbers. To do so, let's multiply $a^4 \cdot a^3$. Observe that $a^4 \cdot a^3$ is the same as

$$\underbrace{(a \cdot a \cdot a \cdot a)}_{\text{4 of these}} \cdot \underbrace{(a \cdot a \cdot a)}_{\text{3 of these}} = \underbrace{a \cdot a \cdot a \cdot a \cdot a \cdot a \cdot a}_{\text{4+3=7 of these}} = a^7.$$

As you can see, the exponents 3 and 4 add up to 7, and the base a remains the same.

Example 2. Multiply.

1) $x^2 \cdot x^9$ 2) $(a^5)(a^7)$ 3) $y^3 \cdot (y^4 \cdot y)$

4) $(x^8)(x^8)(x^8)(x^8)$ 5) $(4a^3)(6a^2)$ 6) $(-9x^6y^2)(5xy^7)$

Solution: 1) $x^2 \cdot x^9 = x^{2+9} = x^{11}$
2) $(a^5)(a^7) = a^{5+7} = a^{12}$
3) $y^3 \cdot (y^4 \cdot y) = y^3 \cdot y^4 \cdot y^1 = y^{3+4+1} = y^8$
4) $(x^8)(x^8)(x^8)(x^8) = x^{8+8+8+8} = x^{32}$
5) $(4a^3)(6a^2) = 4 \cdot 6 \cdot a^3 \cdot a^2 = 24a^{3+2} = 24a^5$
6) $(-9x^6y^2)(5xy^7) = -45x^{6+1}y^{2+7} = -45x^7y^9$

Be careful when the base is numerical. For example, $7^3 \cdot 7^5 = 7^{3+5} = 7^8$ is correct, but $7^3 \cdot 7^5 \overset{??}{=} 49^{3+5} = 49^8$ is incorrect. Remember that the base remains the same; only the exponents add up.

Example 3. Multiply.
1) $4^3 \cdot 4^8$ 2) $3^9(3^4)(3^2)$ 3) 11×11^5

Solution: 1) $4^3 \cdot 4^8 = 4^{3+8} = 4^{11}$ 2) $3^9(3^4)(3^2) = 3^{9+4+2} = 3^{15}$ 3) $11 \times 11^5 = 11^{1+5} = 11^6$

Property 2. When you divide non-zero exponential expressions with the same base, subtract the exponent of the denominator from the exponent of the numerator and keep the same base.

$$\frac{a^m}{a^n} = a^m \div a^n = a^{m-n}$$

We will illustrate Property 2 when m and n are whole numbers and (i) $m > n$, (ii) $m = n$, and (iii) $m < n$.

To begin with, let's divide $\dfrac{a^7}{a^3}$ (note that $m > n$). Notice that $\dfrac{a^7}{a^3}$ is the same as

$$\frac{a \cdot a \cdot a \cdot a \cdot a \cdot a \cdot a}{a \cdot a \cdot a} = \frac{a \cdot a \cdot a \cdot a}{1} = \frac{a^4}{1} = a^4.$$

As you can see, the exponent 4 is obtained by subtracting 3 from 7, and the base stays the same.

Example 4. Divide. Assume that all variables represent non-zero real numbers.
1) $\dfrac{a^{17}}{a^{12}}$ 2) $\dfrac{x^8}{x}$ 3) $y^{23} \div y^{14}$ 4) $\dfrac{36a^{18}b^5}{18a^{17}b^2}$ 5) $\dfrac{-24x^{10}y^{13}}{6x^7y^2}$

Solution: 1) $\dfrac{a^{17}}{a^{12}} = a^{17-12} = a^5$ 2) $\dfrac{x^8}{x} = x^{8-1} = x^7$ 3) $y^{23} \div y^{14} = y^{23-14} = y^9$

4) $\dfrac{36a^{18}b^5}{18a^{17}b^2} = \dfrac{36}{18} \cdot \dfrac{a^{18}}{a^{17}} \cdot \dfrac{b^5}{b^2} = 2a^{18-17}b^{5-2} = 2a^1b^3 = 2ab^3$

5) $\dfrac{-24x^{10}y^{13}}{4x^7y^2} = -4x^{10-7}y^{13-2} = -4x^3y^{11}$

Be careful when the base is numerical. For example, $\frac{8^6}{8^4} = 8^{6-4} = 8^2$ is correct, but $\frac{8^6}{8^4} \overset{??}{=} 1^{6-4} = 1^2$ is incorrect. Remember that the base remains the same; only the exponent of the denominator is subtracted from the exponent of the numerator.

Example 5. Divide.

1) $\frac{8^{12}}{8^5}$ 2) $\frac{13^{10}}{13^9}$ 3) $16^{20} \div 16^{11}$

Solution: 1) $\frac{8^{12}}{8^5} = 8^{12-5} = 8^7$ 2) $\frac{13^{10}}{13^9} = 13^{10-9} = 13^1 = 13$

3) $16^{20} \div 16^{11} = 16^{20-11} = 16^9$

Property 3. Any non-zero number raised to the exponent zero equals one:

$$a^0 = 1 \text{ whenever } a \ne 0.$$

To illustrate, let's consider the expression $\frac{a^n}{a^n}$, where a is any non-zero real number and n is a natural number. We know that $\frac{a^n}{a^n} = 1$. However, by allowing Property 2 to work for this situation we obtain $\frac{a^n}{a^n} = a^{n-n} = a^0$. Since $\frac{a^n}{a^n}$ simplifies to both 1 and a^0, it makes sense to define $a^0 = 1$ whenever a is a non-zero real number. Notice that the expression 0^0 is **undefined**.

Example 6. Evaluate or simplify. Assume that all variables represent non-zero real numbers.

1) 5^0 2) $(2.96)^0$ 3) $(-7)^0$ 4) -7^0
5) x^0 6) $(3a)^0$ 7) $3a^0$ 8) $x^2 y^7 (y^8)^0$

Solution:

1) $5^0 = 1$ 2) $(2.96)^0 = 1$ 3) $(-7)^0 = 1$ 4) $-7^0 = -1(7^0) = -1(1) = -1$
5) $x^0 = 1$ 6) $(3a)^0 = 1$ 7) $3a^0 = 3(1) = 3$ 8) $x^2 y^7 (y^8)^0 = x^2 y^7 (1) = x^2 y^7$

Property 4. If a is any non-zero real number and n is any whole number, then $a^{-n} = \frac{1}{a^n}$.

To illustrate, consider the expression $\frac{a^0}{a^n}$, where a is any non-zero real number and n is any whole number. We know that $\frac{a^0}{a^n} = \frac{1}{a^n}$ since $a^0 = 1$ by Property 3. However, by allowing Property 2 to work, we obtain $\frac{a^0}{a^n} = a^{0-n} = a^{-n}$. Since $\frac{a^0}{a^n}$ simplifies to both $\frac{1}{a^n}$ and a^{-n}, it makes sense to define $a^{-n} = \frac{1}{a^n}$ whenever a is a non-zero real number and n is a whole number.

Example 7. Evaluate or rewrite without negative exponents. Assume that all variables represent non-zero real numbers.

1) 4^{-1} 2) 3^{-2} 3) $(-7)^{-2}$ 4) -7^{-2}

5) m^{-8} 6) y^{-5} 7) $(-8)^{-3}$ 8) -8^{-3}

Solution:

1) $4^{-1} = \dfrac{1}{4^1} = \dfrac{1}{4}$ 2) $3^{-2} = \dfrac{1}{3^2} = \dfrac{1}{9}$

3) $(-7)^{-2} = \dfrac{1}{(-7)^2} = \dfrac{1}{49}$ 4) $-7^{-2} = -1(7^{-2}) = -\dfrac{1}{7^2} = -\dfrac{1}{49}$

5) $m^{-8} = \dfrac{1}{m^8}$ 6) $y^{-5} = \dfrac{1}{y^5}$

7) $(-8)^{-3} = \dfrac{1}{(-8)^3} = \dfrac{1}{-512} = -\dfrac{1}{512}$ 8) $-8^{-3} = -1(8^{-3}) = -\dfrac{1}{8^3} = -\dfrac{1}{512}$

It turns out that $a^m \cdot a^n = a^{m+n}$ holds whenever m and n are **any** two integers. For example, observe that

$$a^{-4} \cdot a^6 = \frac{1}{a^4} \cdot \frac{a^6}{1} = \frac{a^6}{a^4} = a^{6-4} = a^2,$$

which is the same as $a^{-4} \cdot a^6 = a^{(-4)+6} = a^2$. Similarly,

$$a^{-5} \cdot a^{-2} = \frac{1}{a^5} \cdot \frac{1}{a^2} = \frac{1}{a^{5+2}} = \frac{1}{a^7} = a^{-7},$$

which is the same as $a^{-5} \cdot a^{-2} = a^{(-5)+(-2)} = a^{-7}$. Property 2 also holds whenever m and n are **any** two integers.

Example 8. Multiply or divide.

1) $2^{-4} \cdot 2^3$ 2) $9^{-11} \cdot 9^{12}$ 3) $\dfrac{15^{-6}}{15^{-8}}$ 4) $\dfrac{(-4)^9}{(-4)^{10}}$

Solution: 1) $2^{-4} \cdot 2^3 = 2^{-4+3} = 2^{-1} = \dfrac{1}{2}$ 2) $9^{-11} \cdot 9^{12} = 9^{-11+12} = 9^1 = 9$

3) $\dfrac{15^{-6}}{15^{-8}} = 15^{-6-(-8)} = 15^2 = 225$ 4) $\dfrac{(-4)^9}{(-4)^{10}} = (-4)^{9-10} = (-4)^{-1} = \dfrac{1}{-4} = -\dfrac{1}{4}$

Property 5. When an exponential expression is raised to a power, the exponents multiply and the base stays the same:

$$(a^m)^n = a^{mn}$$

To illustrate, consider the expression $(a^7)^4$. Observe that

$$(a^7)^4 = \underbrace{(a^7)(a^7)(a^7)(a^7) = a^{7+7+7+7}}_{\text{by Property 1}} = a^{28},$$

which is just $a^{7 \times 4}$.

Here's a demonstration involving negative exponents:

$$(a^{-3})^3 = \left(\frac{1}{a^3}\right)^3 = \underbrace{\left(\frac{1}{a^3}\right)\left(\frac{1}{a^3}\right)\left(\frac{1}{a^3}\right) = \frac{1}{a^{3+3+3}}}_{\text{by Property 1}} = \frac{1}{a^9} = a^{-9},$$

which is the same as $a^{(-3)(3)} = a^{-9}$.

Example 9. Evaluate or simplify. Assume that all variables represent non-zero real numbers.

1) $(a^3)^6$ 2) $(x^7)^{-2}$ 3) $(y^{-4})^{-1}$ 4) $(a^0)^5$ 5) $(2^3)^2$ 6) $\left[(-3)^2\right]^2$

Solution: 1) $(a^3)^6 = a^{(3)(6)} = a^{18}$ 2) $(x^7)^{-2} = x^{(7)(-2)} = x^{-14} = \frac{1}{x^{14}}$

3) $(y^{-4})^{-1} = y^{(-4)(-1)} = y^4$ 4) $(a^0)^5 = a^{(0)(5)} = a^0 = 1$

5) $(2^3)^2 = 2^{(3)(2)} = 2^6 = 64$ 6) $\left[(-3)^2\right]^2 = (-3)^4 = 81$

Property 6. The exponent of a product is the product of each factor raised to that exponent:

$$(ab)^n = a^n b^n$$

To illustrate, let's consider $(ab)^3$. Observe that $(ab)^3 = (ab)(ab)(ab) = ababab = a^3b^3$ which is what the property gives us. The property also works when n is a negative integer. For example,

$$\underbrace{(ab)^{-2} = \frac{1}{(ab)^2}}_{\text{by Property 4}} = \frac{1}{a^2b^2} = \underbrace{\frac{1}{a^2}\cdot\frac{1}{b^2} = a^{-2}b^{-2}}_{\text{by Property 4}}.$$

Example 10. Simplify.

1) $(xy)^4$ 2) $(3xy)^3$ 3) $(-2a^5b^7)^3$ 4) $(4x^6y^2z^8)^2$ 5) $\left(\frac{2}{5}m^5n\right)^3$

Solution: 1) $(xy)^4 = x^4y^4$
2) $(3xy)^3 = 3^3x^3y^3 = 27x^3y^3$
3) $(-2a^5b^7)^3 = (-2)^3(a^5)^3(b^7)^3 = -8a^{15}b^{21}$
4) $(4x^6y^2z^8)^2 = 4^2(x^6)^2(y^2)^2(z^8)^2 = 16x^{12}y^4z^{16}$
5) $\left(\frac{2}{5}m^5n\right)^3 = \left(\frac{2}{5}\right)^3(m^5)^3(n)^3 = \frac{8}{125}m^{15}n^3$

Property 7. The exponent of a fraction is the fraction whose numerator and denominator is raised to that exponent:

$$\left(\frac{a}{b}\right)^n = \frac{a^n}{b^n}, \; b \neq 0$$

To illustrate, let's simplify the expression $\left(\frac{a}{b}\right)^4$:

$$\left(\frac{a}{b}\right)^4 = \left(\frac{a}{b}\right)\left(\frac{a}{b}\right)\left(\frac{a}{b}\right)\left(\frac{a}{b}\right) = \frac{a^4}{b^4}$$

Example 11. Evaluate or simplify. Assume that all variables represent non-zero real numbers.

1) $\left(\frac{5}{8}\right)^2$ 2) $\left(-\frac{4}{5}\right)^3$ 3) $\left(\frac{x}{y}\right)^5$

4) $\left(\frac{6}{a^4}\right)^2$ 5) $\left(\frac{x^3}{2y^4}\right)^5$ 6) $\left(-\frac{3a^7}{8b^5c^2}\right)^2$

Solution: 1) $\left(\frac{5}{8}\right)^2 = \frac{5^2}{8^2} = \frac{25}{64}$ 2) $\left(-\frac{4}{5}\right)^3 = -\frac{4^3}{5^3} = -\frac{64}{125}$

3) $\left(\frac{x}{y}\right)^5 = \frac{x^5}{y^5}$ 4) $\left(\frac{6}{a^4}\right)^2 = \frac{6^2}{(a^4)^2} = \frac{36}{a^8}$

5) $\left(\frac{x^3}{2y^4}\right)^5 = \frac{(x^3)^5}{(2y^4)^5} = \frac{x^{15}}{32y^{20}}$ 6) $\left(-\frac{3a^7}{8b^5c^2}\right)^2 = \frac{3^2(a^7)^2}{8^2(b^5)^2(c^2)^2} = \frac{9a^{14}}{64b^{10}c^4}$

Now let's look at some examples that uses several properties.

Example 12. Simplify. Assume that all variables represent non-zero real numbers.

1) $3x^4(4x)^2$ 2) $(5a^2)^0(-5a^6)$ 3) $(-2x^4y^3)^4(-3x^8y)$

4) $\frac{7m^{10}}{2n^4}\left(\frac{2m^2}{5n^3}\right)^2$ 5) $\frac{4x^2(3x^3)^2}{-9x^7}$ 6) $\left(\frac{2x^8}{5y^9}\right)^2\left(-\frac{3x^0}{5y^3}\right)$

Solution: 1) $3x^4(4x)^2 = 3x^4(16x^2) = 48x^6$

2) $(5a^2)^0(-5a^6) = 1(-5a^6) = -5a^6$

3) $(-2x^4y^3)^4(-3x^8y) = (16x^{16}y^{12})(-3x^8y) = -48x^{24}y^{13}$

4) $\frac{7m^{10}}{2n^4}\left(\frac{2m^2}{5n^3}\right)^2 = \frac{7m^{10}}{2n^4}\left(\frac{4m^4}{25n^6}\right) = \frac{14m^{14}}{25n^{10}}$

5) $\frac{4x^2(3x^3)^2}{-9x^7} = \frac{4x^2(9x^6)}{-9x^7} = \frac{36x^8}{-9x^7} = -4x^1 = -4x$

6) $\left(\frac{2x^8}{5y^9}\right)^2\left(-\frac{3x^0}{5y^3}\right) = \left(\frac{4x^{16}}{25y^{18}}\right)\left(-\frac{3}{5y^3}\right) = -\frac{12x^{16}}{125y^{21}}$

Summary of the Exponent Properties

1. $a^m \cdot a^n = a^{m+n}$

2. $\dfrac{a^m}{a^n} = a^m \div a^n = a^{m-n}$

3. $a^0 = 1, \; a \neq 0$

4. $a^{-n} = \dfrac{1}{a^n}, \; a \neq 0$

5. $(a^m)^n = a^{mn}$

6. $(ab)^n = a^n b^n$

7. $\left(\dfrac{a}{b}\right)^n = \dfrac{a^n}{b^n}$

Exercises: Chapter 9, Section A

In Examples 1 - 12, evaluate.

1. 5^2

2. $\left(\frac{3}{4}\right)^3$

3. $\left(\frac{9}{7}\right)^3$

4. $\left(-\frac{2}{11}\right)^2$

5. $(-6)^2$

6. -6^2

7. $\left(-\frac{1}{5}\right)^3$

8. $-\left(\frac{1}{3}\right)^5$

9. $(-4)^3$

10. -4^3

11. 3^4

12. 7^1

In Exercises 13 - 18, choose the correct answer.

13. $x^3 \cdot x^4 =$
(a) x^{12} (b) x^7 (c) $2x^{12}$ (d) $2x^7$ (e) x^{81}

14. $(a^{10})(a^2)(a^3) =$
(a) a^{15} (b) a^{60} (c) $3a^{60}$ (d) $3a^{15}$ (e) a^{300}

15. $(2x^3)(4x^7) =$
(a) $6x^{10}$ (b) $8x^{21}$ (c) $8x^{-4}$ (d) $8x^{10}$ (e) $6x^{24}$

16. $(9a^4b^3)(-6a^2b^5) =$
(a) $-54a^8b^{15}$ (b) $-54a^{16}b^{729}$ (c) $-54a^6b^8$ (d) $54a^6b^8$ (e) $54a^8b^{15}$

17. $\left(\frac{1}{3}x^2y^3\right)\left(\frac{9}{10}x^6y\right) =$

(a) $\frac{3}{10}x^{12}y^3$ (b) $\frac{3}{10}x^8y^3$ (c) $\frac{3}{10}x^8y^4$ (d) $\frac{37}{30}x^8y^4$ (e) $\frac{1}{10}x^8y^4$

18. $(m^7)(-n^6m^3)(-mn^4) =$
(a) $-m^{11}n^{10}$ (b) $m^{11}n^{10}$ (c) $m^{14}n^7$ (d) m^8n^{13} (e) $-m^8n^{10}$

In Exercises 19 - 28, evaluate.

19. $\dfrac{5^6}{5^5}$ 20. $\dfrac{2^8}{2^6}$ 21. $\dfrac{(-3)^8}{(-3)^5}$ 22. $\dfrac{(-2)^5}{(-2)^3}$ 23. $\dfrac{4^6}{4^8}$

24. $\dfrac{(-5)^5}{(-5)^6}$ 25. $\dfrac{(-7)^8}{(-7)^{10}}$ 26. $\left(\dfrac{8}{9}\right)^0$ 27. $(-10)^0$ 28. -10^0

In Exercises 29 - 35, choose the correct answer. Assume that all variables represent non-zero real numbers.

29. $\dfrac{x^9}{x^4} =$
(a) 1   (b) x^{13} (c) x^{36} (d) x^{-5} (e) x^5

30. $\dfrac{-35s^7t^4}{-5s^4t} =$
(a) $-7s^3t^4$ (b) $7s^3t^3$ (c) $7s^{11}t^5$ (d) $7s^{-3}t^{-5}$ (e) $\dfrac{5s^3t^3}{7}$

31. $\dfrac{8^2 \cdot 5^3}{8^1 \cdot 5^2} =$
(a) 1   (b) $\dfrac{8}{5}$ (c) $\dfrac{5}{8}$ (d) 40   (e) 2

32. $\dfrac{2^8 \cdot 11^2}{2^9 \cdot 11^1} =$
(a) 1   (b) $\dfrac{11}{2}$ (c) $\dfrac{2}{11}$ (d) 22   (e) $\dfrac{1}{22}$

33. $\dfrac{4^{16} \cdot 3^2}{4^{19}} =$
(a) 9   (b) $\dfrac{9}{64}$ (c) $\dfrac{3}{4}$ (d) $\dfrac{64}{9}$ (e) $\dfrac{1}{276}$

34. $(9x)^0 =$
(a) 9   (b) $9x$ (c) 1   (d) 0   (e) undefined

35. $7t^0 =$
(a) 7   (b) $7t$ (c) 1   (d) 0   (e) undefined

In Exercises 36 - 49, evaluate.

36. 6^{-1} 37. 3^{-4} 38. $(-7)^{-3}$ 39. -7^{-3} 40. $(-8)^{-2}$

41. -8^{-2} 42. -15^{-1} 43. $(2^3)^2$ 44. $(3^2)^2$ 45. $(5^2)^{-1}$

46. $(4^{-3})^2$ 47. $(5^{-1})^{-3}$ 48. $(16^0)^{-2}$ 49. $-(18^8)^0$

In Exercises 50 - 59, write each expression with positive exponents and simplify. Assume that all variables represent non-zero real numbers.

50. x^{-2} 51. y^{-3} 52. $-y^{-6}$ 53. $a^{-1} \cdot a^{-2}$ 54. $t^5 \cdot t^{-4}$

55. $\dfrac{x^3}{x^{-1}}$ 56. $\dfrac{x^{12}y^{-1}}{x^7y^0}$ 57. $\dfrac{-15x^0y^{-1}}{-3x^5y^{-7}}$ 58. $(y^2)^{-6}$ 59. $(t^{-4})^4$

In Exercises 60 - 67, choose the correct answer. Assume that all variables represent non-zero real numbers.

60. $(a^3)^5 =$
(a) a^8 (b) a^{15} (c) $5a^3$ (d) a^2 (e) a^{729}

61. $(x^4)^9 =$
(a) x^{36} (b) x^{13} (c) $9x^{36}$ (d) x^{-5} (e) $9x^4$

62. $(y^{-5})^2 =$
(a) $\dfrac{1}{y^3}$ (b) $\dfrac{1}{y^7}$ (c) $\dfrac{1}{y^{10}}$ (d) y^{10} (e) y^{25}

63. $(t^8)^{-2} =$
(a) $\dfrac{1}{t^{10}}$ (b) t^6 (c) $\dfrac{1}{t^{64}}$ (d) $-t^{16}$ (e) $\dfrac{1}{t^{16}}$

64. $(x^0)^{-2} =$

(a) $\dfrac{1}{x^2}$ (b) 1   (c) −1   (d) x^2 (e) undefined

65. $(2x)^{-5} =$

(a) $\dfrac{1}{2x^5}$ (b) $\dfrac{32}{x^5}$ (c) $-32x^5$ (d) $\dfrac{x^5}{32}$ (e) $\dfrac{1}{32x^5}$

66. $(5t^0)^{-3} =$

(a) $\dfrac{1}{125t}$ (b) $\dfrac{1}{125}$ (c) −125   (d) $\dfrac{125}{t^3}$ (e) $\dfrac{1}{125t^3}$

67. $(7xy^2)^{-1} =$

(a) $\dfrac{1}{7xy^2}$ (b) $\dfrac{7}{xy^2}$ (c) $-7xy^2$ (d) $\dfrac{7x}{y^2}$ (e) $-\dfrac{1}{7xy^2}$

In Exercises 68 - 75, simplify. Assume that all variables represent non-zero real numbers.

68. $\left(\dfrac{a}{b}\right)^4$ 69. $\left(\dfrac{x}{y}\right)^8$ 70. $\left(\dfrac{9}{x^3}\right)^2$ 71. $\left(-\dfrac{5}{a^8}\right)^2$

72. $\left(\dfrac{x}{6y^2}\right)^3$ 73. $\left(\dfrac{10x^4}{y^3}\right)^4$ 74. $\left(\dfrac{1}{mt^2}\right)^4$ 75. $\left(-\dfrac{8s^2}{u^4}\right)^3$

In Exercises 76 - 89, choose the correct answer. Assume that all variables represent non-zero real numbers.

76. $\left(\dfrac{1}{4}m^7n^2\right)^2 =$

(a) $\dfrac{1}{16}m^9n^4$ (b) $\dfrac{1}{16}m^{14}n^4$ (c) $\dfrac{1}{4}m^7n^4$ (d) $16m^{14}n^4$ (e) $\dfrac{1}{2}m^{14}n^4$

77. $2x^4(-3x)^3 =$

(a) $-54x^7$ (b) $54x^7$ (c) $-54x^{12}$ (d) $-18x^7$ (e) $-18x^{12}$

78. $-3a^4(4a^8)^2 =$

(a) $48a^{20}$ (b) $-48a^{14}$ (c) $-48a^{68}$ (d) $-48a^{20}$ (e) $-12a^{20}$

79. $(2a^6)^0(-6a^8)^2 =$
(a) $72a^{22}$ (b) $-6a^{16}$ (c) $36a^{16}$ (d) $72a^{16}$ (e) $36a^{64}$

80. $(8x^3y)^{-2} =$
(a) $\dfrac{1}{8x^3y^2}$ (b) $\dfrac{1}{64x^6y^2}$ (c) $\dfrac{64}{x^6y^2}$ (d) $\dfrac{1}{64x^3y^2}$ (e) $\dfrac{1}{16x^3y^2}$

81. $8x^3y^{-2} =$
(a) $\dfrac{8x^3}{y^2}$ (b) $\dfrac{8}{x^3y^2}$ (c) $\dfrac{1}{8x^3y^2}$ (d) $\dfrac{1}{64x^6y^2}$ (e) $\dfrac{y^2}{8x^3}$

82. $\dfrac{(4s^4t^4)(9s^7)}{18t^3} =$
(a) $2s^{11}t$ (b) $\dfrac{2s^{11}}{t}$ (c) $2s^{28}t$ (d) $\dfrac{1}{2s^{11}t}$ (e) $\dfrac{2}{s^{11}t}$

83. $\dfrac{(12a^3b^2)(-2a^4b)}{9a^2b} =$
(a) $\dfrac{8a^5b^2}{3}$ (b) $\dfrac{3a^5b^2}{8}$ (c) $-\dfrac{8a^5}{3b^2}$ (d) $-\dfrac{8a^{10}b^2}{3}$ (e) $-\dfrac{8a^5b^2}{3}$

84. $\dfrac{108x^{12}y^9}{(-9xy^5)(-4x^4y^0)} =$
(a) $-3x^7y^4$ (b) $3x^7y^4$ (c) $3x^8y^6$ (d) $-\dfrac{1}{3x^7y^4}$ (e) $-\dfrac{x^7y^4}{3}$

85. $(x^{m+7})(x^{3m-6}) =$
(a) x^{3m^2-42} (b) $2x^{4m+1}$ (c) x^{4m+1} (d) x^{4m-1} (e) $2x^{4m-1}$

86. $(y^{7-8t})(y^{2t^2-t+6}) =$
(a) $y^{2t^2+8t+13}$ (b) $y^{2t^2-9t+13}$ (c) $y^{(7-8t)(2t^2-t+6)}$ (d) $2y^{2t^2-9t+13}$ (e) $y^{2t^2+9t+13}$

87. $\dfrac{x^{5n}}{x^{4n}} =$
(a) x^{9n} (b) 1 (c) x^{20n^2} (d) x^n (e) $\dfrac{1}{x^n}$

88. $\dfrac{y^{-a^2+16a-3}}{y^{-a^2+a-17}} =$

(a) $y^{-2a^2+17a-20}$ 　　　(b) y^{15a+14} 　　(c) 1 　　　(d) y^{17a-20} 　　(e) $y^{-15a-14}$

89. $\dfrac{(a^{m-3})(a^{-9m+8})}{a^{4-6m}} =$

(a) a^{-2m+1} 　　　(b) a^{-9m+8} 　　(c) a^{-14m+1} 　　(d) a^{2m-1} 　　(e) 1

Section B. More on Negative Integer Exponents

In this section, we discuss negative exponents further. Recall Property 4 from the previous section:

$$a^{-n} = \frac{1}{a^n}, \; a \neq 0$$

If a is a fraction, this property can be interpreted in a simple way:

Property 8: If a and b are any two non-zero real numbers and n is any integer, then

$$\left(\frac{a}{b}\right)^{-n} = \left(\frac{b}{a}\right)^n = \frac{b^n}{a^n}.$$

Notice that the negative exponent 'flips' (or takes the reciprocal of) the fraction $\frac{a}{b}$, giving us $\frac{b}{a}$. After flipping the fraction, the negative sign disappears. To illustrate,

$$\left(\frac{a}{b}\right)^{-n} = \frac{1}{\left(\frac{a}{b}\right)^n} = \frac{1}{\frac{a^n}{b^n}} = 1 \div \frac{a^n}{b^n} = \frac{1}{1} \div \frac{a^n}{b^n} = \frac{1}{1} \times \frac{b^n}{a^n} = \frac{b^n}{a^n} = \left(\frac{b}{a}\right)^n.$$

Example 1. Evaluate.

1) $\left(\frac{2}{3}\right)^{-1}$ 2) $\left(\frac{1}{7}\right)^{-2}$ 3) $\left(\frac{3}{5}\right)^{-3} \cdot \left(\frac{5}{6}\right)^{-2}$ 4) $\left(\frac{8}{3}\right)^{-2} + 4^{-3}$

Solution: 1) $\left(\frac{2}{3}\right)^{-1} = \left(\frac{3}{2}\right)^1 = \frac{3}{2}$

2) $\left(\frac{1}{7}\right)^{-2} = \left(\frac{7}{1}\right)^2 = 7^2 = 49$

3) $\left(\frac{3}{5}\right)^{-3} \cdot \left(\frac{5}{6}\right)^{-2} = \left(\frac{5}{3}\right)^3 \cdot \left(\frac{6}{5}\right)^2 = \frac{5^3}{3^3} \cdot \frac{6^2}{5^2} = \frac{125}{27} \cdot \frac{36}{25} = \frac{20}{3}$

4) $\left(\frac{8}{3}\right)^{-2} + 4^{-3} = \left(\frac{3}{8}\right)^2 + \frac{1}{4^3} = \frac{9}{64} + \frac{1}{64} = \frac{10}{64} = \frac{5}{32}$

When a fraction has a product in the numerator and/or denominator, negative exponents are easily dealt with.

Rule for applying the 'flipping technique': Whenever you have a fraction whose numerator and denominator are factored, any factor in the numerator that has negative exponent *flips* to the denominator, and any factor in the denominator that has negative exponent *flips* to the numerator. After the expression is *flipped*, the negative sign of the exponent disappears.

Example 2. Evaluate.

1) $\dfrac{5^{-2}}{4^1}$ 2) $\dfrac{2^3}{7^{-2}}$ 3) $\dfrac{8^{-1}}{3^{-3}}$ 4) $\dfrac{6^{-1} \cdot 3^2}{5^3 \cdot 2^{-2}}$

Solution:

1) The negative exponent *flips* the 5^{-2} into the denominator and the -2 becomes 2:

$$\frac{5^{-2}}{4^1} = \frac{1 \cdot 5^{-2}}{4^1} = \frac{1}{4^1 \cdot 5^2} = \frac{1}{4(25)} = \frac{1}{100}$$

2) The negative exponent *flips* the 7^{-2} into the numerator and the -2 becomes 2:

$$\frac{2^3}{7^{-2}} = \frac{2^3}{1 \cdot 7^{-2}} = \frac{2^3 \cdot 7^2}{1} = \frac{8(49)}{1} = \frac{392}{1} = 392$$

3) The 8^{-1} *flips* to the denominator, whereas the 3^{-3} *flips* to the numerator:

$$\frac{8^{-1}}{3^{-3}} = \frac{1 \cdot 8^{-1}}{1 \cdot 3^{-3}} = \frac{1 \cdot 3^3}{1 \cdot 8^1} = \frac{27}{8}$$

4) The 6^{-1} *flips* to the denominator, whereas the 2^{-2} *flips* to the numerator:

$$\frac{6^{-1} \cdot 3^2}{5^3 \cdot 2^{-2}} = \frac{3^2 \cdot 2^2}{6^1 \cdot 5^3} = \frac{9(4)}{6(125)} = \frac{36}{6(125)} = \frac{6}{125}$$

To reiterate: **Rule for applying the flipping technique:** Whenever you have a fraction whose numerator and denominator are factored, any factor in the numerator that has negative exponent *flips* to the denominator, and any factor in the denominator that has negative exponent *flips* to the numerator. After the expression is *flipped*, the negative sign of the exponent disappears.

Example 3. Evaluate.

1) $\dfrac{8^2 \cdot 3^{-1}}{4^2 \cdot 10^{-2}}$ 2) $\dfrac{5^{-2} \cdot 2^{-1}}{5^{-3} \cdot 2^4}$ 3) $\dfrac{-7^2 \cdot 8^{-1}}{3^2 \cdot 4^{-2} \cdot 9^0}$

Solution: 1) $\dfrac{8^2 \cdot 3^{-1}}{4^2 \cdot 10^{-2}} = \dfrac{8^2 \cdot 10^2}{4^2 \cdot 3^1} = \dfrac{64(100)}{16(3)} = \dfrac{400}{3}$

2) $\dfrac{5^{-2} \cdot 2^{-1}}{5^{-3} \cdot 2^4} = \dfrac{5^3}{5^2 \cdot 2^4 \cdot 2^1} = \dfrac{5^3}{5^2 \cdot 2^5} = \dfrac{5}{32}$

3) $\underbrace{\dfrac{-7^2 \cdot 8^{-1}}{3^2 \cdot 4^{-2} \cdot 9^0} = -\dfrac{7^2 \cdot 8^{-1}}{3^2 \cdot 4^{-2} \cdot 9^0}}_{\text{Factor } -1.} = -\dfrac{7^2 \cdot 4^2}{3^2 \cdot 8^1 \cdot 9^0} = -\dfrac{49 \cdot 16}{9 \cdot 8 \cdot 1} = -\dfrac{98}{9}$

Example 4. Rewrite each expression without negative exponents.

1) $2(x+1)^{-1}$ 2) $\dfrac{6x^3}{(x-8)^{-1}}$ 3) $4x^2(5x-2)^{-3}$ 4) $\dfrac{(y+3)^{-2}}{(7y+4)^3}$

Solution:

1) $2(x+1)^{-1} = \dfrac{2(x+1)^{-1}}{1} = \dfrac{2}{(x+1)^1} = \dfrac{2}{x+1}$ 2) $\dfrac{6x^3}{(x-8)^{-1}} = \dfrac{6x^3(x-8)^1}{1} = 6x^3(x-8)$

3) $4x^2(5x-2)^{-3} = \dfrac{4x^2(5x-2)^{-3}}{1} = \dfrac{4x^2}{(5x-2)^3}$ 4) $\dfrac{(y+3)^{-2}}{(7y+4)^3} = \dfrac{1}{(7y+4)^3(y+3)^2}$

Example 5. Rewrite each expression with positive exponents only and simplify. Assume that all variables represent non-zero real numbers.

1) $\left(\dfrac{2}{x}\right)^{-2}$ 2) $\dfrac{2^{-2}}{x}$ 3) $a^5 b^{-5}$ 4) $(a^5 b)^{-5}$

5) $(6m^3 n^{-2})^2$ 6) $(-3x^4 y^{-1})^{-3}$ 7) $(4a^{-2}b^{-4})^3$ 8) $\left(\dfrac{x^2}{3}\right)^{-1} \cdot \left(\dfrac{x^4}{2}\right)^{-2}$

Solution:

1) $\left(\dfrac{2}{x}\right)^{-2} = \left(\dfrac{x}{2}\right)^2 = \dfrac{x^2}{2^2} = \dfrac{x^2}{4}$ 2) $\dfrac{2^{-2}}{x} = \dfrac{1}{2^2 x} = \dfrac{1}{4x}$

3) $a^5 b^{-5} = \dfrac{a^5 b^{-5}}{1} = \dfrac{a^5}{b^5}$ 4) $(a^5 b)^{-5} = \dfrac{(a^5 b)^{-5}}{1} = \dfrac{1}{(a^5 b)^5} = \dfrac{1}{a^{25} b^5}$

5) $(6m^3 n^{-2})^2 = 36m^6 n^{-4} = \dfrac{36m^6 n^{-4}}{1} = \dfrac{36m^6}{n^4}$

6) $(-3x^4 y^{-1})^{-3} = \dfrac{(-3x^4 y^{-1})^{-3}}{1} = \dfrac{1}{(-3x^4 y^{-1})^3} = \dfrac{1}{-27x^{12} y^{-3}} = \dfrac{y^3}{-27x^{12}} = -\dfrac{y^3}{27x^{12}}$

7) $(4a^{-2}b^{-4})^3 = 64a^{-6}b^{-12} = \dfrac{64a^{-6}b^{-12}}{1} = \dfrac{64}{a^6 b^{12}}$

8) $\left(\dfrac{x^2}{3}\right)^{-1} \cdot \left(\dfrac{x^4}{2}\right)^{-2} = \left(\dfrac{3}{x^2}\right)^1 \cdot \left(\dfrac{2}{x^4}\right)^2 = \left(\dfrac{3}{x^2}\right)\left(\dfrac{4}{x^8}\right) = \dfrac{12}{x^{10}}$

Exercises: Chapter 9, Section B

In Exercises 1 - 24, evaluate.

1. $\left(\frac{1}{3}\right)^{-1}$ 2. $\left(\frac{8}{3}\right)^{-2}$ 3. $\left(\frac{4}{7}\right)^{-3}$ 4. $\left(\frac{5}{9}\right)^{-1}$ 5. $\frac{6^2}{5^{-1}}$

6. $\frac{4^1}{3^{-2}}$ 7. $\frac{2^{-3}}{4^2}$ 8. $\frac{7^{-2}}{2^2}$ 9. $\frac{(-9)^{-2}}{(-2)^1}$ 10. $\frac{(-8)^{-1}}{7^2}$

11. $\frac{5^{-2}}{3^{-4}}$ 12. $\frac{8^{-2}}{9^{-3}}$ 13. $\frac{9^{-2}}{-4^{-3}}$ 14. $\frac{-2^{-2}}{(-3)^{-5}}$ 15. $\frac{7^1 \cdot 3^{-2}}{7^{-1} \cdot 3^2}$

16. $\frac{6^{-2} \cdot 5^{-1}}{6^{-1} \cdot 5^0}$ 17. $\frac{9^0 \cdot 6^{-1}}{2^{-4} \cdot 4^0}$ 18. $\frac{10^{-2} \cdot 2^3}{-3^0 \cdot 5^{-1}}$ 19. $\left(\frac{2}{7}\right)^{-2} - \left(\frac{4}{5}\right)^{-1}$

20. $\left(\frac{2}{3}\right)^{-3} - \left(\frac{8}{9}\right)^{-1}$ 21. $\left(\frac{3}{4}\right)^{-3} - 2\left(\frac{9}{2}\right)^{-1}$ 22. $2^4 \cdot 3^0 \cdot 6^{-1}$ 23. $4^2 \cdot 5^{-2}$

24. $3^{-6} \cdot 3^5 \cdot 7^{-1}$

In Exercises 25 - 39, choose the correct answer. Assume that all variables represent non-zero real numbers.

25. $\left(\frac{b}{9}\right)^{-1} =$

(a) $\frac{b}{9}$ (b) $\frac{9}{b}$ (c) $9b$ (d) $\frac{1}{9b}$ (e) $-\frac{b}{9}$

26. $\left(\frac{8}{t}\right)^{-2} =$

(a) $-\frac{64}{t^2}$ (b) $\frac{64}{t^2}$ (c) $64t^2$ (d) $\frac{1}{64t^2}$ (e) $\frac{t^2}{64}$

27. $\left(\frac{4a^3}{7}\right)^{-2} =$

(a) $\frac{49}{16a^6}$ (b) $\frac{49}{16a^5}$ (c) $-\frac{16a^6}{49}$ (d) $\frac{16a^6}{49}$ (e) $\frac{49a^6}{16}$

28. $\left(\dfrac{9}{4b^5}\right)^{-3} =$

(a) $\dfrac{64}{729b^{15}}$ 　　(b) $\dfrac{729}{64b^{15}}$ 　　(c) $\dfrac{64b^8}{729}$ 　　(d) $\dfrac{64b^{15}}{729}$ 　　(e) $-\dfrac{729b^{15}}{64}$

29. $\left(\dfrac{3p^5}{2q^7}\right)^{-5} =$

(a) $\dfrac{32q^{35}}{243p^{25}}$ 　　(b) $\dfrac{243p^{25}}{32q^{35}}$ 　　(c) $\dfrac{32q^{12}}{243p^{10}}$ 　　(d) $\dfrac{2q^{35}}{3p^{25}}$ 　　(e) $-\dfrac{243q^{35}}{32p^{25}}$

30. $5x^{-4}y^6z^0 =$

(a) $\dfrac{5x^4}{y^6}$ 　　(b) $\dfrac{y^6}{5x^4}$ 　　(c) $\dfrac{5y^6z}{x^4}$ 　　(d) $\dfrac{5y^6}{x^4}$ 　　(e) $\dfrac{5y^6}{x^4z}$

31. $(4a^{-3}b^4)^{-3} =$

(a) $\dfrac{a^9}{64b^{12}}$ 　　(b) $\dfrac{b^{12}}{64a^9}$ 　　(c) $\dfrac{a^9}{4b^{12}}$ 　　(d) $\dfrac{a^6}{64b^7}$ 　　(e) $\dfrac{64b^{12}}{a^9}$

32. $\left(\dfrac{x^{-3}}{y^7}\right)^{-2} =$

(a) $\dfrac{x^6}{y^{14}}$ 　　(b) $\dfrac{y^{14}}{x^6}$ 　　(c) x^6y^{14} 　　(d) $\dfrac{1}{x^6y^{14}}$ 　　(e) $-\dfrac{1}{x^6y^{14}}$

33. $\left(\dfrac{3x^{-1}}{4x^0}\right)^{-1} =$

(a) $\dfrac{3x}{4}$ 　　(b) $\dfrac{4x}{3}$ 　　(c) $\dfrac{3}{4x}$ 　　(d) $\dfrac{4}{3x}$ 　　(e) $12x$

34. $\left(\dfrac{x^2}{6}\right)^{-2} \cdot \left(\dfrac{x^4}{2}\right)^{-1} =$

(a) $\dfrac{x^8}{72}$ 　　(b) $\dfrac{72}{x^{16}}$ 　　(c) $72x^8$ 　　(d) $\dfrac{72}{x^{12}}$ 　　(e) $\dfrac{72}{x^8}$

35. $\left(\dfrac{12}{t^7}\right)^{-2} \cdot \left(\dfrac{t^5}{12}\right)^{-3} =$

(a) $\dfrac{12}{t}$ 　　(b) $\dfrac{t^{29}}{12}$ 　　(c) $\dfrac{12}{t^{29}}$ 　　(d) $\dfrac{12^5}{t}$ 　　(e) $\dfrac{144}{t}$

36. $\dfrac{(s^6 t^{-1})^{-1}}{s^3 t^4} =$

(a) $\dfrac{s^9}{t^3}$ 　　　　(b) $\dfrac{1}{s^9 t^3}$ 　　　　(c) $s^9 t^3$ 　　　　(d) $\dfrac{1}{s^9 t^5}$ 　　　　(e) $\dfrac{t^3}{s^3}$

37. $5x^6 y^{-4}(2xy^2)^2 =$
(a) $20x^8$ 　　　　(b) $20x^8 y^8$ 　　　　(c) $20x^8 y^{-8}$ 　　　　(d) $10x^8$ 　　　　(e) $20x^{12} y^{-16}$

38. $(8x^4 y^{-4})^0 (-7x^2 y^{-6})^2 =$
(a) $\dfrac{392x^8}{y^{16}}$ 　　　　(b) $\dfrac{x^4}{49y^{12}}$ 　　　　(c) $\dfrac{49x^4}{y^{12}}$ 　　　　(d) $\dfrac{49y^{12}}{x^4}$ 　　　　(e) $\dfrac{392x^4}{y^8}$

39. $(-2a^{-1} b^0 c^2)^{-3} =$
(a) $\dfrac{8a^3}{c^6}$ 　　　　(b) $-\dfrac{c^6}{8a^3}$ 　　　　(c) $-\dfrac{a^3}{8c^6}$ 　　　　(d) $-\dfrac{a^3 b}{8c^6}$ 　　　　(e) $\dfrac{8a^3}{b^3 c^6}$

Chapter 10:   Polynomials

Section A.   Definitions and Examples of Polynomials

A **monomial** is either a real number (called a **constant monomial**) or a product of a real number with variable(s). Monomials are special types of algebraic expressions (see Chapter 8). Examples of monomials are

$$-9, \quad 4x, \quad -3x^5y, \quad 7.126a^2b^4, \quad \text{and} \quad \frac{13}{10}t^2.$$

The number part of a monomial is called the **coefficient** of the monomial, and the sum of the exponents of the variables called the **degree** of the monomial. For example, $3x^2$ has coefficient 3 and degree 2, and $\frac{4}{5}x^2y^6$ has coefficient $\frac{4}{5}$ and degree $2 + 6 = 8$. The coefficient of $y = 1y$ is 1, and the coefficient of $-t = -1t$ is -1. Constant monomials have degree 0 (except for the constant 0, which has no degree).

Example 1. Find the coefficient and degree of each monomial.

1) $5x^3$ 2) $-8a^2bc^6$ 3) $\frac{7uv}{9}$

Solution: 1) The coefficient is 5 and the degree is 3.

        2) The coefficient is -8 and the degree is $9 = 2 + 1 + 6$.

        3) Notice that $\frac{7uv}{9} = \frac{7}{9}uv$. The coefficient is $\frac{7}{9}$ and the degree is $2 = 1 + 1$.

Two or more monomials are called **like terms** if they have the same **variable parts**. The following pairs of monomials are like terms:

$$\underbrace{6a^2 \text{ and } -7a^2}, \quad \underbrace{-4.18t \text{ and } 18t}, \quad \underbrace{\tfrac{1}{3}x^6y^2 \text{ and } 5y^2x^6}, \quad \text{and} \quad \underbrace{-12 \text{ and } 10.13}.$$

Both variable parts are a^2.   Both variable parts are t. x^6y^2 and y^2x^6 are the same.   Constants are like terms.

Examples of pairs of monomials that are not like terms are:

$$\underbrace{y \text{ and } -y^2}, \quad \underbrace{6a^2x \text{ and } 12ax^2}, \quad \text{and} \quad \underbrace{\tfrac{2}{15}r^5s \text{ and } -\tfrac{1}{2}r^5t}.$$

different exponents.   different exponents. s and t aren't in both terms.

If two or more monomials are like terms, they can be combined into a single monomial.

Rule for combining like terms: Combine the coefficients of the terms, and keep the same variable part.

For example, $-3x + 14x = (-3 + 14)x = 11x$ and $9mn^3 - (-7mn^3) = (9 - (-7))mn^3 = 16mn^3$.

Example 2. Combine like terms.
1) $9x + 13x$ 2) $-x^2y - 15x^2y$ 3) $6st^3 - 17st^3 + 16st^3$

Solution: 1) $9x + 13x = (9 + 13)x = 22x$
   2) $-x^2y - 15x^2y = -1x^2y - 15x^2y = (-1 - 15)x^2y = -16x^2y$
   3) $6st^3 - 17st^3 + 16st^3 = (6 - 17 + 16)st^3 = 5st^3$

A **polynomial** is a sum of monomials. We call each monomial in a polynomial a **term** of the polynomial. If no two terms of a polynomial have the same variable part, then the polynomial is **simplified**.

For example, $5x^2 + 11x - 16$ is a polynomial, and it is simplified. If we write it as
$$5x^2 + 11x + (-16),$$
we see that its terms are $5x^2$, $11x$, and -16. The terms of the polynomial $11xy - 4x - 3y - 6xy$ are $11xy$, $-4x$, $-3y$, and $-6xy$. This polynomial is not simplified since $11xy$ and $-6xy$ have the same variable part. It could be simplified by combining $11xy$ and $-6xy$.

The **degree** of a polynomial is the largest degree of its terms.

Example 3. Find the degree of each polynomial.
1) $-8x^2 - x + 12$ 2) $7x^2 + 6x^4y - 4y^5 - 10$

Solution:
1) The degree is 2:
$$-8x^2 - x + 12 = \underbrace{-8x^2}_{\text{degree 2}} + \underbrace{(-x)}_{\text{degree 1}} + \underbrace{12}_{\text{degree 0}},$$

and the largest degree of the terms is 2.

2) The degree is 5:
$$7x^2 + 6x^4y - 4y^5 - 10 = \underbrace{7x^2}_{\text{degree 2}} + \underbrace{6x^4y}_{\text{degree 5}} + \underbrace{(-4y^5)}_{\text{degree 5}} + \underbrace{(-10)}_{\text{degree 0}},$$

and the largest degree of the terms is 5

If a polynomial has two terms, it is called a **binomial**. If a polynomial has three terms, it is called a **trinomial**. For example, $2x + 3$ and $9y - 6x^2$ are binomials, and $4 + 2t - 9t^2$ and $3a - 5a^2b + ab^2$ are trinomials.

A polynomial of degree 1 is called **linear**. A polynomial of degree 2 is called **quadratic**. For example, the polynomials $3x$, $-x + 4$, and $6a + 5b$ are linear, and the polynomials x^2, $3y^2 - 5y$, and $-\frac{15}{16} + 7t + 9.01t^2$ are quadratic.

Exercises: Chapter 10, Section A

In Exercises 1 - 6, find the coefficient and the degree of each monomial.

1. 4
2. $-5x$
3. $8t$
4. $7y^3$
5. $-8s^4t^3$
6. $\dfrac{-10x^6}{11}$

In Exercises 7 - 10, find the terms of each polynomial and find the coefficient of each term.

7. $3x^2 + 5x - 6$
8. $\dfrac{1}{4}a^3 - a^2$
9. $\dfrac{y^2}{9} - \dfrac{7y}{3} + 8$
10. $\dfrac{3x}{13} + \dfrac{x^2}{12} - \dfrac{1}{2}$

In Exercises 11 - 14, find the degree of each polynomial and state whether the polynomial is linear or quadratic.

11. $2x - 5$
12. $6y^2 + y - 2$
13. $3a - a^2 + 8$
14. $-11 - 9x$

In Exercises 15 - 18, find the degree of each polynomial.

15. $5y - 4x^2$
16. $x^2 + 8x^2y - y^2$
17. $2s^4 + 8s^3t^3 + 9t^4$
18. $-5x^6y^2 + 3xyz^4 + 7x^6 - y^2z^4$

In Exercises 19 - 24, simplify each polynomial.

19. $5x - 3y + 2x + 18y$
20. $-x^2 + 7xy - 16xy + 10$
21. $a^2 + 6ab + (-9a^2) + 2ab$

22. $8st^2 + 4s^2t - st - 19st^2$
23. $16 - 3m^2 - 9m^2n - 23$
24. $x^2 - 3x + 12 + x^2 + 2x - 19$

Section B. Addition and Subtraction of Polynomials

Adding Polynomials

Rule for adding polynomials: To add two or more polynomials, combine their like terms.

For example,

$$\underbrace{(2x + 3) + (-5x + 2) = 2x + 3 + (-5x) + 2}_{\text{Remove the parentheses.}} \quad = \quad \underbrace{2x + (-5x) + 3 + 2 = -3x + 5.}_{\text{Combine like terms.}}$$

Example 1. Add.
1) $(4x - 2) + (6x + 8)$
2) $(-3x^2 + x - 9) + (5x^2 - 7x + 12)$
3) $(5a^2 + 7b^2 - 3) + (-a^2 + 10ab + 9b^2)$
4) $(2y^3 - 7y^2 - 3) + (-9y^2 + 8y) + (8y^3 + 5y^2 - 7y)$
5) $\left(\frac{2}{3}x^2 - 6x + \frac{3}{8}\right) + \left(\frac{1}{9}x^2 + 13x + \frac{7}{12}\right)$

Solution:
1) $4x - 2 + 6x + 8 = 10x + 6$
2) $-3x^2 + x - 9 + 5x^2 - 7x + 12 = 2x^2 - 6x + 3$
3) $5a^2 + 7b^2 - 3 + (-a^2) + 10ab + 9b^2 = 4a^2 + 16b^2 - 3 + 10ab$
4) $2y^3 - 7y^2 - 3 + (-9y^2) + 8y + 8y^3 + 5y^2 - 7y = 10y^3 - 11y^2 + y - 3$
5) $\frac{2}{3}x^2 - 6x + \frac{3}{8} + \frac{1}{9}x^2 + 13x + \frac{7}{12} = \left(\frac{2}{3} + \frac{1}{9}\right)x^2 + (-6 + 13)x + \left(\frac{3}{8} + \frac{7}{12}\right)$

$$= \left(\frac{6}{9} + \frac{1}{9}\right)x^2 + 7x + \left(\frac{9}{24} + \frac{14}{24}\right)$$

$$= \frac{7}{9}x^2 + 7x + \frac{23}{24}$$

Polynomials can added vertically. Let's add $4x^2 + 5x - 7$ and $-x^2 + 5x + 4$ vertically:

$$\begin{array}{r} 4x^2 + 5x - 7 \\ + \quad -x^2 + 5x + 4 \\ \hline 3x^2 + 10x - 3 \end{array} \quad \text{(Add the like terms in each column.)}$$

Example 2. Add.
1) $6x - 4$ and $9x + 7$
2) $-5x^2 + 3xy + y^2$ and $7x^2 - 14xy - 8y^2$
3) $2a^2 - 3$ and $8a^2 + 16a - 7$
4) $5xy^2 + 10x^2 + 14$ and $6y^2 - 12x^2 + 2y - 1$
5) $9a + 3b$, $-a + 4b$, and $-4b - 3a$

Solution:

1)
$$
\begin{array}{r}
6x - 4 \\
+\ \ 9x + 7 \\
\hline
15x + 3
\end{array}
$$

2)
$$
\begin{array}{r}
-5x^2 + 3xy + y^2 \\
+\ \ 7x^2 - 14xy - 8y^2 \\
\hline
2x^2 - 11xy - 7y^2
\end{array}
$$

3)
$$
\begin{array}{r}
2a^2 \qquad -3 \\
+\ \ 8a^2 + 16a - 7 \\
\hline
10a^2 + 16a - 10
\end{array}
$$

4)
$$
\begin{array}{r}
5xy^2 + 10x^2 + 14 \\
+\ \ 6y^2 \qquad - 12x^2 - 1\ + 2y \\
\hline
6y^2 + 5xy^2 - 2x^2 + 13 + 2y
\end{array}
$$

5)
$$
\begin{array}{r}
9a + 3b \\
-a + 4b \\
+\ \ -3a - 4b \\
\hline
5a + 3b
\end{array}
$$

Subtracting Polynomials

Rule for subtracting polynomials: To subtract one polynomial from another, change the sign of each term in the second polynomial, then combine like terms.

For example,

$$
(2x - 5) - (7x - 6) = \underline{2x - 5 - 7x + 6} \qquad = -5x + 1.
$$

$7x$ changed to $-7x$ and -6 changed to 6.

The rule works because $(2x - 5) - (7x - 6)$ is the same as $(2x - 5) + (-1)(7x - 6)$. Observe that the signs of the terms in the second parentheses change as a result of distributing the -1.

Example 3. Subtract.

1) $(8y + 2) - (3y + 12)$ 2) $(-6x^2 + 4x - 9) - (3x^2 - 7x + 2)$
3) $(9a^2 - 3ab + 6b^2) - (-a^2 + ab - 7b^2)$

Solution:

1) $\underbrace{(8y + 2) - (3y + 12) = 8y + 2 - 3y - 12}$ $= 5y - 10$

$3y$ became $-3y$ and 12 became -12.

2) $\underbrace{(-6x^2 + 4x - 9) - (3x^2 - 7x + 2) = -6x^2 + 4x - 9 - 3x^2 + 7x - 2}$ $= -9x^2 + 11x - 11$

$3x^2$ became $-3x^2$, $-7x$ became $7x$, and 2 became -2.

3) $\underbrace{(9a^2 - 3ab + 6b^2) - (-a^2 + ab - 7b^2) = 9a^2 - 3ab + 6b^2 + a^2 - ab + 7b^2}$ $= 10a^2 - 4ab + 13b^2$

$-a^2$ became a^2, ab became $-ab$, and $-7b^2$ became $7b^2$.

As with addition, we can subtract one polynomial from another vertically. Recall that the phrase 'subtract b from a' means $a - b$.

Rule for subtracting polynomials vertically:
1) Set up top and bottom. The polynomial after "from" go on top and the polynomial after "subtract" go on the bottom.
2) Change the sign(s) of the bottom and <u>add</u> that result to the top.

For instance, $(12x - 3) - (5x - 7)$ means that we are subtracting $(5x - 7)$ from $(12x - 3)$. To do this 'vertically', we write:

$$\begin{array}{r} 12x - 3 \quad \text{(top)} \\ - \underline{5x - 7} \quad \text{(bottom)} \end{array} \qquad \text{which becomes} \qquad \begin{array}{r} 12x - 3 \quad \text{(top)} \\ + \underline{-5x + 7} \quad \text{(bottom)} \\ 7x + 4 \end{array}$$

Notice that the subtraction problem turned into an addition problem, and the signs of the terms of the bottom $5x - 7$ changed to $-5x + 7$.

Example 4.
1) Subtract $3a + 5$ from $-a + 3$. 2) Subtract $-6x^2 - 8x$ from $4x^2 + 2x$.
3) Subtract $7y^2 - y + 10$ from $8y^2 - 12$. 4) Subtract $-5x^2 - 3y^2$ from $8y^2 - 9xy$.

Solution:

1)
$$\begin{array}{r} -a + 3 \\ - \underline{3a + 5} \end{array} \quad \text{becomes} \quad \begin{array}{r} -a + 3 \\ + \underline{-3a - 5} \\ -4a - 2 \end{array}$$

2)
$$\begin{array}{r} 4x^2 + 2x \\ - \underline{-6x^2 - 8x} \end{array} \quad \text{becomes} \quad \begin{array}{r} 4x^2 + 2x \\ + \underline{6x^2 + 8x} \\ 10x^2 + 10x \end{array}$$

3)
$$\begin{array}{r} 8y^2 - 12 \\ - \underline{7y^2 - y + 10} \end{array} \quad \text{becomes} \quad \begin{array}{r} 8y^2 - 12 \\ + \underline{-7y^2 + y - 10} \\ y^2 + y - 22 \end{array}$$

4)
$$\begin{array}{r} 8y^2 - 9xy \\ - \underline{-3y^2 - 5x^2} \end{array} \quad \text{becomes} \quad \begin{array}{r} 8y^2 - 9xy \\ + \underline{3y^2 + 5x^2} \\ 11y^2 - 9xy + 5x^2 \end{array}$$

Exercises: Chapter 10, Section B

In Exercises 1 - 20, add or subtract.

1. $(9a + 7) + (-3a + 1)$ 2. $(b - 7) + (6b + 12)$ 3. $(a^2 - 2a) + (4a^2 + 3a)$

4. $(7x + 3) + (x^2 - 9x)$ 5. $(-x^2 + 14y^2) + (-x^2 + 2y)$ 6. $(6mn^2 - 5mn) + (7nm^2 + 3mn)$

7. $(7m^2 - m + 6) + (-m^2 + 15m - 4)$ 8. $(4a - 5b - 2) + (12b - 6ab + 4)$

9. $(p + 3q - 5) + (7 + 9p + 4pq)$ 10. $(6t^2 + 13t - 2) + (7 - 14t + t^2)$

11. $(9x + 1) - (3x + 4)$ 12. $(7a + 2b) - (2a - 3b)$ 13. $(-3s + 8t) - (-4s + t)$

14. $(-2p + 2q) - (7p - q)$ 15. $(x^2 - 8) - (5x - 11)$ 16. $(9uv + 8v) - (-6v + 13u)$

17. $(-x^2 + 10x + 3) - (3x^2 - 2x - 1)$ 18. $(14a^2 - a - 7) - (9a^2 + 4a - 7)$

19. $(5a^2 - 7ab + b^2) - (-3a^2 + 9b^2)$ 20. $(-s^2 - 2st^2 + t^2) - (s^2 - 7t^2)$

In Exercises 21 - 34, choose the correct answer.

21. $(-5x^2 + 18xy) + (7x^2 - 16xy) =$
(a) $2x^2 + 2xy$ (b) $-2x^2 + 2xy$ (c) $2x^2 - 2xy$ (d) $2x^2y$ (e) $12x^2 + 34xy$

22. $(16a^2 - 3a + 15) + (-a^2 + 8a - 29) =$
(a) $15a^2 + 5a - 14$ (b) $16a^2 + 5a + 14$ (c) $15a^2 + 11a - 14$
(d) $15a^2 + 5a + 14$ (e) $6a^3$

23. $(-5x^2 + 18xy) + (7y^2 - 16yx) =$
(a) $-5x^2 - 2xy - 7y^2$ (b) $-5x^2 - 2xy + 7y^2$ (c) $-5x^2 + 2xy + 7y^2$
(d) $2x^2y^2 + 2xy$ (e) $7y^2 - 2xy + 5x^2$

24. $(12a - 15b) - (8b - 22a) =$
(a) $34a + 7b$ (b) $-13a + 23b$ (c) $34a - 23b$ (d) $-10a - 23b$ (e) $34a - 7b$

25. $(3x^2 - 11xy + 4y^2) - (-3x^2 + 5xy - y^2) =$
(a) $6x^4 - 16x^2y^2 + 5y^4$ (b) $6x^2 + 16xy + 5y^2$ (c) $6x^2 - 6xy + 3y^2$
(d) $6x^2 - 16xy + 5y^2$ (e) $-6xy + 5y^2$

26. $(12p + pq - q) - (-3p + 2pq - 9q^2) =$
(a) $15p - pq + 9q^2 - q$ (b) $15p + pq - q + 9q^2$ (c) $9p + 3pq - 9q^2 - q$
(d) $15p + pq - 9q^2 - q$ (e) $9p - pq + 9q^2 - q$

27. $(-4x^2 + 12) + (12 - 3x^2 + 6y^2) =$
(a) $7x^2 + 24 + 6y^2$ (b) $-7x^2 + 6y^2$ (c) $-7x^2 + 6y^2 + 24$
(d) $-7x^2 + 24 - 6y^2$ (e) $7x^2 + 6y^2$

28. $(8x^2 - 13xy - 15x) - (2xy - x - 6xy^2) =$
(a) $8x^2 - 11xy - 14x + 6xy^2$ (b) $8x^2 - 15xy + 14x - 6xy^2$ (c) $8x^2 + 15xy - 14x - 6xy^2$
(d) $8x^2 - 15xy - 14x + 6xy^2$ (e) $8x^2 - 15xy - 14x - 6xy^2$

29. $\left(\frac{2}{3}x^2 + \frac{1}{4}x - \frac{1}{10}\right) + \left(\frac{1}{9}x^2 - \frac{5}{8}x + \frac{2}{3}\right) =$

(a) $\frac{1}{6}x^2 - x - \frac{1}{7}$ (b) $\frac{7}{9}x^2 + \frac{7}{8}x - \frac{17}{30}$ (c) $\frac{7}{9}x^2 + \frac{3}{8}x - \frac{17}{30}$

(d) $\frac{7}{9}x^2 - \frac{3}{8}x + \frac{17}{30}$ (e) $\frac{7}{9}x^2 - \frac{1}{8}x + \frac{23}{30}$

30. $\left(\frac{1}{6}a^2 - ab - \frac{3}{4}b^2\right) - \left(b^2 - \frac{2}{5}ab + \frac{3}{8}a^2\right) =$

(a) $\frac{5}{24}a^2 + \frac{3}{5}ab + \frac{7}{4}b^2$ (b) $-\frac{5}{6}a^2 - \frac{3}{5}ab - \frac{9}{8}b^2$ (c) $-\frac{5}{24}a^2 - \frac{3}{5}ab - b^2$

(d) $-\frac{5}{24}a^2 - \frac{7}{5}ab - \frac{7}{4}b^2$ (e) $-\frac{5}{24}a^2 - \frac{3}{5}ab - \frac{7}{4}b^2$

31. $(0.25x^2 - 1.6xy + 8.034y^2) + (6.15x^2 + 9.8xy - 11.29y^2) =$
(a) $6.04x^2 + 8.2xy + 3.256y^2$ (b) $6.4x^2 - 8.2xy - 3.095y^2$
(c) $6.4x^2 + 8.2xy - 3.256y^2$ (d) $6.4x^2 + 8.2xy + 3.256y^2$
(e) $6.4x^2 + 11.4xy - 3.256y^2$

32. $(7mn + 21.98m - 4.01m^2) - (-16.06mn + 3.2m) =$
(a) $23.06mn + 18.78m + 4.01m^2$ (b) $-4.01m^2 + 23.06mn + 18.78m$
(c) $-4.01m^2 - 9.06mn - 9.81m^2$ (d) $23.06mn - 4.01m^2 + 18.96m$
(e) $-23.06mn + 18.78m - 4.01m^2$

33. $(11x - 10xy) - (7xy - 2y + 6x) + (3x - 19y + xy) =$
(a) $11x - 17xy - 21y$ (b) $8x - 16xy - 17y$ (c) $8x + 16xy - 17y$
(d) $8x - 16xy - 21y$ (e) $-25xy$

34. $(8m + 3) + (9m - 1) - (-5m + 4) =$
(a) $22m - 2$ (b) $22m + 2$ (c) $12m - 2$ (d) $12m + 6$ (e) $-22m + 2$

Section C. Multiplication and Division of Polynomials

Monomial × Monomial

In Chapters 9 and 10, we learned how to multiply monomials together. Let's review how this works.

Example 1. Multiply.

1) $(5x^3y)(3x^7y^2)$ 2) $(-2a^2b^5)(16ab^4)$ 3) $\left(-\frac{2}{9}x^7y^2z\right)\left(-\frac{18}{5}xy^4z^2\right)$

Solution: 1) $(5x^3y)(3x^7y^2) = 15x^{3+7}y^{1+2} = 15x^{10}y^3$

     2) $(-2a^2b^5)(16ab^4) = -32a^{2+1}b^{5+4} = -32a^3b^9$

     3) $\left(-\frac{2}{9}x^7y^2z\right)\left(-\frac{18}{5}xy^4z^2\right) = \frac{4}{5}x^{7+1}y^{2+4}z^{1+2} = \frac{4}{5}x^8y^6z^3$

Monomial × Polynomial

To multiply a monomial by a polynomial, we use the Distributive Property:
$$a(b+c) = ab + ac$$

For example,
$$8x(4x+9) = 8x(4x) + 8x(9) = 32x^2 + 72x \quad \text{and}$$

$$a^2(7a^2 - 6a + 3) = a^2(7a^2) + a^2(-6a) + a^2(3) = 7a^4 - 6a^3 + 3a^2.$$

Example 2. Multiply.

1) $4(7a-6)$ 2) $5x(3x^2-2x+7)$ 3) $-2y^2(6y^2+y-2)$ 4) $-7a^3b^4(-3a^2b^2-4ab^2+7a^2b)$

Solution: 1) $4(7a-6) = 4(7a) + 4(-6) = 28a - 24$

     2) $5x(3x^2-2x+7) = 5x(3x^2) + 5x(-2x) + 5x(7) = 15x^3 - 10x^2 + 35x$

     3) $-2y^2(6y^2+y-2) = -2y^2(6y^2) + (-2y^2)(y) + (-2y^2)(-2) = -12y^4 - 2y^3 + 4y^2$

     4) $-7a^3b^4(-3a^2b^2-4ab^2+7a^2b) = -7a^3b^4(-3a^2b^2) - 7a^3b^4(-4ab^2) - 7a^3b^4(7a^2b)$
$$= 21a^5b^6 + 28a^4b^6 - 49a^5b^5$$

Example 3. Simplify.

1) $2(2x + 1) - 7$ 2) $12a^3 + 3a^2(-a + 2)$ 3) $2(x - 5) + 4(6x - 3)$
4) $a(10 + 3a) - 4a(6 - 7a)$ 5) $-3x(8x + 3y) + 12y(2x - 3y)$

Solution: 1) $2(2x + 1) - 7 = 4x + 2 - 7 = 4x - 5$

2) $3a^2(-a + 2) + 12a^3 = -3a^3 + 6a^2 + 12a^3 = 9a^3 + 6a^2$

3) $2(x - 5) + 4(6x - 3) = 2x - 10 + 24x - 12 = 26x - 22$

4) $a(10 + 3a) - 4a(6 - 7a) = 10a + 3a^2 - 24a + 28a^2 = -14a + 31a^2$

5) $-3x(8x + 3y) + 12y(2x - 3y) = -24x^2 - 9xy + 24yx - 36y^2 = -24x^2 + 15xy - 36y^2$

Binomial × Binomial

To multiply two binomials, say $(A + B)(C + D)$, we distribute both A and B into the second parenthesis and combine. We obtain

$$(A + B)(C + D) = A(C + D) + B(C + D) = \underbrace{AC}_{\text{First terms}} + \underbrace{AD}_{\text{Outer terms}} + \underbrace{BC}_{\text{Inner terms}} + \underbrace{BD}_{\text{Last terms}}$$

This method of multiplying two binomials is often referred to as the **FOIL Method.**

Example 4. Multiply.

1) $(x + 1)(x + 2)$ 2) $(2y - 5)(3y - 1)$ 3) $(7 + 9x)(2 - x^2)$
4) $(3a - 8b)(-a - 4b)$ 5) $(-4x + 7xy)(4y - 8xy)$ 6) $(8a + 3)^2$

Solution:

1) $(x + 1)(x + 2) = \underbrace{x(x)}_{\text{First}} + \underbrace{x(2)}_{\text{Outer}} + \underbrace{1(x)}_{\text{Inner}} + \underbrace{1(2)}_{\text{Last}} = x^2 + \underbrace{2x + x}_{\text{Combine.}} + 2 = x^2 + 3x + 2$

2) $(2y - 5)(3y - 1) = \underbrace{2y(3y)}_{\text{First}} + \underbrace{2y(-1)}_{\text{Outer}} + \underbrace{(-5)(3y)}_{\text{Inner}} + \underbrace{(-5)(-1)}_{\text{Last}}$

$$= 6y^2 \underbrace{-2y - 15y}_{\text{Combine.}} + 5 = 6y^2 - 17y + 5$$

3) $(7 + 9x)(2 - x^2) = 7(2) + 7(-x^2) + 9x(2) + 9x(-x^2) = 14 - 7x^2 + 18x - 9x^3$

4) $(3a - 8b)(-a - 4b) = 3a(-a) + 3a(-4b) + (-8b)(-a) + (-8b)(-4b)$
$$= -3a^2 - 12ab + 8ba + 32b^2$$
$$= -3a^2 - 4ab + 32b^2$$

5) $(-4x + 7xy)(4y - 8xy) = -4x(4y) + (-4x)(-8xy) + 7xy(4y) + 7xy(-8xy)$
$$= -16xy + 32x^2y + 28xy^2 - 56x^2y^2$$

6) $(8a + 3)^2 = (8a + 3)(8a + 3)$
$$= 8a(8a) + 8a(3) + 3(8a) + 3(3)$$
$$= 64a^2 + 24a + 24a + 9$$
$$= 64a^2 + 48a + 9$$

Special Products

Here are some products which often arise:

1. **The Difference of Two Squares:** $(A + B)(A - B) = A^2 - B^2$
2. **The Square of a Sum:** $(A + B)^2 = (A + B)(A + B) = A^2 + 2AB + B^2$
3. **The Square of a Difference:** $(A - B)^2 = (A - B)(A - B) = A^2 - 2AB + B^2$

Let's check these by using the FOIL Method:

$$(A + B)(A - B) = A^2 \underbrace{-AB + AB}_{\text{Combine.}} - B^2 = A^2 - B^2 \;\checkmark$$

$$(A + B)(A + B) = A^2 \underbrace{+AB + AB}_{\text{Combine.}} + B^2 = A^2 + 2AB + B^2 \;\checkmark$$

$$(A - B)(A - B) = A^2 \underbrace{-AB - AB}_{\text{Combine.}} + B^2 = A^2 - 2AB + B^2 \;\checkmark$$

238

For example, $\underbrace{(x+5)(x-5) = (x)^2 - (5)^2}_{\text{Set } A=x \text{ and } B=5 \text{ in Product 1.}} = x^2 - 25$ and

$$(y-12)^2 = \underbrace{(y)^2 - 2(y)(12) + (12)^2}_{\text{Set } A=y \text{ and } B=12 \text{ in Product 3.}} = y^2 - 24y + 144.$$

These examples could also be done by using the FOIL Method directly:

$$(x+5)(x-5) = x^2 - 5x + 5x - 25 = x^2 - 25 \quad \text{and}$$

$$(y-12)^2 = (y-12)(y-12) = y^2 - 12y - 12y + 144 = y^2 - 24y + 144$$

Be careful not to make the following mistakes:

BEWARE: $(A+B)^2 \neq A^2 + B^2$, $(A-B)^2 \neq A^2 + B^2$ and $(A-B)^2 \neq A^2 - B^2$.

Example 5. Multiply.
1) $(x+3)(x-3)$ 2) $(5y-2)(5y+2)$ 3) $(x+4)^2$
4) $(b-8)^2$ 5) $(4+9x)^2$

Solution: 1) $\underbrace{(x+3)(x-3) = (x)^2 - (3)^2}_{\text{Set } A=x \text{ and } B=3 \text{ in Product 1.}} = x^2 - 9$

2) $\underbrace{(5y-2)(5y+2) = (5y)^2 - (2)^2}_{\text{Set } A=5y \text{ and } B=2 \text{ in Product 1.}} = 25y^2 - 4$

3) $\underbrace{(x+4)^2 = (x)^2 + 2(x)(4) + (4)^2}_{\text{Set } A=x \text{ and } B=4 \text{ in Product 2.}} = x^2 + 8x + 16$

4) $\underbrace{(b-8)^2 = (b)^2 - 2(b)(8) + (8)^2}_{\text{Set } A=b \text{ and } B=8 \text{ in Product 3.}} = b^2 - 16b + 64$

5) $\underbrace{(4+9x)^2 = (4)^2 + 2(4)(9x) + (9x)^2}_{\text{Set } A=4 \text{ and } B=9x \text{ in Product 2.}} = 16 + 72x + 81x^2$

Polynomial × Polynomial

To multiply **any** two polynomials, we use the Distributive Property. To demonstrate, let's multiply $x + 3$ by $x^2 + 2x - 3$ horizontally:

$$(x + 3)(x^2 + 2x - 3) = x(x^2) + x(2x) + x(-3) + 3(x^2) + 3(2x) + 3(-3)$$
$$= x^3 + 2x^2 - 3x + 3x^2 + 6x - 9$$
$$= x^3 + 5x^2 + 3x - 9$$

Polynomials can also be multiplied vertically:

$$
\begin{array}{r}
x^2 + 2x - 3 \\
\times \qquad x + 3 \\
\hline
3x^2 + 6x - 9 \\
+ \quad x^3 + 2x^2 - 3x \\
\hline
x^3 + 5x^2 + 3x - 9 \\
\end{array}
$$

(The product of 3 and $x^2 + 2x - 3$.)

(The product of x and $x^2 + 2x - 3$.)

(Add.)

Example 6. Multiply horizontally.

1) $(x + 3)(x^2 + 2x - 3)$
2) $(4a^2 - 5)(2a^2 - 3a + 3)$
3) $(x + 2y - 1)(x - 3y - 1)$
4) $(6t + 1)(2t - 2)(t + 3)$
5) $(4x + 1)^2(4x - 1)$
6) $(2y - 3)^3$

Solution:

1) $(x + 3)(x^2 + 2x - 3) = x(x^2) + x(2x) + x(-3) + 3(x^2) + 3(2x) + 3(-3)$
$$= x^3 + 2x^2 - 3x + 3x^2 + 6x - 9$$
$$= x^3 + 5x^2 + 3x - 9$$

2) $(4a^2 - 5)(2a^2 - 3a + 3) = 4a^2(2a^2) + 4a^2(-3a) + 4a^2(3) + (-5)(2a^2) + (-5)(-3a) + (-5)(3)$
$$= 8a^4 - 12a^3 + 12a^2 - 10a^2 + 15a - 15$$
$$= 8a^4 - 12a^3 + 2a^2 + 15a - 15$$

3) $(x + 2y - 1)(x - 3y - 1)$
$$= x(x) + x(-3y) + x(-1) + 2y(x) + 2y(-3y) + 2y(-1) + (-1)(x) + (-1)(-3y) + (-1)(-1)$$
$$= x^2 - 3xy - x + 2yx - 6y^2 - 2y - x + 3y + 1$$
$$= x^2 - xy - 2x - 6y^2 + y + 1$$

4) $\underbrace{(6t + 1)(2t - 2)(t + 3) = (12t^2 - 10t - 2)(t + 3)}_{\text{FOIL } (6t+1)(2t-2) \text{ first.}} = 12t^3 + 36t^2 - 10t^2 - 30t - 2t - 6$

$$= 12t^3 + 26t^2 - 32t - 6$$

240

5) $(4x+1)^2(4x-1) = (4x+1)\underbrace{(4x+1)(4x-1)}_{\text{Use Product 1.}} = \underbrace{(4x+1)(16x^2-1) = 64x^3 - 4x + 16x^2 - 1}_{\text{Use the FOIL Method.}}$

6) $(2y-3)^3 = (2y-3)(2y-3)(2y-3) = (4y^2 - 12y + 9)(2y-3)$

$$= 4y^2(2y) + 4y^2(-3) + (-12y)(2y) + (-12y)(-3) + 9(2y) + 9(-3)$$
$$= 8y^3 - 12y^2 - 24y^2 + 36y + 18y - 27$$
$$= 8y^3 - 36y^2 + 54y - 27$$

Example 7. Multiply vertically.

1) $(a+2)(a^2 + 4a - 1)$ 2) $(3y-7)(-5y^3 - 3y^2 + 2)$ 3) $(x+2y-3)(2x-3y+5)$

Solution:

1)
$$
\begin{array}{r}
a^2 + 4a - 1 \\
\times \quad\quad a + 2 \\
\hline
2a^2 + 8a - 2 \\
a^3 + 4a^2 - a \quad\quad\\
\hline
a^3 + 6a^2 + 7a - 2
\end{array}
$$

(The product of 2 and $a^2 + 4a - 1$.)
(The product of a and $a^2 + 4a - 1$.)
(Add.)

2)
$$
\begin{array}{r}
-5y^3 - 3y^2 + 2 \\
\times \quad\quad 3y - 7 \\
\hline
35y^3 + 21y^2 \quad\quad - 14 \\
-15y^4 - 9y^3 \quad\quad + 6y \quad\quad \\
\hline
-15y^4 + 26y^3 + 21y^2 + 6y - 14
\end{array}
$$

(The product of -7 and $-5y^3 - 3y^2 + 2$.)
(The product of $3y$ and $-5y^3 - 3y^2 + 2$.)
(Add.)

3)
$$
\begin{array}{r}
x + 2y - 3 \\
\times \quad\quad 2x - 3y + 5 \\
\hline
5x + 10y - 15 \\
-3xy - 6y^2 \quad\quad + 9y \quad\quad \\
2x^2 + 4xy \quad\quad - 6x \quad\quad\quad\quad \\
\hline
2x^2 + xy - 6y^2 - x + 19y - 15
\end{array}
$$

(The product of 5 and $x + 2y - 3$.)
(The product of $-3y$ and $x + 2y - 3$.)
(The product of $2x$ and $x + 2y - 3$.)
(Add.)

Monomial ÷ Monomial

In Chapter 9, we learned how to divide monomials. Let's have a quick review.

Example 8. Divide.

1) $\dfrac{12x^7}{3x^3}$ 2) $(35pq^7) \div (-5pq^2)$ 3) $\dfrac{-42x^2y^{12}}{-6xy^9}$ 4) $(-8x^5y^9z^3) \div (28x^4y^2z)$

Solution: 1) $\dfrac{12x^7}{3x^3} = 4x^4$ 2) $(35pq^7) \div (-5pq^2) = \underbrace{\dfrac{35pq^7}{-5pq^2}}_{\text{Write the problem as a fraction.}} = -7q^5$

3) $\dfrac{-42x^2y^{12}}{-6xy^9} = 7xy^3$ 4) $(-8x^5y^9z^3) \div (28x^4y^2z) = \underbrace{\dfrac{-8x^5y^9z^3}{28x^4y^2z}}_{\text{Write the problem as a fraction.}} = -\dfrac{2}{7}xy^7z^2$

Polynomial ÷ Monomial

To divide a polynomial by a monomial, we will use the properties
$$\frac{A+B}{C} = \frac{A}{C} + \frac{B}{C} \quad \text{and} \quad \frac{A-B}{C} = \frac{A}{C} - \frac{B}{C}.$$

For example,

$$\frac{24x^2+6}{6} = \frac{24x^2}{6} + \frac{6}{6} = 4x^2 + 1 \quad \text{and} \quad \frac{21t^3 - 7t^2 + 14t}{-7t} = \frac{21t^3}{-7t} - \frac{7t^2}{-7t} + \frac{14t}{-7t} = -3t^2 + t - 2.$$

Example 9. Divide.

1) $\dfrac{18x^3 + 21x^2}{3x}$ 2) $\dfrac{25y^2 + 15y}{-5y}$ 3) $\dfrac{-6x^4y^6 - 8x^2y^{10}}{-6x^2y^4}$

4) $(-32a^6b^5 + 12a^9b^{14} - 10a^8b) \div (12a^4b)$

Solution:

1) $\dfrac{18x^3 + 21x^2}{3x} = \dfrac{18x^3}{3x} + \dfrac{21x^2}{3x} = 6x^2 + 7x$

2) $\dfrac{25y^2 + 15y}{-5y} = \dfrac{25y^2}{-5y} + \dfrac{15y}{-5y} = -5y + (-3) = -5y - 3$

3) $\dfrac{-6x^4y^6 - 8x^2y^{10}}{-6x^2y^4} = \dfrac{-6x^4y^6}{-6x^2y^4} - \dfrac{8x^2y^{10}}{-6x^2y^4} = x^2y^2 - \left(\dfrac{4}{-3}y^6\right) = x^2y^2 + \dfrac{4}{3}y^6$

4) Write the problem in fraction form:

$$\frac{-32a^6b^5 + 12a^9b^{14} - 10a^8b}{12a^4b} = \frac{-32a^6b^5}{12a^4b} + \frac{12a^9b^{14}}{12a^4b} - \frac{10a^8b}{12a^4b} = -\frac{8}{3}a^2b^4 + a^5b^{13} - \frac{5}{6}a^4$$

Exercises: Chapter 10, Section C

In Exercises 1 - 23, multiply.

1. $(2x^3)(6x)$

2. $(-6a^5)(-9a)$

3. $(-5st^3)(12s^2t^8)$

4. $4(12a + 3)$

5. $8x^3(9x^4 - 2x)$

6. $7t^2(8t^3 - 6t^2)$

7. $-2p^3(-12p + 8p^3)$

8. $7x^2y^8(-3xy^3 + 4x^5y^2)$

9. $5(3a^2 + 6a - 2)$

10. $-3x^4y^3(5x^2 - 7x^2y^2 + 9y^2)$

11. $(x + 4)(x + 1)$

12. $(t - 3)(t + 8)$

13. $(2y + 5)(3y + 1)$

14. $(2x + 1)(5x + 3)$

15. $(6x - 7)(2x + 3)$

16. $(2y^2 + 7y)(3y - 1)$

17. $(x + 7)(x - 7)$

18. $(8 - 4p)(8 + 4p)$

19. $(2x^2 + 10y)(2x^2 - 10y)$

20. $(x + 4)^2$

21. $(5y - 3)^2$

22. $(x + 3)(x^2 - 2x + 4)$

23. $(5a - 2)(-2a^2 + 7a - 1)$

In Exercises 24 - 38, choose the correct answer.

24. $(-4x^7)(3x^4) =$
(a) $-12x^{11}$
(b) $12x^{11}$
(c) $-12x^{28}$
(d) $-12x^3$
(e) $12x^{28}$

25. $(3a^3b^6)(-ab^2)(8a^5b^3) =$
(a) $-24a^9b^{11}$
(b) $-24a^8b^{11}$
(c) $-24a^{15}b^{36}$
(d) $24a^9b^{11}$
(e) $24a^7b^8$

26. $\left(-\frac{5}{6}ay^{13}\right)(-2a^4y^{11}) =$
(a) $-\frac{5}{3}a^5y^{24}$
(b) $\frac{5}{3}a^5y^{24}$
(c) $\frac{5}{6}a^4y^{143}$
(d) $-\frac{17}{6}a^5y^{24}$
(e) $\frac{5}{3}a^4y^{143}$

27. $4a(5a - 7) =$
(a) $20a^2 - 7$
(b) $20a^2 - 28$
(c) $9a^2 - 11a$
(d) $20a^2 - 28a$
(e) $20a - 28$

28. $-3t^4(5t + 6t^3) =$
(a) $-15t^5 + 6t^3$ (b) $-15t^5 + 18t^7$ (c) $-15t^4 - 18t^{12}$ (d) $-15t^5 - 18t^7$ (e) $-33t^{12}$

29. $6x^3y^4(-2x^2y^5 + 5xy^2) =$
(a) $12x^5y^9 - 30x^4y^6$ (b) $-12x^6y^{20} + 30x^3y^8$ (c) $18x^9y^{15}$
(d) $-12x^5y^9 + 5xy^2$ (e) $-12x^5y^9 + 30x^4y^6$

30. $8x^2(4x^3 - 5x^2 - 11) =$
(a) $32x^5 - 40x^4 - 88x^2$ (b) $32x^5 - 5x^2 - 11$ (c) $32x^6 - 40x^4 - 88$
(d) $32x^5 - 40x^4 - 11$ (e) $32x^4 - 5x - 11$

31. $(3x + 8)(2x - 9) =$
(a) $6x^2 + 11x - 72$ (b) $-5x - 72$ (c) $6x^2 - 11x - 72$
(d) $6x^2 - 72$ (e) $6x^2 - 43x - 72$

32. $(6t - 11)(6t + 11) =$
(a) $6t^2 - 121$ (b) $36t^2 - 121$ (c) $36t^2 + 121$
(d) $36t^2 + 132t - 121$ (e) $36t^2 - 132t - 121$

33. $(3 - 4x)^2 =$
(a) $16x^2 + 9$ (b) $16x^2 - 24x + 9$ (c) $16x^2 - 24x - 9$ (d) $16x^2 - 9$ (e) $4x^2 - 9$

34. $(5x + 3)(2x^2 - x + 5) =$
(a) $10x^3 - x^2 + 22x + 15$ (b) $10x^3 - x^2 - 22x + 15$ (c) $10x^3 + x^2 + 28x + 15$
(d) $10x^3 + 11x^2 + 22x + 15$ (e) $10x^3 + x^2 + 22x + 15$

35. $(2t - 7)^3 =$
(a) $8t^3 - 84t^2 + 294t - 343$ (b) $8t^3 + 84t^2 + 294t + 343$ (c) $8t^3 - 74t^2 + 284t - 343$
(d) $8t^3 - 84t^2 - 294t - 343$ (e) $8t^3 - 343$

36. $(2m + 1)(3m - 2)(m + 10) =$
(a) $6m^3 + 59m^2 - 8m + 20$ (b) $6m^3 + 61m^2 + 8m - 20$ (c) $6m^3 + 61m^2 - 8m - 20$
(d) $6m^3 + 59m^2 - 12m - 20$ (e) $6m^3 - 20$

37. $(x^2 - 4x + 7)(3x^2 + x - 2) =$
(a) $3x^4 + 13x^3 + 23x^2 + x - 14$ (b) $3x^4 - 13x^3 - 27x^2 + 15x - 14$
(c) $3x^4 - 11x^3 - 15x^2 - x + 14$ (d) $3x^4 - 11x^3 + 15x^2 + 15x - 14$
(e) $3x^4 - 13x^3 - 15x^2 + 17x + 14$

38. $(6a + 4b - 5)^2 =$
(a) $36a^2 + 16b^2 + 48ab + 60a + 40b + 25$
(b) $36a^2 + 16b^2 + 48ab - 60a - 40b + 25$
(c) $36a^2 - 16b^2 - 48ab - 60a + 40b - 25$
(d) $36a^2 + 16b^2 + 25$
(e) $20a^2b^2 - 48ab - 60a + 40b - 25$

In Exercises 39 - 49, simplify.

39. $2(5x + 3) + 8(2x - 1)$

40. $-7a^2(a - 5) + 6a^2(3a + 1)$

41. $2p^2(-p^2 + 4p) - 5p(5p^2 - p)$

42. $-10y(3 - 2y) + 8y^2(y + 3) - 7(y^2 + 3)$

43. $3x^2(x + 5y) - 4y(x^2 + 3) - x^2(x - 6)$

44. $(x - 1)(x + 3) + (x + 9)(x + 2)$

45. $(2a - 5)(a + 1) - (a + 2)(2a - 3)$

46. $(y - 5)(y + 5) + (y - 7)(y + 7)$

47. $(x - 2)^2 + (x + 4)^2$

48. $(r - 3) - (r + 7)^2$

49. $(y + 12)^2 + (y - 6)(y + 2)$

In Exercises 51 - 60, divide.

51. $\dfrac{9x^6}{3x}$

52. $\dfrac{-20b^{10}}{-2b^6}$

53. $\dfrac{32xy^7}{-8xy^3}$

54. $\dfrac{16a^5b^3c}{28a^3b^3}$

55. $\dfrac{9x + 27}{3}$

56. $\dfrac{-16y^3 + 18y^2}{2y}$

57. $\dfrac{42x^5 - 18x^{12}}{-6x^4}$

58. $\dfrac{-a^5 - 13x^4}{-a^2}$

59. $\dfrac{-10b^7 + 14b^6 - 2b^3}{2b^2}$

60. $\dfrac{36x^6y^9 + 24x^4y^8 - 16x^{12}y^{10}}{-12x^3y^4}$

In Exercises 61 - 67, choose the correct answer.

61. $\dfrac{-21x^5}{3x^3} =$

(a) $7x^8$ (b) $-7x^8$ (c) $-7x^2$ (d) $7x^2$ (e) -7

62. $\dfrac{-42x^{12}y^{15}}{-7x^{10}y^7} =$

(a) $6x^2y^8$ (b) $-6x^2y^8$ (c) $-6x^2y^{22}$ (d) $6x^{22}y^{22}$ (e) $6xy^8$

63. $\dfrac{30y^5 + 12y^3}{6y^2} =$

(a) $5y^3 + 12y^3$ (b) $30y^5 + 2y$ (c) $7y^4$ (d) $5y^5 + 2y^3$ (e) $5y^3 + 2y$

64. $\dfrac{-8x^4 + 24x^2}{-4x^2} =$

(a) $2x^2 - 24x^2$ (b) $-2x^2 + 6$ (c) $2x^2 - 6$ (d) $2x^2 - 6x$ (e) $26x^2$

65. $\dfrac{28a^5b^2 - 16a^9b^5}{-4a^3b^2} =$

(a) $-7a^2 - 4a^6b^3$ (b) $-7a^2 - 16a^9b^5$ (c) $-7a^2b + 4a^6b^3$
(d) $-7a^2 + 4a^6b^3$ (e) $7a^2 - 4a^6b^3$

66. $\dfrac{36t^5 - 16t^4 + 32t^2}{2t^2} =$

(a) $18t^3 - 8t^2 + 16$ (b) $18t^3 - 16t^4 + 32t^2$ (c) $36t^5 - 16t^4 + 16$
(d) $18t^3 + 8t^2 - 16$ (e) $18t^3 - 8t^2 + 32t$

67. $\dfrac{-6a^3b^4 - 27a^5b^7 + 39a^2b^4}{-3ab^4} =$

(a) $2a^2 - 27a^5b^7 + 39a^2b^4$ (b) $-6a^3b^4 - 27a^5b^7 - 13a$ (c) $2a^2 - 9a^4b^3 + 13a$
(d) $2a^2 + 9a^4b^3 - 13a$ (e) $-2a^2 - 9a^4b^3 - 13a$

Chapter 11:   Factoring Polynomials

Section A. Factoring the Greatest Common Factor

In Chapter 1 (Section E), we discussed factoring natural numbers. Recall that the **factors of a natural number** n are those natural numbers which divide into n without remainder. For example, the factors of 6 are 1, 2, 3, and 6 since $\frac{6}{1} = 6$, $\frac{6}{2} = 3$, $\frac{6}{3} = 2$, and $\frac{6}{6} = 1$. In each case, there is no remainder.

The **factors of a polynomial** P are those polynomials which divide into P without remainder. For instance,

$$\frac{2x^2 + 6x}{1} = 2x^2 + 6x, \quad \frac{2x^2 + 6x}{2x} = x + 3, \quad \frac{2x^2 + 6x}{x} = 2x + 6, \quad \text{and} \quad \frac{2x^2 + 6x}{2} = x^2 + 3x.$$

In each case, the quotients are polynomials. Notice that

$$1(2x^2 + 6x) = 2x^2 + 6x, \quad 2x(x + 3) = 2x^2 + 6x, \quad x(2x + 6) = 2x^2 + 6x, \text{ and } 2(x^2 + 3x) = 2x^2 + 6x.$$

Therefore, 1, $2x^2 + 6x$, $2x$, $x + 3$, x, $2x + 6$, 2, and $x^2 + 3x$ are factors of $2x^2 + 6x$.

The process of writing a polynomial as a product of polynomials is called **factoring**. Our goal in this chapter is to learn different ways of factoring polynomials.

In this section, we will learn how to factor the greatest common factor from a polynomial. Recall from Chapter 1 (Section E) that the **greatest common factor (GCF)** of two or more natural numbers is the largest natural number which is a factor of each of the given numbers. For example, the GCF of 6 and 15 is 3, because 3 is the largest number which divides into both 6 and 15 without a remainder.

The **greatest common factor (GCF)** of two or more monomials is the 'largest' monomial which is a factor of each of the given monomials.

Rule for finding the GCF:
1) The coefficient of the GCF is just the GCF of the coefficients of the given monomials.
2) If variables of the same bases appear in more than one of the monomials, compare variables of the same bases and the choose the variable with the **smallest** exponent.
3) Multiply the results found in 1) and 2).

For example, the GCF of $5x^3$ and $10x^2$ is $5x^2$ because the GCF of 5 and 10 is 5, and x^2 has a smaller exponent than x^3. Notice that

$$\frac{5x^3}{5x^2} = x \quad \text{and} \quad \frac{10x^2}{5x^2} = 2.$$

This means that $5x^2(x) = 5x^3$ and $5x^2(2) = 10x^2$. In other words, $5x^2$ is a factor of both $5x^3$ and $10x^2$.

Similarly, the GCF of $8x^4y^7$ and $20x^3y^{12}$ is $4x^3y^7$; the GCF of 8 and 20 is 4, the smallest exponent of x^4 and x^3 is 3, so x^3 is chosen, and the smallest exponent of y^{12} and y^7 is 7, so y^7 is chosen.

Example 1. Find the GCF.
1) $4x^3$ and $6x^5$ 2) $9y^4$ and $3y^8$ 3) $16a^5b^2$ and $24ab^4$
4) $25b^5$ and $15a^2b^6$ 5) $7x^3y^6$ and $12x^8$ 6) $12x^5$, $9x^7$, and $21x^2$

Solution: 1) $2x^3$ 2) $3y^4$ 3) $8ab^2$ 4) $5b^5$ 5) x^3 6) $3x^2$

A polynomial can have many different factorizations. As we've seen before,

$$\begin{aligned} 2x^2 + 6x &= 1(2x^2 + 6x) \\ &= 2x(x + 3) \\ &= x(2x + 6) \\ &= 2(x^2 + 3x). \end{aligned}$$

We are interested in the factorization whose monomial factor is the GCF of the terms of $2x^2 + 6x$, which is $2x(x + 3)$. Notice that the GCF of $2x^2$ and $6x$ is $2x$, which is a monomial factor of the product $2x(x + 3)$. We say that $2x(x + 3)$ is the **complete factorization** of $2x^2 + 6x$.

Rule for factoring the GCF from a polynomial:
1) Find the GCF of the terms of the polynomial.
2) Divide the polynomial by the GCF.
3) Multiply the GCF by the answer found in 2) to get the original expression.

Let's factor $5x^3 + 10x^2$ completely. Notice that the GCF of $5x^3$ and $10x^2$ is $5x^2$, and

$$\frac{5x^3 + 10x^2}{5x^2} = \frac{5x^3}{5x^2} + \frac{10x^2}{5x^2} = x + 2.$$

Therefore, $5x^3 + 10x^2 = 5x^2(x + 2)$.

Example 2. Factor.
1) $3x + 12$ 2) $6x^2 - 16x^3$ 3) $24a^2b^5 + 16a^5b^3$
4) $9mn^4 - 15m^2$ 5) $x^3 - 8x^2 + 10x$

Solution:

1) The GCF of $3x$ and 12 is 3, and $\dfrac{3x+12}{3} = \dfrac{3x}{3} + \dfrac{12}{3} = x + 4$. Therefore,

$$3x + 12 = 3(x + 4).$$

2) The GCF of $6x^2$ and $16x^3$ is $2x^2$, and $\dfrac{6x^2 - 16x^3}{2x^2} = \dfrac{6x^2}{2x^2} - \dfrac{16x^3}{2x^2} = 3 - 8x$. Therefore,

$$6x^2 - 16x^3 = 2x^2(3 - 8x).$$

3) The GCF of $24a^2b^5$ and $16a^5b^3$ is $8a^2b^3$, and

$$\dfrac{24a^2b^5 + 16a^5b^3}{8a^2b^3} = \dfrac{24a^2b^5}{8a^2b^3} + \dfrac{16a^5b^3}{8a^2b^3} = 3b^2 + 2a^3.$$

Therefore,

$$24a^2b^5 + 16a^5b^3 = 8a^2b^3(3b^2 + 2a^3).$$

4) The GCF of $9mn^4$ and $15m^2$ is $3m$, and $\dfrac{9mn^4 - 15m^2}{3m} = \dfrac{9mn^4}{3m} - \dfrac{15m^2}{3m} = 3n^4 - 5m$.
Therefore,

$$9mn^4 - 15m^2 = 3m(3n^4 - 5m).$$

5) The GCF of x^3, $8x^2$, and $10x$ is x, and $\dfrac{x^3 - 8x^2 + 10x}{x} = \dfrac{x^3}{x} - \dfrac{8x^2}{x} + \dfrac{10x}{x} = x^2 - 8x + 10$.
Therefore,

$$x^3 - 8x^2 + 10x = x(x^2 - 8x + 10).$$

Example 3. Factor.
1) $x(x + 2) + 4(x + 2)$ 2) $a(b^2 - 3) - 2(b^2 - 3)$ 3) $x^2(x - 3)^2 + 5(x - 3)$

Solution:
1) $\underbrace{x(x + 2) + 4(x + 2)}_{\text{Similar to } xy+4y=y(x+4).} = (x + 2)(x + 4)$

2) $\underbrace{a(b^2 - 3) - 2(b^2 - 3)}_{\text{Similar to } ax-2x=x(a-2).} = (b^2 - 3)(a - 2)$

3) $\underbrace{x^2(x - 3)^2 + 5(x - 3)}_{\text{Similar to } x^2y^2+5y=y(x^2y+5).} = (x - 3)\underbrace{[x^2(x - 3) + 5]}_{\text{Simplify.}} = (x - 3)(x^3 - 3x^2 + 5)$

Rule for factoring: Whenever you factor a polynomial, try to factor a GCF first.

Exercises: Chapter 11, Section A

In Exercises 1 - 13, factor the GCF from each polynomial.

1. $5y + 35$ 2. $14b^2 - 7$ 3. $5x^2 + 10x - 20$ 4. $4t^2 + 12t - 28$

5. $3x^3 - 24x^2$ 6. $11p^3 + 5p^2$ 7. $8q^3 + 12q^2$ 8. $18x^4 + 27x^3 - 9x^2$

9. $32y^4 - 16y^3 + 8y^2$ 10. $20a^2b^2 + 22ab^3$ 11. $6s^3t - 5s^3t^2 + s^2t^2$

12. $27p^5q^3 + 3p^4q^6 - 6p^6q$ 13. $15x^2y^3z^3 - 10xy^4z^3 + 35xy^3z^4$

In Exercises 14 - 23, factor completely.

14. $20x^4 + 4x^2 =$
(a) $5x^2(4x^2 + 1)$ (b) $4x(5x^2 + 1)$ (c) $x^2(20x^2 + 1)$ (d) $4x^2(5x^2 + 1)$
(e) $4x(5x^3 + 1)$

15. $6a^3 - 27a^7 =$
(a) $3a^3(2 - 9a^4)$ (b) $2a^3(3 - 9a^4)$ (c) $3a^2(2a - 9a^4)$ (d) $6a^3(1 - 4a^4)$
(e) $3(2a^3 - 9a^4)$

16. $16x^7 + 20x^4 - 28x^2 =$
(a) $2x^2(8x^5 + 10x^2 - 14)$ (b) $x^2(16x^5 + 20x^2 - 28)$ (c) $4x^7(4 + 5x^3 - 7x^5)$
(d) $4x^2(4x^5 - 5x^2 + 7)$ (e) $4x^2(4x^5 + 5x^2 - 7)$

17. $56a^5b^2 - 14a^4b^3 - 7a^5b =$
(a) $7a^4b(8ab - 2b - 1)$ (b) $7a^4b(8ab - 2a^2 - b)$ (c) $7a^4b(8ab - 2b^2 - a)$
(d) $7a^4b(8a - 2b - a^2)$ (e) $7a^4b^2(8a - 2b - ab)$

18. $x^2y - xy^2 + xy =$
(a) $y(x^2 - xy + 1)$ (b) $x(xy - y^2 + 1)$ (c) $xy(x - y)$
(d) $xy(x - y + 1)$ (e) $x^2y^2(y - x + xy)$

19. $2x(x + 1) + 7(x + 1) =$
(a) $(x + 1)(2x + 7)$　　　　(b) $(x + 1)^2(2x + 7)$　　　　(c) $(x + 7)(2x + 1)$
(d) $(x + 1)(2x + 7)^2$　　　　(e) $(x + 1)^2(2x + 7)^2$

20. $6m(n - 12) + 11(n - 12) =$
(a) $(n - 12)^2(6m + 11)$　　　　(b) $(n - 12)(6m - 11)$　　　　(c) $(n - 12)(6m + 11)^2$
(d) $(n - 11)(6m + 12)$　　　　(e) $(n - 12)(6m + 11)$

21. $a(b + 3) - b(b + 3) =$
(a) $(a + b)(b - 3)$　　　　(b) $(a - b)(b + 3)^2$　　　　(c) $(a - b)(b + 3)$
(d) $(a - b)(b - 3)$　　　　(e) $(a - b)^2(b + 3)$

22. $3(x + 5) + (x + 5)^2 =$
(a) $(x + 5)^2(x + 3)$　　　　(b) $(x + 5)(x + 3)$　　　　(c) $(x + 5)(x + 8)$
(d) $(x + 5)(4x + 5)$　　　　(e) $(x + 5)(3x + 1)$

23. $2a(a - 1)^2 + b(a - 1) =$
(a) $(a - 1)(2a^2 + 2a + b)$　　　　(b) $(a - 1)(2a^2 - a + b)$　　　　(c) $(a - 1)^2(2a + b)$
(d) $(a - 1)(2a^2 - 2a + b)$　　　　(e) $(a - 1)(2a + b)$

Section B. Factoring the Difference of Two Squares

Formula for factoring the difference of two squares: $A^2 - B^2 = (A + B)(A - B)$

Recall that a natural number is a perfect square if it is the square of another natural number. Some perfect squares are

$$1 = 1^2, \quad 4 = 2^2, \quad 9 = 3^2, \quad 16 = 4^2, \quad \text{and so on.}$$

A monomial is a **perfect square** if it is the square of another monomial. The following are examples of perfect squares:

$$9x^2 = (3x)^2, \quad 36a^2b^2 = (6ab)^2, \quad t^4 = (t^2)^2, \quad \text{and} \quad 121x^6y^{10} = (11x^3y^5)^2.$$

Observe that the exponent of each variable in the above examples are even numbers. This will always occur in a perfect square. For instance, $4x^5$ is not a perfect square because the exponent 5 is not an even number.

To factor a difference of two squares, use the formula mentioned above. For example,

$$x^2 - 4 = \underbrace{(x)^2 - (2)^2 = (x + 2)(x - 2)}_{\text{Let } A=x \text{ and } B=2 \text{ in the formula.}} \quad \text{and} \quad 25a^2 - 169 = \underbrace{(5a)^2 - (13)^2 = (5a + 13)(5a - 13)}_{\text{Let } A=5a \text{ and } B=13 \text{ in the formula.}}.$$

Example 1. Factor.

1) $x^2 - 1$ 2) $49 - t^2$ 3) $4x^2 - 25$ 4) $100a^2 - 81b^2$
5) $16x^2y^2 - 1$ 6) $m^4 - 36$ 7) $49s^{12} - 64t^{24}$ 8) $x^4y^6z^8 - 121w^2$

Solution:
1) $x^2 - 1 = (x)^2 - (1)^2 = (x + 1)(x - 1)$
2) $49 - t^2 = (7)^2 - (t)^2 = (7 + t)(7 - t)$
3) $4x^2 - 25 = (2x)^2 - (5)^2 = (2x + 5)(2x - 5)$
4) $100a^2 - 81b^2 = (10a)^2 - (9b)^2 = (10a + 9b)(10a - 9b)$
5) $16x^2y^2 - 1 = (4xy)^2 - (1)^2 = (4xy + 1)(4xy - 1)$
6) $m^4 - 36 = (m^2)^2 - (6)^2 = (m^2 + 6)(m^2 - 6)$
7) $49s^{12} - 64t^{24} = (7s^6)^2 - (8t^{12})^2 = (7s^6 + 8t^{12})(7s^6 - 8t^{12})$
8) $x^4y^6z^8 - 121w^2 = (x^2y^3z^4)^2 - (11w)^2 = (x^2y^3z^4 + 11w)(x^2y^3z^4 - 11w)$

If the GCF of a binomial is not 1, factor it out first. Then see if the remaining factor is a difference of two squares. If it is, factor it using the formula. For example,

$$5x^3 - 45x = \underbrace{5x(x^2 - 9)}_{\text{The GCF is } 5x.} = 5x \underbrace{(x + 3)(x - 3)}_{x^2-9 \text{ factored.}}.$$

And so, $5x^3 - 45x$ factors **completely** as $5x(x+3)(x-3)$.

Example 2. Factor completely.

1) $2x^2 - 8$ 2) $16x^3 - x$ 3) $3xy^4 - 27xy^2$

4) $4x^2 - 64$ 5) $ax^5y^3 - 25axy$ 6) $18sm^9n^2 - 242smn^2$

Solution: 1) $2x^2 - 8 = \underbrace{2(x^2 - 4)}_{\text{The GCF is 2.}} = 2\underbrace{(x+2)(x-2)}_{x^2-4 \text{ factored}}$

2) $16x^3 - x = \underbrace{x(16x^2 - 1)}_{\text{The GCF is } x.} = x\underbrace{(4x+1)(4x-1)}_{16x^2-1 \text{ factored}}$

3) $3xy^4 - 27xy^2 = \underbrace{3xy^2(y^2 - 9)}_{\text{The GCF is } 3xy^2.} = 3xy^2\underbrace{(y+3)(y-3)}_{y^2-9 \text{ factored}}$

4) $4x^2 - 64 = \underbrace{4(x^2 - 16)}_{\text{The GCF is 4}} = 4\underbrace{(x+4)(x-4)}_{x^2-16 \text{ factored}}$

5) $ax^5y^3 - 25axy = \underbrace{axy(x^4y^2 - 25)}_{\text{The GCF is } axy.} = axy\underbrace{(x^2y+5)(x^2y-5)}_{x^4y^2-25 \text{ factored}}$

6) $18sm^9n^2 - 242smn^2 = \underbrace{2smn^2(9m^8 - 121)}_{\text{The GCF is } 2smn^2.} = 2smn^2\underbrace{(3m^4+11)(3m^4-11)}_{9m^8-121 \text{ factored}}$

Exercises: Chapter 11, Section B

In Exercises 1 - 12, factor.

1. $x^2 - 4$ 2. $a^2 - 16$ 3. $9 - y^2$ 4. $121t^2 - 1$

5. $64t^2 - 9$ 6. $25p^2 - 36$ 7. $4q^2 - 121$ 8. $x^2 - 64y^2$

9. $81a^2 - b^2$ 10. $144m^4 - n^8$ 11. $36u^6 - 169v^{14}$ 12. $49x^{16}y^2 - 100z^{12}$

In Exercises 13 - 19, factor.

13. $x^2 - 81 =$
(a) $(x + 9)(x - 9)$ (b) $(x + 9)^2$ (c) $(x - 9)^2$ (d) $x(x - 81)$ (e) $x^2 - 9^2$

14. $64 - s^2 =$
(a) $(8 - s)^2$ (b) $(8 + s)^2$ (c) $(8 + s)(8 - s)$ (d) $8(8 - s)$ (e) $(16 + s)(4 - s)$

15. $25a^2 - b^2 =$
(a) $(5a - b)^2$ (b) $(5a + b)(5a - b)$ (c) $(5a + b)^2$
(d) $(5ab + 1)(5ab - 1)$ (e) $(25a + b)(a - b)$

16. $9m^2 - 4 =$
(a) $(9m + 2)(m - 2)$ (b) $(3m + 2)^2$ (c) $(3m + 2)^2$
(d) $(3m - 4)(3m + 1)$ (e) $(3m - 2)(3m + 2)$

17. $100x^2y^4 - 1 =$
(a) $(10xy^2 + 1)(10xy^2 - 1)$ (b) $(10xy^2 - 1)^2$ (c) $(10xy^2 + 1)^2$
(d) $(10x^2y^2 + 1)(10y^2 - 1)$ (e) $(10y^4 + 1)(10x^2 - 1)$

18. $a^6b^8 - 49c^{14} =$
(a) $(a^2b^6 - 7c^7)(a^6b^2 + 7c^7)$ (b) $(a^3b^4 + 7c^7)(a^3b^4 - 7c^7)$ (c) $(a^3b^4 - 7c^7)^2$
(d) $(a^2b^6 + 49c^7)(a^6b^2 - c^7)$ (e) $(a^3b^4 + 49c^7)(a^3b^4 - c^7)$

19. $4s^{16} - 25a^2t^6 =$
(a) $(2s^8 - 5at^3)(2s^8 + 5at^3)$ (b) $(2s^8 + 5at^3)^2$ (c) $(2s^8 + 5at^3)^2$
(d) $(4s^8 - 5at^3)(s^8 + 5at^3)$ (e) $(2s^8 - 25at^3)(2s^8 + at^3)$

In Exercises 20 - 30, factor the binomials completely.

20. $5x^2 - 20$ 21. $7y^2 - 63$ 22. $3m^5 - 48m^3$ 23. $2n^4 - 72n^2$

24. $4a^2 - 16$ 25. $9b^2 - 9$ 26. $16x^2 - 64y^2$ 27. $64x^2 - 4y^2$

28. $x^4y^2 - 100x^2y^2$ 29. $11t^3 - 275x^8t$ 30. $18a^5b^{12} - 98ab^2$

In Exercises 31 - 35, factor the binomials completely.

31. $3x^3 - 75x =$
(a) $3(x^2 + 5)(x - 5)$ (b) $3x(x - 5)^2$ (c) $3x(x + 25)(x - 1)$
(d) $3x(x + 5)(x - 5)$ (e) $3(x^2 + 25)(x - 3)$

32. $20m - 45ms^4 =$
(a) $5(2m + 3s^2)(2 - 3s^2)$ (b) $5m(2 + 3s^2)^2$ (c) $5m(2 - 3s^2)^2$
(d) $5m(4 + s^2)(1 - 9s^2)$ (e) $5m(2 + 3s^2)(2 - 3s^2)$

33. $4x^2 - 64y^2$
(a) $(2x - 8y)^2$ (b) $4(x + 4y)(x - 4y)$ (c) $4(x - 4y)^2$ (d) $4(x - 16y)^2$
(e) $4(x + 16y)(x - y)$

34. $64a^5b^6 - ab^2c^{14} =$
(a) $a(8a^6b^2 + c^7)(8a^2 - c^7)$ (b) $ab^2(16a^2b^2 + c^7)(4a^2b^2 - c^7)$
(c) $ab^2(8a^2b^2 - c^7)^2$ (d) $ab^2(8a^2b^2 + c^7)(8a^2b^2 - c^7)$
(e) $b^2(8a^3b^2 + c^7)(8ab^2 - c^7)$

35. $125ab^2c^3 - 180a^5b^2c^9 =$
(a) $5ab^2c^3(5 + 6a^4c^4)(5 + 6ac^2)$ (b) $5ab^2c^3(5 + 6a^2c^3)^2$ (c) $5ab^2c^3(5 - 6a^2c^3)^2$
(d) $25ab^2c^3(5 + 6a^2c^3)(1 + 6a^2c^3)$ (e) $5ab^2c^3(5 + 6a^2c^3)(5 - 6a^2c^3)$

Section C. Factoring Quadratic Trinomials

Factoring $x^2 + bx + c$

Recall that a quadratic polynomial is a polynomial of degree 2, and a trinomial is a polynomial with 3 terms. To factor a quadratic trinomial, we must realize that any such trinomial comes from multiplying two binomials using the **FOIL Method**. For example

$$(x+4)(x-7) = \overset{F}{\overbrace{x^2}} + \overset{O}{\overbrace{(-7x)}} + \overset{I}{\overbrace{4x}} + \overset{L}{\overbrace{(-28)}}$$
$$= \underbrace{x^2 \quad -3x \quad -28}_{F \quad\; O+I \quad\; L}$$

Notice that the trinomial $x^2 - 3x - 28$ is quadratic. The last term, -28, comes from multiplying the numbers in the factorization, $+4$ and -7, whereas the coefficient of $-3x$ comes from adding the numbers $+4$ and -7.

Rule for factoring $x^2 + bx + c$:
First note that $(x)(x) = x^2$. This will always be the case here and **not** $1(x^2)$. Try to find two integers which multiply to give c and add up to give b. If two such integers are found (call them p and q), then

$$x^2 + bx + c = (x+p)(x+q), \text{ where } p+q = b \text{ and } pq = c.$$

For example, to factor $x^2 + 7x + 12$, we look for two numbers, p and q, such that $pq = +12$ and $p+q = +7$. Think about all possible pairs of numbers which multiply to give $+12$. Notice that both numbers **must** be positive because their product is positive and their sum is positive. Now, observe that

$$12 = 12 \times 1 \quad \text{and} \quad 12 + 1 = 13, \quad \text{no good}$$
$$= 6 \times 2 \quad \text{and} \quad 6 + 2 = 8, \quad \text{no good}$$
$$= 4 \times 3 \quad \text{and} \quad 4 + 3 = 7, \quad \text{GOOD}$$

And so, $x^2 + 7x + 12 = (x+4)(x+3)$, which is the same as $(x+3)(x+4)$. This method of factoring $x^2 + bx + c$ is called the **Reverse FOIL Method**.

Example 1. Factor.
1) $x^2 + 3x + 2$ 2) $y^2 - y - 6$ 3) $x^2 - 2x - 35$
4) $a^2 - 9a + 18$ 5) $t^2 + 10t - 24$ 6) $y^2 + 10y + 25$
7) $m^2 - 18m + 81$ 8) $x^2 - 6x - 40$

Solution:
1)We want two numbers that multiply to give 2 and add up to give 3. Observe that 2 and 1 do the job: $2 \times 1 = 2$ and $2 + 1 = 3$. Therefore, $x^2 + 3x + 2 = (x+2)(x+1)$.

2) We want two numbers that multiply to give –6 and add up to give –1. Let's try –3 and 2:
$(-3) \times 2 = -6$ and $(-3) + 2 = -1$. Therefore, $y^2 - y - 6 = (y - 3)(y + 2)$.

3) $x^2 - 2x - 35 = (x + 5)(x - 7)$ since $5 \times (-7) = -35$ and $5 + (-7) = -2$.

4) Notice that $(-6) \times (-3) = +18$ and $(-6) + (-3) = -9$. Therefore, $a^2 - 9a + 18 = (a - 6)(a - 3)$.

5) Observe that $12 \times (-2) = -24$ and $12 + (-2) = 10$. Therefore, $t^2 + 10t - 24 = (t + 12)(t - 2)$.

6) $y^2 + 10y + 25 = (y + 5)(y + 5) = (y + 5)^2$

7) $m^2 - 18m + 81 = (m - 9)(m - 9) = (m - 9)^2$

8) $x^2 - 6x - 40 = (m + 4)(m - 10)$

   Now we will learn how to factor quadratic trinomials of the form $ax^2 + bx + c$, where $a \neq 1$ and $a > 0$. As before, any trinomial of this form comes from multiplying two binomials using the FOIL Method. For example, recall that

$$(2x + 7)(x - 3) = \overset{F}{\overbrace{2x^2}} + \overset{O}{\overbrace{(-6x)}} + \overset{I}{\overbrace{7x}} + \overset{L}{\overbrace{(-21)}}$$
$$= \underset{F}{\underbrace{2x^2}} + \underset{O+I}{\underbrace{x}} \, \underset{L}{\underbrace{-21}},$$

and the trinomial $2x^2 + x - 21$ is quadratic. Notice that the first term, $2x^2$, comes from multiplying $2x$ and x, whereas the last term, -21, comes from multiplying 7 and –3. Unlike before, the numbers $+7$ and -3 **do not** add up to the coefficient of the middle term, $+1$. This means that we cannot use the Reverse FOIL Method. There are two methods we will learn that will allow us to factor these types of polynomials: the **Trial and Error Method** and the **Grouping Method**.

The Trial and Error Method

   To factor $2x^2 + 5x - 3$, we begin by finding two monomials involving x which multiply to give $2x^2$. There is only one possibility, $2x$ and x. These will be the 'F' terms in FOIL. Next, find two numbers that multiply to give –3. The possibilities are $(+3)(-1)$, $(+1)(-3)$, $(-1)(+3)$, and $(-3)(+1)$. Each pair is a candidate for being the 'L' terms in FOIL. Now, try the different possibilities of factoring:

   $(2x + 3)(x - 1)$ fails since $O + I = (2x)(-1) + 3(x) = +x$ but we want $+5x$,

   $(2x + 1)(x - 3)$ fails since $O + I = (2x)(-3) + 1(x) = -5x$ but we want $+5x$.

However,

   $(2x - 1)(x + 3)$ works because $O + I = (2x)(3) + (-1)(x) = 5x$ is exactly what we want!

Notice that our second attempt, $(2x + 1)(x - 3)$, was close to what we wanted except for the signs. When this happens, just change the signs of your numbers and it will work.

Rule for using the Trial and Error Method: To factor $ax^2 + bx + c$,
1) Find two monomials involving x that multiply to give ax^2 (call them px and qx) and two numbers that multiply to give c (call them m and n).
2) Find the $O + I$ of $(px + m)(qx + n)$ and see if it equals bx. If it does, then you are done. If not, try out other possibilities in Step 1.

Here's another example. Let's factor $4y^2 + 17y + 15$. As before, we need two monomials involving y which multiply to give $4y^2$. There are two possibilities, namely $2y$ and $2y$, and $4y$ and y. Next we find two numbers which multiply to give 15. Both numbers must be positive since there product has to be $+15$ and the middle term of $4y^2 + 17y + 15$ is positive. This leads us to $(+3)(+5)$, $(+15)(+1)$, $(+5)(+3)$, and $(+1)(+15)$. We now try the different possibilities:

$(2y + 3)(2y + 5)$ fails since $O + I = (2y)(5) + 3(2y) = +16y$ but we want $+17y$,

$(2y + 15)(2y + 1)$ fails since $O + I = (2y)(1) + 15(2y) = +32y$ but we want $+17y$,

$(4y + 3)(y + 5)$ fails since $O + I = (4y)(5) + 3(y) = +23y$ but we want $+17y$.

However,

$(4y + 5)(y + 3)$ works since $O + I = (4y)(3) + 5(y) = +17y$.

Example 2. Factor using the Trial and Error Method.
1) $2x^2 + 5x + 2$ 2) $3y^2 - 7y + 4$ 3) $5t^2 - 2t - 7$
4) $4a^2 + 16a + 15$ 5) $16x^2 - 14x - 15$ 6) $20p^2 - 31p + 12$

Solution: 1) $2x^2 + 5x + 2 = \underbrace{(2x + 1)(x + 2)}_{O+I=(2x)(2)+1(x)=5x}$ 2) $3y^2 - 7y + 4 = \underbrace{(3y - 4)(y - 1)}_{O+I=(3y)(-1)+(-4)(y)=-7y}$

3) $5t^2 - 2t - 7 = \underbrace{(5t - 7)(t + 1)}_{O+I=(5t)(1)+(-7)(t)=-2t}$ 4) $4a^2 + 16a + 15 = \underbrace{(2a + 3)(2a + 5)}_{O+I=(2a)(5)+3(2a)=16a}$

5) $16x^2 - 14x - 15 = \underbrace{(8x + 5)(2x - 3)}_{O+I=(8x)(-3)+5(2x)=-14x}$ 6) $20p^2 - 31p + 12 = \underbrace{(4p - 3)(5p - 4)}_{O+I=(4p)(-4)+(-3)(5p)=-31p}$

The Grouping Method

An alternative method of factoring a trinomial $ax^2 + bx + c$ is the **Grouping Method**. To illustrate this method, let's factor $2x^2 + 5x + 2$ (see Example 1 above). The idea is to split up the monomial $5x$ into two monomials. The coefficients of these two monomials are obtained in the

258

following way:

1) Find two numbers which multiply to give $\overbrace{(2)(2)}^{\text{'F' × 'L'}} = 4$ and add up to give $\overbrace{5}^{\text{O+I}}$.

The numbers 4 and 1 do the trick since $(4)(1) = 4$ and $4 + 1 = 5$.

2) Rewrite the trinomial as

$$2x^2 + 5x + 2 = 2x^2 \underbrace{+ 4x + 1x}_{\text{Split up } 5x.} + 2.$$

3) **Group** the first two and the last two terms, then factor the GCF from each group:

$$\underline{2x^2 + 4x} + \underline{1x + 2} = 2x\underline{(x + 2)} + 1\underline{(x + 2)}$$

4) Factor out the polynomial in the parenthesis:

$$2x^2 + 5x + 2 = \underline{2x^2 + 4x} + \underline{1x + 2}$$
$$= 2x\underline{(x + 2)} + 1\underline{(x + 2)} \qquad \text{(Factor the GCF from each group.)}$$
$$= (x + 2)(2x + 1) \qquad \text{(Factor out the } x + 2.\text{)}$$

As you can see, the answer is the same as before.

Rule for using the Grouping Method: To factor $ax^2 + bx + c$,
1) Find two numbers whose product is ac and whose sum is b. Call them m and n.
2) Rewrite bx as $mx + nx$ and obtain $ax^2 + mx + nx + c$.
3) Group the first pair and the last pair of terms: $(ax^2 + mx) + (nx + c)$.
4) Factor the GCF from each group, then factor out the polynomial in parenthesis.

Example 3. Factor using the Grouping Method.
1) $2x^2 - x - 6$ 2) $5y^2 - 17y + 6$ 3) $6t^2 + 7t - 20$
4) $12a^2 + 29a + 15$ 5) $6x^2 - 13x + 6$

Solution:
1) We need to find two numbers which multiply to give $(2)(-6) = -12$ and add up to give -1. Observe that $(-4)(3) = -12$ and $-4 + 3 = -1$, so the numbers we want are -4 and 3. Rewrite $2x^2 - x - 6$ as

$$2x^2 - x - 6 = 2x^2 - 4x + 3x - 6.$$

Next, we group terms, then factor:

$$2x^2 - x - 6 = (2x^2 - 4x) + (3x - 6) \qquad \text{(Group the terms.)}$$
$$= 2x\underline{(x - 2)} + 3\underline{(x - 2)} \qquad \text{(Factor the GCF from each group.)}$$
$$= \underline{(x - 2)}(2x + 3) \qquad \text{(Factor out the } x - 2.\text{)}$$

2) $5y^2 - 17y + 6 = 5y^2 - 15y - 2y + 6$ $((-15)(-2) = 30$ and $-15 + (-2) = -17.)$

$$= (5y^2 - 15y) + (-2y + 6) \quad \text{(Group the terms.)}$$
$$= 5y\underline{(y - 3)} - 2\underline{(y - 3)} \quad \text{(Factor the GCF from each group.)}$$
$$= \underline{(y - 3)}(5y - 2) \quad \text{(Factor out the } y - 3.\text{)}$$

3) $6t^2 + 7t - 20 = 6t^2 + 15t - 8t - 20 \qquad ((15)(-8) = -120 \text{ and } 15 + (-8) = 7.)$
$$= (6t^2 + 15t) + (-8t - 20) \quad \text{(Group the terms.)}$$
$$= 3t\underline{(2t + 5)} - 4\underline{(2t + 5)} \quad \text{(Factor the GCF from each group.)}$$
$$= \underline{(2t + 5)}(3t - 4) \quad \text{(Factor out the } 2t + 5.\text{)}$$

4) $12a^2 + 29a + 15 = 12a^2 + 9a + 20a + 15 \qquad (9 \times 20 = 180 \text{ and } 9 + 20 = 29)$
$$= (12a^2 + 9a) + (20a + 15)$$
$$= 3a\underline{(4a + 3)} + 5\underline{(4a + 3)}$$
$$= \underline{(4a + 3)}(3a + 5)$$

5) $6x^2 - 13x + 6 = 6x^2 - 9x - 4x + 6 \qquad \text{(Why?)}$
$$= (6x^2 - 9x) + (-4x + 6)$$
$$= 3x\underline{(2x - 3)} - 2\underline{(2x - 3)}$$
$$= \underline{(2x - 3)}(3x - 2)$$

Example 3. Factor completely.
1) $2x^2 + 4x + 2$ 2) $5x^3 + 35x^2 + 30x$ 3) $6a^4b^2 - 6a^3b^2 - 120a^2b^2$
4) $10y^5 - 11y^4 - 6y^3$ 5) $36a^4b + 56a^3b - 32a^2b$

Solution: Factor the GCF first, then try to factor further.
1) $2x^2 + 4x + 2 = 2(x^2 + 2x + 1) = 2(x + 1)(x + 1) = 2(x + 1)^2$
2) $5x^3 + 35x^2 + 30x = 5x(x^2 + 7x + 6) = 5x(x + 6)(x + 1)$
3) $6a^4b^2 - 6a^3b^2 - 120a^2b^2 = 6a^2b^2(a^2 - a - 20) = 6a^2b^2(a - 5)(a + 4)$
4) $10y^5 - 11y^4 - 6y^3 = y^3(10y^2 - 11y - 6) = y^3(5y + 2)(2y - 3)$
5) $36a^4b + 56a^3b - 32a^2b = 4a^2b(9a^2 + 14a - 8) = 4a^2b(9a - 4)(a + 2)$

Exercises: Chapter 11, Section C

In Exercises 1 - 20, factor.

1. $x^2 + 7x + 10$ 2. $y^2 - 13y + 30$ 3. $a^2 + a - 56$ 4. $p^2 - 11p - 42$

5. $m^2 + 24m + 144$ 6. $y^2 + 11y + 24$ 7. $b^2 - 18b + 81$ 8. $x^2 + 7x - 18$

9. $b^2 - 13b + 36$ 10. $p^2 - 4p - 21$ 11. $x^2 + 16x + 55$ 12. $q^2 - 15q + 54$

13. $2x^2 + 3x + 1$ 14. $3y^2 + y - 2$ 15. $2y^2 + y - 3$ 16. $5a^2 - a - 4$

17. $14x^2 + 11x + 2$ 18. $8y^2 + 18y + 9$ 19. $4x^2 - 20x + 21$ 20. $6y^2 + 17y + 12$

In Exercises 21 - 28, factor.

21. $x^2 + 7x - 60 =$
(a) $(x - 12)(x + 5)$ (b) $(x + 12)(x + 5)$ (c) $(x - 10)(x + 6)$
(d) $(x - 15)(x + 4)$ (e) $(x - 5)(x + 12)$

22. $t^2 - 22t + 121 =$
(a) $(t - 12)(t - 11)$ (b) $(t - 11)^2$ (c) $(t - 11)(t + 11)$
(d) $(t - 121)(t - 1)$ (e) $(t + 11)^2$

23. $x^2 + 14x + 48 =$
(a) $(x + 6)(x + 8)$ (b) $(x + 12)(x + 4)$ (c) $(x + 16)(x + 3)$
(d) $(x - 6)(x - 8)$ (e) $(x - 6)(x + 8)$

24. $y^2 - y - 30 =$
(a) $(y - 5)(y + 6)$ (b) $(y + 5)(y - 6)$ (c) $(y - 3)(y + 10)$
(d) $(y - 15)(y + 2)$ (e) $(y - 30)(y + 1)$

25. $18t^2 - 19t - 12 =$
(a) $(6t - 3)(3t + 4)$ (b) $(18t - 12)(t + 1)$ (c) $(2t - 3)(9t + 4)$
(d) $(2t + 3)(9t - 4)$ (e) $(9t + 2)(2t - 6)$

26. $6y^2 + 7y - 20 =$
(a) $(2y - 5)(3y + 4)$ (b) $(2y + 4)(3y - 5)$ (c) $(6y + 5)(y - 4)$
(d) $(y + 5)(6y - 4)$ (e) $(2y + 5)(3y - 4)$

27. $25x^2 - 90x + 81 =$
(a) $(5x - 3)(5x - 27)$ (b) $(5x - 9)^2$ (c) $(25x - 9)(x - 9)$
(d) $(5x + 9)(5x - 9)$ (e) $(5x + 9)^2$

28. $16a^2 + 30a + 9 =$
(a) $(8a + 9)(2a + 1)$ (b) $(8a - 3)(2a - 3)$ (c) $(4a + 3)^2$
(d) $(16a + 9)(a + 1)$ (e) $(8a + 3)(2a + 3)$

In Exercises 29 - 39, factor completely.

29. $2x^2 + 6x + 4$ 30. $3x^2 + 15x + 18$ 31. $4a^3 - 8a^2 - 60a$

32. $5u^5 - 55u^4 + 150u^3$ 33. $8v^4 - 40v^3 + 48v^2$ 34. $2x^2y^3 - 6x^2y^2 - 56x^2y$

35. $4m^3n - 12m^2n - 40mn$ 36. $27x^2 + 63x + 18$ 37. $20st^2 + 32st + 12s$

38. $24xy^2 - 24xy - 18x$ 39. $56y^2 + 14y - 21$

In Exercises 40 - 44, factor completely.

40. $4p^3 + 40p^2 + 96p =$
(a) $4(p^2 + 6p)(p + 4)$ (b) $4p(p + 3)(p + 8)$ (c) $(4p + 12)(p^2 + 8p)$
(d) $4p(p + 6)(p + 4)$ (e) $p(4p^2 + 40p + 96)$

41. $3p^3 + 15p^2 - 18p =$
(a) $3p(p + 6)(p - 1)$ (b) $3p(p - 6)(p + 1)$ (c) $(3p - 18)(p^2 + p)$
(d) $4p(p + 3)(p - 2)$ (e) $p(3p^2 + 15p - 18)$

42. $18a^4 + 12a^3 + 2a^2 =$
(a) $2a^2(9a + 1)(a + 1)$ (b) $2a^2(3a + 1)(3a - 1)$ (c) $2a^2(3a + 1)^2$
(d) $2a(3a^2 + 1)(3a + 1)$ (e) $a^2(3a + 1)(6a + 2)$

43. $80x^2y - 120xy + 45y =$
(a) $5y(4y - 3)(4y - 3)$ (b) $5y(4y + 3)(4y - 3)$ (c) $5y(8y - 3)(2y - 3)$
(d) $5y(4y - 9)(4y - 1)$ (e) $4y(20y - 9)(y - 1)$

44. $4x^3y^4 - 4x^3y^3 - 3x^3y^2 =$
(a) $x^3y^2(4y + 3)(y - 1)$ (b) $x^3y^2(2y - 3)(2y + 1)$ (c) $x^3y^2(4y + 1)(y - 3)$
(d) $y^2(2xy + 3)(2xy - 1)$ (e) $x^3y^2(2y + 3)(2y - 1)$

Section D. Factoring Polynomials With Four Terms

In the last section, we used the Grouping Method to factor quadratic trinomials. Rules 3 and 4 of this method can also be used to factor polynomials with four terms. For example, to factor $x^3 + 2x^2 + 5x + 10$, we group the first two and the last two terms. We then proceed as before: factor the GCF from each group, then factor out the polynomial in parenthesis.

$$x^3 + 2x^2 + 5x + 10 = (x^3 + 2x^2) + (5x + 10) \qquad \text{(Group the terms.)}$$
$$= x^2(x + 2) + 5(x + 2) \qquad \text{(Factor the GCF from each group.)}$$
$$= (x + 2)(x^2 + 5) \qquad \text{(Factor out the } x + 2.\text{)}$$

Example 1. Factor.

1) $x^3 + 3x^2 + x + 3$ 2) $2y^3 + 8y^2 - y - 4$ 3) $5n^3 - 30n^2 + 4n - 24$
4) $3p^6 + 12p^4 - 2p^2 - 8$ 5) $7x^2y - 4x^2 + 14y - 8$ 6) $4amx^2 + 24m - 3anx^2 - 18n$

Solution:

1) $x^3 + 3x^2 + x + 3 = (x^3 + 3x^2) + (x + 3)$
$$= x^2(x + 3) + 1(x + 3)$$
$$= (x + 3)(x^2 + 1)$$

2) $2y^3 + 8y^2 - y - 4 = (2y^3 + 8y^2) + (-y - 4)$
$$= 2y^2(y + 4) - 1(y + 4)$$
$$= (y + 4)(2y^2 - 1)$$

3) $5n^3 - 30n^2 + 4n - 24 = (5n^3 - 30n^2) + (4n - 24)$
$$= 5n^2(n - 6) + 4(n - 6)$$
$$= (n - 6)(5n^2 + 4)$$

4) $3p^6 + 12p^4 - 2p^2 - 8 = (3p^6 + 12p^4) + (-2p^2 - 8)$
$$= 3p^4(p^2 + 4) - 2(p^2 + 4)$$
$$= (p^2 + 4)(3p^4 - 2)$$

5) $7x^2y - 4x^2 + 14y - 8 = (7x^2y - 4x^2) + (14y - 8)$
$$= x^2(7y - 4) + 2(7y - 4)$$
$$= (7y - 4)(x^2 + 2)$$

6) $4amx^2 + 24m - 3anx^2 - 18n = (4amx^2 + 24m) + (-3anx^2 - 18n)$
$$= 4m(ax^2 + 6) - 3n(ax^2 + 6)$$
$$= (ax^2 + 6)(4m - 3n)$$

Exercises: Chapter 11, Section D

In Exercises 1 - 9, factor.

1. $t^3 + 4t^2 + 2t + 8$

2. $18a^4 + 27a^3 + 4a + 6$

3. $x^4 + 7x^3 - 3x - 21$

4. $2y^3 - 10y^2 - y + 5$

5. $2x^2 + 2ax + 3x + 3a$

6. $42mn - 77mp + 12n - 22p$

7. $a^2b^2 - a^2t - b^2s + st$

8. $2p^3 - p + 6p^2q - 3q$

9. $80s^4 - 50s^2 - 24s^2y + 15y$

In Exercises 10 - 15, factor.

10. $5x^3 - x^2 + 5x - 1 =$
(a) $(5x - 1)(x + 1)^2$
(b) $(5x - 1)(x^2 + 1)$
(c) $(5x - 1)(x + 1)(x - 1)$
(d) $(5x + 1)(x^2 + 1)$
(e) $(5x + 1)(x - 1)(x + 1)$

11. $2x^3 + 3x^2 + 8x + 12 =$
(a) $(2x + 3)(x + 2)^2$
(b) $(x^2 + 4)(2x + 3)$
(c) $(2x - 3)(x^2 + 4)$
(d) $(2x + 3)^2(x^2 + 4)$
(e) $(2x + 4)(x + 3)(x + 2)$

12. $24a^3 + 15a^2 - 16a - 10 =$
(a) $(3a^2 - 2)(8a + 5)$
(b) $(3a^2 + 2)(8a - 5)$
(c) $(3a^2 - 5)(8a + 2)$
(d) $(3a^2 - 2a)(8a + 5)$
(e) $(3a - 2)(3a + 2)(8a + 5)$

13. $3y - xy + 2ax - 6a =$
(a) $(y + 2a)(3 - x)$
(b) $(y - 2a)(x + 3)$
(c) $(x - 2a)(3 - y)$
(d) $(y - 2a)(x - 3)$
(e) $(y - 2a)(3 - x)$

14. $8a^2 + 20ab + 6ac + 15bc =$
(a) $(4a + 5c)(2a + 3b)$
(b) $(4a + 3c)(2a + 5b)$
(c) $(2a + 3c)(4a + 5b)$
(d) $(4a - 3c)(2a + 5b)$
(e) $(4a^2 + 3c)(2 + 5b)$

15. $27x^3 - 63x - 7y^2 + 3x^2y^2 =$
(a) $(9x - y^2)(3x^2 + 7)$
(b) $(9x^2 + y^2)(3x - 7)$
(c) $(9x + y^2)(3x^2 - 7)$
(d) $(9x + 7)(3x^2 - y^2)$
(e) $(3x^2 - 7)(9x - y^2)$

Section E. Solving Equations by Factoring

Factoring comes in handy when solving equations. A **quadratic equation** (or **second-degree equation**) is an equation that is equivalent to $ax^2 + bx + c = 0$, where a, b, and c are real numbers and $a \neq 0$. Examples of quadratic equations are

$$x^2 + 4x + 3 = 0, \quad 2x^2 - 4x + 2 = 0, \quad 6y^2 = 24, \quad \text{and} \quad 3w(w - 2) = 4.$$

A quadratic equation written in the form $ax^2 + bx + c = 0$ is in **standard form**. The equations $x^2 + 4x + 3 = 0$ and $2x^2 - 4x + 2 = 0$ are in standard form, but the equations $6y^2 = 24$ and $3l(l - 2) = 4$ are not.

Rules for solving a quadratic equation by factoring:
1. Put the equation in standard form: $ax^2 + bx + c = 0$.
2. Factor the quadratic $ax^2 + bx + c$ (if possible).
3. Use the **Zero Product Property**:

> If x and y are real numbers, and if $xy = 0$, then either $x = 0$ or $y = 0$ or both.

The rules mentioned above describe the **Factoring Method** for solving a quadratic equation. Quadratic equations which cannot be solved by factoring will not be discussed here.

For example, let's solve the equation $x^2 - 9x + 20 = 0$. Notice that the equation is in standard form.

We begin by factoring the polynomial: $(x - 4)(x - 5) = 0$

Next, we apply the Zero Product Property:

$$\frac{(x - 4)(x - 5)}{x - 4 = 0 \mid x - 5 = 0} = 0$$

The final step is to solve each equation:

$$\frac{(x - 4)(x - 5)}{\begin{array}{c|c} x - 4 = 0 & x - 5 = 0 \\ +4 \ \ +4 & +5 \ \ +5 \\ \hline x \quad = 4 & x \quad = 5 \end{array}} = 0$$

The **roots** (or **solutions**) of the equation are 4 and 5. Notice that both roots satisfy the equation:
$$(4)^2 - 9(4) + 20 = 16 - 36 + 20 = 0 \quad \text{and} \quad (5)^2 - 9(5) + 20 = 25 - 45 + 20 = 0$$

Example 1. Solve each equation.
1) $x^2 + 7x + 12 = 0$
2) $y^2 + 5y - 24 = 0$
3) $x^2 - 8x + 16 = 0$
4) $10a^2 - 21a + 8 = 0$
5) $9t^2 + 5t = 0$
6) $64p^2 - 9 = 0$

Solution:

1)
$$\frac{(x+4)(x+3)}{}=0$$

$x+4=0$	$x+3=0$
$-4\;-4$	$-3\;-3$
$x\;\;=-4$	$x\;\;=-3$

The solutions are $x=-4$ and $x=-3$.

2)
$$\frac{(y+8)(y-3)}{}=0$$

$y+8=0$	$y-3=0$
$-8\;-8$	$+3\;+3$
$y\;\;=-8$	$y\;\;=3$

The solutions are $y=-8$ and $y=3$.

3)
$$\frac{(x-4)(x-4)}{}=0$$

$x-4=0$	$x-4=0$
$+4\;+4$	$+4\;+4$
$x\;\;=4$	$x\;\;=4$

The solution is $x=4$.

4)
$$\frac{(5a-8)(2a-1)}{}$$

$5a-8=0$	$2a-1=0$
$+8\;+8$	$+1\;+1$
$\frac{5a}{5}=\frac{8}{5}$	$\frac{2a}{2}=\frac{1}{2}$

The solutions are $a=\frac{8}{5}=1\frac{3}{5}$ and $a=\frac{1}{2}$.

5)
$$\frac{t(9t+5)}{}=0$$

$t=0$	$9t+5=0$
	$-5\;-5$
	$\frac{9t}{9}=\frac{-5}{9}$

The solutions are $t=0$ and $t=-\frac{5}{9}$.

6)
$$\frac{(8p+3)(8p-3)}{}=0$$

$8p+3=0$	$8p-3=0$
$-3\;-3$	$+3\;+3$
$\frac{8p}{8}=\frac{-3}{8}$	$\frac{8p}{8}=\frac{3}{8}$

The solutions are $p=-\frac{3}{8}$ and $p=\frac{3}{8}$.

Example 2. Find the roots of each equation.

1) $15x^2=4x$ 2) $36y^2=49$ 3) $x(6x-1)=1$

Solution: Put each equation in standard form, then proceed as before.

1)
$$15x^2=4x$$
$$-4x\;\;-4x$$
$$\overline{15x^2-4x=0}$$

$$\frac{x(15x-4)}{}=0$$

$x=0$	$15x-4=0$
	$+4\;\;+4$
	$\frac{15x}{15}=\frac{4}{15}$

The roots are 0 and $\frac{4}{15}$.

2)
$$36y^2=49$$
$$-49\;-49$$
$$\overline{36y^2-49=0}$$

$$(6y+7)(6y-7)=0$$

$6y+7=0$	$6y-7=0$
$-7\;-7$	$+7\;+7$
$\frac{6y}{6}=\frac{-7}{6}$	$\frac{6y}{6}=\frac{7}{6}$

The roots are $-1\frac{1}{6}$ and $1\frac{1}{6}$.

3)
$$x(6x-1)=1$$
$$6x^2-x=1$$
$$-1\;-1$$
$$\overline{6x^2-x-1=0}$$

$$\frac{(3x+1)(2x-1)}{}=0$$

$3x+1=0$	$2x-1=0$
$-1\;-1$	$+1\;+1$
$\frac{3x}{3}=\frac{-1}{3}$	$\frac{2x}{2}=\frac{1}{2}$

The roots are $-\frac{1}{3}$ and $\frac{1}{2}$.

Next, we give examples of equations that are not quadratic, but we can use the Factoring Method.

Example 3. Solve. Find the sum of the roots of each equation.

1) $2x(x+1)(3x-5) = 0$ 2) $x^3 - 9x = 0$ 3) $7y^4 = -42y^5$

Solution:

1) Since one side of the equation is zero and the other side is factored, we may use the Zero Product Property:

$$2x(x+1)(3x-5) = 0$$

$2x = 0$	$x + 1 = 0$	$3x - 5 = 0$
$\dfrac{2x}{2} = \dfrac{0}{2}$	$-1 \quad -1$	$+5 \quad +5$
$x = 0$	$x = -1$	$\dfrac{3x}{3} = \dfrac{5}{3}$

The roots are $x = 0$, $x = -1$, and $x = \frac{5}{3} = 1\frac{2}{3}$. The sum of the roots is $0 + (-1) + 1\frac{2}{3} = \frac{2}{3}$.

2) One side of the equation is zero. Factor the other side, then proceed as before:

$$x^3 - 9x = 0$$
$$x(x^2 - 9) = 0$$
$$x(x+3)(x-3) = 0$$

$x = 0$	$x + 3 = 0$	$x - 3 = 0$
	$-3 \quad -3$	$+3 \quad +3$
	$x = -3$	$x = 3$

The roots are $x = 0$, $x = -3$, and $x = 3$. Their sum is $0 + (-3) + 3 = 0$.

3) Get one side of the equation equal to zero. Then proceed as before.

$$7y^4 = -42y^5$$
$$\underline{+42y^5 \quad\quad +42y^5}$$
$$7y^4 + 42y^5 = 0$$

$$7y^4(1 + 6y) = 0$$

$7y^4 = 0$	$1 + 6y = 0$
$\dfrac{7y^4}{7} = \dfrac{0}{7}$	$-1 \quad\quad -1$
$y^4 = 0$	$\dfrac{6y}{6} = \dfrac{-1}{6}$
$y = 0$	$y = -\dfrac{1}{6}$

The solutions are $y = 0$ and $y = -\frac{1}{6}$. Their sum is $0 + \left(-\frac{1}{6}\right) = -\frac{1}{6}$.

Exercises: Chapter 11, Section E

In Exercises 1 - 15, solve each quadratic equation.

1. $x^2 - 7x + 12 = 0$

2. $x^2 + 7x + 6 = 0$

3. $y^2 - 9y + 14 = 0$

4. $y^2 - 12y + 32 = 0$

5. $t^2 + 5t - 36 = 0$

6. $t^2 + 8t - 33 = 0$

7. $2x^2 - 11x - 21 = 0$

8. $3x^2 - 25x - 18 = 0$

9. $4m^2 - 23m + 30 = 0$

10. $6m^2 - 19m + 14 = 0$

11. $x^2 + 5x = 0$

12. $x^2 + 16x = 0$

13. $3y^2 - 24y = 0$

14. $b^2 - 25 = 0$

15. $4t^2 - 49 = 0$

In Exercises 16 - 29, find the roots of each equation.

16. $p^2 = 5p$

17. $2q^2 = 16q$

18. $k(k + 15) = -36$

19. $l(l + 10) = -16$

20. $x(5x + 3) = 2$

21. $y(18y - 23) = 6$

22. $x - 10 = -\dfrac{21}{x}$

23. $a - 2 = \dfrac{48}{a}$

24. $\dfrac{8}{x + 1} = \dfrac{x + 6}{3}$

25. $\dfrac{x - 5}{4} = \dfrac{4}{x + 1}$

26. $x^4 - 14x^3 = 0$

27. $2x^3 - 18x^2 + 36x = 0$

28. $100x^4 = 121x^6$

29. $3x^4 = -12x^2(x + 1)$

In Exercises 30 - 33, find the sum of the roots of each equation.

30. $x^2 - 5x - 36 = 0$

31. $y^2 + 6y + 8 = 0$

32. $8a^2 = 32$

33. $k(k + 6) = -5$

Section F. Simplifying Rational Expressions by Factoring

A **rational expression** is an expression of the form $\frac{p}{q}$, where both p and q are polynomials and $q \neq 0$.

Examples of rational expressions are

$$\frac{5}{6}, \quad \frac{x-9}{2x+11}, \quad \frac{5x^2 - 2x - 9}{-8x^3 + 4x + 1}, \quad \text{and} \quad \frac{7x^2 + 2xy - 3y^2}{10y^2 - 4yz + z^2}.$$

Note that every rational number and every polynomial is a rational expression.

Evaluating a Rational Expression

To evaluate a rational expression, replace each variable with its given value (don't forget to follow the order of operations).

Example 1. Evaluate each rational expression.

1) $\dfrac{x-9}{2x+11}$ when $x = 9$ 2) $\dfrac{y^2 - 2y + 3}{-6 + y}$ when $y = 4$ 3) $\dfrac{4a^2 + ab - 5}{2b^3 - ab + a^2}$ when $a = -1$, $b = 3$

Solution: Put parentheses around each variable before you begin.

1) $\dfrac{(9) - 9}{2(9) + 11} = \dfrac{0}{18 + 11} = \dfrac{0}{29} = 0$

2) $\dfrac{(4)^2 - 2(4) + 3}{-6 + (4)} = \dfrac{16 - 8 + 3}{-2} = \dfrac{11}{-2} = -\dfrac{11}{2} = -5\dfrac{1}{2}$

3) $\dfrac{4(-1)^2 + (-1)(3) - 5}{2(3)^3 - (-1)(3) + (-1)^2} = \dfrac{4(1) - 3 - 5}{2(27) + 3 + 1} = \dfrac{4 - 3 - 5}{54 + 3 + 1} = \dfrac{-4}{58} = -\dfrac{2}{29}$

Sometimes a rational expression can be undefined when it is evaluated. For example, the expression $\dfrac{x}{x-8}$ is undefined when $x = 8$ because

$$\frac{8}{(8) - 8} = \frac{8}{0}$$

and zero cannot appear in the denominator of a valid fraction.

Example 2. Is $\dfrac{2y-5}{y^2+6y-27}$ undefined when $y = 3$?

Solution: $\dfrac{2(3)-5}{(3)^2+6(3)-27} = \dfrac{6-5}{9+18-27} = \dfrac{1}{0}$, so it is undefined when $y = 3$.

Rule for determining the values that make a rational expression undefined: Set the denominator equal to zero and solve the equation.

Example 3: Find the values that make the given expression undefined.

1) $\dfrac{x+4}{x-2}$ 2) $\dfrac{x^2-5x+4}{x^2-10x+9}$ 3) $\dfrac{-14}{x^3-x}$

Solution: Set the denominator of each expression to zero and solve.

1) $\quad x - 2 = 0$
$\quad\quad\; +2\quad +2$
$\quad\quad\;\; x \quad\;\; = 2$ The expression is undefined when $x = 2$.

2) $\quad x^2 - 10x + 9 = 0$
$\quad\quad (x-1)(x-9) = 0$

$\quad x - 1 = 0 \;\mid\; x - 9 = 0$
$\quad\quad +1\;\; +1 \mid\quad +9\;\; +9$
$\quad\;\; x \quad\;= 1 \mid x \quad\;\;= 9$ The expression is undefined when $x = 1$ and $x = 9$.

3) $\quad x^3 - x = 0$
$\quad\quad x(x^2 - 1) = 0$
$\quad\quad x(x+1)(x-1) = 0$

$x = 0 \quad x + 1 = 0 \mid x - 1 = 0$
$\quad\quad\quad\; -1\;\; -1 \mid\quad +1\;\; +1$
$\quad\quad\;\; x \quad\;\; = -1 \mid x \quad\;\; = 1$ The expression is undefined when $x = 0$, $x = -1$, and $x = 1$.

Simplifying a Rational Expression

Recall that to simplify a fraction, say $\dfrac{20}{32}$, we factor the numerator and denominator, then cancel out any common factors:

$$\frac{20}{32} = \frac{5 \times \overset{1}{\cancel{4}}}{8 \times \underset{1}{\cancel{4}}} = \frac{5}{8}.$$

A rational expression can be simplified in the same way. For example,

$$\underbrace{\frac{3x+6}{5x+10} = \frac{3\ (x\!\!\!\!\diagup\!\!+2)}{5\ (x+2)} = \frac{3}{5}}_{\text{Defined when } x \neq -2.} \quad \text{and} \quad \underbrace{\frac{15x-30}{x^2+9x-22} = \frac{15\ (x\!\!\!\!\diagdown\!\!2)}{(x+11)\ (x\!\!\!\!\diagdown\!\!2)} = \frac{15}{x+11}}_{\text{Defined when } x \neq -11 \text{ and } x \neq 2.}.$$

If the numerator and denominator of a rational expression are additive inverses of each other, then the expression simplifies to -1. For example,

$$\underbrace{\frac{x-6}{6-x} = -1}_{6-x=-1(x-6)} \quad \text{and} \quad \underbrace{\frac{5y-9}{9-5y} = -1}_{9-5y=-1(5y-9)}.$$

Note that $\frac{x-6}{6-x} = -1$ provided that $x \neq 6$, and $\frac{5y-9}{9-5y} = -1$ provided that $y \neq \frac{9}{5}$.

Example 4. Simplify each rational expression.

1) $\dfrac{2x+8}{6x-12}$
2) $\dfrac{x^2-64}{x^2-16x+64}$
3) $\dfrac{7y-4}{8-14y}$
4) $\dfrac{t^2-2t-63}{18-2t}$

Solution:

1) $\dfrac{2x+8}{6x-12} = \dfrac{\overset{1}{2}\ (x+4)}{\underset{3}{6}\ (x-2)} = \dfrac{x+4}{3(x-2)}$

2) $\dfrac{x^2-64}{x^2-16x+64} = \dfrac{(x+8)\ (x\overset{1}{\cancel{-8}})}{(x-8)\ (\cancel{x}\underset{1}{-8})} = \dfrac{x+8}{x-8}$

3) $\dfrac{7y-4}{8-14y} = \dfrac{1\ (7y\overset{-1}{\cancel{-4}})}{2\ (\cancel{4}\underset{1}{-7y})} = \dfrac{-1}{2} = -\dfrac{1}{2}$

4) $\dfrac{t^2-2t-63}{18-2t} = \dfrac{(t+7)\ (t\overset{-1}{\cancel{-9}})}{2\ (9\underset{1}{\cancel{-t}})} = \dfrac{-(t+7)}{2} = -\dfrac{t+7}{2}$

Example 5. Find the value of k.

1) $\dfrac{x^2+kx-30}{x-6} = x+5, \quad x \neq 6 \text{ and } x \neq 0.$
2) $\dfrac{6x^2+kx+9}{6x-3} = x-3, \quad x \neq \dfrac{1}{2} \text{ and } x \neq 0.$

Solution:
1) Multiply both sides by $x-6$ to clear the fractions:

$$\left(\frac{\cancel{x-6}}{1}\right)\left(\frac{x^2+kx-30}{\cancel{x-6}}\right) = \left(\frac{x-6}{1}\right)(x+5)$$

$$x^2+kx-30 = (x-6)(x+5)$$

272

$$x^2 + kx - 30 = x^2 - x - 30$$

Notice that the right side of the equation equals the left side when $k = -1$.

2) Multiply both sides by $6x - 3$ to clear the fractions:

$$\left(\frac{\cancel{6x - 3}}{1}\right)\left(\frac{6x^2 + kx + 9}{\cancel{6x - 3}}\right) = \left(\frac{6x - 3}{1}\right)(x - 3)$$

$$6x^2 + kx + 9 = (6x - 3)(x - 3)$$
$$6x^2 + kx + 9 = 6x^2 - 21x + 9$$

The right side of the equation equals the left side when $k = -21$.

Exercises: Chapter 11, Section F

In Exercises 1 - 4, evaluate each rational expression (if possible) when $x = 3$.

1. $\dfrac{4x+2}{x+7}$

2. $\dfrac{x^2-5x+5}{7x^2}$

3. $\dfrac{9-2x^2}{4+x-11x^2}$

4. $\dfrac{x-x^2}{3x^2-27}$

In Exercises 5 - 8, evaluate each rational expression (if possible) when $a = -7$.

5. $\dfrac{2a-8}{3a-1}$

6. $\dfrac{a^2-2a+1}{6-a^2}$

7. $\dfrac{a+3a^2}{49-a^2}$

8. $\dfrac{-a^2+5}{4a}$

In Exercises 9 - 12, find the value(s) which make each rational expression undefined.

9. $\dfrac{x-8}{x-12}$

10. $\dfrac{x^2-6x+5}{x^2+12x+27}$

11. $\dfrac{10x+16x^2}{4x^2-1}$

12. $\dfrac{1}{4x^2+16x+15}$

In Exercises 13 - 28, simplify.

13. $\dfrac{2x+4}{3x+6}$

14. $\dfrac{5x+10}{15x+30}$

15. $\dfrac{8y-24}{6y-18}$

16. $\dfrac{9y-36}{3y-12}$

17. $\dfrac{3p^2+8p}{2p^2-p}$

18. $\dfrac{2q-7q^2}{4q^2+q}$

19. $\dfrac{10x^2-15x}{10x-10x^2}$

20. $\dfrac{24y^2-32y}{32y^2-16y}$

21. $\dfrac{x^2+3x+2}{3x+6}$

22. $\dfrac{x^2+8x+15}{4x+20}$

23. $\dfrac{2x^2-8x}{3x^3-48x}$

24. $\dfrac{7x^2-63}{2x^2-6x}$

25. $\dfrac{4t^2-8t-21}{4t^2+12t+9}$

26. $\dfrac{9t^2-30t+25}{6t^2-7t-5}$

27. $\dfrac{7a^2+11a-6}{12-28a}$

28. $\dfrac{16x^3-8x^2}{1-4x^2}$

In Exercises 29 - 34, choose the correct answer.

29. For all $a \neq 0$ and $a \neq 3$, $\dfrac{a^2 + 6a}{a^2 - 3a} =$

(a) -1 (b) $\dfrac{a+6}{a-3}$ (c) $\dfrac{a^2+6}{a^2+3}$ (d) -2 (e) $\dfrac{1+6a}{1-3a}$

30. For all $x \neq -8$, $\dfrac{7x^2 + 56x}{4x + 32} =$

(a) $\dfrac{7}{4}$ (b) $\dfrac{7}{4x}$ (c) $\dfrac{7x}{4} + \dfrac{7}{4}$ (d) $\dfrac{7x}{4}$ (e) $2x$

31. For all $x \neq 0$ and $x \neq 4$, $\dfrac{8x^3 - 32x^2}{16x^4 - 64x^3} =$

(a) $2x$ (b) $\dfrac{2}{x^2}$ (c) 0 (d) $\dfrac{1}{2x}$ (e) $\dfrac{8x^3}{16x^4}$

32. For all $a \neq -\dfrac{3}{2}$, $\dfrac{4a^2 - 4a - 15}{4a + 6} =$

(a) $\dfrac{2a-5}{2}$ (b) $\dfrac{2a+5}{2}$ (c) $a + \dfrac{-4a-15}{4a+6}$ (d) $a - 5$ (e) $\dfrac{-2a+5}{2}$

33. For all $y \neq 3$, if $\dfrac{5y^2 + ky - 6}{y - 3} = 5y + 2$, then $k = ?$
(a) 13 (b) -13 (c) -17 (d) 14 (e) -15

34. For all $x \neq -\dfrac{2}{9}$, if $\dfrac{27x^2 + 42x + k}{9x + 2} = 3x + 4$, then $k = ?$
(a) 7 (b) -8 (c) 8 (d) 4 (e) $-\dfrac{1}{8}$

Section G.   Applications in Geometry

In this section, we solve some geometry problems that rely on factoring.

Recall that the **area** A of a square whose sides have length s is $A = s^2$, and the area A of a rectangle whose length l and whose width w is $A = lw$. The **perimeter** of the square is $P = 4s$ and the perimeter of the rectangle is $P = 2l + 2w$.

Example 1. The area of a rectangle is given by the expression $6st + 18s^4t^4$ square meters. If the width of the rectangle is $6st$ meters, what is its length?

Solution: Set $A = 6st + 18s^4t^4$ and $w = 6st$. Then $A = lw$ gives us $6st + 18s^4t^4 = l(6st)$. We need to solve for l.

$$\frac{6st + 18s^4t^4}{6st} = \frac{(6st)l}{6st}$$

$$\frac{6st(1 + 3s^3t^3)}{6st} = l$$

$$1 + 3s^3t^3 = l$$

The length is $1 + 3s^3t^3$ meters.

Example 2. The area of a rectangle is given by the expression $40s^2t^5 + 20s^4t^6$ square meters. If the length of the rectangle is $2s^2t^2$ meters, what is its width?

Solution: Set $A = 40s^2t^5 + 20s^4t^6$ and $l = 2s^2t^2$. Then $A = lw$ gives us $40s^2t^5 + 20s^4t^6 = (2s^2t^2)w$. We need to solve for w.

$$\frac{40s^2t^5 + 20s^4t^6}{2s^2t^2} = \frac{(2s^2t^2)w}{2s^2t^2}$$

$$\frac{2s^2t^2(20t^3 + 10s^2t^4)}{2s^2t^2} = w \quad \text{(note this factor is \textbf{not} the GCF)}$$

$$20t^3 + 10s^2t^4 = w$$

The width is $20t^3 + 10s^2t^4$ meters.

Example 3. The area of a square is **numerically** equal to its perimeter. What is its width?

Solution: Let x represent the width of the square (which also equals its length). Then its area is x^2 and its perimeter is $4x$. Since they are equal (numerically), we have $x^2 = 4x$. We want to solve for x:

$$x^2 - 4x = 0$$
$$x(x - 4) = 0$$

$x = 0$	$x - 4 = 0$
	$+4 \quad +4$
	$x \quad\quad = 4$

Since we are dealing with length, x cannot equal zero. Therefore, the width is 4 inches.

Example 4. The length of a rectangle is 2 feet longer than its width. If the area of the rectangle is 80 square feet, find its width.

Solution: Let w be the width of the rectangle. Then the length l is $w + 2$ since the length is 2 feet longer than the width. We are given the area $A = 80$. Since $A = lw$, we have:

$$\underbrace{(w + 2)}_{l} \, w = \underbrace{80}_{A}$$

We want to solve for w:

$$w^2 + 2w = 80$$
$$-80 \quad\quad -80$$
$$w^2 + 2w - 80 = 0$$
$$(w - 8)(w + 10) = 0$$

$w - 8 = 0$	$w + 10 = 0$
$+8 \quad +8$	$-10 \quad -10$
$w \quad\quad = 8$	$w \quad\quad = -10$

Since the width cannot be negative, it must be 8 feet.

Exercises: Chapter 11, Section G

In Exercises 1 - 6, solve.

1. The width of a square is w inches. If the area of the square is **numerically** equal to twice its perimeter, find w.
(a) $\frac{1}{2}$ in.   (b) 8 in.   (c) 2 in.   (d) $\frac{1}{4}$ in.   (e) $\frac{1}{8}$ in.

2. The area A of a rectangle is given by the expression $5s^5t^6 + 60s^8t^9$. If the width of the rectangle is $5s^5t^6$, what is its length?
(a) $25s^4t^3$ (b) $25s^5t^6 + 12s^3t^3$ (c) $12s^8t^9$ (d) $1 + 12s^3t^3$ (e) $60s^8t^9$

3. The area of a square whose length is x is equal to the area of a rectangle whose length is $3x$ and width is $x - 2$. Find x.
(a) 0   (b) 2   (c) 3   (d) 1   (e) $\frac{1}{3}$

4. The area of a rectangle is given by the expression $40x^3y^4 + 80x^7y^4$ square meters. If the length of the rectangle is $10x^2y^3$ meters, what is its width?
(a) $40xy + 80x^5y$ (b) $4x^2y + 8x^5y$ (c) $4xy + 8x^5y$ (d) $4xy + 8x^5y^5$
(e) $4xy^4 + 8x^5y$

5. The length of a rectangle is 3 ft. longer than its width. If the area is 40 ft.^{2}, the width is:
(a) 8 ft.   (b) 5 ft.   (c) 2 ft.   (d) 3 ft.   (e) 10 ft.

6. The width of a rectangle is 5 ft. shorter than its length. If the area is 14 ft.^{2}, the width is:
(a) 2 ft.   (b) 7 ft.   (c) 3 ft.   (d) 1 ft.   (e) 4 ft.

In right triangle ABC, angle C is a right angle, c is the longest side of the triangle (called the **hypotenuse**), and a and b are the shorter sides (called the **legs**). The **Pythagorean Theorem** states that $a^2 + b^2 = c^2$.

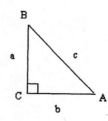

7. The sides of a right triangle are x, $x - 1$, and $x - 2$. Find x.
(a) 5   (b) 1   (c) 4   (d) 7   (e) 3

8. The sides of a right triangle are x, $x - 1$, and $x - 8$. Find the shortest side.
(a) 5   (b) 12   (c) 13   (d) 7   (e) 9

Chapter 12:   Radicals and Rational Exponents

Section A. Radicals

Square Roots

Recall from Chapter 4 that if a and b are real numbers and $b^2 = a$, then b is a **square root** of a. For example, both -5 and 5 are square roots of 25 because $5^2 = 25$ and $(-5)^2 = 25$.

Every positive number has two square roots, a positive one and a negative one. The positive square root of a positive number n is called the **principal square root** of n, and is written using the **radical symbol** as $\sqrt{n}$ (we call n the **radicand**).

For example, $\sqrt{25} = 5$ and $\sqrt{64} = 8$. The negative square root of n is written as $-\sqrt{n}$. Thus, $-\sqrt{16} = -4$ and $-\sqrt{81} = -9$. Negative numbers do not have square roots. For example, $\sqrt{-1}$ and $\sqrt{-64}$ are undefined.

Here are some square roots of perfect squares:

$\sqrt{1} = 1$	$\sqrt{49} = 7$	$\sqrt{169} = 13$
$\sqrt{4} = 2$	$\sqrt{64} = 8$	$\sqrt{196} = 14$
$\sqrt{9} = 3$	$\sqrt{81} = 9$	$\sqrt{225} = 15$
$\sqrt{16} = 4$	$\sqrt{100} = 10$	$\sqrt{256} = 16$
$\sqrt{25} = 5$	$\sqrt{121} = 11$	$\sqrt{289} = 17$
$\sqrt{36} = 6$	$\sqrt{144} = 12$	$\sqrt{324} = 18$

The list above only includes the (principal) square roots of perfect squares. However, every positive number has a principal square root (see Chapter 4).

If a is a positive integer which is *not* a perfect square, then $\sqrt{a}$ is an irrational number. For example, $\sqrt{15}$ and $\sqrt{76}$ are irrational since 15 and 76 are not perfect squares.

Cube Roots

If a and b be two real numbers and $b^3 = a$, then b is called a **cube root** of a. For example, 2 is a cube root of 8 since $2^3 = 8$. In fact, 2 is the **only** (real) cube root of 8. Similarly, -2 is a cube root of -8 because $(-2)^3 = -8$. Again, -2 is the **only** (real) cube root of -8.

Every real number has a unique (real) cube root. This root is called the **principal cube root**. We write 'b is the **cube root** of a' symbolically as $b = \sqrt[3]{a}$. Just like for square roots, we call the term 'a' under the **cube root symbol** the **radicand**.

A **perfect cube** is a natural number which is the cube of another natural number. Examples of perfect cubes are 1, 8, 27, and so on.

Here is a list of some cube roots of perfect cubes:

$$\sqrt[3]{1} = 1 \qquad\qquad \sqrt[3]{216} = 6$$
$$\sqrt[3]{8} = 2 \qquad\qquad \sqrt[3]{343} = 7$$
$$\sqrt[3]{27} = 3 \qquad\qquad \sqrt[3]{512} = 8$$
$$\sqrt[3]{64} = 4 \qquad\qquad \sqrt[3]{729} = 9$$
$$\sqrt[3]{125} = 5 \qquad\qquad \sqrt[3]{1,000} = 10$$

Numbers such as $\sqrt[3]{2}$, $\sqrt[3]{7.4456}$, and $\sqrt[3]{-\pi}$ exist as well. For instance, we could approximate the value of $\sqrt[3]{2}$ by setting $x = \sqrt[3]{2}$, which is the same as $x^3 = 2$, and choose numbers for x which, when cubed, is close to 2. We will discuss this further in the next section.

Rule: If a is a positive integer which is *not* a perfect cube, then $\sqrt[3]{a}$ is an irrational number.

For example, $\sqrt[3]{2}$, $\sqrt[3]{26}$, and $\sqrt[3]{55}$ are irrational numbers.

Radicals

Suppose that a and b are real numbers and $n > 1$ is a natural number. If $b^n = a$, then we say that b is an nth **root** of a. For example, -3 and 3 are fourth roots of 81 since $(-3)^4 = 81$ and $3^4 = 81$, and the **only** fifth root of 32 is 2 because $2^5 = 32$.

If a is a real number which has an nth root, then the **principal n^{th} root of a**, written as $\sqrt[n]{a}$, is the nth root that has the same sign as a. For example,

$$\underbrace{\sqrt[4]{81} = 3}_{3^4=81} \quad \text{and} \quad \underbrace{\sqrt[5]{-32} = -2.}_{(-2)^5=-32}$$

The natural number n is called the **index** of the radical and a is called the **radicand**. Note that a square root is a radical of index 2, and a cube root is a radical of index 3.

Observe that $\sqrt[3]{-64} = -4$, but $\sqrt{-64}$ doesn't exist because $x^2 \ne -64$ for any real number x. The general rule is:

Rule for roots to exist:
1) If the index of a radical is an even number, then the radicand must be non-negative. In this case, the radical will be non-negative.
2) If the index is an odd number, then the radicand can be any real number. The sign of the radical is the same as the sign of the radicand.

281

For instance, $\sqrt[5]{-1}$ exists because it has index 5, which is an odd number. In fact, $\sqrt[5]{-1} = -1$ (both the radicand and the radical are negative). On the other hand, $\sqrt[6]{-1}$ does not exist.because it has index 6, which is an even number

Example 1. State the index and radicand. Evaluate each radical.

1) $\sqrt{16}$ 2) $\sqrt[3]{125}$ 3) $\sqrt[4]{625}$ 4) $\sqrt[7]{-1}$ 5) $\sqrt[3]{-64}$ 6) $\sqrt[4]{256}$

Solution: 1) The index is 2, the radicand is 16, and $\sqrt{16} = 4$ since $4^2 = 16$.
              2) The index is 3, the radicand is 125, and $\sqrt[3]{125} = 5$ since $5^3 = 125$.
              3) The index is 4, the radicand is 625, and $\sqrt[4]{625} = 5$ because $5^4 = 625$.
              4) The index is 5, the radicand is -1, and $\sqrt[7]{-1} = -1$ because $(-1)^7 = -1$.
              5) The index is 3, the radicand is -64, and $\sqrt[3]{-64} = -4$ since $(-4)^3 = -64$.
              6) The index is 4, the radicand is 256, and $\sqrt[4]{256} = 4$ because $4^4 = 256$.

A natural number is called a **perfect n^{th} power** if it is the nth power of a natural number. Here are some more commonly seen radicals of perfect n^{th} powers:

Fourth roots	Fifth roots	Sixth roots
$\sqrt[4]{1} = 1$	$\sqrt[5]{1} = 1$	$\sqrt[6]{1} = 1$
$\sqrt[4]{16} = 2$	$\sqrt[5]{32} = 2$	$\sqrt[6]{64} = 2$
$\sqrt[4]{81} = 3$	$\sqrt[5]{243} = 3$	$\sqrt[6]{729} = 3$
$\sqrt[4]{256} = 4$		
$\sqrt[4]{625} = 5$		

The next rule generalizes a rule that we've mentioned for square roots and cube roots.

Rule: If a is a positive integer which is *not* a perfect n^{th} power, then $\sqrt[n]{a}$ is an irrational number. For example, $\sqrt[4]{17}$ and $\sqrt[7]{1,000}$ are irrational numbers because 17 is not a perfect fourth root and $1,000$ is not a perfect seventh root.

Exercises: Chapter 12, Section A

In Exercises 1 - 16, evaluate.

1. $\sqrt{81}$

2. $\sqrt{289}$

3. $-\sqrt{25}$

4. $-\sqrt{144}$

5. $\sqrt[3]{8}$

6. $\sqrt[3]{-216}$

7. $-\sqrt[3]{64}$

8. $-\sqrt[3]{-729}$

9. $\sqrt[5]{32}$

10. $\sqrt[4]{81}$

11. $-\sqrt[5]{1}$

12. $-\sqrt[4]{256}$

13. $\sqrt[3]{-27}$

14. $\sqrt[4]{16}$

15. $-\sqrt[5]{-243}$

16. $\sqrt[3]{1,000}$

In Exercises 17 - 24, state whether or not the root exists.

17. $\sqrt[3]{216}$

18. $\sqrt{25}$

19. $\sqrt[4]{-16}$

20. $-\sqrt[4]{16}$

21. $-\sqrt[4]{-16}$

22. $\sqrt[3]{-243}$

23. $\sqrt[8]{0}$

24. $\sqrt[6]{-1}$

In Exercises 25 - 32, evaluate (if possible).

25. $\sqrt[4]{16}$

26. $\sqrt[3]{-35}$

27. $\sqrt[3]{9}$

28. $\sqrt[6]{64}$

29. $\sqrt[3]{-1}$

30. $\sqrt[3]{-26}$

31. $\sqrt{115}$

32. $\sqrt[3]{206}$

Section B. Approximating Radicals

Every positive number has an nth root. Numbers such as $\sqrt{3}$, $\sqrt[3]{2}$, and $\sqrt[4]{17}$ do exist, but they are irrational numbers. You can never write down the decimal value for any of them because they are non-terminating and non-repeating decimals. However, you can approximate their values.

In Chapter 4, we saw how to approximate a square root. The same method applies to radicals in general. For example, let's approximate the value of $\sqrt[3]{2}$ to the nearest hundredth. Notice that $\sqrt[3]{2}$ is between 1 and 2 because $1^3 = 1$, $2^3 = 8$, and $\left(\sqrt[3]{2}\right)^3 = 2$. Furthermore, $\sqrt[3]{2}$ is closer to 1 than it is to 2. Let's pick two numbers which are close to 1, say 1.2 and 1.3, and cube them:

$$(1.2)^3 = 1.728 \quad \text{and} \quad (1.3)^3 = 2.197$$

Since 2 is between 1.728 and 2.197, we know that the value of $\sqrt[3]{2}$ is between 1.2 and 1.3. Let's cube 1.25 and 1.26:

$$(1.25)^3 = 1.953125 \quad \text{and} \quad (1.26)^3 = 2.000376$$

Now we see that $\sqrt[3]{2}$ is between 1.25 and 1.26 because 2 is between 1.953125 and 2.000376. We need one more decimal place to approximate $\sqrt[3]{2}$ to the nearest hundredth. Let's cube 1.258 and 1.259:

$$(1.258)^3 = 1.990865512 \quad \text{and} \quad (1.259)^3 = 1.995616979$$

Therefore, $\sqrt[3]{2}$ is between 1.259 and 1.26, which rounds off to 1.26. Using the method of ''zeroing in' on the value of the radical, we can approximate it to any decimal place that we'd like.

Example 1. Find two consecutive integers for which the given radical is between.
1) $\sqrt{46}$ 2) $\sqrt[3]{38}$ 3) $\sqrt[5]{287}$

Solution:
1) $6^2 = 36$, $7^2 = 49$, and 46 is between 36 and 49. Therefore, $\sqrt{46}$ is between 6 and 7.
2) $3^3 = 27$, $4^3 = 64$, and 38 is between 27 and 64. Therefore, $\sqrt[3]{38}$ is between 3 and 4.
3) $\sqrt[5]{287}$ is between 3 and 4 since $3^5 = 243$, $4^5 = 1,024$, and 287 is between 243 and 1,024.

Example 2. Determine the integer which closest to each radical.
1) $\sqrt{190}$ 2) $\sqrt[3]{115}$ 3) $\sqrt[3]{6,801}$ 4) $\sqrt[4]{43,885}$

Solution:
1) Observe that $13^2 = 169$ and $14^2 = 196$. Since 190 is closer to 196 than it is to 169, $\sqrt{190}$ is closest to 14.
2) Notice that $4^3 = 64$ and $5^3 = 125$. Since 115 is closer to 125 than it is to 64, $\sqrt[3]{115}$ is closest to 5.

3) Let's take fifth powers of some numbers:

$$4^5 = 1,024, \quad \underbrace{5^5 = 3,125, \quad \text{and} \quad 6^5 = 7,776}.$$

6,801 is between 3,125 and 7,776.

Since $6,801$ is closer to $7,776$, $\sqrt[5]{6,801}$ is closest to 6.

Exercises: Chapter 12, Section B

In Exercises 1 - 10, choose the correct answer.

1. Which two integers is $\sqrt{73}$ between?
(a) 6 and 7   (b) 7 and 8   (c) 8 and 9   (d) 9 and 10   (e) 10 and 11

2. Which two integers is $\sqrt{410}$ between?
(a) 18 and 19   (b) 19 and 20   (c) 20 and 21   (d) 21 and 22   (e) 22 and 23

3. Which two integers is $\sqrt[3]{1,569}$ between?
(a) 9 and 10   (b) 10 and 11   (c) 11 and 12   (d) 12 and 13   (e) 13 and 14

4. Which two integers is $\sqrt[3]{14,840}$ between?
(a) 10 and 11   (b) 11 and 12   (c) 12 and 13   (d) 13 and 14   (e) 14 and 15

5. Which integer is closest to $\sqrt{1,825}$?
(a) 40   (b) 41   (c) 42   (d) 43   (e) 44

6. Which integer is closest to $\sqrt[3]{6,133}$?
(a) 15   (b) 16   (c) 17   (d) 18   (e) 19

7. Which integer is closest to $\sqrt[5]{26,000}$?
(a) 6   (b) 7   (c) 8   (d) 9   (e) 10

8. Which integer is closest to $\sqrt[4]{4,703}$?
(a) 6   (b) 7   (c) 8   (d) 9   (e) 10

9. Which integer is closest to $\sqrt{28,324}$?
(a) 165   (b) 166   (c) 167   (d) 168   (e) 169

10. Which integer is closest to $\sqrt[3]{13,033}$?
(a) 23   (b) 24   (c) 25   (d) 26   (e) 27

Section C. Simplifying Radicals

Next we list some properties of radicals. Similar properties were discussed in Chapter 4 for square roots.

Property 1. Suppose that a is any real number.
1. If n is an even number, then $\sqrt[n]{a^n} = |a|$.
2. If n is an odd number, then $\sqrt[n]{a^n} = a$.

For example, $\sqrt[3]{7^3} = 7$ and $\sqrt[8]{(-31)^8} = |-31| = 31$.

Example 1. Evaluate using Property 1.

1) $\sqrt[4]{12^4}$ 2) $\sqrt[5]{(-19)^5}$ 3) $\sqrt{(-78)^2}$ 4) $\sqrt[3]{(-16)^3}$

Solution: 1) $\sqrt[4]{12^4} = |12| = 12$ 2) $\sqrt[5]{(-19)^5} = -19$

3) $\sqrt{(-78)^2} = |-78| = 78$ 4) $\sqrt[3]{(-16)^3} = -16$

Property 2. If $\sqrt[n]{a}$ and $\sqrt[n]{b}$ are well-defined, then $\sqrt{a} \times \sqrt{b} = \sqrt{a \times b}$.

For example, $\sqrt[3]{4} \times \sqrt[3]{2} = \sqrt[3]{4 \times 2} = \sqrt[3]{8} = 2$ and $\sqrt[4]{16 \times 81} = \sqrt[4]{16} \times \sqrt[4]{81} = 2 \times 3 = 6$. Notice that

$$\sqrt[4]{-16} \times \sqrt[4]{-81} \neq \sqrt[4]{(-16) \times (-81)}$$

since $\sqrt[4]{-16}$ and $\sqrt[4]{-81}$ are undefined, even though $\sqrt[4]{(-16) \times (-81)}$ is well defined:

$$\sqrt[4]{(-16) \times (-81)} = \sqrt[4]{1,296} = 6$$

Example 2. Simplify using Property 2.

1) $\sqrt[4]{8} \times \sqrt[4]{2}$ 2) $\sqrt[3]{216 \times 64}$ 3) $\sqrt[5]{(-32)(-243)}$ 4) $\sqrt[4]{100} \times \sqrt[4]{100}$

Solution: 1) $\sqrt[4]{8} \times \sqrt[4]{2} = \sqrt[4]{8 \times 2} = \sqrt[4]{16} = 2$

2) $\sqrt[3]{216 \times 64} = \sqrt[3]{216} \times \sqrt[3]{64} = 6 \times 4 = 24$

3) $\sqrt[5]{(-32)(-729)} = \sqrt[5]{-32} \times \sqrt[5]{-243} = (-2) \times (-3) = 6$

4) $\sqrt[4]{100} \times \sqrt[4]{100} = \sqrt[4]{100 \times 100} = \sqrt[4]{10,000} = 10$

Property 3. If $\sqrt[n]{a}$ and $\sqrt[n]{b}$ are well-defined and $\sqrt[n]{b} \neq 0$, then $\sqrt[n]{\dfrac{a}{b}} = \dfrac{\sqrt[n]{a}}{\sqrt[n]{b}}$.

For example, $\sqrt[3]{\dfrac{8}{125}} = \dfrac{\sqrt[3]{8}}{\sqrt[3]{125}} = \dfrac{2}{5}$ and $\dfrac{\sqrt[4]{405}}{\sqrt[4]{5}} = \sqrt[4]{\dfrac{405}{5}} = \sqrt[4]{81} = 3$.

Example 3. Simplify using Property 3.

1) $\sqrt[4]{\dfrac{81}{16}}$ 2) $\sqrt[3]{\dfrac{-64}{-1,000}}$ 3) $\dfrac{\sqrt[4]{6}}{\sqrt[4]{96}}$

Solution: 1) $\sqrt[4]{\dfrac{81}{16}} = \dfrac{\sqrt[4]{81}}{\sqrt[4]{16}} = \dfrac{3}{2}$ 2) $\sqrt[3]{\dfrac{-64}{-1,000}} = \underbrace{\sqrt[3]{\dfrac{8}{125}}}_{\text{Simplify the fraction.}} = \dfrac{\sqrt[3]{8}}{\sqrt[3]{125}} = \dfrac{2}{5}$

       3) $\dfrac{\sqrt[4]{6}}{\sqrt[4]{96}} = \underbrace{\sqrt[4]{\dfrac{6}{96}} = \sqrt[4]{\dfrac{1}{16}}}_{\text{Simplify the fraction.}} = \dfrac{\sqrt[4]{1}}{\sqrt[4]{16}} = \dfrac{1}{2}$

Property 4. If $\sqrt[n]{a}$ is well-defined, then $\left(\sqrt[n]{a}\right)^n = a$.

For example, $\left(\sqrt[6]{28}\right)^6 = 28$ and $\left(\sqrt[5]{-712.03}\right)^5 = -712.03$.

Example 4. Simplify using Property 4.

1) $\left(\sqrt{19}\right)^2$ 2) $\left(\sqrt[3]{72}\right)^3$ 3) $\left(\sqrt[3]{-104}\right)^3$ 4) $\left(\sqrt[7]{y}\right)^7$

Solution: 1) 19   2) 72   3) –104   4) y

Simplifying Radicals

Recall that to simplify a square root, you first factor the radicand so that one of the factors is a perfect square. Then you apply Property 2. For example,

$$\sqrt{162} = \sqrt{81 \times 2} = \sqrt{81} \times \sqrt{2} = 9 \times \sqrt{2} = 9\sqrt{2}.$$

Simplifying any radical works in a similar way.

Rule for simplifying the radical of a number:
1) Factor the radicand so that one of the factors is a perfect n^{th} power.
2) Apply Property 2.

Example 5. Simplify.

1) $\sqrt[3]{40}$ 2) $\sqrt[4]{80}$ 3) $-\sqrt[4]{162}$ 4) $\sqrt[3]{-64}$

Solution: 1) $\sqrt[3]{40} = \sqrt[3]{8 \times 5} = \sqrt[3]{8} \times \sqrt[3]{5} = 2\sqrt[3]{5}$
           2) $\sqrt[4]{80} = \sqrt[4]{16 \times 5} = \sqrt[4]{16} \times \sqrt[4]{5} = 2\sqrt[4]{5}$

$3) - \sqrt[4]{162} = - \sqrt[4]{81 \times 2} = - \sqrt[4]{81} \times \sqrt[4]{2} = -3\sqrt[4]{2}$

$4) \sqrt[5]{-64} = \sqrt[5]{(-32) \times 2} = \sqrt[5]{-32} \times \sqrt[5]{2} = -2\sqrt[5]{2}$

Next we will simplify radicals whose radicand is a monomial (**assume that all variables represent non-negative numbers**). To simplify $\sqrt{x^7}$, we divide the exponent of the variable by the index of the radical:

$$7 \div 2 = 3 \text{ R } 1$$

The quotient, 3, tells us that the the number of x's that come out of the radical, and the remainder, 1, tells us how many x's remain in the radical. Therefore, $\sqrt{x^7} = x^3 \sqrt{x^1} = x^3 \sqrt{x}$.

To simplify $\sqrt[5]{y^{23}}$, we divide $23 \div 5 = 4 \text{ R } 3$. This tells us that 4 y's come out of the radical, and 3 y's stay in the radical:

$$\sqrt[5]{y^{23}} = y^4 \sqrt[5]{y^3}$$

Rule for simplifying the radical of a variable raised to an exponent: Divide exponent ÷ index. The quotient is the number of variables that come out of the radical, and the remainder is the number of variables that remain the radical.

Example 6. Simplify. Assume that the variables represent non-negative numbers.

1) $\sqrt{x^5}$　　　2) $\sqrt{y^{14}}$　　　3) $\sqrt[3]{x^{13}}$　　　4) $\sqrt[4]{x^{31}}$

Solution:　1) $\underbrace{\sqrt{x^5} = x^2 \sqrt{x^1}}_{5 \div 2 = 2 \, R \, 1} = x^2 \sqrt{x}$　　　2) $\underbrace{\sqrt{y^{14}} = y^7}_{14 \div 2 = 7 \, R \, 0}$

3) $\underbrace{\sqrt[3]{x^{13}} = x^4 \sqrt[3]{x^1}}_{13 \div 3 = 4 \, R \, 1} = x^4 \sqrt[3]{x}$　　　4) $\underbrace{\sqrt[4]{x^{31}} = x^7 \sqrt[4]{x^3}}_{31 \div 4 = 7 \, R \, 3}$

If the radicand of a radical is a monomial, then simplify it in pieces. To demonstrate, let's simplify $\sqrt{18x^6 y^{11}}$. First simplify $\sqrt{18}$: $\sqrt{18} = \sqrt{9} \times \sqrt{2} = 3\sqrt{2}$. Next simplify the square root of the variable factors: $\underbrace{\sqrt{x^6} = x^3}_{6 \div 2 = 3 \, R \, 0}$ and $\underbrace{\sqrt{y^{11}} = y^5 \sqrt{y^1}}_{11 \div 2 = 5 \, R \, 1}$. Now multiply the simplified pieces together:

$$\sqrt{18x^6 y^{11}} = \left(3\sqrt{2}\right)(x^3)\left(y^5 \sqrt{y}\right) = 3x^3 y^5 \sqrt{2y}$$

Example 7. Simplify. Assume that all variables represent non-negative numbers.

1) $\sqrt{4x^2 y^8}$　　　2) $\sqrt[3]{32a^{14} b^6}$　　　3) $\sqrt[4]{81x^3 y^{12}}$

Solution:

1) $\sqrt{4x^2y^8} = 2xy^4$ since $\sqrt{4} = 2$, $\underbrace{\sqrt{x^2} = x}_{2\div2=1\ R\ 0}$, and $\underbrace{\sqrt{y^8} = y^4}_{8\div2=4\ R\ 0}$.

2) $\sqrt[3]{32a^{14}b^6} = 2a^4b^3\sqrt[3]{4a^2}$ because $\sqrt[3]{32} = \sqrt[3]{8} \times \sqrt[3]{4} = 2\sqrt[3]{4}$, $\underbrace{\sqrt[3]{a^{14}} = a^4\sqrt[3]{a^2}}_{14\div3=4\ R\ 2}$, and $\underbrace{\sqrt[3]{b^6} = b^2}_{6\div3=2\ R\ 0}$.

3) $\sqrt[4]{81x^3y^{12}} = 9y^3\sqrt[4]{x^3}$ since $\sqrt[4]{81} = 3$, $\underbrace{\sqrt[4]{x^3}\ \text{is simplified}}_{3\div4=0\ R\ 3}$, and $\underbrace{\sqrt[4]{y^{12}} = y^3}_{12\div4=3\ R\ 0}$.

Simplifying radicals which fractional radicands works the same way: simplify it in pieces. For example, if x represents a non-negative number and y represents a positive number, then

$$\sqrt[3]{\frac{x^7}{54y^{14}}} = \frac{x^2}{3y^4}\sqrt[3]{\frac{x}{2y^2}} \text{ because } \underbrace{\sqrt[3]{x^7} = x^2\sqrt[3]{x}}_{7\div3=2\ R\ 1}, \underbrace{\sqrt[3]{54} = 3\sqrt[3]{2}}_{\sqrt[3]{54}=\sqrt[3]{27}\,\sqrt[3]{2}=3\sqrt[3]{2}}, \text{ and } \underbrace{\sqrt[3]{y^{14}} = y^4\sqrt[3]{y^2}}_{14\div3=4\ R\ 2}.$$

Example 8. Simplify. Assume that all variables represent positive numbers.

1) $\sqrt[4]{\dfrac{64a^7}{b^4}}$　　2) $\sqrt[3]{\dfrac{125}{x^5y}}$　　3) $\sqrt{\dfrac{40a^2}{49}}$　　4) $\sqrt[5]{\dfrac{-32s^9}{t^{11}}}$

Solution: 1) $\sqrt[4]{\dfrac{64a^7}{b^4}} = \dfrac{2a\sqrt[4]{4a^3}}{b}$ since $\underbrace{\sqrt[4]{64} = 2\sqrt[4]{4}}_{\sqrt[4]{64}=\sqrt[4]{16}\,\sqrt[4]{4}=2\sqrt[4]{4}}$, $\underbrace{\sqrt[4]{a^7} = a\sqrt[4]{a^3}}_{7\div4=1\ R\ 3}$, and $\underbrace{\sqrt[4]{b^4} = b}_{4\div4=1\ R\ 0}$.

2) $\sqrt[3]{\dfrac{125}{x^5y}} = \dfrac{5}{x\sqrt[3]{x^2y}}$ because $\sqrt[3]{125} = 5$, $\underbrace{\sqrt[3]{x^5} = x\sqrt[3]{x^2}}_{5\div3=1\ R\ 2}$, and $\sqrt[3]{y}$ is already simplified.

3) $\sqrt{\dfrac{40a^2}{49}} = \dfrac{2a\sqrt{10}}{7}$ since $\sqrt{40} = 2\sqrt{10}$, $\underbrace{\sqrt{a^2} = a}_{2\div2=1\ R\ 0}$, and $\sqrt{49} = 7$.

4) $\sqrt[5]{\dfrac{-32s^9}{t^{11}}} = -\dfrac{2s\sqrt[5]{s^4}}{t^2\sqrt[5]{t}}$ because $\sqrt[5]{-32} = -2$, $\underbrace{\sqrt[5]{s^9} = s\sqrt[5]{s^4}}_{9\div5=1\ R\ 4}$, and $\underbrace{\sqrt[5]{t^{11}} = t^2\sqrt[5]{t}}_{11\div5=2\ R\ 1}$.

Notice that $-\dfrac{2s\sqrt[5]{s^4}}{t^2\sqrt[5]{t}} = -\dfrac{2s}{t^2} \cdot \dfrac{\sqrt[5]{s^4}}{\sqrt[5]{t}} = -\dfrac{2s}{t^2}\sqrt[5]{\dfrac{s^4}{t}}$.

Example 9. Perform the indicated operation and simplify. Assume that all variables represent positive numbers.

1) $\sqrt{7} \cdot \sqrt{7}$

2) $\sqrt{2x^2} \cdot \sqrt{6x^4}$

3) $\left(\sqrt{2b^3}\right)^2$

4) $\left(7\sqrt[3]{5}\right)\left(3\sqrt[3]{6}\right)$

5) $\sqrt[3]{9a^2} \cdot \sqrt[3]{-9a^7}$

6) $\sqrt[3]{16xy^5} \cdot \sqrt[3]{4x^4y}$

7) $\left(5\sqrt[3]{2}\right)^3$

8) $\dfrac{\sqrt{72x^{14}}}{\sqrt{8x^9}}$

9) $\dfrac{\sqrt{120a^{11}b^8}}{\sqrt{12a^9b^9}}$

Solution:

1) $\sqrt{7} \cdot \sqrt{7} = \sqrt{7 \cdot 7} = \sqrt{49} = 7$. Alternatively, $\sqrt{7} \cdot \sqrt{7} = \left(\sqrt{7}\right)^2 = 7$ by Property 4.

2) $\sqrt{2x^2} \cdot \sqrt{6x^4} = \sqrt{2x^2 \cdot 6x^4} = \underbrace{\sqrt{12x^6} = 2x^3\sqrt{3}}_{\sqrt{12}=2\sqrt{3} \text{ and } \sqrt{x^6}=x^3.}$

3) $\left(\sqrt{2b^3}\right)^2 = 2b^3$ by Property 4.

4) $\left(7\sqrt[3]{5}\right)\left(3\sqrt[3]{6}\right) = 7 \times 3 \times \sqrt[3]{5} \times \sqrt[3]{6} = 21\sqrt[3]{30}$

5) $\sqrt[3]{9a^2} \cdot \sqrt[3]{-9a^7} = \sqrt[3]{(9a^2)(-9a^7)} = \sqrt[3]{-81a^9} = -3a^3\sqrt[3]{3}$ since $\sqrt[3]{-81} = -3\sqrt[3]{3}$ and $\sqrt[3]{a^9} = a^3$.

6) $\sqrt[3]{16xy^5} \cdot \sqrt[3]{4x^4y} = \sqrt[3]{(16xy^5)(4x^4y)} = \underbrace{\sqrt[3]{64x^5y^6} = 4xy^2\sqrt[3]{x^2}}_{\sqrt[3]{64}=4,\ \sqrt[3]{x^5}=x\sqrt[3]{x^2},\ \text{and } \sqrt[3]{y^6}=y^2.}$

7) Using the fact that $(5x)^3 = 5^3x^3$, we have $\underbrace{\left(5\sqrt[3]{2}\right)^3 = 5^3 \cdot \left(\sqrt[3]{2}\right)^3}_{\text{Think of } \sqrt[3]{2} \text{ as } x.} = 125 \cdot 2 = 250$.

8) $\dfrac{\sqrt{72x^{14}}}{\sqrt{8x^9}} = \sqrt{\dfrac{72x^{14}}{8x^9}} = \sqrt{9x^5} = 3x^2\sqrt{x}$ because $\sqrt{9} = 3$ and $\sqrt{x^5} = x^2\sqrt{x}$.

9) $\dfrac{\sqrt{120a^{11}b^8}}{\sqrt{12a^9b^9}} = \sqrt{\dfrac{120a^{11}b^8}{12a^9b^9}} = \sqrt{\dfrac{10a^2}{b}} = \dfrac{a\sqrt{10}}{\sqrt{b}}$

Exercises: Chapter 12, Exercise C

In Exercises 1 - 20, choose the correct answer. Assume all variables represent positive numbers.

1. $\sqrt{18} \cdot \sqrt{18} =$
(a) 18   (b) 9   (c) 12   (d) 6   (e) 24

2. $\sqrt{4x^2} =$
(a) $2x^2$ (b) $4x$ (c) $2x$ (d) x^2 (e) 2

3. $\sqrt{\dfrac{y^2}{36}} =$
(a) $\dfrac{y}{36}$ (b) $\dfrac{y}{6}$ (c) $\dfrac{y^2}{6}$ (d) $\dfrac{y}{18}$ (e) $\dfrac{y^2}{36}$

4. $\sqrt[3]{(27)(125)} =$
(a) 14   (b) 15   (c) 6   (d) 8   (e) 16

5. $\sqrt[4]{\dfrac{81}{625}} =$
(a) $\dfrac{9}{25}$ (b) $\dfrac{3}{625}$ (c) $\dfrac{81}{5}$ (d) $\dfrac{3}{5}$ (e) $\dfrac{9}{5}$

6. $\sqrt{56} =$
(a) $14\sqrt{2}$ (b) $2\sqrt{15}$ (c) $2\sqrt{10}$ (d) $3\sqrt{7}$ (e) $2\sqrt{14}$

7. $\sqrt[3]{-4,000} =$
(a) $-10\sqrt[3]{-4}$ (b) $-100\sqrt[3]{4}$ (c) $-40\sqrt[3]{10}$ (d) $-4\sqrt[3]{10}$ (e) $4\sqrt[3]{10}$

8. $\sqrt[3]{\dfrac{72}{125}} =$
(a) $\dfrac{2\sqrt[3]{9}}{5}$ (b) $\dfrac{9\sqrt[3]{2}}{5}$ (c) $\dfrac{6\sqrt[3]{2}}{5}$ (d) $\dfrac{2\sqrt[3]{9}}{25}$ (e) $10\sqrt[3]{9}$

9. $\sqrt[4]{\dfrac{1}{80}} =$
(a) $\dfrac{2}{\sqrt[4]{5}}$ (b) $\dfrac{1}{5\sqrt[4]{2}}$ (c) $\dfrac{1}{2\sqrt[4]{5}}$ (d) $\dfrac{1}{4\sqrt[4]{5}}$ (e) $\dfrac{1}{2\sqrt{5}}$

10. $\sqrt{5} \cdot \sqrt{10} =$
(a) $2\sqrt{5}$
(b) $5\sqrt{2}$
(c) $2\sqrt{10}$
(d) $10\sqrt{5}$
(e) $5\sqrt{10}$

11. $\left(3\sqrt{11}\right)^2 =$
(a) $9\sqrt{11}$
(b) 66
(c) 33
(d) 99
(e) $11\sqrt{3}$

12. $\left(-5\sqrt[3]{4}\right)\left(-2\sqrt[3]{16}\right) =$
(a) -28
(b) 40
(c) -40
(d) -20
(e) 20

13. $\sqrt{16x^2 y^{11}} =$
(a) $4y^5\sqrt{xy}$
(b) $xy^{11}\sqrt{4x}$
(c) $4xy^5\sqrt{y}$
(d) $4x^2 y^5\sqrt{y}$
(e) $2xy^5\sqrt{y}$

14. $\sqrt[4]{96ab^6} =$
(a) $2b\sqrt[4]{6ab^2}$
(b) $6b\sqrt[4]{2ab^2}$
(c) $2ab\sqrt[4]{6b^2}$
(d) $4b^3\sqrt[4]{6a}$
(e) $2b\sqrt[4]{6a^2 b^2}$

15. $\sqrt[3]{72x^7 y^{14}} =$
(a) $6x^3 y^7\sqrt[3]{2x}$
(b) $2x^2 y^4\sqrt[3]{9xy^2}$
(c) $6x^2 y^4\sqrt[3]{xy^2}$
(d) $2x^3 y^7\sqrt[3]{9x}$
(e) $9xy^2\sqrt[3]{2x^2 y^4}$

16. $\sqrt{\dfrac{4b^5}{3a^2}} =$
(a) $\dfrac{2b^2\sqrt{b}}{3a}$
(b) $\dfrac{2b^4}{a^2}\sqrt{\dfrac{b}{3}}$
(c) $\dfrac{b^2}{a}\sqrt{\dfrac{2b}{3}}$
(d) $\dfrac{2b^2}{a}\sqrt{\dfrac{b}{3}}$
(e) $\dfrac{2b^4}{a\sqrt{3}}$

17. $\sqrt{8x^2 y} \cdot \sqrt{5x^3 y^2} =$
(a) $2xy\sqrt{10xy}$
(b) $2x^2 y\sqrt{10}$
(c) $10x^2 y\sqrt{2xy}$
(d) $2x^2\sqrt{10y}$
(e) $2x^2 y\sqrt{10xy}$

18. $\sqrt[3]{16x^5} \cdot \sqrt[3]{3x^3 y^7} =$
(a) $2x^2 y^4\sqrt[3]{6x^2}$
(b) $6x^2 y^4\sqrt[3]{2x^2}$
(c) $2x^2 y^4\sqrt[3]{6}$
(d) $2x^2 y^2\sqrt[3]{6x^2}$
(e) $2x^2 y^2\sqrt{6x^2 y}$

19. $\dfrac{\sqrt{49y^{12}}}{\sqrt{7y^5}} =$
(a) $7y^7$
(b) $y^7\sqrt{7}$
(c) $y^3\sqrt{7y}$
(d) $7y^3\sqrt{y}$
(e) $\dfrac{y^3\sqrt{y}}{7}$

20. $\dfrac{\sqrt[3]{2m^6}}{\sqrt[3]{500n^{16}}} =$

(a) $\dfrac{m^2}{5n^5\sqrt[3]{2n}}$ 　　(b) $\dfrac{5m^2\sqrt[3]{2}}{n^5\sqrt[3]{n}}$ 　　(c) $\dfrac{m^3}{5n^8\sqrt[3]{5}}$ 　　(d) $\dfrac{m^2\sqrt[3]{n}}{5n^5\sqrt[3]{2n}}$ 　　(e) $\dfrac{m^2}{\sqrt[3]{5n^5}}$

In Exercises 21 - 36, simplify. Assume all variables represent positive numbers.

21. $\sqrt{32}$ 　　　　　　22. $-\sqrt{72}$ 　　　　　　23. $\sqrt[3]{500}$ 　　　　　　24. $\sqrt{y^5}$

25. $\sqrt[5]{x^{13}}$ 　　　　　　26. $\sqrt{18x^6}$ 　　　　　　27. $\sqrt[3]{54y^5}$ 　　　　　　28. $\sqrt{8a^2b^9}$

29. $\sqrt[3]{27m^8n^3}$ 　　30. $\sqrt[5]{-256a^6b^2}$ 　　31. $\sqrt{\dfrac{54x^3}{y^4}}$ 　　32. $\sqrt[3]{\dfrac{a^9}{125b^7}}$

In Exercises 33 - 44, multiply or divide and simplify. Assume all variables represent non-negative numbers.

33. $\sqrt{5} \cdot \sqrt{10}$ 　　34. $\sqrt[3]{14} \cdot \sqrt[3]{6}$ 　　35. $\sqrt[3]{100x^2} \cdot \sqrt[3]{10x^4}$ 　　36. $\left(\sqrt{5x^4}\right)^2$

37. $\left(3x\sqrt{2}\right)^2$ 　　38. $\left(\sqrt[3]{12x}\right)\left(18\sqrt[3]{4x}\right)$ 　　39. $\left(2\sqrt[3]{7b}\right)^3$ 　　40. $\dfrac{\sqrt{16x^5}}{\sqrt{8x^4}}$

41. $\dfrac{\sqrt[3]{4x^3}}{\sqrt[3]{32x^9}}$ 　　42. $\dfrac{\sqrt{12xy^{10}}}{\sqrt{11x^7y^2}}$

Section D.   Addition and Subtraction of Radicals

In Chapter 4, we learned how to combine square roots. Recall that if two or more square roots have the same radicand, then we call them **like roots**. For example, $6\sqrt{3}$ and $7\sqrt{3}$ are like roots, but $5\sqrt{2}$ and $2\sqrt{5}$ are not like roots.

More generally, if two or more radicals have the same radicand and the same index, then they are called **like roots**. For example, $5\sqrt[3]{16}$ and $8\sqrt[3]{16}$ are like roots, as well as $-4\sqrt[5]{6a^2}$ and $8a\sqrt[5]{6a^2}$. On the other hand, $7\sqrt[4]{8x}$ and $-16\sqrt[4]{8}$ are not like roots because they have different radicands, and $-\sqrt[4]{9x^3}$ and $5\sqrt{9x^3}$ are not like roots because they have different indices.

Like roots can be added or subtracted to form a single root.

Rule for combining like roots: Combine the numbers outside the radical symbols, then multiply it by the original radical.

For example,

$$19\sqrt[3]{6} + 4\sqrt[3]{6} = 23\sqrt[3]{6} \quad \text{and} \quad 6\sqrt{3x} + 17\sqrt{3x} - 20\sqrt{3x} = 3\sqrt{3x}.$$

Add 19+4, then multiply by $\sqrt[3]{6}$.　　　　Combine 6+17−20, then multiply by $\sqrt{3x}$.

Observe that $8\sqrt[4]{3} + 2\sqrt[4]{6}$ cannot be combined into a single root since $8\sqrt[4]{3}$ and $2\sqrt[4]{6}$ are not like roots. Similarly, $\sqrt{x} + 3x^2 - 11\sqrt{2x}$ cannot be combined because $\sqrt{x}$, $3x^2$, and $-11\sqrt{2x}$ are not like roots.

Sometimes we can simplify the given radicals and produce like roots. For example,

$$4\sqrt[3]{2} + 19\sqrt[3]{54} = 4\sqrt[3]{2} + 19\left(3\sqrt[3]{2}\right) = 4\sqrt[3]{2} + 57\sqrt[3]{2} = 61\sqrt[3]{2}.$$

These aren't like roots.　　　　　　These are like roots!

Simplify $\sqrt[3]{54} = \sqrt[3]{27} \times \sqrt[3]{2} = 3\sqrt[3]{2}$.

Example 1. Combine and simplify.
1) $8\sqrt[3]{15} - 3\sqrt[3]{15}$　　　　2) $-14\sqrt{10x} + 3\sqrt{10x} - 18\sqrt{10x}$
3) $13\sqrt[3]{4} + 6\sqrt[3]{32}$　　　　4) $9x\sqrt[3]{3x} + 12\sqrt[3]{-3x^4} + 11x\sqrt[3]{375x}$

Solution:
1) $8\sqrt[3]{15} - 3\sqrt[3]{15} = (8-3)\sqrt[3]{15} = 5\sqrt[3]{15}$
2) $-14\sqrt{10x} + 3\sqrt{10x} - 18\sqrt{10x} = (-14+3-18)\sqrt{10x} = -29\sqrt{10x}$
3) $13\sqrt[3]{4} + 6\sqrt[3]{32} = 13\sqrt[3]{4} + 6\left(2\sqrt[3]{4}\right) = 13\sqrt[3]{4} + 12\sqrt[3]{4} = (13+12)\sqrt[3]{4} = 25\sqrt[3]{4}$

$\sqrt[3]{32} = \sqrt[3]{8} \times \sqrt[3]{4} = 2\sqrt[3]{4}$

4) $9x\sqrt[3]{3x} + 12\sqrt[3]{-3x^4} + 11x\sqrt[3]{375x} = 9x\sqrt[3]{3x} + 12\left(-x\sqrt[3]{3x}\right) + 11x\left(5\sqrt[3]{3x}\right)$

$\sqrt[3]{-3x^4} = -x\sqrt[3]{3x}$ and $\sqrt[3]{375x} = 5\sqrt[3]{3}$.

$$= 9x\sqrt[3]{3x} - 12x\sqrt[3]{3x} + 55x\sqrt[3]{3x} = (9x - 12x + 55x)\sqrt[3]{3x} = 52x\sqrt[3]{3x}$$

Example 2. Combine and simplify.

1) $\sqrt[3]{6} + 3\sqrt[3]{64} - 11\sqrt[3]{6}$ 2) $8\sqrt{9n} - \sqrt{4n} - 13\sqrt{9n^2}$, where $n \geq 0$.

Solution:

1) $\sqrt[3]{6} + 3\sqrt[3]{64} - 11\sqrt[3]{6} = \sqrt[3]{6} + 3(4) - 11\sqrt[3]{6} = \sqrt[3]{6} + 12 - 11\sqrt[3]{6} = -10\sqrt[3]{6} + 12$

Simplify $\sqrt[3]{64} = 4$.   Combine $\sqrt[3]{6} - 11\sqrt[3]{6} = -10\sqrt[3]{6}$.

2) $8\sqrt{9n} - \sqrt{4n} - 13\sqrt{9n^2} = 8(3\sqrt{n}) - 2\sqrt{n} - 13(3n) = 24\sqrt{n} - 2\sqrt{n} - 39n = 22\sqrt{n} - 39n$

Simplify $\sqrt{9n} = \sqrt{9}\sqrt{n} = 3\sqrt{n}$, $\sqrt{4n} = \sqrt{4}\sqrt{n} = 2\sqrt{n}$, and $\sqrt{9n^2} = \sqrt{9}\sqrt{n^2} = 3n$.   Combine $24\sqrt{n} - 2\sqrt{n} = 22\sqrt{n}$.

Next we will practice evaluating algebraic expressions which contain radicals.

Example 3. Find the value of each expression.

1) $2x^2 + 5\sqrt{x} - 4\sqrt{9x}$ when $x = 4$ 2) $a^2\sqrt{3a + b} - \sqrt{10a - 2b}$ when $a = 6$ and $b = -2$
3) $\sqrt{2a^2 + 6b}$ when $a = -4$ and $b = 2$.

Solution: First put parenthesis around each variable, then replace each variable with its given value.

1) $2(4)^2 + 5\sqrt{4} - 4\sqrt{9(4)} = 2(16) + 5(2) - 4\sqrt{36} = 32 + 10 - 24 = 18$
2) $(6)^2\sqrt{3(6) + (-2)} - \sqrt{10(6) - 2(-2)} = 36\sqrt{16} - \sqrt{64} = 36(4) - 8 = 136$
3) $\sqrt{2(-4)^2 + 6(2)} = \sqrt{32 + 12} = \sqrt{44} = 2\sqrt{11}$

Exercises: Chapter 12, Exercise D

In Exercises 1 - 13, combine. Assume all variables represent non-negative numbers.

1. $2\sqrt{10} + 15\sqrt{10}$

2. $8\sqrt[3]{9} - 20\sqrt[3]{9}$

3. $-3\sqrt[3]{7} + 12\sqrt[3]{7}$

4. $\sqrt{12} + \sqrt{27}$

5. $\sqrt[3]{16} + 2\sqrt[3]{24}$

6. $14\sqrt[3]{54} - \sqrt[3]{2}$

7. $4\sqrt{6x} + \sqrt{54x}$

8. $\sqrt{3y^3} - 6y\sqrt{3y}$

9. $\sqrt[3]{27x^3} + \sqrt{16x^2}$

10. $-3\sqrt[4]{16a^4} + 11a$

11. $6x\sqrt[3]{5x} + \sqrt[3]{40x^4}$

12. $5\sqrt[3]{2} - 12\sqrt[3]{16} + 6\sqrt[3]{54}$

13. $x\sqrt{2x} - 9\sqrt{50x^3} - \sqrt{2x^3}$

In Exercises 14 - 25, choose the correct answer. Assume all variables represent non-negative numbers.

14. $-3\sqrt{5} + 9\sqrt{5} - \sqrt{5} =$
(a) $5\sqrt{5}$
(b) $5\sqrt{15}$
(c) $-5\sqrt{5}$
(d) $4\sqrt{5}$
(e) $-2\sqrt{15}$

15. $6\sqrt[3]{7} - 4\sqrt[3]{-7} =$
(a) $10\sqrt[3]{7}$
(b) $2\sqrt[3]{7}$
(c) $10\sqrt[3]{-7}$
(d) 0
(e) $10\sqrt{7}$

16. $8\sqrt{8} - \sqrt{32} =$
(a) $16\sqrt{2} - 2\sqrt{4}$
(b) $20\sqrt{2}$
(c) $7\sqrt{-24}$
(d) $4\sqrt{2}$
(e) $12\sqrt{2}$

17. $9\sqrt{10} - 3\sqrt{81} + 2\sqrt{40} =$
(a) $8\sqrt{-31}$
(b) $5\sqrt{10} - 27$
(c) $11\sqrt{10} - 27$
(d) $13\sqrt{10} - 27$
(e) $-14\sqrt{10}$

18. $-10\sqrt[3]{16} + 3\sqrt[3]{250} =$
(a) $5\sqrt[3]{2}$
(b) $-5\sqrt[3]{2}$
(c) $-7\sqrt[3]{266}$
(d) $35\sqrt[3]{2}$
(e) $-5\sqrt{2}$

19. $4\sqrt[3]{216} - 2\sqrt[3]{4,000} =$
(a) $4\sqrt[3]{4}$
(b) -16
(c) $24 - 20\sqrt[3]{4}$
(d) $24 - 10\sqrt[3]{4}$
(e) $10 - 20\sqrt[3]{2}$

20. $3x\sqrt{2x} + \sqrt{8x^3} =$
(a) $6x^2\sqrt{2x}$ (b) $5x\sqrt{2x}$ (c) $3x\sqrt{10x}$ (d) $(2+3x)\sqrt{2x}$ (e) can't combined

21. $\sqrt{32x^2} - 19x\sqrt{2} =$
(a) $5x\sqrt{2}$ (b) -5 (c) $-5x\sqrt{2}$ (d) $-15x\sqrt{2}$ (e) can't combined

22. $2\sqrt[3]{3x^4} + 18x\sqrt[3]{24x} =$
(a) $(2+36x)\sqrt[3]{x}$ (b) $20x\sqrt[3]{3x}$ (c) can't combined   (d) $38x\sqrt[3]{3x}$ (e) $30x\sqrt[3]{3x}$

23. Find the value of $2\sqrt{x} - 5x\sqrt{x} + 3x^2$ when $x = 4$.
(a) 12   (b) -12 (c) 84   (d) 42   (e) 22

24. Find the value of $(4x^2 + x)\sqrt{9x} - 13\sqrt{x}$ when $x = 9$.
(a) 204   (b) $2,858$ (c) 291   (d) $2,958$ (e) $3,058$

25. Find the value of $\sqrt{3a^2 - b} + \sqrt{a^2 - b^2}$ when $a = 4$ and $b = -3$.
(a) $5 + \sqrt{51}$ (b) $\sqrt{56}$ (c) $7 + \sqrt{51}$ (d) $3\sqrt{5} - 5$ (e) $-5 + \sqrt{51}$

Section E. Multiplication and Division of Radicals

In this section, we will learn how to multiply and divide radical expressions.

Multiplying Radicals

Recall: $\sqrt[n]{a} \cdot \sqrt[n]{b} = \sqrt[n]{a \cdot b}$

Example 1. Multiply and simplify.

1) $\left(4\sqrt{3}\right)\left(8\sqrt{3}\right)$ 2) $\left(-3\sqrt{5}\right)\left(6\sqrt{10}\right)$ 3) $\left(4\sqrt[3]{6}\right)\left(-5\sqrt[3]{20}\right)$

4) $9\left(3 - 2\sqrt{5}\right)$ 5) $7\sqrt{3}\left(2\sqrt{3} + 4\sqrt{2}\right)$ 6) $2\sqrt[3]{3}\left(\sqrt[3]{9} - 7\sqrt[3]{3x}\right)$

Solution:

1) $\left(4\sqrt{3}\right)\left(8\sqrt{3}\right) = 4 \cdot 8 \cdot \sqrt{3} \cdot \sqrt{3} = 32\sqrt{9} = 32(3) = 96$

2) $\left(-3\sqrt{5}\right)\left(6\sqrt{10}\right) = -3 \cdot 6 \cdot \sqrt{5} \cdot \sqrt{10} = \underbrace{-18\sqrt{50} = -18\left(5\sqrt{2}\right)}_{\sqrt{50} = \sqrt{25}\,\sqrt{2} = 5\sqrt{2}} = -90\sqrt{2}$

3) $\left(4\sqrt[3]{6}\right)\left(-5\sqrt[3]{20}\right) = 4 \cdot (-5) \cdot \sqrt[3]{6} \cdot \sqrt[3]{20} = \underbrace{-20\sqrt[3]{120} = -20\left(2\sqrt[3]{15}\right)}_{\sqrt[3]{120} = \sqrt[3]{8}\,\sqrt[3]{15} = 2\sqrt[3]{15}} = -40\sqrt[3]{15}$

4) Notice that the expression $3 - 2\sqrt{5}$ does not combine into a single radical. We need to use the Distributive Property:

$$9\left(3 - 2\sqrt{5}\right) = 9(3) + 9\left(-2\sqrt{5}\right) = 27 - 18\sqrt{5}$$

Be careful! The expression $27 - 18\sqrt{5}$ does not combine to $9\sqrt{5}$ because 27 and $9\sqrt{5}$ are not like roots.

5) Use the Distributive Property:

$$7\sqrt{3}\left(2\sqrt{3} + 4\sqrt{2}\right) = 7\sqrt{3}\left(2\sqrt{3}\right) + 7\sqrt{3}\left(4\sqrt{2}\right) = 14\sqrt{9} + 28\sqrt{6}$$

$$= 14(3) + 28\sqrt{6} = 42 + 28\sqrt{6}$$

Be careful! The expression $42 + 28\sqrt{6}$ does not combine to $70\sqrt{6}$ because 42 and $28\sqrt{6}$ are not like roots.

6) $2\sqrt[3]{3}\left(\sqrt[3]{9} - 7\sqrt[3]{3x}\right) = 2\sqrt[3]{3}\left(\sqrt[3]{9}\right) + 2\sqrt[3]{3}\left(-7\sqrt[3]{3x}\right) = 2\sqrt[3]{27} - 14\sqrt[3]{9x}$

$$= 2(3) - 14\sqrt[3]{9x} = 6 - 14\sqrt[3]{9x}$$

In the next set of examples, we use the FOIL Method to multiply.

Example 2. Multiply and simplify.

1) $\left(\sqrt{3}+4\right)\left(\sqrt{3}-2\right)$ 2) $\left(4\sqrt{2}-5\right)\left(2\sqrt{5}-1\right)$ 3) $\left(2\sqrt{6x}+3\right)\left(4\sqrt{6x}+5\right)$

4) $\left(1-8\sqrt[3]{4}\right)\left(6-2\sqrt[3]{2}\right)$ 5) $\left(-\sqrt[3]{3x^2}+2\right)\left(\sqrt[3]{2x}+5\right)$ 6) $\left(x\sqrt[4]{7}+3\right)\left(x\sqrt[4]{7}+1\right)$

Solution:

1) $\left(\sqrt{3}+4\right)\left(\sqrt{3}-2\right) = \left(\sqrt{3}\right)\left(\sqrt{3}\right)-2\left(\sqrt{3}\right)+4\left(\sqrt{3}\right)+4(-2)$ (by the FOIL Method)

$$= \sqrt{9}-2\sqrt{3}+4\sqrt{3}-8$$
$$= 3-2\sqrt{3}+4\sqrt{3}-8$$
$$= -5+2\sqrt{3}$$

2) $\left(4\sqrt{2}-5\right)\left(2\sqrt{5}-1\right) = 4\sqrt{2}\left(2\sqrt{5}\right)+4\sqrt{2}(-1)-5\left(2\sqrt{5}\right)-5(-1)$

$$= 8\sqrt{10}-4\sqrt{2}-10\sqrt{5}+5$$

3) $\left(2\sqrt{6x}+3\right)\left(4\sqrt{6x}+5\right) = 2\sqrt{6x}\left(4\sqrt{6x}\right)+\left(2\sqrt{6x}\right)(5)+3\left(4\sqrt{6x}\right)+3(5)$

$$= 8\sqrt{36x^2}+10\sqrt{6x}+12\sqrt{6x}+15$$
$$= 8x(6x)+10\sqrt{6x}+12\sqrt{6x}+15$$
$$= 48x^2+22\sqrt{6x}+15$$

4) $\left(1-8\sqrt[3]{4}\right)\left(6-2\sqrt[3]{2}\right) = 1(6)+1\left(-2\sqrt[3]{2}\right)-8\sqrt[3]{4}(6)-8\sqrt[3]{4}\left(-2\sqrt[3]{2}\right)$

$$= 6-2\sqrt[3]{2}-48\sqrt[3]{4}+16\sqrt[3]{8}$$
$$= 6-2\sqrt[3]{2}-48\sqrt[3]{4}+16(2)$$
$$= 6-2\sqrt[3]{2}-48\sqrt[3]{4}+32$$
$$= 38-2\sqrt[3]{2}-48\sqrt[3]{4}$$

5) $\left(-\sqrt[3]{3x^2}+2\right)\left(\sqrt[3]{2x}+5\right) = -\sqrt[3]{3x^2}\left(\sqrt[3]{2x}\right)-\sqrt[3]{3x^2}(5)+2\left(\sqrt[3]{2x}\right)+2(5)$

$$= -\sqrt[3]{6x^3}-5\sqrt[3]{3x^2}+2\sqrt[3]{2x}+10$$
$$= -x\sqrt[3]{6}-5\sqrt[3]{3x^2}+2\sqrt[3]{2x}+10$$

6) $\left(x\sqrt[4]{7}+3\right)\left(x\sqrt[4]{7}+1\right) = \left(x\sqrt[4]{7}\right)\left(x\sqrt[4]{7}\right)+x\sqrt[4]{7}(1)+3\left(x\sqrt[4]{7}\right)+3(1)$

$$= \left(x^2\sqrt[4]{49}\right)+x\sqrt[4]{7}+3x\sqrt[4]{7}+3$$
$$= \left(x^2\sqrt[4]{49}\right)+4x\sqrt[4]{7}+3$$

Example 3. Use the formula $(A+B)(A-B)=A^2-B^2$ to multiply.

1) $\left(\sqrt{13}+2\right)\left(\sqrt{13}-2\right)$ 2) $\left(\sqrt{15}-\sqrt{14}\right)\left(\sqrt{15}+\sqrt{14}\right)$

3) $\left(2\sqrt{7x}+3y\right)\left(2\sqrt{7x}-3y\right)$, where $x \geq 0$.

Solution: 1) Let $A = \sqrt{13}$ and $B = 2$ in the formula.

$$\left(\sqrt{13} + 2\right)\left(\sqrt{13} - 2\right) = \left(\sqrt{13}\right)^2 - (2)^2 = 13 - 4 = 9$$

2) Let $A = \sqrt{15}$ and $B = \sqrt{14}$ in the formula.

$$\left(\sqrt{15} - \sqrt{14}\right)\left(\sqrt{15} + \sqrt{14}\right) = \left(\sqrt{15}\right)^2 - \left(\sqrt{14}\right)^2 = 15 - 14 = 1$$

3) Let $A = 2\sqrt{7x}$ and $B = 3y$ in the formula.

$$\left(2\sqrt{7x} + 3y\right)\left(2\sqrt{7x} - 3y\right) = \left(2\sqrt{7x}\right)^2 - (3y)^2 = 2^2\left(\sqrt{7x}\right)^2 - 9y^2$$
$$= 4(7x) - 9y^2 = 28x - 9y^2$$

Dividing Radicals

Recall: $\dfrac{\sqrt[n]{a}}{\sqrt[n]{b}} = \sqrt[n]{\dfrac{a}{b}}$

Example 4. Divide and simplify.

1) $\dfrac{\sqrt{60}}{\sqrt{15}}$
2) $\dfrac{7\sqrt{28}}{21\sqrt{14}}$
3) $\dfrac{20\sqrt[3]{56}}{12\sqrt[3]{7}}$

Solution: 1) $\dfrac{\sqrt{60}}{\sqrt{15}} = \sqrt{\dfrac{60}{15}} = \sqrt{4} = 2$

2) $\dfrac{7\sqrt{28}}{21\sqrt{14}} = \dfrac{7}{21}\sqrt{\dfrac{28}{14}} = \dfrac{1}{3}\sqrt{2} = \dfrac{1}{3} \cdot \dfrac{\sqrt{2}}{1} = \dfrac{\sqrt{2}}{3}$

3) $\dfrac{20\sqrt[3]{56}}{12\sqrt[3]{7}} = \dfrac{20}{12}\sqrt[3]{\dfrac{56}{7}} = \dfrac{5}{3}\sqrt[3]{8} = \dfrac{5}{3}(2) = \dfrac{5}{3}\left(\dfrac{2}{1}\right) = \dfrac{10}{3}$

Sometimes the numerator and/or denominator of a radical expression contains more than one radical.

Example 5. Simplify.

1) $\dfrac{\sqrt{12} + 3\sqrt{3}}{5}$
2) $\dfrac{2\sqrt{20} - 7\sqrt{45}}{34}$
3) $\dfrac{4 + 12\sqrt[3]{40}}{16}$
4) $\dfrac{-5 + \sqrt{200}}{-25}$

Solution:

1) $\underbrace{\dfrac{\sqrt{12} + 3\sqrt{3}}{5} = \dfrac{2\sqrt{3} + 3\sqrt{3}}{5}}_{\text{Simplify } \sqrt{12}.} = \dfrac{5\sqrt{3}}{5} = \dfrac{\sqrt{3}}{1} = \sqrt{3}$

301

2) $\dfrac{2\sqrt{20}-7\sqrt{45}}{34} = \dfrac{2\left(2\sqrt{5}\right)-7\left(3\sqrt{5}\right)}{34} = \dfrac{4\sqrt{5}-21\sqrt{5}}{34} = \dfrac{-17\sqrt{5}}{34} = -\dfrac{\sqrt{5}}{2}$

Simplify $\sqrt{20}$ and $\sqrt{45}$.

3) $\dfrac{4+12\sqrt[3]{40}}{16} = \dfrac{4+12\left(2\sqrt[3]{5}\right)}{16} = \dfrac{4+24\sqrt[3]{5}}{16} = \dfrac{4\left(1+6\sqrt[3]{5}\right)}{16} = \dfrac{1+6\sqrt[3]{5}}{4}$

Simplify $\sqrt[3]{40}$.   Factor the numerator the same way as 4+24x.

4) $\dfrac{-5+\sqrt{200}}{-25} = \dfrac{-5+10\sqrt{2}}{-25} = \dfrac{5\left(-1+2\sqrt{2}\right)}{-25} = \dfrac{-1+2\sqrt{2}}{-5}$

Simplify $\sqrt{200}$, then factor $-5+10\sqrt{2}$ the same way as $-5+10x$.

Exercises: Chapter 12, Section E

In Exercises 1 - 30, multiply and simplify. Assume that all variables represent non-negative numbers.

1. $\sqrt{3}\left(5\sqrt{3}\right)$

2. $2\sqrt{6x}\left(7\sqrt{6x}\right)$

3. $\left(4\sqrt[3]{9}\right)\left(3\sqrt{2}\right)$

4. $\left(-3\sqrt[3]{16a}\right)\left(\sqrt[3]{4a^2}\right)$

5. $\sqrt{2}\left(3\sqrt{2}+4\right)$

6. $2\sqrt{3}\left(7\sqrt{3}-5\right)$

7. $6\sqrt{5}\left(\sqrt{5}-4\sqrt{20}\right)$

8. $3\sqrt{3}\left(4\sqrt{3}+5\sqrt{27}\right)$

9. $\sqrt[3]{2}\left(\sqrt[3]{3}+6\right)$

10. $\sqrt[3]{5}\left(\sqrt[3]{6}-2\right)$

11. $\sqrt[3]{16}\left(\sqrt[3]{2}+5\sqrt[3]{3}\right)$

12. $\sqrt[3]{12}\left(3\sqrt[3]{3}-5\sqrt[3]{6}\right)$

13. $\left(\sqrt{2}+\sqrt{3}\right)\left(\sqrt{2}+3\sqrt{3}\right)$

14. $\left(2\sqrt{3}-\sqrt{5}\right)\left(\sqrt{3}-\sqrt{5}\right)$

15. $\left(4\sqrt{6}-\sqrt{3}\right)\left(\sqrt{6}+5\sqrt{3}\right)$

16. $(\sqrt{x}+7)(\sqrt{x}-4)$

17. $\left(8+\sqrt{y}\right)\left(6-\sqrt{y}\right)$

18. $(5-2\sqrt{t})(3+\sqrt{t})$

19. $\left(\sqrt[3]{2}-7\right)\left(\sqrt[3]{2}+2\right)$

20. $\left(\sqrt[3]{3}+2\right)\left(\sqrt[3]{3}-4\right)$

21. $(\sqrt[3]{x}-5)(\sqrt[3]{x}-7)$

22. $\left(\sqrt{6}-\sqrt{3}\right)\left(\sqrt{6}+\sqrt{3}\right)$

23. $\left(\sqrt{5}+7\right)\left(\sqrt{5}-7\right)$

24. $\left(2\sqrt{3}+4\right)\left(2\sqrt{3}-4\right)$

25. $(\sqrt{x}+8)(\sqrt{x}-8)$

26. $(\sqrt{a}-3b)(\sqrt{a}+3b)$

27. $\left(12\sqrt{y}+1\right)\left(12\sqrt{y}-1\right)$

28. $\left(\sqrt{6}+\sqrt{2}\right)^2$

29. $\left(\sqrt{10}-4\right)^2$

30. $\left(\sqrt{11}-6\sqrt{3}\right)^2$

In Exercises 31 - 39, choose the correct answer. Assume that all variables represent non-negative numbers.

31. $\sqrt{10a^2}\cdot\sqrt{10a^3}=$
(a) $10a^2\sqrt{a}$ (b) $a^2\sqrt{10a}$ (c) $50a^2\sqrt{2a}$ (d) $10a\sqrt{a}$ (e) $10a^2$

32. $3\sqrt{11}\left(2\sqrt{11}-5\sqrt{3}\right)=$
(a) $66-15\sqrt{11}$ (b) $-9\sqrt{88}$ (c) $56+7\sqrt{2}$ (d) $66-15\sqrt{33}$ (e) $51\sqrt{33}$

33. $2\sqrt{6}\left(8+\sqrt{12}\right)=$
(a) $16\sqrt{72}$ (b) $16\sqrt{6}+6\sqrt{2}$ (c) $18\sqrt{78}$ (d) $16\sqrt{6}+12\sqrt{2}$ (e) $28\sqrt{8}$

34. $\sqrt{5x}\left(3\sqrt{x}+\sqrt{5}\right)=$
(a) $5x\sqrt{3}+5\sqrt{x}$ (b) $3\sqrt{5x}+5\sqrt{x}$ (c) $3\sqrt{5x}+x\sqrt{5}$ (d) $3x\sqrt{5}+5\sqrt{x}$
(e) $3x^2\sqrt{5}+5x$

35. $\left(\sqrt{15}+3\right)\left(\sqrt{15}-7\right)=$
(a) $-6-4\sqrt{15}$ (b) $-10\sqrt{15}$ (c) $-3\sqrt{15}-21$ (d) -6 (e) $-6-4\sqrt{30}$

36. $\left(3-2\sqrt{10}\right)\left(4\sqrt{10}-2\right)=$
(a) -6 (b) $-86+16\sqrt{10}$ (c) $16\sqrt{10}+86$ (d) $32\sqrt{5}-86$ (e) $-70\sqrt{10}$

37. $\left(9\sqrt{2}+\sqrt{3}\right)^2=$
(a) 165 (b) $165+18\sqrt{6}$ (c) 21 (d) $162+\sqrt{3}+18\sqrt{6}$ (e) $165+21\sqrt{6}$

38. $\left(8+\sqrt{2}\right)\left(8-\sqrt{2}\right)=$
(a) 62 (b) 60 (c) 6 (d) 66 (e) 68

39. $\left(2x-\sqrt{5y}\right)\left(2x+\sqrt{5y}\right)=$
(a) $4x^2+5y$ (b) $4x^2-25y^2$ (c) $2x^2-5y$ (d) $2x^2-25y^2$ (e) $4x^2-5y$

In Exercises 40 - 52, divide and simplify.

40. $\dfrac{\sqrt{200}}{\sqrt{2}}$ 41. $\dfrac{8\sqrt{75}}{4\sqrt{3}}$ 42. $\dfrac{12\sqrt[3]{18}}{9\sqrt[3]{6}}$ 43. $\dfrac{10\sqrt[3]{2}}{15\sqrt[3]{54}}$

44. $\dfrac{2\sqrt{7}+8\sqrt{28}}{9}$ 45. $\dfrac{3\sqrt{18}-2\sqrt{2}}{14}$ 46. $\dfrac{6\sqrt{4}-5\sqrt{25}}{13}$

47. $\dfrac{-\sqrt{9}+4\sqrt{81}}{11}$ 48. $\dfrac{10+\sqrt{32}}{2}$ 49. $\dfrac{8\sqrt{3}-12\sqrt{2}}{4}$

50. $\dfrac{9\sqrt{5}+12\sqrt{7}}{3}$ 51. $\dfrac{-4+\sqrt{200}}{2}$ 52. $\dfrac{-12-\sqrt{18}}{-6}$

Section F. Rationalization

Suppose we are given a fraction which contains a radical in the denominator and we want to remove it. The process of converting a given fraction into an equivalent one which has a denominator **without** a radical is called **rationalizing the denominator**.

For example, let's rationalize the denominator of $\dfrac{11}{\sqrt{6}}$. The goal is to remove the $\sqrt{6}$ from the denominator. Notice that $\left(\sqrt{6}\right)\left(\sqrt{6}\right) = \left(\sqrt{6}\right)^2 = 6$, and 6 is not a radical. Therefore,

$$\underbrace{\frac{11}{\sqrt{6}} = \frac{11}{\sqrt{6}}\left(\frac{\sqrt{6}}{\sqrt{6}}\right) = \frac{11\sqrt{6}}{\left(\sqrt{6}\right)^2} = \frac{11\sqrt{6}}{6}}_{\text{The idea is that } \left(\sqrt{6}\right)^2 = 6.}$$

Example 1. Rationalize the denominator. Assume that all variables represent positive numbers.

1) $\dfrac{1}{\sqrt{2}}$ 2) $\dfrac{7}{\sqrt{7}}$ 3) $\dfrac{6}{5\sqrt{3}}$ 4) $\dfrac{4}{\sqrt{20}}$

5) $\dfrac{6\sqrt{3}}{\sqrt{18}}$ 6) $\sqrt{\dfrac{7}{24y^2}}$ 7) $\dfrac{4}{9\sqrt{3x}}$

Solution:

1) $\dfrac{1}{\sqrt{2}} = \dfrac{1}{\sqrt{2}}\left(\dfrac{\sqrt{2}}{\sqrt{2}}\right) = \dfrac{\sqrt{2}}{\left(\sqrt{2}\right)^2} = \dfrac{\sqrt{2}}{2}$

2) $\dfrac{7}{\sqrt{7}} = \dfrac{7}{\sqrt{7}}\left(\dfrac{\sqrt{7}}{\sqrt{7}}\right) = \dfrac{7\sqrt{7}}{\left(\sqrt{7}\right)^2} = \dfrac{7\sqrt{7}}{7} = \sqrt{7}$

3) $\underbrace{\dfrac{6}{5\sqrt{3}} = \dfrac{6}{5\sqrt{3}}\left(\dfrac{\sqrt{3}}{\sqrt{3}}\right) = \dfrac{6\sqrt{3}}{5\left(\sqrt{3}\right)^2}}_{\text{We only need to put } \sqrt{3}, \text{ not } 5\sqrt{3}.} = \dfrac{6\sqrt{3}}{5(3)} = \dfrac{6\sqrt{3}}{15} = \dfrac{2\sqrt{3}}{5}$

4) $\dfrac{4}{\sqrt{20}} = \dfrac{4}{\sqrt{20}}\left(\dfrac{\sqrt{20}}{\sqrt{20}}\right) = \dfrac{4\sqrt{20}}{\left(\sqrt{20}\right)^2} = \underbrace{\dfrac{4\sqrt{20}}{20} = \dfrac{4\left(2\sqrt{5}\right)}{20}}_{\text{Simplify } \sqrt{20}.} = \dfrac{8\sqrt{5}}{20} = \dfrac{2\sqrt{5}}{5}$

Another way to do this example is to simplify $\sqrt{20}$ first, then rationalize the denominator:

$$\underbrace{\frac{4}{\sqrt{20}} = \frac{4}{2\sqrt{5}} = \frac{2}{1\sqrt{5}}}_{\text{Simplify } \sqrt{20}.} = \underbrace{\frac{2}{\sqrt{5}}\left(\frac{\sqrt{5}}{\sqrt{5}}\right) = \frac{2\sqrt{5}}{\left(\sqrt{5}\right)^2} = \frac{2\sqrt{5}}{5}}_{\text{Rationalize the denominator.}}$$

5) $\underbrace{\dfrac{6\sqrt{3}}{\sqrt{18}} = \dfrac{6\sqrt{3}}{3\sqrt{2}} = \dfrac{2\sqrt{3}}{\sqrt{2}}}_{\text{Simplify first.}} = \underbrace{\dfrac{2\sqrt{3}}{\sqrt{2}}\left(\dfrac{\sqrt{2}}{\sqrt{2}}\right) = \dfrac{2\sqrt{6}}{\left(\sqrt{2}\right)^2} = \dfrac{2\sqrt{6}}{2}}_{\text{Rationalize the denominator.}} = \dfrac{\sqrt{6}}{1} = \sqrt{6}$

6) $\sqrt{\dfrac{7}{24y^2}} = \underbrace{\dfrac{\sqrt{7}}{\sqrt{24y^2}} = \dfrac{\sqrt{7}}{2y\sqrt{6}}}_{\text{Simplify first.}} = \left(\dfrac{\sqrt{7}}{2y\sqrt{6}}\right)\left(\dfrac{\sqrt{6}}{\sqrt{6}}\right) = \dfrac{\sqrt{42}}{2y\left(\sqrt{6}\right)^2} = \dfrac{\sqrt{42}}{2y(6)} = \dfrac{\sqrt{42}}{12y}$

7) $\dfrac{4}{9\sqrt{3x}} = \left(\dfrac{4}{9\sqrt{3x}}\right)\left(\dfrac{\sqrt{3x}}{\sqrt{3x}}\right) = \dfrac{4\sqrt{3x}}{9\left(\sqrt{3x}\right)^2} = \dfrac{4\sqrt{3x}}{9(3x)} = \dfrac{4\sqrt{3x}}{27x}$

If the denominator of a fraction is a binomial expression, we rationalize it in a different way. For example, let's rationalize the denominator of the fraction $\dfrac{3}{2+\sqrt{2}}$. Notice that the denominator is a binomial because it has two terms which are not like roots. We multiply the numerator and denominator of the fraction by the **conjugate** of $2+\sqrt{2}$, which is just $2-\sqrt{2}$. In general, the **conjugate** of the binomial $A + B$ is $A - B$.

Multiplying a binomial by its conjugate can be easily done using the Difference of Squares Formula:

$$(A + B)(A - B) = A^2 - B^2$$

Let's see what happens in our example:

$\dfrac{3}{2+\sqrt{2}} = \underbrace{\left(\dfrac{3}{2+\sqrt{2}}\right)\left(\dfrac{2-\sqrt{2}}{2-\sqrt{2}}\right) = \dfrac{3\left(2-\sqrt{2}\right)}{(2)^2 - \left(\sqrt{2}\right)^2}}_{\text{Set } A=2 \text{ and } B=\sqrt{2} \text{ in the formula to obtain } A^2-B^2=(2)^2-\left(\sqrt{2}\right)^2.} = \dfrac{3\left(2-\sqrt{2}\right)}{4-2} = \dfrac{3\left(2-\sqrt{2}\right)}{2} = \dfrac{6-3\sqrt{2}}{2}$

As you can see, the denominator of the answer has no radicals in it.

Example 2. Rationalize the denominator.

1) $\dfrac{6}{-\sqrt{5}+2}$

2) $\dfrac{4+\sqrt{6}}{4-\sqrt{6}}$

3) $\dfrac{\sqrt{x}-2\sqrt{5}}{\sqrt{x}-\sqrt{5}}$, where $x > 0$ and $x \neq 5$.

Solution:

1) The conjugate of $-\sqrt{5}+2$ is $-\sqrt{5}-2$.

$$\frac{6}{-\sqrt{5}+2} = \frac{6}{-\sqrt{5}+2}\left(\frac{-\sqrt{5}-2}{-\sqrt{5}-2}\right) = \frac{6\left(-\sqrt{5}-2\right)}{\left(-\sqrt{5}\right)^2 - (2)^2}$$

$$= \frac{6\left(-\sqrt{5}-2\right)}{5-4} = \frac{6\left(-\sqrt{5}-2\right)}{1}$$

$$= 6\left(-\sqrt{5}-2\right) = -6\sqrt{5}-12$$

2) The conjugate of $4-\sqrt{6}$ is $4+\sqrt{6}$.

$$\frac{4+\sqrt{6}}{4-\sqrt{6}} = \left(\frac{4+\sqrt{6}}{4-\sqrt{6}}\right)\left(\frac{4+\sqrt{6}}{4+\sqrt{6}}\right) = \frac{16+4\sqrt{6}+4\sqrt{6}+\left(\sqrt{6}\right)^2}{(4)^2 - \left(\sqrt{6}\right)^2}$$

$$= \frac{16+4\sqrt{6}+4\sqrt{6}+6}{16-6} = \frac{22+8\sqrt{6}}{10}$$

$$= \frac{2\left(11+4\sqrt{6}\right)}{2(5)} = \frac{11+4\sqrt{6}}{5}$$

3) The conjugate of $\sqrt{x}-\sqrt{5}$ is $\sqrt{x}+\sqrt{5}$.

$$\frac{\sqrt{x}-2\sqrt{5}}{\sqrt{x}-\sqrt{5}} = \left(\frac{\sqrt{x}-2\sqrt{5}}{\sqrt{x}-\sqrt{5}}\right)\left(\frac{\sqrt{x}+\sqrt{5}}{\sqrt{x}+\sqrt{5}}\right)$$

$$= \frac{\left(\sqrt{x}\right)^2 + \sqrt{5x} - 2\sqrt{5x} - 2\left(\sqrt{5}\right)^2}{\left(\sqrt{x}\right)^2 - \left(\sqrt{5}\right)^2}$$

$$= \frac{x+\sqrt{5x}-2\sqrt{5x}-10}{x-5} = \frac{x-\sqrt{5x}-10}{x-5}$$

Exercises: Chapter 12, Section F

In Exercises 1 - 20, rationalize the denominator and simplify.

1. $\dfrac{3}{\sqrt{2}}$

2. $\dfrac{13}{\sqrt{26}}$

3. $\dfrac{10}{\sqrt{8}}$

4. $\dfrac{8}{3\sqrt{20}}$

5. $\dfrac{-12}{5\sqrt{24}}$

6. $\sqrt{\dfrac{1}{5}}$

7. $\sqrt{\dfrac{14}{3}}$

8. $\sqrt{\dfrac{11}{12}}$

9. $\dfrac{3}{\sqrt{x}}$, $x > 0$

10. $\dfrac{2}{3\sqrt{2y}}$, $y > 0$

11. $\dfrac{5}{4\sqrt{10x^2}}$, $x > 0$

12. $\dfrac{\sqrt{8}}{\sqrt{9x}}$, $x > 0$

13. $\dfrac{\sqrt{16t}}{\sqrt{21}}$, $t > 0$

14. $\dfrac{1}{\sqrt{2} + 1}$

15. $\dfrac{1}{\sqrt{5} - 2}$

16. $\dfrac{4}{2\sqrt{3} - 3}$

17. $\dfrac{1 + \sqrt{2}}{2 - \sqrt{2}}$

18. $\dfrac{\sqrt{7} - \sqrt{10}}{\sqrt{7} + \sqrt{10}}$

19. $\dfrac{4 + \sqrt{x}}{2 - \sqrt{x}}$, $x > 0, x \neq 4$

20. $\dfrac{\sqrt{x} - \sqrt{7y}}{\sqrt{x} + \sqrt{5y}}$, $x > 0, y > 0, x \neq 5y$

In Exercises 21 - 26, choose the correct answer.

21. $\dfrac{20}{3\sqrt{15}} =$

(a) $\dfrac{4\sqrt{15}}{9}$

(b) $\dfrac{4\sqrt{15}}{5}$

(c) $\dfrac{20}{3}$

(d) $\dfrac{4}{3\sqrt{3}}$

(e) $\dfrac{4\sqrt{3}}{3}$

22. $\dfrac{7}{\sqrt{12}} =$

(a) $\dfrac{7\sqrt{6}}{3}$

(b) $\dfrac{7\sqrt{3}}{12}$

(c) $\dfrac{7\sqrt{3}}{6}$

(d) $\dfrac{7}{3}$

(e) $\dfrac{7\sqrt{12}}{6}$

23. If $x > 0$, then $\dfrac{16}{9\sqrt{5x}} =$

(a) $\dfrac{16\sqrt{5x}}{45x}$

(b) $\dfrac{16}{5}$

(c) $\dfrac{80\sqrt{x}}{45x}$

(d) $\dfrac{16\sqrt{5x}}{405x}$

(e) $\dfrac{16\sqrt{5}}{5x}$

308

24. $\dfrac{\sqrt{7}+4}{\sqrt{7}-4} =$

(a) $-\dfrac{23+8\sqrt{7}}{9}$ (b) -1 (c) $\dfrac{-23+8\sqrt{7}}{9}$ (d) $-\dfrac{21}{9}$ (e) $\dfrac{23-8\sqrt{7}}{9}$

25 If x represents a non-negative number other than 1, then $\dfrac{\sqrt{x}+1}{\sqrt{x}-1} =$

(a) -1 (b) $\dfrac{3\sqrt{x}+1}{x-1}$ (c) $\dfrac{x+2\sqrt{x}+1}{x+1}$ (d) $\dfrac{x+1}{x-1}$ (e) $\dfrac{x+2\sqrt{x}+1}{x-1}$

26. Assume x and y are positive numbers and $y \neq 9x$. Then $\dfrac{\sqrt{x}}{3\sqrt{x}-\sqrt{y}} =$

(a) $\dfrac{3x+\sqrt{xy}}{9x^2-y^2}$ (b) $\dfrac{3x+xy}{9x-y}$ (c) $\dfrac{3x+\sqrt{xy}}{9x-y}$ (d) $\dfrac{1}{3-\sqrt{y}}$ (e) $\dfrac{9x+\sqrt{xy}}{9x-y}$

Section G.   Some Quadratic and Square Root Equations

Next we will learn how to solve different types of equations which contain exponents and radicals.

Quadratic Equations

In Section E of Chapter 11, we learned how to solve quadratic equations by factoring. Now we will learn how to solve quadratic equations of the form $x^2 = a$, where a is any non-negative number. Suppose we want to solve the equation $x^2 = 49$. We could solve this by subtracting 49 on both sides of the equation, then use factoring. An easier way is to use the **Square Root Property**:

If $a \geq 0$, then the equation $x^2 = a$ has solutions $x = -\sqrt{a}$ and $x = \sqrt{a}$. In abbreviated form, $x = \pm \sqrt{a}$.

Notice that both $x = -\sqrt{a}$ and $x = \sqrt{a}$ are solutions to the equation $x^2 = a$ because $(-\sqrt{a})^2 = a$ and $(\sqrt{a})^2 = a$.

Getting back to our equation, the solutions to $x^2 = 49$ are $x = \pm \sqrt{49} = \pm 7$. Equivalently, the solution set is $\{-7, 7\}$.

Example 1. Solve.
1) $x^2 = 100$ 2) $y^2 - 9 = 0$ 3) $5t^2 - 20 = 0$
4) $(y + 2)^2 = 25$ 5) $3(x - 5)^2 = 12$ 6) $-8a^2 - 360 = 0$

Solution:

1) By the Square Root Property, $x = \pm \sqrt{100} = \pm 10$.

2) First we need to get y^2 by itself, then we use the Square Root Property.

$$
\begin{aligned}
y^2 - 9 &= 0 \\
+9 &\quad +9 \\
\hline
y^2 &= 9 \\
y = \pm \sqrt{9} &= \pm 3
\end{aligned}
$$

3) First we need to get t^2 by itself, then we use the Square Root Property.

$$
\begin{aligned}
5t^2 - 20 &= 0 \\
+20 &\quad +20 \\
\hline
\frac{5t^2}{5} &= \frac{20}{5} \\
t^2 &= 4 \\
t = \pm \sqrt{4} &= \pm 2
\end{aligned}
$$

4) The Square Root Property allows us to remove the square in **any** equation of the form $x^2 = a$, where $a \geq 0$. The equation $(y + 2)^2 = 25$ can be solved in the same way as the others (think of $y + 2$ as x and 25 as a in the property):

310

$$(y+2)^2 = 25$$
$$y+2 = \pm\sqrt{25}$$
$$y+2 = \pm 5$$

Now we need to find the values of y. We separate the equation $y + 2 = \pm 5$ in two and solve each of them:

$$
\begin{array}{ccc}
y + 2 = -5 & \quad\text{and}\quad & y + 2 = 5 \\
\underline{-2 \quad -2} & & \underline{-2 \quad -2} \\
y = -7 & & y = 3
\end{array}
$$

5) First isolate the squared expression, then proceed as before.

$$\frac{3(x-5)^2}{3} = \frac{12}{3}$$

$$(x-5)^2 = 4$$
$$x - 5 = \pm\sqrt{4}$$
$$x - 5 = \pm 2$$

$$
\begin{array}{ccc}
x - 5 = -2 & \quad\text{and}\quad & x - 5 = 2 \\
\underline{+5 \quad +5} & & \underline{+5 \quad +5} \\
x = 3 & & x = 7
\end{array}
$$

6) Solve for a^2 first:

$$
\begin{array}{c}
-8a^2 - 360 = 0 \\
\underline{+360 \quad +360} \\
\dfrac{-8a^2}{-8} = \dfrac{360}{-8} \\
a^2 = -45
\end{array}
$$

The Square Root Property doesn't apply here because the square of a real number cannot be negative. This equation has no real roots.

Square Root Equations

A **square root equation** is an equation in which the variable appears in the radicand of a square root. For example,

$$\sqrt{x+5} = 7, \quad \sqrt{x} = -2, \quad \frac{4\sqrt{y-6}+2}{3} = 8, \quad\text{and}\quad \frac{24}{\sqrt{a}} = 8$$

are square root equations. Some square root equations have no solution. For example, $\sqrt{x} = -2$ has no solution since a square root cannot be negative.

Rule for solving a square root equation:
1) Isolate the square root term.
2) Square both sides of the equation.
3) Solve for the variable, then check your answer.

Example 2. Solve. Make sure to check your answers.

1) $\sqrt{x+5} = 7$ 2) $\sqrt{3x} = -6$ 3) $5 + \sqrt{2y-1} = 11$

4) $\dfrac{24}{\sqrt{a}} = 8$ 5) $\dfrac{6}{\sqrt{x^2+4}} = 2$ 6) $1 - 2\sqrt{t} = 7$

Solution:

1)
$$\sqrt{x+5} = 7$$
$$\left(\sqrt{x+5}\right)^2 = (7)^2$$
$$x + 5 = 49$$
$$\underline{ -5 \quad -5}$$
$$x \quad = 44$$

Check: $\sqrt{x+5} = 7$
$$\sqrt{44+5} \overset{?}{=} 7$$
$$\sqrt{49} \overset{\checkmark}{=} 7$$

2)
$$\sqrt{3x} = -6$$
$$\left(\sqrt{3x}\right)^2 = (-6)^2$$
$$\frac{3x}{3} = \frac{36}{3}$$
$$x = 12$$

Check: $\sqrt{3x} = -6$
$$\sqrt{3(12)} \overset{?}{=} -6$$
$$\sqrt{36} \neq -6$$

No solution.

3) Isolate the square root expression, then proceed as before.

$$5 + \sqrt{2y-1} = 11$$
$$\underline{-5 \qquad\qquad -5}$$
$$\sqrt{2y-1} = 6$$

$$\left(\sqrt{2y-1}\right)^2 = (6)^2$$
$$2y - 1 = 36$$
$$\underline{+1 \qquad +1}$$
$$\frac{2y}{2} = \frac{37}{2}$$

Check: $5 + \sqrt{2y-1} = 11$
$$5 + \sqrt{2\left(\frac{37}{2}\right) - 1} \overset{?}{=} 11$$
$$5 + \sqrt{37 - 1} \overset{?}{=} 11$$
$$5 + 6 \overset{\checkmark}{=} 11$$

4) Multiply both sides of the equation by $\sqrt{a}$ first.

$$\frac{24}{\sqrt{a}} = 8$$
$$\frac{24}{\sqrt{a}}(\sqrt{a}) = 8(\sqrt{a})$$
$$\frac{24}{8} = \frac{8\sqrt{a}}{8}$$
$$3 = \sqrt{a}$$
$$(3)^2 = (\sqrt{a})^2$$
$$9 = a$$

Check: $\dfrac{24}{\sqrt{a}} = 8$
$$\frac{24}{\sqrt{9}} \overset{?}{=} 8$$
$$\frac{24}{3} \overset{\checkmark}{=} 8$$

5) Multiply both sides of the equation by $\sqrt{x^2+4}$, then isolate the square root.

$$\left(\frac{6}{\sqrt{x^2+4}}\right)\sqrt{x^2+4} = 2\left(\sqrt{x^2+4}\right)$$

312

$$6 = 2\sqrt{x^2 + 4}$$

$$\frac{6}{2} = \frac{2\sqrt{x^2 + 4}}{2}$$

$$3 = \sqrt{x^2 + 4}$$

$$3^2 = \left(\sqrt{x^2 + 4}\right)^2$$

$$9 = x^2 + 4 \qquad \text{(Solve for } x^2.)$$
$$\underline{-4 \qquad -4}$$
$$5 = x^2 \qquad \text{(Solve for } x.)$$
$$\pm\sqrt{5} = x$$

Check: a) $x = -\sqrt{5}:$ $\qquad \dfrac{6}{\sqrt{x^2 + 4}} = 2 \qquad\qquad$ b) $x = \sqrt{5}:$ $\qquad \dfrac{6}{\sqrt{x^2 + 4}} = 2$

$$\frac{6}{\sqrt{\left(-\sqrt{5}\right)^2 + 4}} \overset{?}{=} 2 \qquad\qquad\qquad \frac{6}{\sqrt{\left(\sqrt{5}\right)^2 + 4}} \overset{?}{=} 2$$

$$\frac{6}{\sqrt{5 + 4}} \overset{?}{=} 2 \qquad\qquad\qquad\qquad \frac{6}{\sqrt{5 + 4}} \overset{?}{=} 2$$

$$\frac{6}{\sqrt{9}} \overset{?}{=} 2 \qquad\qquad\qquad\qquad \frac{6}{\sqrt{9}} \overset{?}{=} 2$$

$$\frac{6}{3} \overset{\checkmark}{=} 2 \qquad\qquad\qquad\qquad \frac{6}{3} \overset{\checkmark}{=} 2$$

6) Isolate the square root expression: $\qquad \cancel{1} - 2\sqrt{t} = 7$
$$\underline{-\cancel{1} \qquad\qquad -1}$$
$$\frac{-2\sqrt{t}}{-2} = \frac{6}{-2}$$

$$\sqrt{t} = -3$$
$$\left(\sqrt{t}\right)^2 = (-3)^2$$
$$t = 9$$

Check: $\qquad 1 - 2\sqrt{t} = 7$
$$1 - 2\sqrt{9} \overset{?}{=} 7$$
$$1 - 2(3) \overset{?}{=} 7$$
$$1 - 5 \neq 7$$

Therefore, the equation has no solution.

Exercises: Chapter 12, Section G

In Exercises 1 - 25, solve each equation.

1. $x^2 = 4$

2. $t^2 - 36 = 0$

3. $y^2 - 40 = 0$

4. $(x + 7)^2 = 1$

5. $(a - 1)^2 - 3 = -3$

6. $2(t + 11)^2 - 12 = 20$

7. $\sqrt{x + 2} = 5$

8. $\sqrt{5x - 7} = 9$

9. $\sqrt{x - 1} = -8$

10. $\dfrac{20}{\sqrt{x}} = 4$

11. $4\sqrt{m - 2} + 3 = 11$

12. $\dfrac{16}{\sqrt{t^2 - 3}} = 4$

13. $y^2 = 121$
(a) $y = 11$ and $y = -12$
(b) $y = \pm 11$
(c) $y = \pm 12$
(d) $y = \pm\dfrac{121}{2}$
(e) $y = \pm\sqrt{11}$

14. $a^2 - 169 = 0$
(a) $a = \pm 13$
(b) $a = \pm\dfrac{169}{2}$
(c) $a = 13$ only
(d) $a = \pm 15$
(e) $a = \pm\sqrt{13}$

15. $a^2 = 200$
(a) $a = \pm 2\sqrt{10}$
(b) $a = 10\sqrt{2}$ only
(c) $a = \pm 100$
(d) $a = \pm 16$
(e) $a = \pm 10\sqrt{2}$

16. $5n^2 - 100 = 0$
(a) $n = \pm 2\sqrt{5}$
(b) $n = \pm 10$
(c) $n = \pm 5\sqrt{2}$
(d) $n = \pm 2$
(e) $n = 2\sqrt{5}$ only

17. $(y - 4)^2 = 49$
(a) $y = 3$ and $y = -11$
(b) $y = 11$ only
(c) $y = \pm\sqrt{33}$
(d) $y = -3$ and $y = 11$
(e) $y = 4 \pm \sqrt{7}$

18. $(x - 2)^2 + 5 = 30$
(a) $x = 7$ and $x = -3$
(b) $x = 7$ only
(c) $x = \pm\sqrt{21}$
(d) $x = -7$ and $x = 3$
(e) no real roots

19. $-22 + 8(y - 6)^2 = 10$
(a) $y = 4$ and $y = 8$
(b) $y = -8$ and $y = -4$
(c) $y = -8$ and $y = 4$
(d) $y = 6 \pm 2\sqrt{6}$
(e) no real roots

20. $\sqrt{4y} = 8$

(a) $y = 8$ (b) $y = \pm 16$ (c) $y = 32$ (d) $y = 16$ (e) no solution

21. $\sqrt{-3 + 4a} = 7$

(a) $a = -13$ (b) $a = 13$ (c) $a = \pm 13$ (d) $a = 11\frac{1}{2}$ (e) no solution

22. $\sqrt{3a + 5} - 4 = 1$

(a) $a = \frac{3}{20}$ (b) $a = -6\frac{2}{3}$ (c) $a = 10$ (d) $a = 6\frac{2}{3}$ (e) no solution

23. $\sqrt{6y - 1} + 9 = 4$

(a) $y = 4$ (b) $y = -10\frac{2}{3}$ (c) $y = 32$ (d) $y = 16$ (e) no solution

24. $\frac{9}{\sqrt{t}} = 18$

(a) $t = \frac{1}{2}$ (b) $t = -\frac{1}{4}$ (c) $t = \frac{1}{4}$ (d) $t = -\frac{1}{2}$ (e) no solution

25. $\frac{21}{\sqrt{x^2 + 4}} = 7$

(a) $x = \pm 5$ (b) $x = \pm 25$ (c) $x = \sqrt{5}$ only   (d) $x = \pm \sqrt{5}$ (e) $x = \pm \frac{\sqrt{5}}{5}$

Section H. Rational Exponents

Every radical can be written in terms of a **rational exponent**. In this section, we learn how to compute expressions containing rational exponents. There are three rules to follow.

Rule 1: Let a be a real number and suppose that $n > 1$ is an integer. Then $a^{\frac{1}{n}} = \sqrt[n]{a}$, provided that $\sqrt[n]{a}$ is a real number.

Since $\frac{1}{n}$ is a rational number, we call it a **rational exponent**. Notice that the denominator of the exponent becomes the index of the radical. Hence, we have

$$a^{\frac{1}{2}} = \sqrt{a}, \quad a^{\frac{1}{3}} = \sqrt[3]{a}, \quad a^{\frac{1}{4}} = \sqrt[4]{a}, \quad \text{etc.}$$

Example 1. Evaluate.

1) $4^{\frac{1}{2}}$ 2) $8^{\frac{1}{3}}$ 3) $81^{\frac{1}{4}}$ 4) $\left(\frac{4}{25}\right)^{\frac{1}{2}}$

5) $-169^{\frac{1}{2}}$ 6) $(-169)^{\frac{1}{2}}$ 7) $(-125)^{\frac{1}{3}}$ 8) $-125^{\frac{1}{3}}$

Solution:

1) $4^{\frac{1}{2}} = \sqrt{4} = 2$ 2) $8^{\frac{1}{3}} = \sqrt[3]{8} = 2$

3) $81^{\frac{1}{4}} = \sqrt[4]{81} = 3$ 4) $\left(\frac{4}{25}\right)^{\frac{1}{2}} = \sqrt{\frac{4}{25}} = \frac{2}{5}$

5) $-169^{\frac{1}{2}} = -\sqrt{169} = -13$ 6) $(-169)^{\frac{1}{2}} = \sqrt{-169}$ does not exist.

7) $(-125)^{\frac{1}{3}} = \sqrt[3]{-125} = -5$ 8) $-125^{\frac{1}{3}} = -\sqrt[3]{125} = -5$

Example 2. Rewrite each expression in terms of radicals.

1) $a^{\frac{1}{2}}$ 2) $b^{\frac{1}{7}}$ 3) $y^{\frac{1}{3}}$

Solution: 1) $\sqrt{a}$ 2) $\sqrt[7]{b}$ 3) $\sqrt[3]{y}$

Example 3. Rewrite each expression in terms of rational exponents.

1) $\sqrt{17}$ 2) $\sqrt[4]{26}$ 3) $\sqrt[5]{-\frac{2}{3}}$ 4) $\sqrt[3]{10.74}$ 5) $\sqrt[4]{b}$

Solution: 1) $17^{\frac{1}{2}}$ 2) $26^{\frac{1}{4}}$ 3) $\left(-\frac{2}{3}\right)^{\frac{1}{5}}$ 4) $10.74^{\frac{1}{3}}$ 5) $b^{\frac{1}{4}}$

Rule 2: Let a be a real number and suppose that $n > 1$ is any integer. If m is a positive integer and the fraction $\frac{m}{n}$ is in lowest terms, then

$$a^{\frac{m}{n}} = (\sqrt[n]{a})^m = \sqrt[n]{a^m},$$

provided that $\sqrt[n]{a}$ exists.

Since $\frac{m}{n}$ is a rational number, we call it a **rational exponent**. Notice that the numerator of the exponent becomes the exponent of the radical, whereas the denominator of the exponent becomes the index of the radical. Furthermore, notice that if $m = 1$, we get Definition 1.

Example 4. Evaluate.

1) $16^{\frac{3}{2}}$ 2) $27^{\frac{4}{3}}$ 3) $16^{\frac{7}{4}}$ 4) $-49^{\frac{3}{2}}$ 5) $(-49)^{\frac{3}{2}}$ 6) $-125^{\frac{4}{3}}$

Solution: 1) $16^{\frac{3}{2}} = \left(\sqrt{16}\right)^3 = (4)^3 = 64$ 2) $27^{\frac{4}{3}} = \left(\sqrt[3]{27}\right)^4 = (3)^4 = 81$

3) $16^{\frac{7}{4}} = \left(\sqrt[4]{16}\right)^7 = (2)^7 = 128$ 4) $-49^{\frac{3}{2}} = -\left(\sqrt{49}\right)^3 = -(7)^3 = -343$

5) $(-49)^{\frac{3}{2}} = \left(\sqrt{-49}\right)^3$ does not exist..   6) $-125^{\frac{4}{3}} = -\left(\sqrt[3]{125}\right)^4 = -(5)^4 = -625$

Example 5. Rewrite each expression in terms of radicals.

1) $x^{\frac{2}{3}}$ 2) $m^{\frac{3}{4}}$ 3) $t^{\frac{7}{10}}$

Solution: 1) $\sqrt[3]{a^2}$ 2) $\sqrt[4]{m^3}$ 3) $\sqrt[10]{t^7}$

Example 6. Rewrite each expression in terms of rational exponents.

1) $\sqrt[4]{x^3}$ 2) $\left(\sqrt{7}\right)^4$ 3) $\left(\sqrt[8]{b}\right)^6$ 4) $\sqrt[3]{(-9y)^2}$ 5) $\left(\sqrt[3]{-8x}\right)^5$

Solution: 1) $x^{\frac{3}{4}}$ 2) $7^{\frac{2}{4}}$ 3) $b^{\frac{6}{8}}$ 4) $(-9y)^{\frac{2}{3}}$ 5) $(-8x)^{\frac{5}{3}}$

Rule 3: Let $a \neq 0$ be a real number and suppose that $n > 1$ is any integer. Then

$$a^{-\frac{m}{n}} = \frac{1}{a^{\frac{m}{n}}} = \frac{1}{\left(\sqrt[n]{a}\right)^m} = \frac{1}{\sqrt[n]{a^m}},$$

provided that $\sqrt[n]{a}$ exists.

Example 7. Evaluate.

1) $100^{-\frac{1}{2}}$ 2) $216^{-\frac{2}{3}}$ 3) $32^{-\frac{4}{5}}$ 4) $\left(\frac{81}{16}\right)^{-\frac{1}{4}}$ 5) $\frac{2^3}{9^{-\frac{1}{2}}}$ 6) $\frac{27^{-\frac{1}{3}}}{7}$

Solution:

1) $100^{-\frac{1}{2}} = \frac{1}{100^{\frac{1}{2}}} = \frac{1}{\sqrt{100}} = \frac{1}{10}$ 2) $216^{-\frac{2}{3}} = \frac{1}{216^{\frac{2}{3}}} = \frac{1}{\left(\sqrt[3]{216}\right)^2} = \frac{1}{(6)^2} = \frac{1}{36}$

3) $32^{-\frac{4}{5}} = \frac{1}{32^{\frac{4}{5}}} = \frac{1}{\left(\sqrt[5]{32}\right)^4} = \frac{1}{2^4} = \frac{1}{16}$ 4) $\left(\frac{81}{16}\right)^{-\frac{1}{4}} = \left(\frac{16}{81}\right)^{\frac{1}{4}} = \sqrt[4]{\frac{16}{81}} = \frac{2}{3}$

Recall: $\left(\frac{a}{b}\right)^{-n} = \left(\frac{b}{a}\right)^n$

5) $\dfrac{2^3}{9^{-\frac{1}{2}}} = \dfrac{2^3 \cdot 9^{\frac{1}{2}}}{1} = \dfrac{8 \cdot \sqrt{9}}{1} = 8 \cdot 3 = 24$ $\underbrace{\phantom{\dfrac{2^3}{9^{-\frac{1}{2}}}}}$

Negative exponents flip.

6) $\dfrac{27^{-\frac{1}{3}}}{7} = \dfrac{1}{7 \cdot 27^{-\frac{1}{3}}} = \dfrac{1}{7 \cdot \sqrt[3]{27}} = \dfrac{1}{7 \cdot 3} = \dfrac{1}{21}$ $\underbrace{\phantom{\dfrac{27^{-\frac{1}{3}}}{7} = \dfrac{1}{7 \cdot 27^{-\frac{1}{3}}}}}$

Negative exponents flip.

Example 8. Rewrite each expression in terms of radicals.

1) $a^{-\frac{1}{2}}$ 　　2) $m^{-\frac{2}{3}}$ 　　3) $x^{-\frac{3}{5}}$ 　　4) $y^{-\frac{7}{4}}$ 　　5) $(3x)^{-\frac{1}{2}}$

Solution: 　1) $\dfrac{1}{\sqrt{a}}$ 　　2) $\dfrac{1}{\sqrt[3]{m^2}}$ 　　3) $\dfrac{1}{\sqrt[5]{x^3}}$ 　　4) $\dfrac{1}{\sqrt[4]{y^7}}$ 　　5) $\dfrac{1}{\sqrt{3x}}$

Example 9. Rewrite each expression in terms of rational exponents.

1) $\dfrac{1}{\sqrt[3]{t}}$ 　　2) $\dfrac{1}{\sqrt[4]{x^3}}$ 　　3) $\dfrac{1}{\sqrt{y^5}}$ 　　4) $\dfrac{1}{\left(\sqrt[3]{6x}\right)^2}$

Solution: 　1) $t^{-\frac{1}{3}}$ 　　2) $x^{-\frac{3}{4}}$ 　　3) $y^{-\frac{5}{2}}$ 　　4) $(6x)^{-\frac{2}{3}}$

Exercises: Chapter 12, Exercise H

In Exercises 1 - 16, evaluate.

1. $49^{\frac{1}{2}}$

2. $125^{\frac{1}{3}}$

3. $81^{\frac{3}{4}}$

4. $36^{\frac{3}{2}}$

5. $(-32)^{\frac{2}{5}}$

6. $-32^{\frac{2}{5}}$

7. $(-27)^{\frac{5}{3}}$

8. $-27^{\frac{5}{3}}$

9. $16^{-\frac{1}{2}}$

10. $49^{-\frac{3}{2}}$

11. $64^{-\frac{2}{3}}$

12. $625^{-\frac{1}{4}}$

13. $(-27)^{-\frac{2}{3}}$

14. $-27^{-\frac{2}{3}}$

15. $\left(\frac{4}{49}\right)^{-\frac{1}{2}}$

16. $\left(-\frac{1,000}{27}\right)^{-\frac{1}{3}}$

In Exercises 17 - 36, choose the correct answer. Assume that all variables represent non-negative numbers.

17. $49^{\frac{1}{2}} =$
(a) 7   (b) 14   (c) $\frac{49}{2}$ (d) 9   (e) 16

18. $32^{\frac{1}{5}} =$
(a) 6   (b) 4   (c) $\frac{32}{5}$ (d) 2   (e) 3

19. $64^{\frac{2}{3}} =$
(a) 8   (b) $\frac{128}{3}$ (c) 64   (d) 16   (e) 512

20. $(-125)^{\frac{4}{3}} =$
(a) -625 (b) -20 (c) $\frac{500}{3}$ (d) 625   (e) does not exist

21. $\left(\frac{25}{4}\right)^{\frac{3}{2}} =$

(a) $\frac{125}{4}$ (b) $\frac{75}{16}$ (c) $\frac{125}{8}$ (d) $\frac{25}{8}$ (e) $\left(\sqrt[3]{\frac{25}{4}}\right)^2$

22. $\left(-\dfrac{1}{32}\right)^{\frac{3}{5}} =$

(a) $-\dfrac{1}{8}$ (b) $\dfrac{1}{8}$ (c) $\left(\sqrt[3]{-\dfrac{1}{32}}\right)^{5}$ (d) -8 (e) does not exist

23. $49^{-\frac{1}{2}} =$

(a) $\dfrac{1}{7}$ (b) -7 (c) $-\dfrac{1}{7}$ (d) $-\dfrac{49}{2}$ (e) $\dfrac{1}{49\sqrt{7}}$

24. $216^{-\frac{2}{3}} =$

(a) -144 (b) -36 (c) $\dfrac{1}{36}$ (d) $-\dfrac{1}{36}$ (e) $\dfrac{1}{216\sqrt{216}}$

25. $(-4)^{-\frac{1}{2}} =$

(a) $-\dfrac{1}{2}$ (b) $\dfrac{1}{2}$ (c) -2 (d) 2 (e) does not exist

26. $-4^{-\frac{1}{2}} =$

(a) $\dfrac{1}{2}$ (b) $-\dfrac{1}{2}$ (c) -2 (d) 2 (e) does not exist

27. $\dfrac{25^{-\frac{1}{2}}}{4} =$

(a) $\dfrac{1}{10}$ (b) $\dfrac{7}{10}$ (c) 10 (d) $\dfrac{1}{20}$ (e) does not exist

28. $\dfrac{49^{\frac{1}{2}}}{125^{-\frac{1}{3}}} =$

(a) $5\sqrt{7}$ (b) $\dfrac{1}{35}$ (c) 35 (d) $\dfrac{7}{5}$ (e) does not exist

29. $a^{\frac{4}{3}} =$

(a) $\left(\sqrt[4]{a}\right)^{3}$ (b) $\left(\sqrt[3]{a}\right)^{4}$ (c) $\dfrac{1}{\sqrt[4]{a^{3}}}$ (d) $\dfrac{1}{\left(\sqrt[3]{a}\right)^{4}}$ (e) $\dfrac{3}{4a}$

30. $(5x)^{\frac{3}{2}} =$

(a) $5\sqrt{x^{3}}$ (b) $\sqrt{5x^{3}}$ (c) $\sqrt{125x^{3}}$ (d) $\sqrt[3]{25x^{2}}$ (e) $\sqrt[3]{5x^{2}}$

31. $t^{-\frac{9}{4}} =$
(a) $\sqrt[9]{t^4}$ 　　　(b) $\dfrac{1}{\sqrt[9]{t^4}}$ 　　　(c) $-\sqrt[4]{t^9}$ 　　　(d) $\sqrt[4]{t^9}$ 　　　(e) $\dfrac{1}{\sqrt[4]{t^9}}$

32. $6^{\frac{1}{3}} =$
(a) $\sqrt[3]{36}$ 　　　(b) 2 　　　(c) $\sqrt{6}$ 　　　(d) $\sqrt[3]{6}$ 　　　(e) 3

33. $(-64)^{\frac{3}{2}} =$
(a) -216 　　　(b) -32^3 　　　(c) -512 　　　(d) -16 　　　(e) does not exist

34. $-64^{\frac{3}{2}} =$
(a) -216 　　　(b) 512 　　　(c) -512 　　　(d) -16 　　　(e) does not exist

35. $\left(\sqrt[3]{9}\right)^2 =$
(a) $9^{\frac{2}{3}}$ 　　　(b) $9^{\frac{3}{2}}$ 　　　(c) 9 　　　(d) $9^{\frac{1}{6}}$ 　　　(e) does not exist

36. $\left(\sqrt[3]{-12x}\right)^2 =$
(a) $(12x)^{\frac{2}{3}}$ 　　　(b) $(-12x)^{\frac{2}{3}}$ 　　　(c) $(-12x)^{\frac{5}{2}}$ 　　　(d) $-12x^{\frac{5}{2}}$ 　　　(e) $-12x^{\frac{2}{3}}$

321

Chapter 13: Graphing Equations in Two Variables

Section A. The Rectangular Coordinate System

On a piece of paper, draw two number lines, one vertical and the other horizontal. These number lines are called the **coordinate axes** for our **rectangular coordinate system**. The **vertical axis** will be called the **y-axis** and the **horizontal axis** will be called the **x-axis**. The point where both axes intersect (the x-axis and the y-axis) is 0. Label the x-axis so that the numbers are increasing from left to right, and label the y-axis so that the numbers are increasing as you go upward:

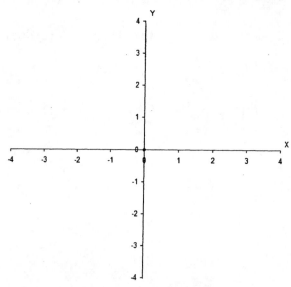

Notice that only the integers have been labeled on each axis. However, **any** real number can be located on each axis. The rectangular coordinate system drawn above is also called the *xy*-**plane**.

We want to graph points in the rectangular coordinate system. First, we need to understand what a point is. An **ordered pair** is a pair of real numbers, written as (x, y), where x is the x **coordinate** (or **abscissa**) and y is the y **coordinate** (or **ordinate**). In particular, the ordered pair $(0, 0)$ is called the **origin**. This is where the axes cross each other.

For example, $(1, -3)$ is an ordered pair with x-coordinate 1 and y coordinate -3. To draw a picture of this ordered pair, begin at the origin and go 1 unit to the right (along the positive x-axis, since 1 is the x coordinate and it is positive). Then go down by 3 units (since -3 is the y coordinate and it is negative). After doing this, draw a dot. This is the **graph** of the ordered pair $(1, -3)$, or simply the **point** $(1, -3)$. We say that we have **plotted** the point $(1, -3)$ (see the next figure).

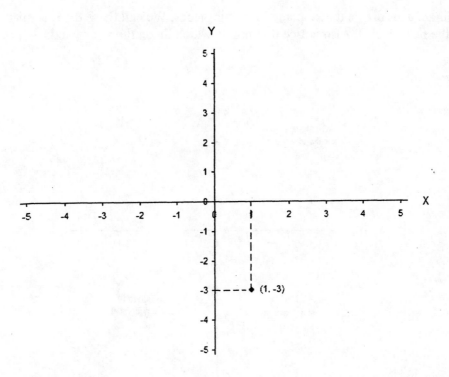

Example 1. Plot the given points.

1) $(4, 7)$ 2) $(2, -2)$ 3) $(-2, 3)$

4) $(-3, -3)$ 5) $(0, 1)$ 6) $(-5, 0)$

Solution:

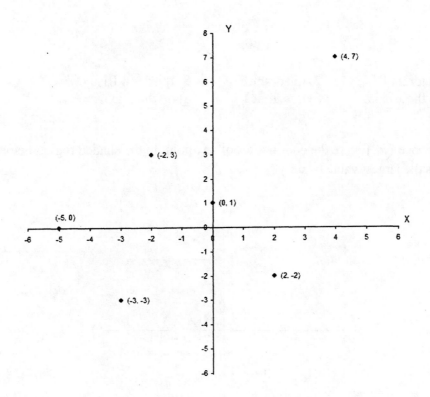

The coordinate axes divide the *xy*-plane into four pieces. We call these the **quadrants** of the *xy*-plane (see the next figure). Also notice that points which lie on the *x*- or *y*-axis do not lie in a quadrant.

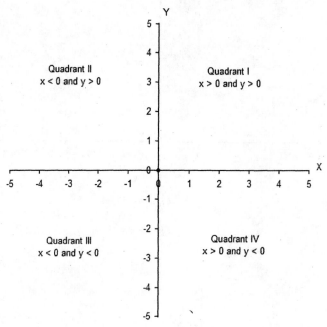

Example 2. Determine the quadrant where each point is located. If any point is not in a quadrant, state the axis it is on.

1) $\left(3, -6\right)$ 2) $\left(-8, 11\right)$ 3) $\left(-1, -6\right)$
4) $\left(2, 0\right)$ 5) $\left(4, 2\right)$ 6) $\left(0, -4\right)$

Solution: 1) quadrant IV   2) quadrant II   3) quadrant III
             4) on the *x*-axis   5) quadrant I   6) on the *y*-axis

Example 3. Suppose $\left(x, y\right)$ are the coordinates of any point in the shaded region below, or on its borders. What is the largest value of $x + y$?

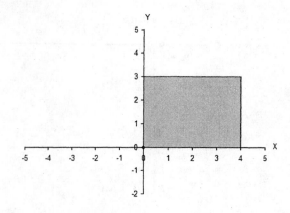

Solution: The expression $x + y$ achieves its largest value at the point which has the largest x coordinate **and** the largest y coordinate possible. In the figure, this point is $(4, 3)$. Therefore, the largest value of $x + y$ is $4 + 3 = 7$.

Exercises: Chapter 13, Section A

In Exercises 1 - 8, plot each point in the rectangular coordinate system.

1. $(2, 1)$ 2. $(3, -4)$ 3. $(-4, -3)$ 4. $(6, 2)$

5. $(3, 0)$ 6. $(-1, 1)$ 7. $(0, 2)$ 8. $(-4, 0)$

In Exercises 9 - 15, choose the correct answer.

9. Which quadrant is $(-3, -6)$ in?
(a) quadrant I   (b) quadrant II   (c) quadrant III   (d) quadrant IV   (e) none of these

10. Which quadrant is $(5, 2)$ in?
(a) quadrant I   (b) quadrant II   (c) quadrant III   (d) quadrant IV   (e) none of these

11. Which quadrant is $(3, -18)$ in?
(a) quadrant I   (b) quadrant II   (c) quadrant III   (d) quadrant IV   (e) none of these

12. Which quadrant is $(-2, 14)$ in?
(a) quadrant I   (b) quadrant II   (c) quadrant III   (d) quadrant IV   (e) none of these

13. Where is $(6, -3)$ located?
(a) quadrant I   (b) on the y-axis   (c) quadrant II   (d) quadrant III   (e) quadrant IV

14. Where is $(0, 11)$ located?
(a) quadrant I   (b) on the y-axis   (c) quadrant II   (d) quadrant III   (e) on the x-axis

15. Where is $(-4, 0)$ located?
(a) quadrant I   (b) on the y-axis   (c) quadrant II   (d) quadrant III   (e) on the x-axis

In Exercises 16 - 18, (x, y) are the coordinates of any point in the shaded region or on its borders (see the next page).

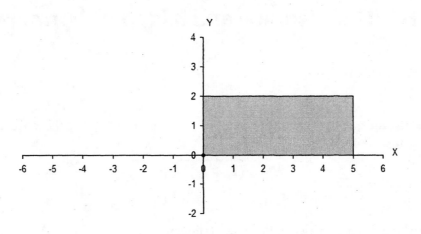

16. What is the largest value of $x + y$?
(a) 7   (b) 5   (c) 2   (d) 10   (e) 3

17. What is the smallest value of $x + y$?
(a) 5   (b) 2   (c) 0   (d) 7   (e) 3

18. What is the largest value of $x + y^2$?
(a) 41   (b) 13   (c) 4   (d) 27   (e) 9

Section B.   The Distance and Midpoint Formulas

The Distance Formula

To find the **distance**, d, between the points (x_1, y_1) and (x_2, y_2) in the xy-plane, we use the **Distance Formula**:

$$d = \sqrt{(x_2 - x_1)^2 + (y_2 - y_1)^2}$$

Example 1. Find the distance between the given points.
1) $(1, 0)$ and $(1, 5)$ 2) $(0, -2)$ and $(0, 1)$
3) $(1, -2)$ and $(-3, 6)$ 4) $(-2, -5)$ and $(-1, -7)$

Solution:
1) If we set $(x_1, y_1) = (1, 0)$ and $(x_2, y_2) = (1, 5)$, then $x_1 = 1$, $y_1 = 0$, $x_2 = 1$, and $y_2 = 5$.
Now, put these values into the Distance Formula:

$$d = \sqrt{(x_2 - x_1)^2 + (y_2 - y_1)^2} = \sqrt{(1 - 1)^2 + (5 - 0)^2}$$
$$= \sqrt{(0)^2 + (5)^2} = \sqrt{0 + 25} = \sqrt{25} = 5$$

2) Set $(x_1, y_1) = (0, -2)$ and $(x_2, y_2) = (0, 1)$. Then $x_1 = 0$, $y_1 = -2$, $x_2 = 0$, and $y_2 = 1$.
Put these values into the Distance Formula:

$$d = \sqrt{(x_2 - x_1)^2 + (y_2 - y_1)^2} = \sqrt{(0 - 0)^2 + (1 - (-2))^2}$$
$$= \sqrt{(0)^2 + (3)^2} = \sqrt{0 + 9} = \sqrt{9} = 3$$

3) Let $(x_1, y_1) = (1, -2)$ and $(x_2, y_2) = (-3, 6)$. Then

$$d = \sqrt{(x_2 - x_1)^2 + (y_2 - y_1)^2} = \sqrt{(-3 - 1)^2 + (6 - (-2))^2}$$
$$= \sqrt{(-3 - 1)^2 + (6 + 2)^2} = \sqrt{(-4)^2 + (8)^2} = \sqrt{16 + 64}$$
$$= \sqrt{80} = \sqrt{16}\sqrt{5} = 4\sqrt{5}.$$

4) Let $(x_1, y_1) = (-2, -5)$ and $(x_2, y_2) = (-1, -7)$. Then

$$d = \sqrt{(x_2 - x_1)^2 + (y_2 - y_1)^2} = \sqrt{(-1 - (-2))^2 + (-7 - (-5))^2}$$
$$= \sqrt{(-1 + 2)^2 + (-7 + 5)^2} = \sqrt{(1)^2 + (-2)^2} = \sqrt{1 + 4} = \sqrt{5}.$$

Example 2. Triangle ABC has vertices $A(0, 4)$, $B(3, 0)$, and $C(0, 0)$.
1) Find the length of $\overline{AC}$.   2) Find the length of $\overline{BC}$.
3) Find the length of $\overline{AB}$.   4) Is triangle ABC a right triangle?

Solution:

1) Let $A = (x_1, y_1) = (0, 4)$ and $C = (x_2, y_2) = (0, 0)$. Then
$$d = \sqrt{(x_2 - x_1)^2 + (y_2 - y_1)^2} = \sqrt{(0 - 0)^2 + (0 - 4)^2}$$
$$= \sqrt{0^2 + (-4)^2} = \sqrt{0 + 16} = \sqrt{16} = 4.$$

2) Let $B = (x_1, y_1) = (3, 0)$ and $C = (x_2, y_2) = (0, 0)$. Then
$$d = \sqrt{(x_2 - x_1)^2 + (y_2 - y_1)^2} = \sqrt{(0 - 3)^2 + (0 - 0)^2}$$
$$= \sqrt{(-3)^2 + 0^2} = \sqrt{9 + 0} = \sqrt{9} = 3.$$

3) Let $A = (x_1, y_1) = (0, 4)$ and $B = (x_2, y_2) = (3, 0)$. Then
$$d = \sqrt{(x_2 - x_1)^2 + (y_2 - y_1)^2} = \sqrt{(3 - 0)^2 + (0 - 4)^2}$$
$$= \sqrt{3^2 + (-4)^2} = \sqrt{9 + 16} = \sqrt{25} = 5.$$

4) Triangle ABC is a right triangle because the lengths of the sides satisfy the Pythagorean Theorem:
$$4^2 + 3^2 \overset{\checkmark}{=} 5^2$$

The Midpoint Formula

The midpoint of a line segment is the point on the segment which divides it into two equal segments (see the next figure). Notice that the distance from point A to point M is **equal to** the distance from point M to point B.

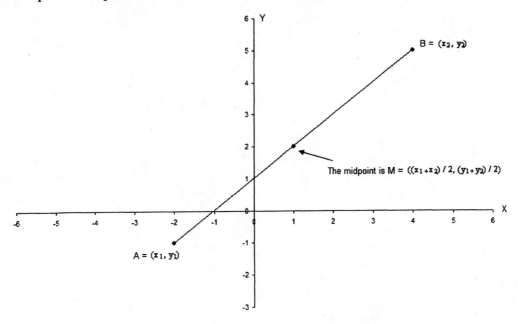

329

The **midpoint**, M, of the line segment with endpoints $A = (x_1, y_1)$ and $B = (x_2, y_2)$ is

$$M = \left(\frac{x_1 + x_2}{2}, \frac{y_1 + y_2}{2} \right).$$

Example 3. Find the midpoint of $\overline{AB}$, where $A = (4, 3)$ and $B = (2, 9)$.

Solution:
Let $(x_1, y_1) = (4, 3)$ and $(x_2, y_2) = (2, 9)$. Then the midpoint of $\overline{AB}$ is

$$\left(\frac{x_1 + x_2}{2}, \frac{y_1 + y_2}{2} \right) = \left(\frac{4+2}{2}, \frac{3+9}{2} \right) = \left(\frac{6}{2}, \frac{12}{2} \right) = (3, 6).$$

Exercises: Chapter 13, Section B

In Exercises 1 - 4, find the distance between the given points.

1. $(1, 0)$ and $(4, 4)$
(a) $\sqrt{41}$ (b) $\sqrt{26}$ (c) 5   (d) 7   (e) $\sqrt{7}$

2. $(-2, -1)$ and $(8, -1)$
(a) $\sqrt{10}$ (b) $\sqrt{104}$ (c) 8   (d) 10   (e) $2\sqrt{10}$

3. $(6, -5)$ and $(-3, 1)$
(a) $\sqrt{117}$ (b) $\sqrt{97}$ (c) $3\sqrt{5}$ (d) 3   (e) 5

4. $(-6, 7)$ and $(-6, 3)$
(a) 2   (b) 4   (c) $4\sqrt{10}$ (d) $2\sqrt{2}$ (e) $2\sqrt{61}$

In Exercises 5 - 8, choose the correct answer.

5. Find the length of $\overline{AB}$, where $A = (2, -9)$ and $B = (-1, 4)$.
(a) $\sqrt{170}$ (b) 16   (c) $\sqrt{168}$ (d) 13   (e) $\sqrt{178}$

6. Find the length of $\overline{MN}$, where $M = (0, 3)$ and $N = (-5, 17)$.
(a) $\sqrt{221}$ (b) 15   (c) $\sqrt{211}$ (d) 19   (e) $\sqrt{425}$

7. In triangle PQR, point P has coordinates $(4, -11)$ and point R has coordinates $(2, -13)$. Find the length of $\overline{PR}$.
(a) 8   (b) 4   (c) $2\sqrt{145}$ (d) $2\sqrt{13}$ (e) $2\sqrt{2}$

8. The vertices of rectangle $ABCD$ are $A(0, 7)$, $B(5, 7)$, $C(5, 0)$, and $D(0, 0)$. Find the length of the diagonal $\overline{AC}$.
(a) $\sqrt{73}$ (b) 12   (c) $\sqrt{74}$ (d) $\sqrt{2}$ (e) $37\sqrt{2}$

In Exercises 9 - 12, triangle TUV has vertices $T(6, 1)$, $U(-2, 3)$, and $V(0, -3)$.

9. Find the length of $\overline{TU}$.   10. Find the length of $\overline{UV}$.   11. Find the length of $\overline{TV}$.

12. Is triangle TUV a right triangle?

13. Triangle ABC has vertices $A(4, -1)$, $B(2, -7)$, and $C(8, 0)$. Find the length of the shortest side of the triangle.

14. Right triangle XYZ has vertices $X(2, 1)$, $Y(2, 7)$, and $Z(10, 1)$. Find the length of the hypotenuse.

In Exercises 15 - 18, find the midpoint of the line segment whose endpoints are given.

15. $A = (2, 0)$ and $B = (4, 4)$
(a) $(3, 2)$ (b) $(3, -2)$ (c) $(6, 4)$ (d) $(1, 2)$ (e) $(2, 3)$

16. $P = (-5, 4)$ and $Q = (-11, 9)$
(a) $(-16, 13)$ (b) $\left(8, -\frac{13}{2}\right)$ (c) $\left(-8, \frac{13}{2}\right)$ (d) $\left(-6, \frac{5}{2}\right)$
(e) $\left(-6, \frac{13}{2}\right)$

17. $X = (7, -3)$ and $Y = (0, -16)$
(a) $(7, -19)$ (b) $\left(\frac{7}{2}, -\frac{19}{2}\right)$ (c) $\left(-\frac{7}{2}, -\frac{13}{2}\right)$ (d) $\left(\frac{7}{2}, \frac{19}{2}\right)$
e) $\left(-\frac{7}{2}, -\frac{19}{2}\right)$

18. $M = (1.5, -3.25)$ and $N = (-0.25, 4.8)$
(a) $(0.875, 4.025)$ (b) $(-0.875, -4.025)$ (c) $(1.25, 1.55)$
(d) $(-0.625, -0.775)$ (e) $(0.625, 0.775)$

Section C. Graphing Linear Equations in Two Variables

Equations such as

$$y = 3x - 2, \quad y = -\frac{1}{5}x + 1, \quad x + 4y - 7 = 0, \quad \text{and} \quad 5x = -9y + 7$$

are examples of **linear equations in two variables**, x and y. They are linear because the variables x and y have exponent (or degree) equal to 1.

A **solution** to an equation in two variables, x and y, is an ordered pair (a, b) which satisfies the equation when we replace x by a and y by b. For example, the ordered pair $(0, 1)$ is a solution to $y = 2x + 1$ since

$$1 \overset{\surd}{=} 2(0) + 1.$$

However, the ordered pair $(-3, 2)$ is not a solution to $y = 2x + 1$ because

$$2 \neq 2(-3) + 1.$$

We are interested in finding the solutions to our equation and plotting them in the rectangular coordinate system.

Rule for finding solutions: Choose different numbers for your x-value and then find the y-value which corresponds to each.

The table below gives solutions for the equation $y = 2x + 1$.

x	$y = 2x + 1$	Solution
0	$2(0) + 1 = 1$	$(0, 1)$
1	$2(1) + 1 = 3$	$(1, 3)$
-1	$2(-1) + 1 = -1$	$(-1, -1)$
2	$2(2) + 1 = 5$	$(2, 5)$

The numbers that are chosen for x are easy to compute with. In fact, we could have chosen any real number for x. For example, if we choose $x = 5.13$, then $y = 2(5.13) + 1 = 11.26$. This gives us a solution $(5.13, 11.26)$. Unfortunately, this pair would not be easy to graph, since it has decimals in its coordinates.

Since there are infinitely many real numbers to choose for x, there are infinitely many solutions to this equation. If we find **all** of the solutions and plot them in the xy-plane, we obtain the graph of a straight line (see the next figure).

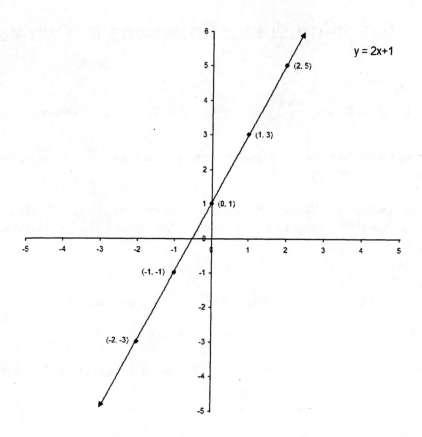

The line is a graphical representation of all of the solutions to the equation $y = 2x + 1$. If a point lies on the line, then it must satisfy the equation. For example, the point $(-2, 0)$ is not on the line and $0 \neq 2(-2) + 1$. However, the point $(-2, -3)$ is on the line and $-3 = 2(-2) + 1$. We name the line according to its equation, $y = 2x + 1$ in this case.

Example 1. Find the solutions to $y = 3x - 7$ when $x = -1, 0,$ and 2.

Solution:
1) When $x = -1$, we get $y = 3(-1) - 7 = -3 - 7 = -10$. Therefore, $\left(-1, \ -10\right)$ is a solution.
2) When $x = 0$, we get $y = 3(0) - 7 = 0 - 7 = -7$. Therefore, $\left(0, \ -7\right)$ is a solution.
3) When $x = 2$, we get $y = 3(2) - 7 = 6 - 7 = -1$. Therefore, $\left(2, \ -1\right)$ is a solution.

Example 2. Find the solutions to $4x - y = -6$ when $x = -2, 1,$ and 3.

Solution: Solve for y:

$$\begin{aligned} \cancel{4x} - y &= -6 \\ -\cancel{4x} \qquad\quad -4x & \qquad \text{(Isolate the } y \text{ term.)} \\ \hline -y &= -6 - 4x \\ -1(-y) &= -1(-6 - 4x) \qquad \text{(Solve for } y.) \\ y &= 6 + 4x \end{aligned}$$

1) When $x = -2$, we get $y = 6 + 4(-2) = 6 - 8 = -2$. Therefore, $\left(-2, \ -2\right)$ is a solution.

334

2) When $x = 1$, we get $y = 6 + 4(1) = 6 + 4 = 10$. Therefore, $(1, 10)$ is a solution.

3) When $x = 3$, we get $y = 6 + 4(3) = 6 + 12 = 18$. Therefore, $(3, 18)$ is a solution.

Example 3. Determine which points are on the line whose equation is $y = \frac{3}{4}x + 2$.

1) $(0, 2)$　　　2) $(-2, 1)$　　　3) $\left(\frac{1}{2}, 6\frac{1}{4}\right)$　　　4) $\left(-4, -\frac{1}{4}\right)$

Solution: Substitute the x- and y-value of each point into the equation and check to see if the result is true.

1) $(0, 2)$ is on the line because $2 \overset{\checkmark}{=} \frac{3}{4}(0) + 2$.

2) Notice that $\frac{3}{4}(-2) + 2 = \frac{3}{4}\left(-\frac{2}{1}\right) + 2 = -\frac{3}{2} + \frac{4}{2} = \frac{1}{2}$. Therefore, $(-2, 1)$ is not on the line since

$$1 \neq \frac{3}{4}(-2) + 2 = \frac{1}{2}.$$

3) Observe that $\frac{3}{4}\left(\frac{1}{2}\right) + 2 = \frac{3}{8} + 2 = 2\frac{3}{8}$. Therefore, $\left(\frac{1}{2}, 6\frac{1}{4}\right)$ is not on the line since

$$6\frac{1}{4} \neq \frac{3}{4}\left(\frac{1}{2}\right) + 2 = 2\frac{3}{8}.$$

4) $\left(-4, -\frac{1}{4}\right)$ is not on the line because

$$-\frac{1}{4} \neq \frac{3}{4}(-4) + 2.$$

Example 4. Find 3 solutions to each equation and graph each line.

1) $y = 3x - 1$　　　2) $y = -\frac{1}{2}x + 2$　　　3) $-\frac{2}{3}x + y + 4 = 0$

Solution:

1)

x	$y = 3x - 1$	Solution
-1	$3(-1) - 1 = -4$	$(-1, -4)$
0	$3(0) - 1 = -1$	$(0, -1)$
1	$3(1) - 1 = 2$	$(1, 2)$

The graph is on the next page.

335

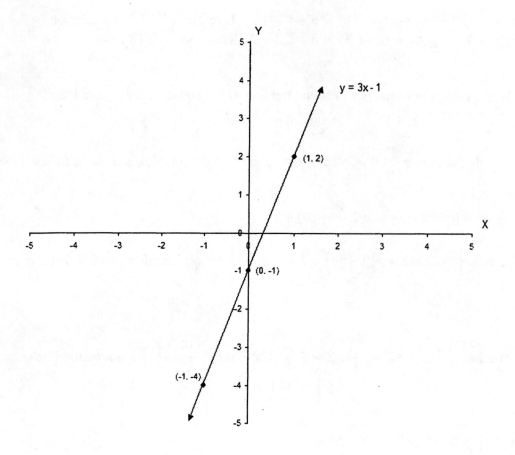

2) Since the denominator of $-\dfrac{1}{2}$ is 2, we will choose x-values that are multiples of 2. This will prevent fractions from appearing in our solutions.

x	$y = -\dfrac{1}{2}x + 2$	Solution
-2	$-\dfrac{1}{2}(-2) + 2 = 3$	$(-2, 3)$
0	$-\dfrac{1}{2}(0) + 2 = 2$	$(0, 2)$
2	$-\dfrac{1}{2}(2) + 2 = 1$	$(2, 1)$

The graph is on the next page.

y = -1/2 x + 2

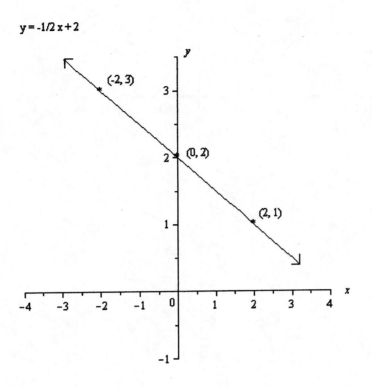

3) First solve for y by itself:

$$-\tfrac{2}{3}x + y + 4 = 0$$
$$+\tfrac{2}{3}x \qquad -4 \qquad +\tfrac{2}{3}x - 4$$
$$y \qquad = \tfrac{2}{3}x - 4$$

Since the denominator of $\tfrac{2}{3}$ is 3, we will choose x-values that are multiples of 3.

x	$y = \tfrac{2}{3}x - 4$	Solution
-3	$\tfrac{2}{3}(-3) - 4 = -6$	$(-3, -6)$
0	$\tfrac{2}{3}(0) - 4 = -4$	$(0, -4)$
3	$\tfrac{2}{3}(3) - 4 = -2$	$(3, -2)$

The graph is on the next page.

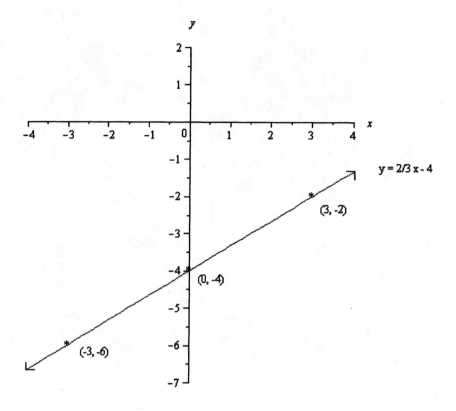

y = 2/3 x - 4

(3, -2)

(0, -4)

(-3, -6)

As we will see, the graph of every linear equation in two variables is a line. Furthermore, every linear equation in x and y can be written in the form

$$Ax + By + C = 0,$$

where A, B, and C are real numbers. This is called the **general form** of a linear equation in x and y.

Example 5. Determine whether or not the given equation is linear. If it is, put it in the general form.
1) $3x + 6y = 1$ 2) $x = 7y^2$ 3) $-5y = 14x + 3$

Solution: 1) $3x + 6y = 1$ is linear. In general form, it is $3x + 6y - 1 = 0$.
        2) $x = 7y^2$ is not linear because the degree of $7y^2$ is 2.
        3) $-5y = 14x + 3$ is linear. In general form, it is $14x + 5y + 3 = 0$.

Example 6. If the point $\left(a, \; -13\right)$ is on the graph of $-3x + 5 = y$, find the value of a.

Solution: Set $x = a$ and $y = -13$ in the equation and solve for a:

$$-3a + 5 = -13$$
$$\underline{\quad -5 \quad -5}$$
$$\frac{-3a}{-3} = \frac{-18}{-3}$$
$$a = 6$$

338

Example 7. If the point $(2, k)$ is on the line whose equation is $5x + 2y - 1 = 0$, find the value of k.

Solution: Set $x = 2$ and $y = k$ in the equation and solve for k:

$$5(2) + 2(k) - 1 = 0$$
$$10 + 2k - 1 = 0$$
$$9 + 2k = 0$$
$$\underline{-9 \qquad\quad -9}$$
$$\frac{2k}{2} = \frac{-9}{2}$$

$$k = -\frac{9}{2} = -4\frac{1}{2}$$

Exercises: Chapter 13, Section C

In Exercises 1 - 8, determine whether or not the given point is on the line whose equation is given.

1. $(4, 5)$; $y = 3x - 7$ 2. $(2, 3)$; $y = 2x - 1$ 3. $(0, -6)$; $y = x - 6$

4. $(-3, 8)$; $y = -4x - 4$ 5. $(5, 3)$; $y = -\frac{3}{5}x + 2$ 6. $(2, -5)$; $y = \frac{1}{4}x + 7$

7. $(0, 0)$; $-x + 8y = 0$ 8. $(2, 2)$; $4x - 3y - 6 = 0$

In Exercises 9 - 14, graph the line whose equation is given.

9. $y = 2x + 3$ 10. $y = \frac{1}{5}x - 2$ 11. $y = -\frac{3}{7}x + 2$

12. $y = x - 6$ 13. $2x + 5y - 5 = 0$ 14. $x - 2y + 1 = 0$

In Exercises 15 - 18, determine whether or not the given equation is linear.

15. $y = -4x - 3$ 16. $x^2 - 6y + 2 = 0$ 17. $x - 6y + 2 = 0$ 18. $\dfrac{1}{2x + y} = -5$

In Exercises 19 - 24, choose the correct answer.

19. A solution to the equation $y = 3x - 5$ is:
(a) $(2, 4)$ (b) $(-1, 8)$ (c) $(0, -5)$ (d) $(-6, 23)$ (e) $(4, 2)$

20. A solution to the equation $-x + 6y + 3 = 0$ is:
(a) $(3, 0)$ (b) $(0, -2)$ (c) $(2, -6)$ (d) $\left(3, \frac{1}{6}\right)$ (e) $\left(\frac{1}{6}, 3\right)$

21. Which of the following is not a solution to the equation $9y + x = -18$?
(a) $(-18, 0)$ (b) $(0, 2)$ (c) $(0, -2)$ (d) $(9, -3)$ (e) $\left(2, -2\frac{2}{9}\right)$

22. Which of the following is not a solution to the equation $3x - 11y + 33 = 0$?

(a) $(-11, 0)$ (b) $(0, 3)$ (c) $\left(6, 4\frac{7}{11}\right)$ (d) $(0, 0)$ (e) $\left(-3, -2\frac{2}{11}\right)$

23. If the point $(-3, m)$ is on the line whose equation is $y = 8x + 2$, find the value of m.

(a) -20 (b) 20 (c) -22 (d) $-\frac{5}{8}$ (e) 24

24. If the point $(p, 12)$ is on the line whose equation is $-6x + \frac{3}{2}y - 5 = 0$, find the value of p.

(a) $2\frac{1}{6}$ (b) $-2\frac{1}{6}$ (c) $\frac{1}{6}$ (d) $-51\frac{1}{3}$ (e) $-6\frac{1}{2}$

Section D. The Slope and Equation of a Line

The Slope Formula

We want to explore the relationship between linear equations and lines. The formula which tells the story is the Slope Formula. The **slope** of the line containing the points (x_1, y_1) and (x_2, y_2), where $x_1 \neq x_2$, is

$$m = \frac{y_2 - y_1}{x_2 - x_1} = \frac{\Delta y}{\Delta x} = \frac{\text{rise}}{\text{run}}.$$

Δy tells you how many units to go up or down (rise)

Δx tells you how many units to go to the right or left (run).

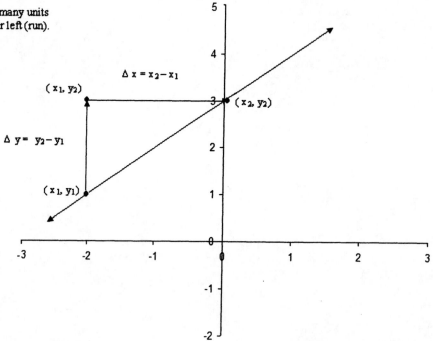

The 'Δ' symbol is the greek letter 'delta' and means 'the change in'. Thus, Δy (read as 'delta y') means 'the change in the y-value, and Δx (read as 'delta x') means 'the change in the x-value.

To compute the change in the value of the variables, subtract its initial value from its final value. For example, let T be the variable representing temperature. If the initial temperature is $T_1 = 60°C$ and the final temperature is $T_2 = 45°C$, then the change in the temperature is

$$\Delta T = T_2 - T_1 = 45°C - 60°C = -15°C.$$

In other words, the temperature *decreased* by 15°C.

Let's find the slope of the line containing $(1, 0)$ and $(2, 3)$, then use the slope to find the

342

coordinates of a third point on it. To find the slope, set $(x_1, y_1) = (1, 0)$ and $(x_2, y_2) = (2, 3)$. Then $x_1 = 1$, $y_1 = 0$, $x_2 = 2$, and $y_2 = 3$. Put these values into the Slope Formula:

$$m = \frac{y_2 - y_1}{x_2 - x_1} = \frac{3 - 0}{2 - 1} = \frac{+3}{+1} = 3.$$

The slope of the line is 3. How do we use the slope to find a third point on it?

Rules for using Δy and Δx to find a point on a line:
1) If Δy is **positive** (so the y-value increased), then you go **up** by Δy units.
2) If Δy is **negative** (so the y-value decreased), then you go **down** by Δy units.
3) If Δx is **positive** (so the x-value increased), then you go **to the right** by Δx units.
4) If Δx is **negative** (so the x-value decreased), then you go **to the left** by Δx units.
5) If $\Delta y = 0$, then the y-value didn't change.

In our example, $\Delta y = y_2 - y_1 = +3$ and $\Delta x = x_2 - x_1 = +1$. If we begin at the point $(1, 0)$ and go up by 3 units (because $\Delta y = +3$), then go across to the right by 1 unit (because $\Delta x = +1$), we end up at $(2, 3)$, which we already know is on the line. Let's use Δy and Δx to obtain another point. Starting at $(2, 3)$, go up by 3 units, then go across to the right by 1 unit. We end up at the point $(3, 6)$ (see the next figure).

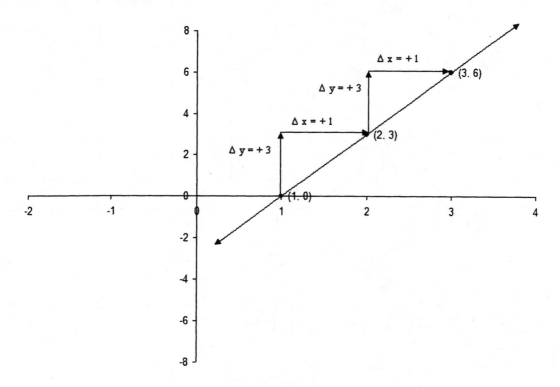

Example 1. Find the slope of the line containing the given points. Graph the line and use the slope to find two additional points on the line.
1) $(4, -1)$ and $(1, 3)$ 2) $(-2, 5)$ and $(-3, 0)$

343

Solution:

1) Let $(x_1, y_1) = (4, -1)$ and $(x_2, y_2) = (1, 3)$. Then $x_1 = 4$, $y_1 = -1$, $x_2 = 1$, and $y_2 = 3$. Plug these into the Slope Formula:

$$m = \frac{y_2 - y_1}{x_2 - x_1} = \frac{3 - (-1)}{1 - 4} = \frac{+4}{-3} = -\frac{4}{3}$$

To find two additional points on the line, let $\Delta y = +4$ and $\Delta x = -3$. Starting at the point $(1, 3)$, go up by 4 units and go across to the left by 3 units. After doing this two times, we obtain the points $(-2, 7)$ and $(-5, 11)$ (see the next figure).

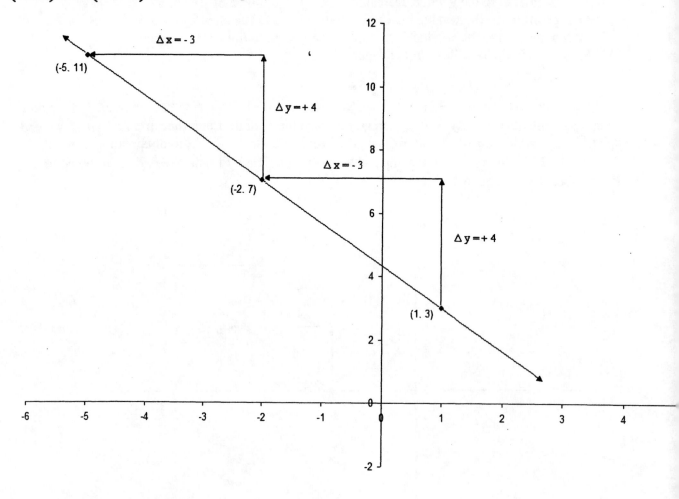

2) Let $(x_1, y_1) = (-2, 5)$ and $(x_2, y_2) = (-3, 0)$. Then

$$m = \frac{y_2 - y_1}{x_2 - x_1} = \frac{0 - 5}{-3 - (-2)} = \frac{-5}{-1} = 5.$$

To find two additional points on the line, let $\Delta y = -5$ and $\Delta x = -1$. Starting at the point $(-3, 0)$, go down by 5 units and go across to the left by 1 unit. After doing this twice, we obtain the points $(-4, -5)$ and $(-5, -10)$ (see the next figure).

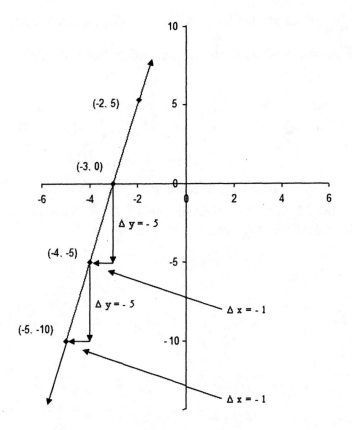

Example 2. Find the slope (if it exists) of the line containing the given points.

1) $\left(4, 2\right)$ and $\left(-1, 2\right)$ 2) $\left(-4, 3\right)$ and $\left(-4, 5\right)$

Solution:

1) Let $\left(x_1, y_1\right) = \left(4, 2\right)$ and $\left(x_2, y_2\right) = \left(-1, 2\right)$. Then

$$m = \frac{y_2 - y_1}{x_2 - x_1} = \frac{2 - 2}{-1 - 4} = \frac{0}{-5} = 0.$$

The graph is a horizontal line which crosses the y-axis at $(0, 2)$ (graph it and see for yourself).

In general, if a line has slope zero, then it is a horizontal line and vice-versa.

2) Since the x coordinates are the same, there is an **undefined** slope: if we set $\left(x_1, y_1\right) = \left(-4, 3\right)$ and $\left(x_2, y_2\right) = \left(-4, 5\right)$, then

$$m = \frac{y_2 - y_1}{x_2 - x_1} = \frac{5 - 3}{-4 - (-4)} = \frac{+2}{0}, \text{ which is undefined.}$$

The graph is a vertical line which crosses the x-axis at (−4, 0) (graph it and see for yourself).

In general, if a line has an undefined slope, then it is a vertical line and vice-versa.

Example 3. Graph the line containing the point (x_1, y_1) and whose slope is m.

1) $(x_1, y_1) = (1, -2)$ and $m = \frac{3}{2}$ 2) $(x_1, y_1) = (4, 0)$ and $m = -\frac{6}{5}$

Solution:

1) Since $m = \frac{+3}{+2}$, we have $\Delta y = +3$ and $\Delta x = +2$. Starting at $(x_1, y_1) = (1, -2)$, we go up by 3 units and go across to the right by 2 units. We obtain the point $(3, 1)$. Now that we have two points, we can graph the line (see the next figure).

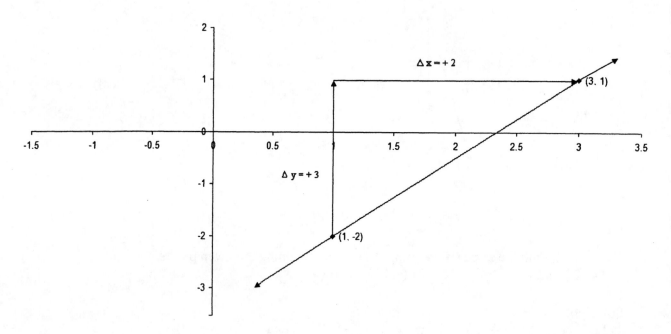

2) The slope is $m = -\frac{6}{5} = \frac{-6}{+5}$. We have $\Delta y = -6$ and $\Delta x = +5$. Starting at $(x_1, y_1) = (4, 0)$, go down by 6 units and go across to the right by 5 units. We get $(9, -6)$. We can now graph the line (see the figure on the next page). Note that we can use $m = \frac{+6}{-5}$ as well.

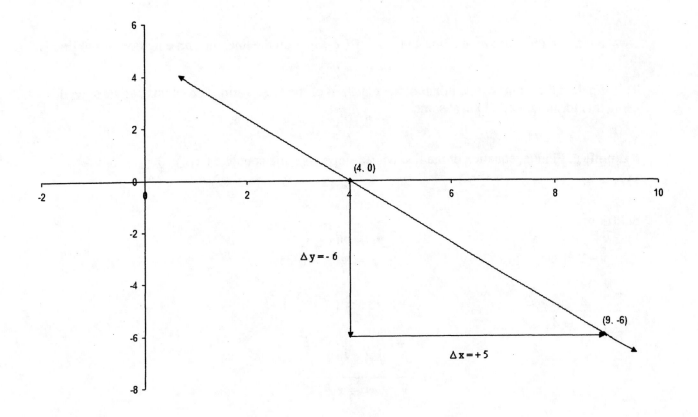

Example 4. The slope of the line containing $(a, 3)$ and $(4, 1)$ is 5. Find the value of a.

Solution: Let $(x_1, y_1) = (a, 3)$ and $(x_2, y_2) = (4, 1)$. Then

$$m = \frac{y_2 - y_1}{x_2 - x_1} = \frac{1 - 3}{4 - a} = \frac{-2}{4 - a}.$$

We are given that the slope is 5, so $\frac{-2}{4 - a} = 5$. Solve for a:

$$\frac{-2}{4 - a} = \frac{5}{1}$$

$$5(4 - a) = -2$$
$$20 - 5a = -2$$
$$\underline{-20 \qquad\quad -20}$$
$$\frac{-5a}{-5} = \frac{-22}{-5}$$

$$a = \frac{22}{5} = 4\frac{2}{5}$$

The Point-Slope Form

If we are given the slope m of a line and a point (x_1, y_1) on the line, then an equation of the line is

$$y - y_1 = m(x - x_1).$$

This is called the **Point-Slope Form** of the equation of the line. Various problems can be solved using this formula. Let's look at some.

Example 5. Find an equation of the line whose slope is m and contains (x_1, y_1).

1) $m = 4$; $(x_1, y_1) = (1, 2)$ 2) $m = \frac{3}{7}$; $(x_1, y_1) = (-3, 5)$

Solution:

1)
$$y - y_1 = m(x - x_1)$$
$$y - 2 = 4(x - 1)$$
$$y - 2 = 4x - 4$$
$$\underline{+2 \qquad +2}$$
$$y \quad = 4x - 2$$

2)
$$y - y_1 = m(x - x_1)$$
$$y - 5 = \frac{3}{7}(x - (-3))$$
$$y - 5 = \frac{3}{7}\left(x + \frac{3}{1}\right)$$
$$y - 5 = \frac{3}{7}x + \frac{9}{7}$$
$$\underline{+5 \qquad +5}$$
$$y \quad = \frac{3}{7}x + \frac{44}{7}$$

Example 6. Find an equation of the line containing the given points.

1) $(4, -2)$ and $(5, 1)$ 2) $(-3, 8)$ and $(9, 4)$.

Solution: When you are given two points, first find the slope of the line by using the Slope Formula. Then use the Point-Slope Form to get the equation.

1) Let $(x_1, y_1) = (4, -2)$ and $(x_2, y_2) = (5, 1)$. Then $m = \frac{y_2 - y_1}{x_2 - x_1} = \frac{1 - (-2)}{5 - 4} = \frac{3}{1} = 3$.
Therefore, the equation is:

$$y - y_1 = m(x - x_1)$$

$$y - (-2) = 3(x - 4)$$
$$y + 2 = 3x - 12$$
$$\underline{-2 \qquad -2}$$
$$y = 3x - 14$$

2) Let $(x_1, y_1) = (-3, 8)$ and $(x_2, y_2) = (9, 4)$.
Then $m = \frac{y_2 - y_1}{x_2 - x_1} = \frac{4 - 8}{9 - (-3)} = \frac{-4}{12} = -\frac{1}{3}$. Therefore, the equation is:

$$y - y_1 = m(x - x_1)$$

$$y - 8 = -\frac{1}{3}(x - (-3))$$

$$y - 8 = -\frac{1}{3}\left(x + \frac{3}{1}\right)$$

$$y - 8 = -\frac{1}{3}x - 1$$
$$\underline{+8 \qquad\qquad +8}$$
$$y = -\frac{1}{3}x + 7$$

The Slope-Intercept Form

When we find an equation of a line, we write our answer in the form $y = mx + b$. This is called the **slope-intercept form** of the equation. The number m is the slope of the line and b is the y coordinate of the y-intercept. The y-**intercept** of a line is the point where the line crosses the y-axis.

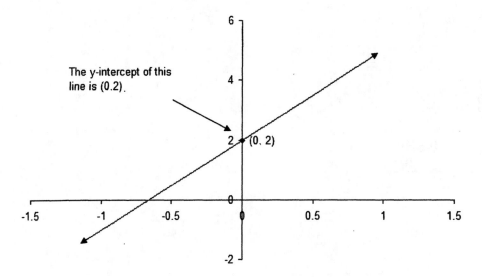

Notice that the y-intercept is of the form $(0, b)$, where b is a real number. There are lines which do not have a y-intercept, namely vertical lines which are parallel to the y-axis. We will discuss vertical lines later.

Example 7. Find an equation of the line whose slope is 5 and whose y-intercept is $(0, 3)$.

Solution: We are given $m = 5$ and $b = 3$. Putting these values into $y = mx + b$ gives us the equation $y = 5x + 3$.

Example 8. Find an equation of the line whose slope is $\frac{11}{12}$ and whose y-intercept is $(0, -3)$.

Solution: We are given $m = \frac{11}{12}$ and $b = -3$. Putting these values into $y = mx + b$ gives us the equation $y = \frac{11}{12}x + (-3)$, which becomes $y = \frac{11}{12}x - 3$

Example 9. Find the slope and y-intercept of the line whose equation is given.

1) $y = \frac{11}{3}x + 5$ 2) $y = -x - 12$ 3) $6x - 7y + 4 = 0$ 4) $-2y + 20 = -10x$

Solution: To find the slope and y-intercept of a line when we are given an equation, we put the equation in the form $y = mx + b$. The slope is m and the y-intercept is $(0, b)$.

1) The equation $y = \frac{11}{3}x + 5$ is in the form $y = mx + b$. Since $m = \frac{11}{3}$ and $b = 5$, the slope is $\frac{11}{3}$ and the y-intercept is $(0, 5)$.

2) The equation $y = -x - 12$ is in the form $y = mx + b$, and $m = -1$ and $b = -12$. Therefore, the slope is -1 and the y-intercept is $(0, -12)$.

3) Solve for y:

$$6x - 7y + 4 = 0$$
$$\underline{+7y \qquad\quad +7y}$$
$$\frac{6x}{7} + \frac{4}{7} = \frac{7y}{7}$$

The slope is $\frac{6}{7}$ and the y-intercept is $\left(0, \frac{4}{7}\right)$.

4) Solve for y:

$$-2y + 20 = -10x$$
$$\underline{\quad -20 \qquad\quad -20}$$
$$\frac{-2y}{-2} = \frac{-10x - 20}{-2}$$

$$y = \frac{-10x}{-2} - \frac{20}{-2}$$

$$y = 5x + 10$$

The slope is 5 and the y-intercept is $(0, 10)$.

The *x*-intercept is the point where a line crosses the *x*-axis.

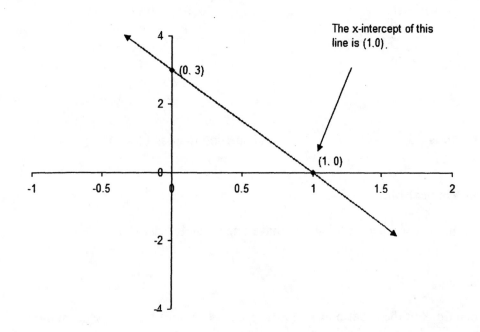

The x-intercept of this line is (1.0).

Notice that such a point must be of the form $\left(a,\ 0\right)$, where a is a real number. Not every line has an *x*-intercept (for example, any horizontal line which is parallel to the *x*-axis has no *x*-intercept).

Rule for finding intercepts:
1) To find the *y*-intercept, you set $x = 0$ in the equation and solve for *y*.
2) To find the *x*-intercept, you set $y = 0$ in the equation and solve for *x*.

Example 10. Find the intercepts of the line.
1) $2x - 3y + 6 = 0$ 2) $-x + 5y + 9 = 0$

Solution:
1) *y*-intercept: Set $x = 0$ and solve for *y*.   *x*-intercept: Set $y = 0$ and solve for *x*.

$$2(0) - 3y + 6 = 0 \qquad\qquad 2x - 3(0) + 6 = 0$$
$$-3y + \cancel{6} = 0 \qquad\qquad\qquad 2x + \cancel{6} = 0$$
$$\underline{-\cancel{6} \quad -6} \qquad\qquad\qquad \underline{-\cancel{6} \quad -6}$$
$$\frac{-\cancel{3}y}{-\cancel{3}} = \frac{-6}{-3} \qquad\qquad\qquad \frac{\cancel{2}x}{\cancel{2}} = \frac{-6}{2}$$
$$y = 2 \qquad\qquad\qquad\qquad x = -3$$

The *y*-intercept is $\left(0,\ 2\right)$.   The *x*-intercept is $\left(-3,\ 0\right)$.

2) y-intercept: Set $x = 0$ and solve for y.

$$-(0) + 5y + 9 = 0$$
$$5y + 9 = 0$$
$$\underline{-9 \quad -9}$$
$$\frac{5y}{5} = \frac{-9}{5}$$
$$y = -\frac{9}{5}$$

The y-intercept is $\left(0, -\frac{9}{5}\right)$.

x-intercept: Set $y = 0$ and solve for x.

$$-x + 5(0) + 9 = 0$$
$$-x + 9 = 0$$
$$\underline{-9 \quad -9}$$
$$\frac{-x}{-1} = \frac{-9}{-1}$$
$$x = 9$$

The x-intercept is $(9, 0)$.

Horizontal and Vertical Lines

Next we graph some linear equations that only have one variable 'visible'.

Example 11. Graph: $y = 4$

Solution: We can think of the equation $y = 4$ as $y = 0x + 4$. Notice that whatever number we choose for x, the y-value will always be equal to 4. Furthermore, the slope is 0.

x	$y = 4$	Solution
0	4	(0, 4)
1	4	(1, 4)
−1	4	(−1, 4)

The graph that we obtain is a horizontal line whose y-intercept is (0, 4) (see the next figure).

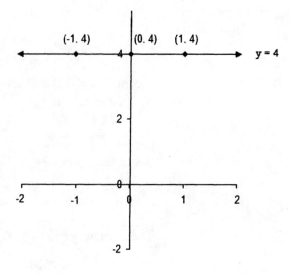

In general, the graph of the equation $y = b$ is a horizontal line whose y-intercept is $(0, b)$ and whose slope equals 0.

Example 12. Graph: $x = -2$

Solution: We can think of the equation $x = -2$ as $x = -2 + 0y$. No matter what the y-value is, the x-value will always equal -2.

$x = -2$	y	Solution
-2	-1	$(-2, -1)$
-2	0	$(-2, 0)$
-2	1	$(-2, 1)$

The graph is a vertical line whose x-intercept is $(-2, 0)$ (see the next figure). Vertical lines have **undefined slope**.

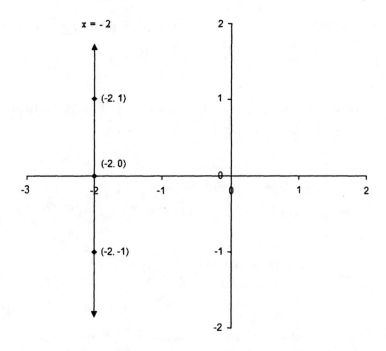

In general, the graph of the equation $x = a$ is a vertical line whose x-intercept is $(a, 0)$. Every vertical line has an undefined slope.

353

Exercises: Chapter 13, Section D

In Exercises 1 - 6, find the slope of the line containing the given points.

1. $(3, 4)$ and $(1, 8)$ 2. $(2, -7)$ and $(0, 8)$ 3. $(-6, 5)$ and $(-8, 1)$

4. $(-9, 3)$ and $(2, -11)$ 5. $(-5, 1)$ and $(-1, 1)$ 6. $(9, 0)$ and $(7, -3)$

In Exercises 7 - 19, choose the correct answer.

7. The slope of the line containing $(0, -2)$ and $(n, 3)$ is 1. Find the value of n.
   (a) $\frac{1}{5}$ (b) $-\frac{1}{5}$ (c) -5 (d) 5 (e) 1

8. The slope of the line containing $(1, y)$ and $(-3, 6)$ is $\frac{2}{3}$. Find the value of y.
   (a) $-8\frac{2}{3}$ (b) $8\frac{2}{3}$ (c) $\frac{3}{26}$ (d) $-\frac{3}{26}$ (e) $3\frac{1}{3}$

9. The slope of the line containing $(a, -2)$ and $(3, -5)$ is -6. Find the value of a.
   (a) $2\frac{1}{2}$ (b) 5 (c) $-\frac{2}{5}$ (d) $-2\frac{1}{2}$ (e) $-3\frac{1}{2}$

10. Which point is on a line whose slope is $\frac{1}{4}$ and contains $(1, 2)$?
    (a) $(-5, 3)$ (b) $(5, 3)$ (c) $(0, 1)$ (d) $(-2, 0)$ (e) $(9, 6)$

11. Which point is on a line whose slope is -2 and contains $(3, -1)$?
    (a) $(3, 0)$ (b) $(5, 5)$ (c) $(5, -5)$ (d) $(-2, 4)$ (e) $(4, -6)$

12. Find an equation of the line whose slope is 6 and contains $(2, 9)$.
    (a) $y = 6x + 3$ (b) $y = 6x - 8$ (c) $y = 6x - 5$ (d) $y = \frac{1}{6}x + \frac{5}{6}$
    (e) $y = 6x - 3$

13. Find an equation of the line whose slope is $\frac{2}{7}$ and contains $(-4, 6)$.
    (a) $y = \frac{2}{7}x + \frac{2}{7}$ (b) $y = \frac{2}{7}x + \frac{1}{7}$ (c) $y = \frac{2}{7}x + 7\frac{1}{7}$ (d) $y = \frac{2}{7}x - 1$
    (e) $y = \frac{2}{7}x + 6\frac{6}{7}$

14. Find an equation of the line with no slope and contains $(-6, -3)$.

(a) $x = -3$ (b) $y = x + 3$ (c) $y = -3$ (d) $x = -6$ (e) $y = x - 3$

15. Find an equation of the line with slope 0 and contains $(9, -5)$.

(a) $x = 9$ (b) $y = x - 14$ (c) $y = -5$ (d) $x = 4$ (e) $y = -9$

16. Find an equation of the line containing $(2, -5)$ and $(0, 3)$.

(a) $y = 4x - 3$ (b) $y = -\frac{1}{4}x + 3$ (c) $y = -4x - 5$ (d) $y = -4x + 3$

(e) $y = -x + 3$

17. Find an equation of the line containing $(-1, -1)$ and $(5, 5)$.

(a) $y = x$ (b) $y = -x$ (c) $y = 2x$ (d) $y = x - 1$ (e) $y = -x + 1$

18. Find an equation of the line containing $(8, 2)$ and $(-3, 2)$.

(a) $y = x - 6$ (b) $y = \frac{1}{4}x$ (c) $y = 2$ (d) $y = x + 2$ (e) $y = 0$

19. Find an equation of the line containing $(5, -12)$ and $(5, 3)$.

(a) $y = x + 5$ (b) $x = 0$ (c) $y = 5$ (d) $x = 5$ (e) $y = x - 7$

In Exercises 20 - 30, find the slope and y-intercept of the line whose equation is given.

20. $y = 3x + 6$ 21. $y = \frac{4}{11}x - \frac{3}{11}$ 22. $y = -8x - 1$ 23. $2x + 6y = 12$

24. $8x - 3y + 24 = 0$ 25. $-5x - 3y + 2 = 0$ 26. $-4x + y - 6 = 0$

27. $y = -1$ 28. $x = 5$ 29. $x = -8$ 30. $y = 3$

In Exercises 31 - 41, choose the correct answer.

31. The y-intercept of the line $x - 5y - 10 = 0$ is:

(a) $(0, 2)$ (b) $(0, -2)$ (c) $\left(0, \frac{1}{2}\right)$ (d) $\left(0, -\frac{1}{2}\right)$ (e) $(0, 10)$

32. The x-intercept of the line $-12x + 2y - 8 = 0$ is:

(a) $\left(-\frac{2}{3}, 0\right)$ (b) $\left(\frac{2}{3}, 0\right)$ (c) $\left(\frac{3}{2}, 0\right)$ (d) $\left(-\frac{3}{2}, 0\right)$ (e) $(4, 0)$

33. The y-intercept of the line $y = 7$ is:

(a) $(0, 7)$ (b) $(0, -7)$ (c) $(0, 0)$ (d) $(7, 0)$ (e) $(-7, 0)$

34. The x-intercept of the line $x = -2$ is:

(a) $(0, 2)$ (b) $(0, -2)$ (c) $(0, 0)$ (d) $(2, 0)$ (e) $(-2, 0)$

35. The y-intercept of the line $\frac{3}{8}y - 11x = -12$ is:

(a) $(0, 32)$ (b) $\left(0, -4\frac{1}{2}\right)$ (c) $(0, -32)$ (d) $\left(0, -\frac{1}{32}\right)$ (e) $\left(0, 1\frac{1}{12}\right)$

36. Which equation represents a line that crosses the origin?

(a) $y = 2x - 3$ (b) $y = -x + 6$ (c) $y = \frac{x}{8}$ (d) $y = 9x + 1$ (e) $y = \frac{3x}{4} - 5$

37. The x-intercept of the line $15 - 3x + \frac{5}{9}y = 0$ is:

(a) $(-5, 0)$ (b) $(5, 0)$ (c) $\left(\frac{1}{5}, 0\right)$ (d) $(-27, 0)$ (e) $\left(\frac{3}{5}, 0\right)$

38. Which statement about the line $7x + y + 1 = 0$ is true?

(a) The slope is 7.   (b) The x-intercept is $\left(\frac{1}{7}, 0\right)$.   (c) The y-intercept is $(0, 1)$.

(d) The slope is $\frac{1}{7}$.   (e) It contains the point $(-1, 6)$.

39. Which statement about the line $y = 8x - 13$ is false?

(a) The slope is 8.   (b) The x-intercept is $\left(-1\frac{5}{8}, 0\right)$.   (c) The y-intercept is $(0, -13)$.

(d) It does not go through the origin.   (e) It contains the point $(2, 3)$.

40. Which statement about the line $2x = \frac{1}{8}y - 9$ is true?

(a) The slope is 2.   (b) The x-intercept is $\left(4\frac{1}{2}, 0\right)$.   (c) The y-intercept is $\left(0, 1\frac{1}{8}\right)$.

(d) The slope is 16.   (e) The point $(7, 16)$ is on the line.

41. Which statement about the line $x - 16y = 0$ is false?

(a) The slope is 1.   (b) The x-intercept is $(0, 0)$.   (c) The y-intercept is $(0, 0)$.

(d) It contains the point $(-32, -2)$.   (e) The slope is $\frac{1}{16}$.

Section E.   Parallel and Perpendicular Lines

Parallel Lines

Two lines are **parallel** if they never intersect.

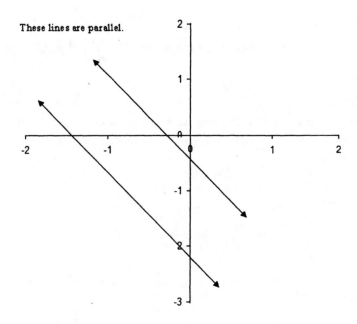

These lines are parallel.

If $y = m_1x + b_1$ and $y = m_2x + b_2$ are the equations of two non-vertical lines and $b_1 \neq b_2$ (so the lines don't have the same y-intercept), then these lines are parallel if and only if $m_1 = m_2$; that is, if and only if they have equal slopes.

For example, the lines $y = 4x - 4$ and $y = 4x + 15$ are parallel because they both have slope 4, and they have different y-intercepts are different. Notice that horizontal lines are parallel to each other, and vertical lines are parallel to each other.

Example 1. Are the lines parallel?
1) $y = 3x + 1$ and $y = 3x - 5$ 2) $y = x - 4$ and $y = -2x$
3) $y = 5$ and $y = -2$ 4) $2x + 5y - 1 = 0$ and $-2x - 5y + 7 = 0$

Solution:
1) Both lines have slope 3 and have different y-intercepts, $(0, 1)$ and $(0, -5)$. Therefore, they are parallel.
2) $y = x - 4$ has slope 1, and $y = -2x$ has slope –2. Therefore, the lines are not parallel.
3) Both lines are horizontal and they have different y-intercepts. Therefore, they are parallel.
4) We need to get both equations in slope-intercept form:

$$2x + 5y - 1 = 0 \qquad\qquad -2x - 5y + 7 = 0$$
$$\underline{ -5y \qquad -5y} \qquad\qquad \underline{ +5y \qquad +5y}$$
$$\frac{2x}{-5} - \frac{1}{-5} = \frac{-5y}{-5} \qquad\qquad \frac{-2x}{5} + \frac{7}{5} = \frac{5y}{5}$$

$$-\frac{2}{5}x + \frac{1}{5} = y \qquad\qquad -\frac{2}{5}x + \frac{7}{5} = y$$

Since both lines have slope $-\frac{2}{5}$ and the y-intercepts are different, the lines are parallel.

Example 2. Find an equation of the line containing the point $(2, 1)$ and parallel to the line $y = -6x + 5$.

Solution: We use the Point-Slope Form: $y - y_1 = m(x - x_1)$. We are given $(x_1, y_1) = (2, 1)$, but we are not given the slope m. We know that the line we want is parallel to $y = -6x + 5$. Therefore, it must have the same slope as $y = -6x + 5$, which is -6. Substituting $x_1 = 2$, $y_1 = 1$, and $m = -6$ into the Point-Slope Form gives us:

$$y - y_1 = m(x - x_1)$$
$$y - 1 = -6(x - 2)$$
$$y - 1 = -6x + 12$$
$$\underline{+1 \qquad\qquad +1}$$
$$y = -6x + 13$$

Observe that the y-intercept of our line is different from the y-intercept of the given line. This guarantees that the lines are different.

Example 3. In the xy-plane, line $\overleftrightarrow{AB}$ is parallel to line $\overleftrightarrow{PQ}$. If the slope of $\overleftrightarrow{AB}$ is $\frac{4}{5}$ and the slope of $\overleftrightarrow{PQ}$ is $\frac{a-6}{15}$, find the value of a.

Solution: Since the lines are parallel, their slopes are equal.

$$\frac{4}{5} = \frac{a-6}{15}$$

$$4(15) = 5(a-6) \qquad \text{(after cross multiplying)}$$
$$60 = 5a - 30$$
$$\underline{+30 \qquad\quad +30}$$
$$\frac{90}{5} = \frac{5a}{5}$$

$$18 = a$$

Perpendicular Lines

Two lines are **perpendicular** if they intersect and form right angles (recall that a **right angle** is an angle whose measurement is 90°).

These lines are perpendicular.

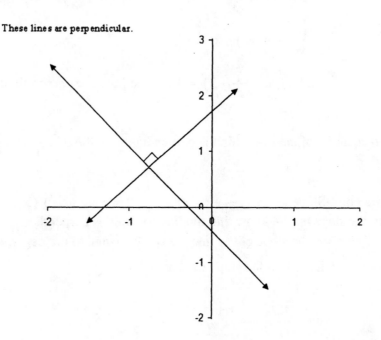

If $y = m_1 x + b_1$ and $y = m_2 x + b_2$ are the equations of two lines (neither is vertical nor horizontal), then these lines are perpendicular if and only if $m_1 m_2 = -1$; that is, if and only if their slopes multiply to give -1. Another way to interpret this is by saying that m_2 is the **negative reciprocal** of m_1.

For example, the line $y = \frac{7}{5}x + 2$ is perpendicular to the line $y = -\frac{5}{7}x - 10$ because their slopes multiply to give -1: $\frac{7}{5}\left(-\frac{5}{7}\right) = -1$. Observe that $-\frac{5}{7}$ is the negative reciprocal of $\frac{7}{5}$. Note that every horizontal line is perpendicular to every vertical line and vice versa.

Example 4. Are the given lines perpendicular?
1) $y = 4x - 2$ and $y = -\frac{1}{4}x + 1$ 2) $y = \frac{2}{5}x - 1$ and $y = -\frac{1}{3}x + 3$
3) $x = 5$ and $y = -2$ 4) $x - 3y - 8 = 0$ and $-3x - y + 5 = 0$

Solution:
1) The slope of $y = 4x - 2$ is 4 and the slope of $y = -\frac{1}{4}x + 1$ is $-\frac{1}{4}$. Since $4\left(-\frac{1}{4}\right) = -1$, the lines are perpendicular.
2) The slope of $y = \frac{2}{5}x - 1$ is $\frac{2}{5}$ and slope of $y = -\frac{1}{3}x + 3$ is $-\frac{1}{3}$. Since $\frac{2}{5}\left(-\frac{1}{3}\right) = -\frac{2}{15} \neq -1$, the lines are not perpendicular.
3) $x = 5$ is a vertical line and $y = -2$ is a horizontal line. They are perpendicular,

4) We need to get both equations in slope-intercept form:

$$x - 3y - 8 = 0 \qquad\qquad -3x - y + 5 = 0$$
$$\underline{+3y \qquad\quad +3y} \qquad\qquad \underline{+y \qquad\qquad +y}$$
$$\frac{x}{3} - \frac{8}{3} = \frac{3y}{3} \qquad\qquad\qquad -3x + 5 = y$$

$$\frac{1}{3}x - \frac{8}{3} = y$$

Therefore, the slopes are $\frac{1}{3}$ and -3, and $\frac{1}{3}(-3) = -1$. The lines are perpendicular.

Example 5. Find an equation of the line which is perpendicular to the line $\frac{1}{2}x + \frac{5}{6}y - 1 = 0$ and contains the point $(-8, -5)$.

Solution: We use the Point-Slope Form: $y - y_1 = m(x - x_1)$. We are given $(x_1, y_1) = (-8, -5)$, but we are not given the slope m. We know that the line we want is perpendicular to $\frac{1}{2}x + \frac{5}{6}y - 1 = 0$. Therefore, the slope of the line we want is equal to the negative reciprocal of the slope of $\frac{1}{2}x + \frac{5}{6}y - 1 = 0$. Let's find the slope of $\frac{1}{2}x + \frac{5}{6}y - 1 = 0$:

$$\frac{1}{2}x + \frac{5}{6}y - 1 = 0$$
$$\underline{\quad -\frac{5}{6}y \qquad\quad -\frac{5}{6}y}$$
$$\frac{1}{2}x - 1 = -\frac{5}{6}y$$

$$-\frac{6}{5}\left(\frac{1}{2}x - 1\right) = -\frac{6}{5}\left(-\frac{5}{6}y\right)$$

$$-\frac{3}{5}x + \frac{6}{5} = y$$

And so, the slope of $\frac{1}{2}x + \frac{5}{6}y - 1 = 0$ is $-\frac{3}{5}$. Therefore, the slope of the line we want is $\frac{5}{3}$. Substituting $x_1 = -8$, $y_1 = -5$, and $m = -\frac{3}{5}$ into the Point-Slope Form gives us:

$$y - y_1 = m(x - x_1)$$
$$y - (-5) = \frac{5}{3}(x - (-8))$$

$$y + 5 = \frac{5}{3}\left(x + \frac{8}{1}\right)$$

$$y + 5 = \frac{5}{3}x + \frac{40}{3}$$
$$\underline{\quad -5 \qquad\qquad -5}$$
$$y = \frac{5}{3}x + \frac{25}{3}$$

Example 6. In the xy-plane, line $\overleftrightarrow{MN}$ is perpendicular to line $\overleftrightarrow{ST}$. If the slope of $\overleftrightarrow{MN}$ is $-\frac{3}{4}$ and the slope of $\overleftrightarrow{ST}$ is $\frac{20}{9y}$, find the value of y.

Solution: The slopes of these perpendicular lines multiply to give -1:

$$-\frac{3}{4}\left(\frac{20}{9y}\right) = -1$$

$$-\frac{5}{3y} = \frac{-1}{1}$$

$$\frac{-\cancel{3}y}{-\cancel{3}} = \frac{-5}{-3}$$

$$y = \frac{5}{3}$$

Exercises: Chapter 13, Section E

In Exercises 1 - 12, determine whether the given pair of equations represent parallel lines, perpendicular lines or neither.

1. $y = 2x - 12$ and $y = 2x + 8$

2. $y = 7x + 5$ and $y = 7x - 2$

3. $y = -\frac{4}{9}x$ and $y = \frac{9}{4}x + 1$

4. $y = \frac{3}{5}x - 1$ and $y = -\frac{5}{3}x + 12$

5. $y = -\frac{3}{8}x + 6$ and $y = -\frac{8}{3}x + 6$

6. $y = -3x + 11$ and $y = 3x + 8$

7. $-2x + y = 0$ and $6x - 3y - 1 = 0$

8. $x - y - 8 = 0$ and $2x - 2y - 5 = 0$

9. $9x - 5y + 6 = 0$ and $-5x - y = 0$

10. $x = 2$ and $y = 9$

11. $8x - 3y - 7 = 0$ and $-3x - 5y = 0$

12. $y = 0$ and $y = -6$

In Exercises 13 - 24, choose the correct answer.

13. Find an equation of the line containing $(1, 0)$ and parallel to $y = x + 2$.
    (a) $y = x + 3$ (b) $y = x - 2$ (c) $y = x$ (d) $y = x - 1$ (e) $y = -x + 1$

14. Find an equation of the line containing $(-3, 5)$ and parallel to $4x + 3y - 9 = 0$.
    (a) $y = \frac{4}{3}x + 9$ (b) $y = -\frac{4}{3}x + 1$ (c) $y = -\frac{4}{3}x + 9$ (d) $y = 4x + 17$
    (e) $y = \frac{3}{4}x + \frac{29}{4}$

15. Find an equation of the line containing $(7, -1)$ and parallel to $x = 6$.
    (a) $y = -1$ (b) $y = 6$ (c) $x = 7$ (d) $x = -1$ (e) $x + y = 6$

16. Find an equation of the line containing $(0, 2)$ and perpendicular to $y = 8x - 3$.
    (a) $y = 8x + 2$ (b) $y = \frac{1}{8}x + 2$ (c) $y = -\frac{1}{8}x - 3$ (d) $y = -\frac{1}{8}x + 2$
    (e) $y = 8x - 3$

362

17. Find an equation of the line containing $(5, 9)$ and perpendicular to $-7x - 5y + 12 = 0$.

(a) $y = \frac{1}{7}x + \frac{58}{7}$ (b) $y = -\frac{5}{7}x + \frac{88}{7}$ (c) $y = \frac{5}{7}x + \frac{38}{7}$ (d) $y = \frac{7}{5}x + 16$

(e) $y = \frac{5}{7}x - \frac{16}{7}$

18. Find an equation of the line containing $(-3, -4)$ and perpendicular to $x = 2$.

(a) $y = -4$ (b) $y = 2$ (c) $x = -3$ (d) $x = -4$ (e) $x + y = -7$

19. Line $\overleftrightarrow{AB}$ is parallel to line $\overleftrightarrow{CD}$. If the slope of $\overleftrightarrow{AB}$ is 5 and the slope of $\overleftrightarrow{CD}$ is $\frac{a}{6}$, find the value of a.

(a) $\frac{6}{5}$ (b) $\frac{5}{6}$ (c) $\frac{1}{30}$ (d) 30   (e) $-\frac{6}{5}$

20. Line $\overleftrightarrow{PQ}$ is parallel to line $\overleftrightarrow{RS}$. If the slope of $\overleftrightarrow{PQ}$ is $\frac{x+3}{2}$ and the slope of $\overleftrightarrow{RS}$ is $-\frac{2x}{9}$, find the value of x.

(a) $-\frac{27}{13}$ (b) $-\frac{13}{27}$ (c) $-\frac{27}{5}$ (d) $-\frac{3}{13}$ (e) $-\frac{27}{16}$

21. Line $\overleftrightarrow{EF}$ is perpendicular to line $\overleftrightarrow{GH}$. If the slope of $\overleftrightarrow{EF}$ is $9t + 2$ and the slope of $\overleftrightarrow{GH}$ is -4, find the value of t.

(a) $\frac{7}{36}$ (b) $-\frac{36}{7}$ (c) $-\frac{2}{3}$ (d) $\frac{1}{4}$ (e) $-\frac{7}{36}$

22. Line $\overleftrightarrow{AB}$ is perpendicular to line $\overleftrightarrow{CD}$. If the slope of $\overleftrightarrow{AB}$ is $\frac{2a}{a-3}$ and the slope of $\overleftrightarrow{CD}$ is 1, find the value of a.

(a) -1 (b) -3 (c) 1   (d) 2   (e) 0

23. Line $\overleftrightarrow{ST}$ is a horizontal line and is parallel to $\overleftrightarrow{UV}$. If the slope of $\overleftrightarrow{UV}$ is $7x - 14$, find the value of x.

(a) -2 (b) $-\frac{1}{2}$ (c) $\frac{1}{2}$ (d) 2   (e) 0

24. Line $\overleftrightarrow{XY}$ is a vertical line and is perpendicular to line $\overleftrightarrow{PQ}$. If the slope of $\overleftrightarrow{PQ}$ is $20y + 15$, find the value of y.

(a) $\frac{3}{4}$ (b) $-\frac{3}{4}$ (c) $-\frac{4}{3}$ (d) $\frac{4}{3}$ (e) 0

Section F.   Systems of Equations

A **system of linear equations** is a set of two or more linear equations, each containing one or more variables. For example, the pair

$$x - y = 5$$
$$x + y = -3$$

is a system of linear equations consisting of two equations and two variables. We call this a 2×2 **system** (the first 2 is the number of equations, and the second 2 is the number of variables).

A **solution** to a 2×2 system of linear equations in x and y is an ordered pair (a, b) which solves **both equations** in the system when we replace x by a and y by b.

A solution to the system

$$x - y = 5$$
$$x + y = -3$$

is $(1, -4)$ because when we replace x by 1 and y by –4 in both equations, both equations are true:

$$x - y = 5 \qquad\qquad x + y = -3$$
$$(1) - (-4) = 5 \ \checkmark \qquad\qquad (1) + (-4) = -3 \ \checkmark$$

Graphically, a solution to a 2×2 system is a point where the lines intersect each other (see the next figure).

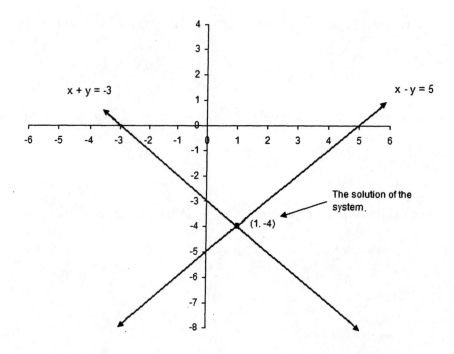

There are 2 × 2 systems which have infinitely many solutions. An example of such a system is:

$$2x + 3y = 6$$
$$-4x - 6y = -12$$

Notice, for instance, that $(6, -2)$ and $(3, 0)$ are solutions to both equations:

$$2(6) + 3(-2) \overset{\checkmark}{=} 6 \qquad \text{and} \qquad 2(3) + 3(0) \overset{\checkmark}{=} 6$$
$$-4(6) - 6(-2) \overset{\checkmark}{=} -12 \qquad\qquad -4(3) - 6(0) \overset{\checkmark}{=} -12$$

In fact, any solution to the first equation is also a solution to the second one.

There are also 2 × 2 linear systems which have no solution. For example, the system

$$x = 3 + y$$
$$x = 5 + y$$

has no solution. There are no values of x and y that solve both equations simultaneously.

Example 1. Decide whether or not the ordered pair $(-2, 3)$ is a solution to the given system.

1) $x - y = -5$ 2) $-x = y + 5$ 3) $4y = 3x + 18$
    $2x + y = -1$ $6x + y = 0$ $x - 7y = 12$

Solution: Remember that a solution to a 2 × 2 system must solve **both equations**.
1) Replace x by –2 and y by 3 in both of the equations. Since $(-2) - (3) \overset{\checkmark}{=} -5$ and $2(-2) + (3) \overset{\checkmark}{=} -1$, $(-2, 3)$ is a solution to the system.
2) If we replace x by –2 and y by 3 in the first equation, we obtain $-(-2) \neq (3) + 5$. Therefore, $(-2, 3)$ is not a solution to the system.
3) Notice that $4(3) \overset{\checkmark}{=} 3(-2) + 18$, but $(-2) - 7(3) \neq 12$. Therefore, $(-2, 3)$ is not a solution to the system.

The Substitution Method

A 2 × 2 linear system can be solved algebraically by using the Substitution Method. To demonstrate how the method works, let's solve the following system:

$$y = 3x - 1$$
$$x + y = 3$$

First, notice that the variable y is by itself in the first equation. Replace the y-variable in the **second equation** by $3x - 1$; that is, **substitute** $3x - 1$ into the second equation for y. By doing so, the second equation becomes:

$$x + \overbrace{(3x - 1)}^{y} = 3$$

Next, solve for x:

$$x + (3x - 1) = 3$$
$$4x - 1 = 3$$
$$\underline{+1 \quad +1}$$
$$\frac{4x}{4} = \frac{4}{4}$$
$$x = 1$$

Now, we find y by replacing x by 1 in either one of the equations in the system. Let's use the first equation since y is already by itself:

$$y = 3x - 1 = 3(1) - 1 = 3 - 1 = 2$$

The solution to the system is $(1, 2)$.

To use the Substitution Method, a variable in at least one equation in the system must be by itself.

Example 2. Solve each system.

1) $2x - 7y = 2$ 2) $-8x + 3y - 2 = 0$ 3) $y = 10 - 6x$ 4) $9y - 7 = x$
    $x = 3y + 4$ $y = 4x - 1$ $y = -3 - 6x$ $5x = 45y - 35$

Solution:

1) In the second equation, the variable x is by itself. Substitute $3y + 4$ into the first equation for x:

$$2 \overset{x}{\overbrace{(3y + 4)}} - 7y = 2$$
$$6y + 8 - 7y = 2$$
$$-y + 8 = 2$$
$$\underline{-8 \quad -8}$$
$$\frac{-y}{-1} = \frac{-6}{-1}$$

$$y = 6$$

To find x, replace y by 6 in either one of the equations in the system. The second one is easier to work with since x is already by itself:

$$x = 3y + 4 = 3(6) + 4 = 18 + 4 = 22$$

The solution to the system is $(22, 6)$.

2) Substitute $4x - 1$ into the first equation for y:

$$-8x + 3 \overset{y}{\overbrace{(4x - 1)}} - 2 = 0$$
$$-8x + 12x - 3 - 2 = 0$$
$$4x - 5 = 0$$
$$\underline{+5 \quad +5}$$
$$\frac{4x}{4} = \frac{5}{4}$$

$$x = \frac{5}{4}$$

We find y by replacing x by $\frac{5}{4}$ in the second equation:

$$y = 4x - 1 = \frac{4}{1}\left(\frac{5}{4}\right) - 1 = 5 - 1 = 4$$

The solution is $\left(\frac{5}{4}, 4\right)$.

3) The variable y is by itself in **both** equations. Therefore, set the right hand side of each equation equal to one another and solve for x:

$$
\begin{array}{r}
\overbrace{10 - 6x}^{y} = -3 - 6x \\
+\,6x \qquad\quad +\,6x \\
\hline
10 \qquad = -3 \ ??
\end{array}
$$

The variable x dropped out and we have two **unequal numbers** equal to one another, which is absurd. When this happens, the system has **no solution**.

4) The variable x is by itself in the first equation. Substitute $9y - 7$ into the second equation for x:

$$
\begin{array}{r}
5\,\overbrace{(9y - 7)}^{x} = 45y - 35 \\
45y - 35 = 45y - 35 \\
-45y \qquad\quad -45y \\
\hline
-35 = \qquad -35 \ ??
\end{array}
$$

This time, the variable y dropped out and we obtained two numbers equal to one another which **really are** equal. When this happens, the system has **infinitely many solutions**.

Notice that the Substitution Method worked nicely in these examples because at least one equation in each system had a variable by itself. Next

The Elimination Method

The Substitution Method worked nicely in the previous examples because each system contained an equation with x or y by itself. Not all 2×2 linear systems come this way. For example, the system

$$
\begin{aligned}
6x + 5y &= 1 \\
-8x + 2y &= -3
\end{aligned}
$$

does not have an equation with one variable by itself. We **could** solve for x or y in one of the equations, then substitute and solve as before. However, this would require some messy algebra (try it!).

An alternative way of solving a 2×2 linear system is to apply the Elimination Method. To demonstrate, let's solve the following system:

$$x + y = 5$$
$$x - y = -7$$

We begin by noticing that the columns of the system contain like terms: the first column contains the x terms, the second contains the y terms, and the third contains the constant terms. Also note that the equals signs are aligned. Since $+y$ and $-y$ are additive inverses of each other, we can **eliminate** the y terms by adding the two equations together. This allows us to solve for x:

$$
\begin{array}{r}
x + y = 5 \\
+ \quad x - y = -7 \\
\hline
\dfrac{2x}{2} = \dfrac{-2}{2} \\
x = -1
\end{array}
$$

To find y, replace x by -1 in the first equation (it doesn't matter which equation you choose).

$$
\begin{array}{r}
x + y = 5 \\
-1 + y = 5 \\
+1 \qquad +1 \\
\hline
y = 6
\end{array}
$$

The solution to the system is $(-1, 6)$.

Rule: To use the Elimination Method, the columns of the system must contain like terms, and at least one of the variable columns contains additive inverses.

Example 3. Solve each system.

1) $-6x + 5y = -1$
   $6x + y = 13$

2) $7x + 2y = -2$
   $-x + 3y = 3$

3) $6x + 5y = 1$
   $-8x + 2y = -3$

4) $y = -7x + 12$
   $y = -7x + 4$

Solution:

1) The columns of the system contain like terms, the equal signs are aligned, and $-6x$ and $+6x$ are additive inverses of each other. We eliminate the x terms by adding the two equations together:

$$
\begin{array}{r}
-6x + 5y = -1 \\
+ \quad 6x + y = 13 \\
\hline
\dfrac{6y}{6} = \dfrac{12}{6} \\
y = 2
\end{array}
$$

To find x, replace y by 2 in the first equation.

$$
\begin{array}{r}
-6x + 5y = -1 \\
-6x + 5(2) = -1 \\
-6x + 10 = -1 \\
-10 \quad -10 \\
\hline
\dfrac{-6x}{-6} = \dfrac{-11}{-6} \\
\\
x = \dfrac{11}{6}
\end{array}
$$

The solution to the system is $\left(\frac{11}{6}, 2\right)$.

2) The columns contain like terms and the equal signs are aligned, but we do not have additive inverses. We make the x terms additive inverses by multiplying the second equation by 7, then eliminate the x terms in the new system:

$$\begin{array}{lll}
7x + 2y & = -2 \\
7(-x + 3y) & = 7(3)
\end{array}
\qquad \text{becomes} \qquad
\begin{array}{ll}
7x + 2y & = -2 \\
+\ -7x + 21y & = 21 \\
\hline
\dfrac{23y}{23} & = \dfrac{19}{23}
\end{array}$$

To find x, replace y by $\frac{19}{23}$ in the first equation:
$$7x + 2y = -2$$
$$7x + \frac{2}{1}\left(\frac{19}{23}\right) = -2$$
$$7x + \frac{38}{23} = -2$$
$$\frac{23}{1}\left(7x + \frac{38}{23}\right) = \frac{23}{1}(-2) \qquad \text{(Clear the fractions.)}$$

$$\begin{array}{rcl}
161x + 38 & = & -46 \\
-38 & & -38 \\
\hline
\dfrac{161x}{161} & = & \dfrac{-84}{161}
\end{array}$$

$$x = -\frac{84}{161} = -\frac{12}{23}$$

The solution to the system is $\left(-\frac{12}{23}, \frac{19}{23}\right)$.

3) Once again, we do not have additive inverses. In order to make the x terms additive inverses of each other, first realize that the LCM of 6 and 8 is 24. To produce $24x$ in the first equation, multiply it by 4; to produce $-24x$ in the second equation, multiply it by 3. Add the new equations together to eliminate the x terms:

$$\begin{array}{ll}
4(6x + 5y) = 4(1) \\
3(-8x + 2y) = 3(-3)
\end{array}
\qquad \text{becomes} \qquad
\begin{array}{ll}
24x + 20y = 4 \\
+ \quad -24x + 6y = -9 \\
\hline
\dfrac{26y}{26} = \dfrac{-5}{26} \\
y = -\dfrac{5}{26}
\end{array}$$

To find x, replace y by $-\frac{5}{26}$ in the first equation:
$$6x + 5y = 1$$
$$6x + \frac{5}{1}\left(-\frac{5}{26}\right) = 1$$
$$6x - \frac{25}{26} = 1$$

$$\frac{26}{1}\left(6x - \frac{25}{26}\right) = \frac{26}{1}(1) \qquad \text{(Clear the fractions.)}$$

$$156x - 25 = 26$$
$$\underline{+25 \quad +25}$$
$$\frac{156x}{156} = \frac{51}{156}$$

$$x = \frac{51}{156} = \frac{17}{52}$$

The solution to the system is $\left(\frac{17}{52}, -\frac{5}{26}\right)$.

4) To eliminate the y terms, multiply the second equation by -1 to get additive inverses.

$$y = -7x + 12 \qquad \text{becomes}$$
$$-1(y) = -1(-7x + 4)$$

$$\begin{array}{r} y = -7x + 12 \\ + \quad -y = 7x - 4 \\ \hline 0 = \quad 8 \text{ ??} \end{array}$$

Recall that if you solve a system and a variable drops out, leaving two unequal numbers, the system has **no solution**.

Exercises: Chapter 13, Section F

In Exercises 1 - 8, determine whether or not $(-3, -1)$ is a solution to the given system.

1. $y = x + 2$
   $y = 4x + 11$

2. $y = -4x - 13$
   $y = 2x + 5$

3. $y = 3x + 8$
   $y = -7x + 2$

4. $y = 6x$
   $y = -x - 4$

5. $2x - y + 5 = 0$
   $3x - 3y + 6 = 0$

6. $-4x + 3y - 9 = 0$
   $-7x + 8y - 13 = 0$

7. $x + y = -4$
   $x - 5y = 0$

8. $9x + 2y = -30$
   $4x - 3y = 12$

In Exercises 9 - 12, solve the system by using the Substitution Method.

9. $y = 3x + 5$
   $x + 2y = 17$

10. $-x + 2y = -5$
    $y = -3x + 1$

11. $x = 7 + 4y$
    $x + 3y - 4 = 0$

12. $y = -9x - 1$
    $6x + y + 12 = 0$

In Exercises 13 - 16, solve the system by using the Elimination Method.

13. $x + y = 6$
    $x - y = -2$

14. $x - y = 8$
    $x + y = 2$

15. $-2x - 5y = 0$
    $4x + 6y = 8$

16. $-7x + 10y = 1$
    $3x - 5y = 6$

In Exercises 17 - 25, choose the correct answer.

17. The solution to the system $\quad x - 2y = 10 \quad$ is:
    $\qquad\qquad\qquad\qquad\quad 5x + 2y = 8$

(a) $\left(3, -\frac{7}{2}\right)$ (b) $\left(-3, \frac{7}{2}\right)$ (c) $\left(3, -\frac{13}{2}\right)$ (d) $\left(-3, \frac{13}{2}\right)$ (e) $(2, -3)$

18. The solution to the system $3x + 2y = 0 \quad$ is:
    $\qquad\qquad\qquad\qquad\quad 4x - 11 = y$

(a) $(-2, -3)$ (b) $(2, 3)$ (c) $(2, -3)$ (d) $(-3, 2)$
(e) $(4, -6)$

19. The solution to the system $\quad y = 12x + 3 \quad$ is
$$-x + 2y = 8$$

(a) $\left(\frac{5}{23}, \frac{14}{23}\right)$ (b) $\left(\frac{2}{23}, \frac{27}{23}\right)$ (c) $\left(\frac{93}{23}, \frac{2}{23}\right)$ (d) $\left(\frac{2}{23}, \frac{93}{23}\right)$

(e) $\left(-\frac{2}{23}, \frac{45}{23}\right)$

20. Which of the following is not a solution to the system $\quad 9x - 11y = 6 \quad$?
$$-18x + 22y = -12$$

(a) $\left(0, -\frac{6}{11}\right)$ (b) $\left(-2, -\frac{24}{11}\right)$ (c) $\left(3, -\frac{21}{11}\right)$ (d) $\left(1, \frac{3}{11}\right)$

(e) $\left(\frac{2}{3}, 0\right)$

21. Find the solution to the system: $\quad -9x + y = 0$
$$9x - y = 2$$

(a) $\left(-1, -9\right)$ (b) $\left(0, 0\right)$ (c) $\left(-3, 27\right)$ (d) $\left(2, 18\right)$ (e) no solution

22. What is the y value of the solution to the system $\quad x = -y + 7$?
$$x = 16y - 1$$

(a) $\frac{8}{15}$ (b) $\frac{6}{17}$ (c) $\frac{17}{8}$ (d) $\frac{8}{17}$ (e) $-\frac{8}{17}$

23. The solution to the system $\quad 8x + 9y = -3 \quad$ is:
$$-2x + 4y = 1$$

(a) $\left(-\frac{21}{50}, \frac{1}{25}\right)$ (b) $\left(\frac{1}{25}, -\frac{21}{50}\right)$ (c) $\left(-\frac{42}{25}, \frac{1}{25}\right)$ (d) $\left(\frac{7}{25}, -\frac{23}{50}\right)$
(e) no solution

24. Which system has infinitely many solutions?
(a) $y = -x + 1$ (b) $4x = 11y - 3$ (c) $x - 2y = -14$ (d) $3x = 2 + 8y$ (e) $x = 2y$
$\quad x = -y - 1$ $\quad 33y = 12x + 9$ $\quad 6x + y = 8$ $\quad 3y - 2x = 0$ $\quad y = -x$

25. Which system has the solution $\left(6, -11\right)$?
(a) $y = -x - 5$ (b) $-m + 2n = 28$ (c) $y + 3 = 2x$ (d) $3x = 7 - y$ (e) $x + y = -5$
$\quad x = -y + 5$ $\quad n = -3m + 7$ $\quad -4y = 8 + 7x$ $\quad y = 4x - 13$ $\quad x - y = 17$

Section G. Graphing Quadratic Equations in Two Variables

A **quadratic equation** in two variables, x and y, is an equation of the form $y = ax^2 + bx + c$, where a, b, and c are real numbers, and $a \neq 0$. Examples of quadratic equations are

$$y = x^2 - 3x - 4, \quad y = 9x^2 - 1, \quad \text{and} \quad y = -5x^2 + 10x.$$

Our goal in this section is to learn how to graph quadratic equations. Recall from Section C that the graph of the linear equation $y = mx + b$ is a line whose slope is m and whose y-intercept is $(0, b)$. Solutions to such an equation are just points on the line. For example, the point $(-1, 3)$ is on the line $y = -2x + 1$ because $3 = -2(-1) + 1$.

Similarly, solutions to a quadratic equation in x and y are points on its graph. For example, the point $(2, -6)$ is on the graph of $y = x^2 - 3x - 4$ since replacing x by 2 and y by -6 gives $-6 = (2)^2 - 3(2) - 4$ which is true.

On the other hand, $(3, 0)$ is not on the graph of $y = 9x^2 - 1$ since $0 \neq 9(3)^2 - 1$.

Example 1. Is $(4, -2)$ on the graph of $y = 2x^2 - 8x + 14$?

Solution: Replace x by 4 and y by 2 in the equation:

$$-2 \stackrel{?}{=} 2(4)^2 - 8(4) + 14$$
$$-2 \stackrel{?}{=} 2(16) - 32 + 14$$
$$-2 \stackrel{?}{=} 32 - 32 + 14$$
$$-2 \neq 14$$

Therefore, $(4, -2)$ not on the graph of $y = 2x^2 - 8x + 14$.

Example 2. Is $(-7, 9)$ on the graph of $y = (x + 4)^2$?

Solution: Replace x by -7 and y by 9 in the equation:

$$9 \stackrel{?}{=} (-7 + 4)^2$$
$$9 \stackrel{?}{=} (-3)^2$$
$$9 \stackrel{\checkmark}{=} 9$$

Therefore, $(-7, 9)$ is on the graph of $y = (x + 4)^2$.

Example 3. The point $(a, 6)$ is on the graph of $y = x^2 - 30$. What are the possible values of a?

Solution: Replace x by a and y by b in the equation, then solve for a.

$$6 = a^2 - 30$$
$$\underline{+30 \qquad +30}$$
$$36 = a^2$$
$$\pm\sqrt{36} = a$$
$$\pm 6 = a$$

Example 4. What are the x-intercepts of the graph of $y = x^2 - 2x - 24$?

Solution: The x-intercepts are the points where the graph crosses the x-axis; their y-values are 0. To find the x-intercepts, replace y by 0 in the equation, then solve for x.

$$x^2 - 2x - 24 = 0$$
$$\underline{(x + 4)(x - 6) = 0}$$
$$x + 4 = 0 \quad x - 6 = 0$$
$$\underline{-4 \quad -4 \quad\quad +6 \quad +6}$$
$$x \quad = -4 \quad x \quad = 6$$

The x-intercepts are $(-4,\, 0)$ and $(6,\, 0)$.

Next we graph some quadratic equations.

Example 5. Graph: $y = x^2$

Solution: First, we find some solutions to the equation, then we plot them and graph.

x	$x^2 = y$	Solutions
-2	$(-2)^2 = 4$	$(-2,\, 4)$
-1	$(-1)^2 = 1$	$(-1,\, 1)$
0	$(0)^2 = 0$	$(0,\, 0)$
1	$(1)^2 = 1$	$(1,\, 1)$
2	$(2)^2 = 4$	$(2,\, 4)$

The graph is on the next page.

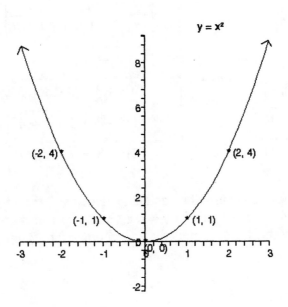

This graph is called a **parabola**. Notice that it has a U-shape.

Vertical Shifting

Some graphs of quadratic equations can be obtained by vertically shifting the graph of $y = x^2$.

Rule for vertical shifting: Suppose c is a positive number.
1) The graph of the equation $y = x^2 + c$ is obtained by shifting the graph of $y = x^2$ **upward** by c units.
2) The graph of the equation $y = x^2 - c$ is obtained by shifting the graph of $y = x^2$ **downward** by c units.

Example 6. Graph $y = x^2 + 3$.

Solution: The graph of $y = x^2 + 3$ is obtained by shifting the graph of $y = x^2$ **upward** by 3 units. Let's see why this shift occurs by looking at the tables for the solutions to $y = x^2$ and $y = x^2 + 3$.

x	$y = x^2$	Solutions
–2	$(-2)^2 = 4$	(–2, 4)
–1	$(-1)^2 = 1$	(–1, 1)
0	$(0)^2 = 0$	(0, 0)
1	$(1)^2 = 1$	(1, 1)
2	$(2)^2 = 4$	(2, 4)

and

x	$y = x^2 + 3$	Solutions
–2	$(-2)^2 + 3 = 4 + 3 = 7$	(–2, 7)
–1	$(-1)^2 + 3 = 1 + 3 = 4$	(–1, 4)
0	$(0)^2 + 3 = 0 + 3 = 3$	(0, 3)
1	$(1)^2 + 3 = 1 + 3 = 4$	(1, 4)
2	$(2)^2 + 3 = 4 + 3 = 7$	(2, 7)

Observe that the same x-values are used for each table. However, the y-values for $y = x^2 + 3$ are each 3 more than the corresponding y-values for $y = x^2$. Graphically, this means that the points for $y = x^2 + 3$ can be obtained by shifting the points for $y = x^2$ upward by 3 units.

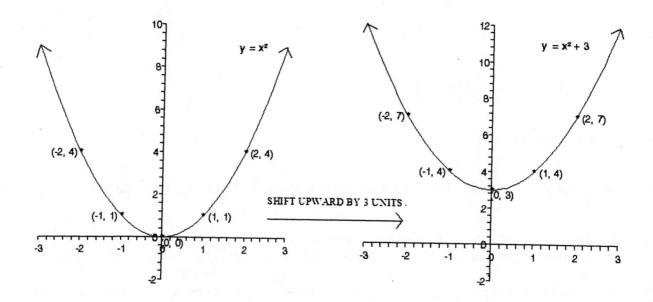

Horizontal Shifting

Some graphs of quadratic equations can be obtained by horizontally shifting the graph of $y = x^2$.

Rule for horizontal shifting: Suppose c is a positive number.
1) The graph of the equation $y = (x + c)^2$ is obtained by shifting the graph of $y = x^2$ **to the left** by c units.
2) The graph of the equation $y = (x - c)^2$ is obtained by shifting the graph of $y = x^2$ **to the right** by c units.

376

Example 7. Graph $y = (x+3)^2$.

Solution: The graph of $y = (x+3)^2$ is obtained by shifting the graph of $y = x^2$ **to the left** by 3 units. Let's see why this shift occurs by looking at the tables for the solutions to $y = x^2$ and $y = (x+3)^2$.

x	$y = x^2$	Solutions
-2	$(-2)^2 = 4$	$(-2, 4)$
-1	$(-1)^2 = 1$	$(-1, 1)$
0	$(0)^2 = 0$	$(0, 0)$
1	$(1)^2 = 1$	$(1, 1)$
2	$(2)^2 = 4$	$(2, 4)$

and

x	$y = (x+3)^2$	Solutions
-5	$(-5+3)^2 = (-2)^2 = 4$	$(-5, 4)$
-4	$(-4+3)^2 = (-1)^2 = 1$	$(-4, 1)$
-3	$(-3+3)^2 = (0)^2 = 0$	$(-3, 0)$
-2	$(-2+3)^2 = (1)^2 = 1$	$(-2, 1)$
-1	$(-1+3)^2 = (2)^2 = 4$	$(-1, 4)$

Notice that the same y-values arise in both tables, but the x-values for $y = (x+3)^2$ are each 3 less than the corresponding x-values for $y = x^2$. Graphically, this means that the points for $y = (x+3)^2$ can be obtained by shifting the points for $y = x^2$ to the left by 3 units.

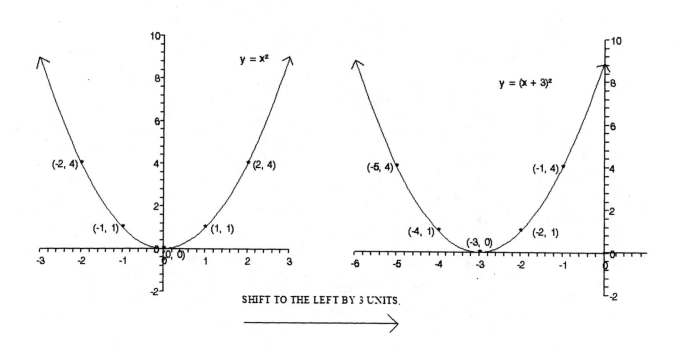

SHIFT TO THE LEFT BY 3 UNITS.

Reflection About the x-Axis

The graph of $y = -x^2$ is obtained by **reflecting the graph** of $y = x^2$ **about the x-axis**. In other words, the graph of $y = -x^2$ is an upside down U-shape (a dome).

Example 8. Graph $y = -x^2$.

Solution: Find some solutions, then graph.

x	$y = -x^2$	Solutions
-2	$-(-2)^2 = -4$	$(-2, -4)$
-1	$-(-1)^2 = -1$	$(-1, -1)$
0	$-(0)^2 = 0$	$(0, 0)$
1	$-(1)^2 = -1$	$(1, -1)$
2	$-(2)^2 = -4$	$(2, -4)$

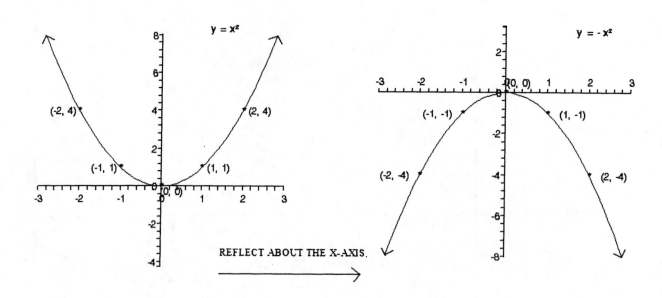

REFLECT ABOUT THE X-AXIS.

Combining the Techniques

Example 9. Graph $y = (x - 3)^2 + 1$.

Solution: First shift the graph of $y = x^2$ **to the right** by 3 units to get the graph of $y = (x - 3)^2$, then shift the graph of $y = (x - 3)^2$ **upward** by 1 unit to obtain the graph of $y = (x - 3)^2 + 1$.

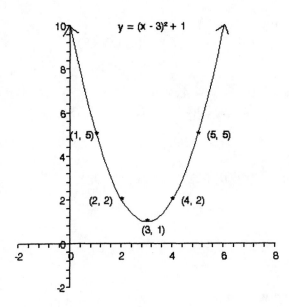

Exercises: Chapter 13, Section G

In Exercises 1 - 9, choose the correct answer.

1. Which ordered pair is a solution to the equation $y = x^2 + 3x - 2$?
(a) $(0, 2)$ (b) $(-1, 0)$ (c) $(4, 26)$ (d) $(-4, 26)$ (e) $(3, 14)$

2. Which ordered pair is a solution to the equation $y = (x - 7)^2 + 12$?
(a) $(0, 37)$ (b) $(2, 37)$ (c) $(-1, 48)$ (d) $(7, 11)$ (e) $(5, 18)$

3. Which ordered pair is not a solution to the equation $y = x^2 - 4x - 9$?
(a) $(0, -9)$ (b) $(4, -9)$ (c) $(-3, 12)$ (d) $(6, 3)$ (e) $(-2, -13)$

4. Which point is not on the graph of $y = (x + 8)^2 - 2$?
(a) $(-8, 2)$ (b) $(-8, -2)$ (c) $(-6, 2)$ (d) $(0, 62)$ (e) $(2, 98)$

5. Which point is on the graph of $y = x^2 + x - 20$?
(a) $(-3, 14)$ (b) $(-5, 0)$ (c) $(2, 14)$ (d) $(7, 46)$ (e) $(0, 0)$

6. If the point $(a, 9)$ on the graph of $y = x^2$, then what is a?
(a) ± 81 (b) ± 9 (c) ± 3 (d) 3 only   (e) $\pm \sqrt{3}$

7. If the point $(2, t)$ on the graph of $y = x^2 + 9x - 22$, then what is t?
(a) -11 and 2 (b) -2 and 11 (c) 44 (d) -1 (e) 0

8. What are the x-intercepts of the graph of $y = x^2 - 6x - 55$?
(a) $(-5, 0)$ and $(11, 0)$ (b) $(-11, 0)$ and $(5, 0)$ (c) $(-11, 0)$ and $(-5, 0)$
(d) $(-6, 0)$ and $(5, 0)$ (e) There are no x-intercepts.

9. What are the x-intercepts of the graph of $y = (x - 8)^2$?
(a) $(-8, 0)$ and $(8, 0)$ (b) $(-8, 0)$ only   (c) $(8, 0)$ only
(d) $(64, 0)$ only   (e) There are no x-intercepts.

In Exercises 10 - 15, choose the equation that matches the given graph.

10.

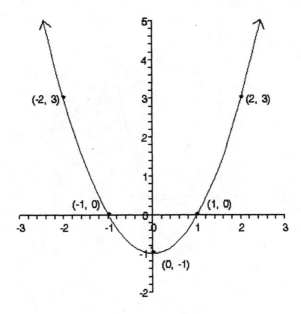

(a) $y = x^2 - 1$ (b) $y = x^2 + 1$ (c) $y = (x + 1)^2$

(d) $y = (x - 1)^2$ (e) $y = (x - 1)^2 + 1$

11.

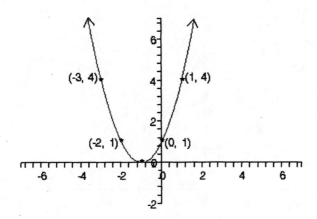

(a) $y = (x + 1)^2$ (b) $y = (x - 1)^2$ (c) $y = x^2 - 1$

(d) $y = x^2 + 1$ (e) $y = -x^2 + 1$

12.

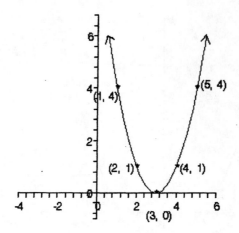

(a) $y = x^2 - 3$
(d) $y = (x - 3)^2$

(b) $y = x^2 + 3$
(e) $y = 3x^2$

(c) $y = (x + 3)^2$

13.

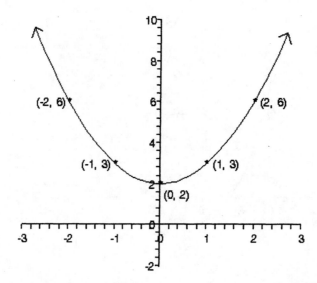

(a) $y = x^2 - 2$
(d) $y = (x - 2)^2$

(b) $y = x^2 + 2$
(e) $y = 2x^2$

(c) $y = (x + 2)^2$

14.

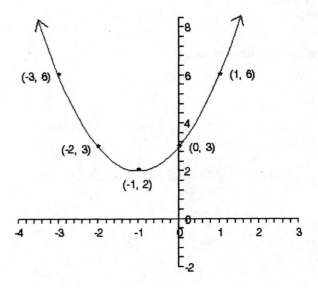

(a) $y = (x-1)^2 + 2$ (b) $y = (x+1)^2 - 2$ (c) $y = (x+1)^2 + 2$
(d) $y = (x-1)^2 - 2$ (e) $y = (x+2)^2 + 2$

15.

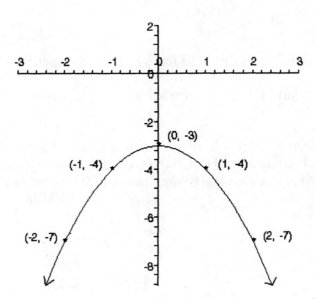

(a) $y = -x^2 - 3$ (b) $y = -(x-3)^2$ (c) $y = -x^2 + 3$
(d) $y = -(x+3)^2$ (e) $y = -(x^2 - 3)$

Practice Prealgebra Tests

Here are some practice Prealgebra tests for you to try.

Practice Prealgebra Test A

1) Evaluate: $(2 - 4)^2 - (12 \div 6 - 2 \times 6)$
(a) –4   (b) 12   (c) 4   (d) –12   (e) 14

2) Tamara earned $30 in tips working as a waitress from four of her favorite customers. If three of her customers gave her $7 each, how much did she received from her fourth customer?
(a) 9   (b) 23   (c) 7   (d) 21   (e) 2

3) Danny purchases 9 feet of wire. He cuts it into 3 pieces. If each of the first 2 pieces are 27 inches long, how many inches is the third piece?
(a) 3   (b) 54   (c) 27   (d) 9   (e) 2

4) How much does it cost to carpet a room that is 13 feet by 11 feet if carpeting cost $5 per square foot?
(a) $1,000   (b) $55   (c) $715   (d) $120   (e) $500

5) On Wednesday morning at 9:00 AM, Jan's favorite stock was valued at $108. At the end of each hour, beginning at 9:00 AM and ending at 1:00 PM, he recorded the following changes in the value of the stock: +5, –7, –4, +13. What was the value of the stock at 1:00 PM that day?
(a) $115   (b) $108   (c) $114   (d) $109   (e) $106

6) Simplify. $\dfrac{3}{\dfrac{5}{3} - \dfrac{3}{2}}$

(a) 6   (b) 2   (c) 10   (d) 18   (e) $\dfrac{1}{2}$

7) A jar of instant coffee contains $16\frac{1}{3}$ ounces of coffee. How many cups of coffee containing $1\frac{1}{6}$ ounces of coffee can be made?
(a) 18   (b) $\frac{1}{3}$ (c) 22   (d) 3   (e) 14

8) An electrician earns \$35 an hour. He worked $8\frac{1}{2}$ hours on Monday, $4\frac{2}{5}$ hours on Wednesday, and $7\frac{1}{4}$ hours on Friday. How much did he earned for the three days?
(a) \$665   (b) \$708   (c) \$700   (d) \$705.25   (e) \$505

9) Francis spends $\frac{1}{5}$ of his money and loses $\frac{3}{4}$ of the remainder. If he has 50¢ left, how much money did he start with?
(a) 83¢   (b) \$2.50   (c) \$2   (d) \$5   (e) \$3.05

10) What is the cost of $5\frac{1}{3}$ pounds of ham if the cost is \$3 per pound?
(a) \$1.78   (b) \$30   (c) \$16   (d) \$9   (e) \$3

11) Write the product $(4 \times 10^{-6})(8 \times 10^{2})$ in scientific notation.
(a) 3.2×10^{-3} (b) 3.2×10^{4} (c) 3.2×10^{-5} (d) 3.2×10^{-4}
(e) 3.2×10^{-11}

12) A supermaket manager buys a carton of 12 boxes of juice for \$18.60. He sells each box for \$2.99. What is his profit?
(a) \$15.61   (b) \$17.28   (c) \$204.60   (d) \$18.60   (e) \$37.01

13) A printing company charges 11¢ per copy for the first 13 copies, 10¢ per copy for the next 20 copies, and 8¢ for each additional copy. What is the cost, in dollars, of making 40 copies?
(a) \$2.99   (b) \$3.43   (c) \$2.56   (d) \$3.99   (e) \$1.43

14) Jenny went shopping for beauty supplies last week. She bought a bar of 12.5 ounces of soap, $1\frac{1}{4}$ pounds of mineral salts, and four sticks of anti-perspirant, of weight 2.875 ounces each. How many ounces (oz.) of beauty supplies did Jenny buy?
(a) 26 oz.   (b) 54 oz.   (c) 44 oz.   (d) 56 oz.   (e) 24 oz..

15) Write 0.00267 in scientific notation.
(a) 2.67×10^{2} (b) 2.67×10^{3} (c) 2.67×10^{-4} (d) 2.67×10^{-2}
(e) 2.67×10^{-3}

16) Which of the following is an irrational number?
(a) $\sqrt{36}$ (b) $\sqrt{13}$ (c) $\sqrt{144}$ (d) $\sqrt{25}$ (e) $\sqrt{81}$

17) Evaluate the expression $\dfrac{\sqrt{100-64}}{100-\sqrt{64}}$ and simplify.

(a) $\dfrac{3}{32}$ (b) $\dfrac{1}{6}$ (c) 0   (d) $\dfrac{3}{46}$ (e) 1

18) Which two integers is $\sqrt{84}$ between?

(a) 6 and 7   (b) 9 and 10   (c) 8 and 9   (d) 7 and 8   (e) 10 and 11

19) Which integer is closest to $\sqrt{675}$?

(a) 26   (b) 23   (c) 25   (d) 27   (e) 24

20) Simplify: $9\sqrt{125} + 4\sqrt{20} - \sqrt{5}$

(a) $240\sqrt{5}$ (b) $8\sqrt{5}$ (c) $52\sqrt{5}$ (d) $12\sqrt{5}$ (e) $13\sqrt{5}$

21) If 4 shirts cost $95, how much does it cost to buy 9 shirts?

(a) $237.50   (b) $213.75   (c) $855   (d) $190   (e) $195

22) A college has a faculty to student ratio of 2 to 18. If the college has 13,500 students, how many faculty members are there?

(a) $15,000   (b) $750   (c) $1,500   (d) $6,7500   (e) $1,350

23) The width and length a 3 inch by 4 inch picture are enlarged proportionally. If the length is enlarged to 17 in., what is the enlarged width?

(a) $12\dfrac{3}{4}$ in.   (b) $22\dfrac{2}{3}$ in.   (c) 16 in.   (d) 15 in.   (e) $23\dfrac{1}{4}$ in.

24) The ratio 19 to p is 5 to 8. Find p.

(a) 22   (b) $11\dfrac{7}{8}$ (c) 9   (d) $30\dfrac{4}{5}$ (e) $2\dfrac{2}{19}$

25) Marlon burns x calories for every y miles that he runs. How much calories (written as a formula) would Marlon burn if he runs z miles?

(a) $\dfrac{y}{x}z$ (b) yz (c) xz (d) xyz (e) $\dfrac{x}{y}z$

26) What percent of 35 is 14?

(a) 250%   (b) 28%   (c) 40%   (d) 70%   (e) 35%

27) Distilled water is poured into a beaker containing 27 ml.of phosphoric acid to form an acid-water solution. How much water must be added to form a solution that is 45% acid?

(a) 17 ml.   (b) 90 ml.   (c) 54 ml.   (d) 33 ml.   (e) 55 ml.

28) In a large class, there are 62 boys, which represents 31% of the students in the class. How many girls are in the class?

(a) 100   (b) 138   (c) 200   (d) 38   (e) 69

29) A computer sells for $560 plus an 9% sales tax. What is the total price of the computer?

(a) $610.40   (b) $509.60   (c) $569   (d) $560   (e) $50.40

30) A college consists of 14,000 students. The students can be put into four categories: those who have black hair, those have blond hair, those who have brunette hair, and those who have no hair (bald). If 55% of the students have black hair, 24% of the students are blond, and the number of students who are brunettes is a third of the number of students who are blond. How many students have no hair (bald)?

(a) 7,900   (b) 11,060   (c) 1,120   (d) 2,000   (e) 1,820

In Excercise 31 - 34, the following applies: Marvin got these scores on 6 quizzes: 90, 82, 52, 71, 85, and 94.

31) What is the mean score?

(a) 75   (b) 92   (c) 83   (d) 79   (e) 80.5

32) What is the median score?

(a) 90   (b) 82   (c) 83.5   (d) 71   (e) 85

33) What is the mode?

(a) 94   (b) 85   (c) none   (d) 82   (e) 71

34) If Marvin took another quiz and he got 0, which of the following is affected the most?

(a) mean   (b) median   (c) mode   (d) all   (e) none

35) A car travels x miles in 9 hours and then y miles in 21 hours. What is an expression for the car's average rate (speed), in miles per hour, for the entire distance traveled?

(a) $\dfrac{21}{x+y}$ (b) $\dfrac{30}{x+y}$ (c) $x+y$ (d) $x-y$ (e) $\dfrac{x+y}{30}$

36) Cathy took four practice tests. If she received scores 77, 93, and 87 on the first 3 tests, what score must she had earned on the fourth test to have an average of 89?

(a) 64   (b) 99   (c) 74   (d) 89   (e) 80

37) Andrea's average score on 5 tests is 86. Her lowest score is 56, and the professor will drop that score. What is Andrea's new average?
(a) 74.8   (b) 90   (c) 93.5   (d) 96   (e) 72

38) Andrew drove for 4 hours at an average speed of 46 miles per hour and for the next 5 hours at an average speed of 64 miles per hour. What was Andrew's average speed, in miles per hour, during the entire trip?
(a) 56   (b) 110   (c) 12.22   (d) 55   (e) 51.75

Practice Prealgebra Test B

1) Evaluate: $(4 + 2)^2 \div 6 \times 6 - 6 \div 6 + 6$

(a) 11   (b) 41   (c) 42   (d) 7   (e) $5\frac{1}{3}$

2) Dan bought a bed for $900. He gave a deposit of $350 and he paid $200 when the bed arrived. He paid the rest in 5 installments. How much was each installment?

(a) $350   (b) $70   (c) $500   (d) $550   (e) $180

3) Luke purchases 4 feet of rope. He cuts it into 2 pieces. If one piece is 28 inches long, how long is the other piece?

(a) 10   (b) 54   (c) 27   (d) 9   (e) 20

4) How many 6 inch square blocks can be use to partition a wall that is 12 square feet?

(a) 2   (b) 4   (c) 48   (d) 144   (e) 1,728

5) On a very cold winters day, the temperature at 3:00 PM was $5°F$. By 6:30 PM, the temperature was $-1°F$. By how much did the temperature change?

(a) $5°F$ (b) $7°F$ (c) $4°F$ (d) $6°F$ (e) $1°F$

6) Simplify: $\dfrac{9 - \frac{1}{2}}{\frac{5}{6} + 2}$

(a) 3   (b) 2   (c) $10\frac{4}{5}$ (d) $\frac{1}{3}$ (e) $24\frac{1}{12}$

7) What is the cost of $5\frac{1}{4}$ pounds of rice if the cost is $1.50 per pound?

(a) $78.80   (b) $78.75   (c) $3.50   (d) $7.00   (e) $7.88

8) A plumber has a piece of pipe $12\frac{1}{2}$ feet long. He needs $\frac{2}{5}$ of the pipe to repair a sink. What length must he cut off from the piece of pipe to do the repair?

(a) 5 ft.   (b) $\frac{1}{5}$ ft.   (c) 2 ft.   (d) $\frac{2}{5}$ ft.   (e) $2\frac{1}{2}$ ft.

9) At 7:00 AM, Marvin mowed $\frac{1}{4}$ of his lawn. Later that morning, his brother Paul mowed $\frac{4}{5}$ of the lawn that Marvin didn't mow. How much of the lawn has not been mowed?

(a) $\frac{3}{5}$ (b) $\frac{3}{20}$ (c) $\frac{9}{20}$ (d) $\frac{1}{5}$ (e) 0

10) An interior designer ordered cloth materials for 6 windows. Each window has 2 drapery panels. How many yards of material should the designer order if each panel requires $1\frac{3}{4}$ yards of material?
(a) 12 yds.   (b) $3\frac{1}{2}$ yds.   (c) $10\frac{1}{2}$ yds.   (d) 21 yds.   (e) 8 yds.

11) Write the sum $(3.0 \times 10^{-2}) + (8.0 \times 10^{2}) + 7.0 + (7.0 \times 10^{-1})$ in decimal notation.
(a) 807.73   (b) 8,077.3   (c) 0.25   (d) 0.018   (e) 2.5

12) A box of screws weighs 245 ounces (oz.). If each screw weighs 1.25 oz., how many screws are in the box?
(a) 306   (b) 245   (c) 196   (d) 1   (e) 760

13) A library charges 10¢ per copy for the first 20 copies, 8¢ per copy for the next 30 copies, and 5¢ for each additional copy. What is the cost, in dollars, of making 69 copies?
(a) $4.40   (b) $5.35   (c) $2.56   (d) $8.85   (e) $3.45

14) Rachel went grocery shopping last week. She bought 8 ounces (oz.) of spices, $4\frac{1}{4}$ pounds (lbs.) of onions, and 6.75 lbs. of flour. How many pounds of groceries did Rachel buy?
(a) 19 lbs.   (b) 68 lbs.   (c) 11 lbs.   (d) 18 lbs.   (e) $11\frac{1}{2}$ lbs.

15) Write 23,311.5 in scientific notation.
(a) 2.33×10^{5} (b) 2.33115×10^{-4} (c) 2.33115×10^{6} (d) 2.33115×10^{4}
(e) 2.33115×10^{-3}

16) Which of the following is a rational number?
(a) $\sqrt{71}$ (b) $\sqrt{13}$ (c) $\sqrt{12}$ (d) $\sqrt{81}$ (e) $\sqrt{15}$

17) Evaluate the expression $\dfrac{\sqrt{100 \times 64} + 1}{\sqrt{49} - \sqrt{16}}$ and simplify.

(a) $26\frac{2}{3}$ (b) $\frac{1}{3}$ (c) 27   (d) $\dfrac{81}{\sqrt{33}}$ (e) 30

18) Which two integers is $\sqrt{33}$ between?
(a) 6 and 7   (b) 5 and 6   (c) 4 and 5   (d) 7 and 8   (e) 3 and 4

19) Which integer is closest to $\sqrt{67}$?
(a) 8   (b) 9   (c) 7   (d) 6   (e) 10

20) Simplify: $\left(9\sqrt{3}\right)\left(7\sqrt{3}\right)$
(a) $63\sqrt{3}$ (b) $\sqrt{189}$ (c) 63 (d) 3 (e) 189

21) A woman worked for 8 hours and earned $141.60. What was her hourly wage?
(a) $17 (b) $676.80 (c) $18 (d) $17.70 (e) $17.50

22) In a restaurant, 4 out of every 21 customer drink soda. If the restaurant has 168 customers, what is the number of customers who *do not* drink soda?
(a) 32 (b) 136 (c) 882 (d) 2 (e) 166

23) If a map has a scale, where 1 inch represents 6 miles, how many miles would $2\frac{3}{4}$ inches represent?
(a) 11 mi. (b) $2\frac{2}{11}$ mi. (c) $16\frac{1}{2}$ mi. (d) 13 mi. (e) 12 mi..

24) In a cake recipe, the ratio of sugar to flour is $\frac{2}{3}$. If 7 cups of flour are used, how many cups of sugar are used?
(a) 21 (b) $10\frac{1}{2}$ (c) 6 (d) 4 (e) $4\frac{2}{3}$

25) A basket ball team won 4 times as many games as it lost. How many games did it lose if it played a total of 50 games?
(a) 13 (b) 40 (c) 12 (d) 11 (e) 10

26) A bottle contains 100 ml. of hydrochloric acid. If 52.5 ml. of the hydrochloric acid is used for an experiment. What percent of acid is used?
(a) 100% (b) 52.5% (c) 47.5% (d) 40% (e) 0.5%

27) Which of the following is not equivalent to 2%?
(a) 0.02 (b) 2 out of a hundred (c) 20 hundredths (d) $\frac{2}{100}$ (e) 2 hundredths.

28) If 0.13% interest is given on a savings account, then the interest written as a decimal is:
(a) 0.0013 (b) 13 (c) 1300 (d) 1.3 (e) 0.013

29) A sweater that is selling for $22.50 is reduced by 20%. What is the new price of the sweater?
(a) $27 (b) $21.50 (c) $20 (d) $18 (e) $2.50

30) A certain school's enrollment decreased 5% this year over last year's enrollment. If the school now has 4,750 students enrolled, how many students were enrolled last year?
(a) 2,500   (b) 4,988   (c) 95,000   (d) 2,000   (e) 5,000

31) The average test score for 4 tests was 95. What was the sum of the test scores?
(a) 47.5   (b) 285   (c) 380   (d) 24   (e) 26

32) Ray's average score on three tests is 85. He took two more tests and got scores 87 and 78. What is Ray's new average?
(a) 82.5   (b) 84   (c) 86   (d) 33.5   (e) $83\frac{1}{3}$

33) Elena took four practice tests. If she received scores 77, 94, and 96 on the first 3 tests, what score must she had earned on the fourth test to have an average of 89?
(a) 83   (b) 97   (c) 74   (d) 89   (e) 80

34) A truck travels 5 miles in s hours and then 7 miles in t hours. What is an expression for the truck's average rate (speed), in miles per hour, for the entire distance traveled?
(a) $\dfrac{12}{s+t}$ (b) $\dfrac{35}{s+t}$ (c) $\dfrac{s+t}{35}$ (d) $\dfrac{5+s}{7+t}$ (e) $\dfrac{s+t}{12}$

35) Last semester, Kate took four tests in Biology. She remembered the average of all four test was 88. She recalled receiving scores, 87, 94, and 77, but she forgot the fourth score. What was Kate's score her fourth test?
(a) 82   (b) 90   (c) 90.5   (d) 94   (e) 92

36) What is the average of 6 numbers whose sum is 597?
(a) 99.5   (b) 99   (c) 3,582   (d) 89   (e) 84

In Excercise 37 - 38, the following applies: Johnson got these scores on 7 quizzes: 96, 58, 66, 90, 84, 87, and 90.

37) What is the median score?
(a) 90   (b) 87   (c) 85.5   (d) 96   (e) 66

38) What is the mode?
(a) 96   (b) 90   (c) 87   (d) 58   (e) 84

392

Practice Prealgebra Test C

1) Evaluate: $(7 - 2)^2 - (12 \div 3 - 6 \times 12)$
(a) 6   (b) 43   (c) 93   (d) 49   (e) 15

2) Martha earned $24 in tips working as a waitress from three of her favorite customers. If two of her customers gave her $6 each, how much did she received from her third customer?
(a) 12   (b) 8   (c) 14   (d) 0   (e) 2

3) Bob purchases 20 feet of wire. He cuts it into 3 pieces. If each of the first 2 pieces is 20 inches long, how many inches is the third piece?
(a) 3   (b) 200   (c) 80   (d) 9   (e) 40

4) How much does it cost to carpet a room that is 15 feet by 14 feet if carpeting cost $7 per square foot?
(a) $1,000   (b) $30   (c) $210   (d) $1200   (e) $1,470

5) On Tuesday morning at 10:00 AM, Ned's favorite stock was valued at $56. At the end of each hour, beginning at 10:00 AM and ending at 3:00 PM, he recorded the following changes in the value of the stock: −4, +6, −5, +1, +3. What was the value of the stock at 3:00 PM that day?
(a) $105   (b) $75   (c) $114   (d) $57   (e) $56

6) Simplify. $\dfrac{\frac{1}{2}}{\frac{1}{4} + \frac{5}{3}}$

(a) $\frac{1}{12}$ (b) 1   (c) $\frac{6}{23}$ (d) 18   (e) $\frac{23}{24}$

7) A jar of cocoa contains 15 ounces of cocoa. How many cups of cocoa containing $2\frac{1}{7}$ ounces of cocoa can be made?
(a) 8   (b) 7   (c) 32   (d) 3   (e) 14

8) A drummer earns $45 an hour. He worked $5\frac{1}{4}$ hours on Monday, $5\frac{4}{5}$ hours on Wednesday, and $9\frac{1}{2}$ hours on Friday. How much did he earned for the three days?
(a) $924.75   (b) $282.27   (c) $560   (d) $745.25   (e) $856.50

9) Pierre spends $\frac{5}{8}$ of his money and loses $\frac{1}{6}$ of the remainder. If he has 80¢ left, how much money did he start with?

(a) 96¢   (b) $2.50   (c) $2.56   (d) $3   (e) $2

10) What is the cost of $6\frac{1}{2}$ pounds of fish if the cost is $3.50 per pound?

(a) $2   (b) $34   (c) $19   (d) $22.75   (e) $1.86

11) Write the product $(2 \times 10^{-1})(9 \times 10^4)$ in scientific notation.

(a) 1.8×10^{-3} (b) 1.8×10^3 (c) 1.8×10^{-5} (d) 1.8×10^{-4}
(e) 1.8×10^4

12) A supermaket manager buys a carton of 24 boxes of juice for $40.78. He sells each box for $2.50. What is his profit?

(a) $15.61   (b) $19.22   (c) $22.60   (d) $96   (e) $30

13) A printing company charges 15¢ per copy for the first 15 copies, 10¢ per copy for the next 25 copies, and 7¢ for each additional copy. What is the cost, in dollars, of making 75 copies?

(a) $2.37   (b) $7.20   (c) $2.06   (d) $3.19   (e) $3.43

14) Bob went shopping for tools. He bought a screwdriver weighing of 4.5 ounces, a sledge hammer weighing $6\frac{1}{2}$ pounds, and a measuring tape weighing 7.5 ounces. What is the weight in pounds of the tools?

(a) 26 oz.   (b) 54 oz.   (c) 44 oz.   (d) $7\frac{1}{4}$ lbs.   (e) 24 oz.

15) Write 0.000305 in scientific notation.

(a) 3.05×10^{-4} (b) 3.05×10^3 (c) 3.05×10^4 (d) 3.05×10^{-2}
(e) 3.05×10^{-5}

16) Which of the following is an irrational number?

(a) $\sqrt{36}$ (b) $\sqrt{144}$ (c) $\sqrt{38}$ (d) $\sqrt{25}$ (e) $\sqrt{100}$

17) Evaluate the expression $\dfrac{\sqrt{200+25}}{\sqrt{100}-\sqrt{49}}$ and simplify.

(a) 15   (b) $\frac{1}{7}$ (c) 15   (d) $\dfrac{15}{\sqrt{51}}$ (e) 5

18) Which two integers is $\sqrt{50}$ between?

(a) 6 and 7   (b) 9 and 10   (c) 8 and 9   (d) 7 and 8   (e) 10 and 11

19) Which integer is closest to $\sqrt{175}$
(a) 12   (b) 13   (c) 10   (d) 11   (e) 15

20) Simplify: $6\sqrt{50} - 2\sqrt{72} + \sqrt{2}$
(a) $20\sqrt{2}$ (b) $19\sqrt{2}$ (c) $33\sqrt{2}$ (d) $12\sqrt{2}$ (e) $13\sqrt{2}$

21) If 5 shirts cost $195, how much does it cost to buy 4 shirts?
(a) $156   (b) $213.75   (c) $48.75   (d) $243.75   (e) $105

22) A college has a faculty to student ratio of 3 to 5. If the college has 1,500 students, how many faculty members are there?
(a) $500   (b) $600   (c) $1,500   (d) $300   (e) $900

23) The width and length a 12 inch by 16 inch picture are enlarged proportionally. If the length is enlarged to 18 in., what is the enlarged width?
(a) $10\frac{3}{4}$ in.   (b) $10\frac{2}{3}$ in.   (c) $13\frac{1}{2}$ in.   (d) 14 in.   (e) 24 in.

24) The ratio 45 to x is 9 to 7. Find x.
(a) 21   (b) $10\frac{2}{3}$ (c) 9   (d) 35   (e) $57\frac{6}{7}$

25) Mike burns l calories for every m miles that he runs. How much calories (written as a formula) would Mike burn if he runs n miles?
(a) $\frac{m}{l}n$ (b) lm (c) mn (d) lmn (e) $\frac{l}{m}n$

26) What percent of 15 is 69?
(a) 230%   (b) 460%   (c) 40%   (d) 21.7%   (e) 31%

27) Distilled water is poured into a beaker containing 60 ml. of hydrochloric acid to form an acid-water solution. How much water must be added to form a solution that is 25% acid?
(a) 180 ml.   (b) 90 ml.   (c) 54 ml.   (d) 30 ml.   (e) 55 ml.

28) In a large class, there are 72 boys, which represents 40% of the students in the class. How many girls are in the class?
(a) 103   (b) 108   (c) 200   (d) 28   (e) 69

29) An stereo sells for $706 plus an $8\frac{1}{2}$% sales tax. What is the total price of the stereo?

(a) $20.40   (b) $645.99   (c) $766.01   (d) $260   (e) $50.40

30) A school consists of 6,000 students. The students can be put into four categories: those who have black hair, those have blond hair, those who have brunette hair, and those who have no hair (bald). If 60% of the students have black hair, 28% of the students are blond, and the number of students who are brunettes is a fourth of the number of students who are blond. How many students have no hair (bald)?

(a) 7,900   (b) 3,600   (c) 1,120   (d) 300   (e) 1,680

In Excercise 31 - 34, the following applies: Steven got these scores on 6 quizzes: 99, 71, 72, 80, 86, and 72.

31) What is the mean score?

(a) 75   (b) 92   (c) 80   (d) 78   (e) 85

32) What is the median score?

(a) 99   (b) 76   (c) 83.5   (d) 71   (e) 85

33) What is the mode?

(a) 94   (b) 85   (c) none   (d) 82   (e) 72

34) If Steven took another quiz and he got 0, which of the following is affected the most?

(a) none   (b) median   (c) mode   (d) all   (e) mean

35) A car travels x miles in 5 hours and then y miles in 13 hours. What is an expression for the car's average rate (speed), in miles per hour, for the entire distance traveled?

(a) $\frac{65}{x+y}$ (b) $\frac{18}{x+y}$ (c) $x+y$ (d) $x-y$ (e) $\frac{x+y}{18}$

36) Carl took four practice tests. If he received scores 64, 99, and 68 on the first 3 tests, what score must he had earned on the fourth test to have an average of 74?

(a) 64   (b) 65   (c) 74   (d) 89   (e) 80

37) Debra's average score on 4 tests is 81. Her lowest score is 75, and the professor will drop that score. What is Debra's new average?

(a) 83   (b) 90   (c) 92   (d) 86   (e) 72

38) David drove for 6 hours at an average speed of 61 miles per hour and for the next 3 hours at an average speed of 55 miles per hour. What was David's average speed, in miles per hour, during the

entire trip?
    (a) 56   (b) 58   (c) 12   (d) 59   (e) 57

Practice Algebra Tests

Here are some practice Algebra tests for you to try. These types of questions seem to occur often on the test. Make sure that you can solve them! Of course, other examples can show up on the exam as well that are not included in these practice tests.

Practice Algebra Test A

1) Last semester a class at Harvard University took a trip to a power plant in New York City. Inside the plant the students encountered a large circular wheel which spins between two large magnets. The formula for the area (A) of the circular wheel is given by $A = \pi r^2$, where r is the radius and π = 3.14. The area of the circular wheel whose radius equals 10.5 meters is:

(a) 32.97 m.^{2} (b) 103.526 m.^{2} (c) 346.185 m.^{2} (d) 314 m.^{2}
(e) 314.785 m.^{2}

2) If a number is doubled, the result is 3 less than triple the number. The number is:
(a) –3   (b) 3   (c) 6   (d) –6   (e) 1

3) A train travels 45 miles in x hours and then 95 miles in y hours. What is an expression for the train's average rate (speed), in miles per hour, for the entire distance traveled?

(a) $\dfrac{x+y}{140}$ (b) $\dfrac{140}{x+y}$ (c) $\dfrac{24x}{95y}$ (d) $\dfrac{45x+95y}{140}$ (e) $\dfrac{140}{45x+95y}$

4) What is the sum of the polynomials, $6x^3y^5 - 4x^2y^2 + x^2y$ and $-7x^3y^5 - 6x^2y^2$?
(a) $-x^3y^5 + 10x^2y^2 + x^2y$ (b) $-x^3y^5 - 10x^2y^2 + x^2y$ (c) $-x^3y^5 - 9x^2y^2$
(d) $13x^3y^5 - 10x^2y^2 + x^2y$ (e) $-13x^3y^5 - 11x^2y^2$

5) What is the simplified form of $-7x^2 - 10y - (-8x^2 - 5y)$?
(a) $-x^2 + 5y$ (b) $x^2 - 5y$ (c) $15x^2 - 15y$ (d) $x^2 + 5y$ (e) $-x^2 + 15y$

6) If the expression $2x^2 + kx - 12$ is equal to 6 when $x = -2$, then $k = ?$
(a) –2   (b) 2   (c) 10   (d) –5   (e) –12

7) If $3(5x - 9) - 3x = 8 - 2x$, then $x = ?$
(a) $2\frac{1}{2}$ (b) $-2\frac{1}{3}$ (c) $2\frac{1}{5}$ (d) $3\frac{1}{3}$ (e) 2

8) The operation $\circ$ is defined as $a \circ b = a^3 + 3b$. If $-3 \circ x = 0$, then $x = ?$
(a) -7 (b) 9 (c) -9 (d) 3 (e) 27

9) If $-\frac{5}{6} + \frac{3}{4} = -5x + 1\frac{2}{3}$, then $x = ?$

(a) $1\frac{6}{7}$ (b) $2\frac{7}{24}$ (c) $2\frac{1}{4}$ (d) $3\frac{7}{20}$ (e) $\frac{7}{20}$

10) Jessica took five exams last semester. If she received scores of 73, 87, 84, and 89 on the first four of them, what score must she had earned on the fifth exam to have had an average of 85?
(a) 70   (b) 95   (c) 92   (d) 90   (e) 82

11) Tom Johnson is 1 year less than twice as old as his sister. If the sum of their ages is 14 years, then Tom's age is:
(a) 4   (b) 2   (c) 6   (d) 5   (e) 9

12) Marcella has a base salary of \$250 per week. In addition, she receives a commission of 12% of her sales. Last week her total earnings was \$520. What was Marcella's total sales for the week?
(a) \$2,005   (b) \$2,050   (c) \$2,250   (d) \$5,550   (e) \$780

13) For all nonzero r, s, and t values, the simplified form of $\frac{-50r^6 s^4 t^6}{-5r^8 s^2 t^7}$ in terms of positive exponents is:
(a) $\frac{10s}{rt}$ (b) $\frac{10s^2}{r^2 t}$ (c) $-\frac{10s^2}{r^2 t}$ (d) $\frac{10}{st}$ (e) $\frac{10s^2}{r^2}$

14) The area of a rectangle is $3s^4 t^6 + 24s^8 t^8$ square meters. If the width is $3s^2 t^2$ meters, then the length, in meters, of the rectangle is:
(a) $s^2 t^4 + 8s^6 t^6$ (b) $\frac{s^2 t}{3}$ (c) $8st$ (d) $9s^2 t^4$ (e) $s^2 t^3 + 8s^4 t^4$

15) If $\frac{5}{2x - 7} = \frac{3}{x - 2}$, then $x = ?$
(a) 7   (b) -2 (c) -11 (d) 6   (e) 11

16) The ratio $(x - 1)$ to 6 is $(x - 8)$ to 4. Find x.
(a) -22 (b) 44   (c) 22   (d) 11   (e) -11

17) If $x = -2$ and $y = -2$, what is the value of the expression $-4x^3y^2 - 5xy$?
(a) -108 (b) 108 (c) 801 (d) -148 (e) 148

18) If $x = -2$, what is the value of $\dfrac{x^6 - 1}{x^3 - 1}$?
(a) 7 (b) 2 (c) 4 (d) -7 (e) 1

19) If $3x^2 - 7x + 2 = 0$, then a solution to this equation is:
(a) $x = -\dfrac{1}{3}$ (b) $x = -2$ (c) $x = \dfrac{1}{2}$ (d) $x = 3$ (e) $x = 2$

20) Factor the following expression completely: $4x^3y^3z^5 - 20xy^2z^2 + 12x^2y^2z$
(a) $4x^2y^2z(x^2y^2z^4 - 5z^2 + 3x)$ (b) $4xy^2z^2(x^2yz^4 - 5yz + 3xyz)$
(c) $4xy^2z(x^2yz^4 - 5z + 3x)$ (d) $4xy^2z(x^2yz^4 - 5z + 3xz)$
(e) $4xy^2z(x^2yz^4 + 5z + 3x)$

21) What is a factor of the expression $5x^5 + 5x^4 - 10x^3$?
(a) $2x + 1$ (b) $5x + 3$ (c) $3x + 1$ (d) $x + 2$ (e) $x + 1$

22) Simplify the following expression: $\sqrt[3]{\dfrac{1}{8}}$

(a) 2 (b) $\dfrac{2}{3}$ (c) $\dfrac{1}{2}$ (d) $\dfrac{1}{8}$ (e) $\dfrac{1}{4}$

23) Simplify the following expression: $\sqrt{75} + 2\sqrt{300} - \dfrac{1}{3}\sqrt{27}$
(a) 3 (b) $5\sqrt{3}$ (c) $16\sqrt{3}$ (d) $24\sqrt{3}$ (e) $\sqrt{3}$

24) Which of the following is a factor of $x^2 - 5x - 14$?
(a) $x + 7$ (b) $x - 7$ (c) $x - 2$ (d) $x + 14$ (e) $x - 5$

25) For all $x \geq 0$, $x \neq 1$, the radical expression $\dfrac{\sqrt{x}}{\sqrt{x} - 1}$ is equivalent to:

(a) $\dfrac{x}{x - 1}$ (b) $\dfrac{x}{x + 1}$ (c) $\dfrac{\sqrt{x}}{x - 1}$ (d) $\dfrac{x + \sqrt{x}}{x - 1}$ (e) $\dfrac{\sqrt{x}}{x + 1}$

26) For $x \neq -\dfrac{1}{2}$, $\dfrac{2x^2 - 5x - 3}{2x + 1} = ?$
(a) $x - 2$ (b) $x + 5$ (c) $x - 3$ (d) $x + 1$ (e) $x - 4$

27) For $x \neq -\frac{1}{5}$, $\frac{15x^2 + kx - 3}{5x + 1} = 3x - 3$. Find k.

(a) 4   (b) −15   (c) 3   (d) 1   (e) −12

28) If $x^{-3} = -\frac{1}{27}$, then what is x?

(a) 3   (b) 9   (c) −9   (d) −3   (e) 4

29) $\left(\frac{1}{3}\right)^{-2} + 4^{\frac{1}{2}} = ?$

(a) 2   (b) 6   (c) 11   (d) 9   (e) 13

30) If $\frac{6}{\sqrt{3x}} = \sqrt{x}$, then $x = ?$

(a) $\frac{6}{\sqrt{3}}$ (b) $\pm\sqrt{2}$ (c) ± 3 (d) 12   (e) 1

31) What are (x, y) coordinates of the point where the line determined by the equation $y = 2x + 3$ intersects the line $y = -x + 6$?

(a) (−1, 3)   (b) (1, 5)   (c) (1, 1)   (d) (0, 3)   (e) (5, 1)

32) The slope of the line with the equation $9x = 3y + 9$ is:

(a) 9   (b) 2   (c) 3   (d) −3   (e) 1

33) An equation of the line that contains the points with (x, y) coordinates (2, 3) and (0, −1) is:

(a) $y = 2x - 1$ (b) $y = -2x - 1$ (c) $y = -2x + 1$ (d) $y = 3x + 1$

(e) $y = 3x - 1$

34) The distance between the two points (3, 3) and (−1, 0) is:

(a) 3   (b) 5   (c) $\sqrt{11}$ (d) $\sqrt{7}$ (e) 7

35) An equation of the straight line that passes through the point (1, 3) and which is parallel to the line $y = 3x + 1$ is:

(a) $y = -\frac{1}{3}x + 3\frac{1}{3}$ (b) $y = 3x + 3$ (c) $y = 2x - 6$ (d) $y = 3x + 6$

(e) $y = 3x$

36) An equation of the straight line that passes through the point (2, −2) and which is perpendicular to the line $y = x - 6$ is:

(a) $y = -x$ (b) $y = -x + 1$ (c) $y = x + 6$ (d) $y = -x + 3$ (e) $y = -2x$

37) Simplify the following expression: $\sqrt{8x^3y^4}$

(a) $\sqrt{4xy}$ (b) $4x^3y^4$ (c) $2xy^2\sqrt{2x}$ (d) $2xy^2\sqrt{2}$ (e) $8x^2y^2$

38) If $5x - 14 = 0.2x + 0.4$, then $x = ?$

(a) -3 (b) 2.1 (c) 6 (d) 3 (e) 2

Practice Algebra Test B

1) At a simple interest rate r, an amount of money P grows to an amount A in t years according to the equation $A = P(1 + rt)$. What is A after 5 years if P was $1,400.00$ and the interest rate was 8% (use $r = 0.08$)?
(a) $1,860.00$ (b) $1,960.00$ (c) $1,560.00$ (d) $1,440.00$ (e) $1,920.00$

2) If three times a number is increased by 15, the result is 99. The number is:
(a) 18   (b) 28   (c) 38   (d) −28   (e) 26

3) A car travels 19 miles in p hours and then 33 miles in q hours. What is an expression for the car's average rate (speed), in miles per hour, for the entire distance traveled?
(a) $\dfrac{p+q}{52}$ (b) $\dfrac{14}{p+q}$ (c) $\dfrac{52}{p+q}$ (d) $\dfrac{19p+33q}{52}$ (e) $\dfrac{52}{19p+33q}$

4) What is the sum of the polynomials $x^5y^7 + 8x^3y - 2y^2$ and $-16x^5y^7 + 9y^2$?
(a) $-15x^5y^7 + 8x^3y + 7y^2$ (b) $-17x^5y^7 + 8x^3y - 7y^2$ (c) $15x^5y^7 + 8x^3y + 7y^2$
(d) $-15x^{10}y^{14} + 8x^3y + 7y^4$ (e) $-15x^5y^7 + 8x^3y - 7y^2$

5) What is the simplified form of $-4x + 8y^2 - (3y^2 - 2x)$?
(a) $2x - 5y^2$ (b) $-6x + 5y^2$ (c) $5y^2 + 2x$ (d) $6x + 5y^2$ (e) $-2x + 5y^2$

6) If the expression $7x^2 + kx - 12$ is equal to 6 when $x = 3$, then $k = ?$
(a) −15   (b) 12   (c) 15   (d) −18   (e) −16

7) If $4(x - 1) + x = 6 - x$, then $x = ?$
(a) $\dfrac{3}{5}$ (b) $1\dfrac{1}{2}$ (c) $2\dfrac{1}{3}$ (d) $1\dfrac{2}{3}$ (e) $1\dfrac{2}{3}$

8) The operation $*$ is defined as $a * b = 2a - b$. If $1 * x = -7$, then $x = ?$
(a) −9   (b) 9   (c) −15   (d) 12   (e) −13

9) If $\dfrac{7}{9} - \dfrac{4}{5} = 4x + \dfrac{1}{3}$, then $x = ?$

(a) $-\dfrac{2}{45}$ (b) $\dfrac{2}{45}$ (c) $1\dfrac{1}{45}$ (d) $-\dfrac{4}{45}$ (e) $\dfrac{4}{45}$

10) Danielle took five exams last semester. If she received scores of 92, 86, 95, and 83 on the first four of them, what score must she had earned on the fifth exam to have had an average of 87?
(a) 79   (b) 89   (c) 90   (d) 75   (e) 73

11) Timothy's father is 1 year less than twice as old as he is. If the sum of their ages is 77 years, then Timothy's age is:
(a) 27   (b) 34   (c) 26   (d) 24   (e) 16

12) Anthony has a base salary of $400 per week. In addition, he receives a commission of 12% of his sales. Last week his total earnings was $730. What was Anthony's total sales for the week?
(a) $3,333.00   (b) $6,083.00   (c) $4,800.00   (d) $1,750   (e) $2,750

13) Simplify the expression $\frac{-16r^5s^2t^7}{-8r^6s^2t^5}$ in terms of positive exponents (assume all variables are nonzero valued).

(a) $-\frac{2t^2}{r}$ (b) $\frac{2t^2}{r}$ (c) $\frac{2st^2}{r}$ (d) $2rt^2$ (e) $\frac{2r}{t^2}$

14) The area of a rectangle is $18s^2t + 6st^6$ square meters (m.^{2}). If the length is $3st$ meters, then the width, in meters, of the rectangle is:
(a) $6 + 2t^5$ (b) $6s + 6st^6$ (c) $6s + 2t^6$ (d) $6s + 2t^5$ (e) $54s^3t^2 + 18s^2t^7$

15) If $\frac{x-4}{x+2} = \frac{2}{7}$, then $x = ?$

(a) $\frac{5}{33}$ (b) $1\frac{4}{5}$ (c) $6\frac{1}{5}$ (d) $6\frac{2}{5}$ (e) $-6\frac{2}{5}$

16) The ratio 10 to 3 is 3 to x. Find x.
(a) $\frac{3}{5}$ (b) $3\frac{1}{3}$ (c) $\frac{3}{10}$ (d) $1\frac{1}{9}$ (e) $\frac{9}{10}$

17) If $x = -4$ and $y = 3$, what is the value of the expression $4y^2 - 6x^3$?
(a) 420   (b) 348   (c) -240   (d) -420   (e) -348

18) If $x = 3$, what is the value of $\frac{x^3 + 1}{x^6 - 1}$?

(a) $\frac{1}{24}$ (b) $-\frac{1}{26}$ (c) $\frac{1}{26}$ (d) $\frac{4}{91}$ (e) $\frac{10}{17}$

19) If $3x^2 + 36x + 108 = 0$, then the solution to this equation is:
(a) $x = 6$ (b) $x = -6$ (c) $x = 4$ (d) $x = -9$ (e) $x = -4$

20) Factor the following expression completely: $28x^4y^8z^3 + 14x^7y^5z^4 - 21x^3y^6z^3$

(a) $7x^3y^5z^3(4xy^3 + 2x^4z - 3y)$ (b) $7x^2y^6z^3(4y^3 + 2x^3z - 3)$

(c) $7x^4y^5z^3(4y^3 + 2x^3z - 3y)$ (d) $14x^3y^5z^3(2xy^3 + x^4z - 7y)$

(e) $7x^3y^5z^4(4xy^3 + 2x^4 - 3y)$

21) What is a factor of the expression $4x^3 - 20x^2 - 96x$?

(a) $x - 3$ (b) $x + 3$ (c) $x + 8$ (d) $x + 4$ (e) $x + 6$

22) Simplify the following expression: $\sqrt[3]{-\dfrac{125}{8}}$

(a) $\dfrac{2}{5}$ (b) $2\dfrac{1}{2}$ (c) $-1\dfrac{1}{2}$ (d) $-\dfrac{2}{5}$ (e) $-2\dfrac{1}{2}$

23) Simplify the following expression: $4\sqrt{8} - 6\sqrt{9} + 3\sqrt{50}$

(a) $15\sqrt{2} - 1$ (b) $-18 - 7\sqrt{2}$ (c) $5\sqrt{2}$ (d) $23\sqrt{2} - 18$ (e) $23\sqrt{2} - 6\sqrt{3}$

24) Which of the following is a factor of $x^2 + 14x + 48$?

(a) $x + 12$ (b) $x + 4$ (c) $x + 6$ (d) $x + 3$ (e) $x - 8$

25) For all $x \geq 0$, $x \neq 9$, the radical expression $\dfrac{\sqrt{x}}{\sqrt{x} - 3}$ is equivalent to:

(a) $\dfrac{3\sqrt{x}}{x - 9}$ (b) $\dfrac{x + 3\sqrt{x}}{x^2 - 9}$ (c) $\dfrac{x + 3\sqrt{x}}{x - 9}$ (d) $-\dfrac{1}{3}$ (e) $\dfrac{(x + 3)\sqrt{x}}{x - 9}$

26) For $x \neq -\dfrac{1}{4}$, $\dfrac{4x^2 + 5x + 1}{4x + 1} = ?$

(a) $2x - 2$ (b) $3x + 5$ (c) $2x + 1$ (d) $x + 1$ (e) $x + 4$

27) For $x \neq -6$, $\dfrac{3x^2 + kx - 24}{x + 6} = 3x - 4$. Find k.

(a) -14 (b) 14 (c) 22 (d) -22 (e) 17

28) If $x^4 = \left(\dfrac{16}{81}\right)^{-1}$, then what is x?

(a) $1\dfrac{1}{2}$ (b) $\dfrac{2}{3}$ (c) $-1\dfrac{1}{2}$ (d) $2\dfrac{1}{4}$ (e) $\dfrac{2}{9}$

29) $\left(\dfrac{1}{5}\right)^{-2} + 64^{\frac{1}{2}} = ?$

(a) 13 (b) 23 (c) 33 (d) $8\dfrac{1}{25}$ (e) $7\dfrac{24}{25}$

30) If $\dfrac{1}{\sqrt{x+1}} = \dfrac{\sqrt{x+1}}{3}$, then $x = ?$

(a) 4   (b) –3   (c) 2   (d) –2   (e) –1

31) What are (x, y) coordinates of the point where the line determined by the equation $y = 2x + 5$ intersects the line $y = -3x - 15$?

(a) (4, 13)   (b) (–4, –3)   (c) (–2, 1)   (d) (2, 9)   (e) (–4, –4)

32) The slope of the line with the equation $7x - 12y + 16 = 0$ is:

(a) 7   (b) $-\dfrac{7}{12}$ (c) $1\dfrac{5}{7}$ (d) $\dfrac{7}{12}$ (e) $-\dfrac{7}{16}$

33) An equation of the line that contains the points with (x, y) coordinates $(-4, -3)$ and $(-1, 6)$ is:

(a) $y = 3x - 8$ (b) $y = \dfrac{1}{3}x - 1\dfrac{1}{3}$ (c) $y = -3x + 2$ (d) $y = 3x + 7$

(e) $y = 3x + 9$

34) The distance between the two points $(0, 7)$ and $(\sqrt{6}, 2)$ is:

(a) 61   (b) 11   (c) $\sqrt{61}$ (d) $\sqrt{31}$ (e) 31

35) An equation of the straight line that passes through the point $(5, 5)$ and which is parallel to the line $y = 8x - 13$ is:

(a) $y = 8x - 35$ (b) $y = 8x + 45$ (c) $y = \dfrac{1}{8}x + 4\dfrac{3}{8}$ (d) $y = \dfrac{1}{4}x + 5$

(e) $y = 8x + 30$

36) The equation of the straight line that passes through the point $(0, -4)$ and which is perpendicular to the line $y = -x + 8$ is:

(a) $y = x - 8$ (b) $y = x - 4$ (c) $y = -x - 4$ (d) $y = x + 8$

(e) $y = 4x + 8$

37) Simplify the following expression: $\sqrt{32a^3b^8}$

(a) $4ab^2\sqrt{2a}$ (b) $16ab^4\sqrt{a}$ (c) $4a^3b^4\sqrt{2}$ (d) $4a^2b^4\sqrt{2ab}$ (e) $4ab^4\sqrt{2a}$

38) If $3.2x - 4.6 = 0.6x + 0.34$, then $x = ?$

(a) –2.3   (b) –1.9   (c) 1.9   (d) 1.4   (e) 2

Practice Algebra Test C

1) In the study of optics, the focal length f of a lens is given by the formula $\frac{1}{f} = \frac{1}{d_1} + \frac{1}{d_2}$, where d_1 is the distance from the object to the lens and d_2 is the distance from the lens to the image. If $d_1 = 5$ meters (m.) and $d_2 = 3\frac{1}{3}$ meters (m.), then $f = ?$

(a) 2 m.   (b) 7 m.   (c) 13 m.   (d) $\frac{1}{2}$ m.   (e) $3\frac{3}{4}$ m.

2) Five times a number exceeds the number by 28. What is the number?

(a) 21   (b) $4\frac{2}{3}$ (c) 8   (d) 7   (e) 6

3) A bus travels 190 miles in x hours and then 35 miles in y hours. What is an expression for the bus' average rate (speed), in miles per hour, for the entire distance traveled?

(a) $\frac{x+y}{225}$ (b) $\frac{225}{x+y}$ (c) $\frac{155}{x+y}$ (d) $\frac{35x + 190y}{225}$ (e) $\frac{225}{35x + 190y}$

4) What is the sum of the polynomials $8x^4y^3 - 6x^3y$ and $x^3y - 19x^4y^3$?

(a) $5x^3y + 11x^4y^3$ (b) $-5x^3y + 11x^4y^3$ (c) $9x^3y - 25x^4y^3$ (d) $-5x^3y - 27x^4y^3$

(e) $-5x^3y - 11x^4y^3$

5) What is the simplified form of $2x + 9y - (-3x + 18y)$?

(a) $5x + 9y$ (b) $5x - 9y$ (c) $-x + 27y$ (d) $5x + 17y$ (e) $-4xy$

6) If the expression $11x^2 + 3x - k$ is equal to 0 when $x = 2$, then $k = ?$

(a) 46   (b) 60   (c) 50   (d) 30   (e) −50

7) If $4(3 - x) + 3 = 7x$, then $x = ?$

(a) $1\frac{4}{11}$ (b) $\frac{11}{15}$ (c) 5   (d) $\frac{9}{11}$ (e) $-1\frac{4}{11}$

8) The operation $*$ is defined as $a * b = 7a - 2b^2$. If $x * (-1) = 12$, then $x = ?$

(a) $1\frac{3}{7}$ (b) −2   (c) 2   (d) −3   (e) 4

9) If $\frac{1}{4} - \frac{1}{8} = \frac{1}{2}x + 2$, then $x = ?$

(a) $-2\frac{3}{4}$ (b) $3\frac{1}{2}$ (c) −4   (d) $-3\frac{3}{4}$ (e) $4\frac{1}{4}$

10) Pat took five exams last semester. If he received scores of 72, 91, 76, and 86 on the first four of them, what score must he had earned on the fifth exam to have had an average of 81?
(a) 75   (b) 70   (c) 82   (d) 65   (e) 80

11) Nancy's mother is 10 years more than twice her age. If the sum of their ages is 70 years, then Nancy's age is:
(a) 30   (b) 20   (c) 16   (d) 25   (e) 50

12) Jerry has a base salary of $700 per week. In addition, he receives a commission of 6% of his sales. Last week his total earnings was $940. What was Jerry's total sales for the week?
(a) $4,000   (b) $6,000   (c) $144   (d) $3,500   (e) $400

13) Simplify the expression $\dfrac{-48r^5s^7}{12r^4s^{10}}$ in terms of positive exponents (assume all variables are non-zero valued).

(a) $-\dfrac{4r}{s^3}$ (b) $-\dfrac{4r}{s^2}$ (c) $-\dfrac{s^3}{4r}$ (d) $\dfrac{4r^3}{s^2}$ (e) $\dfrac{r}{4s^3}$

14) The area of a rectangle is $27s^4t^3 - 18s^2t^4$ square meters. If the width is $9s^2t$ meters, then the length of the rectangle is:
(a) $3st - 2t^3$ (b) $3s^2t^2 - 18s^2t^4$ (c) $3s^2t^2 - 2t$ (d) $3s^2t^2 - 2t^3$
(e) $243s^6t^4 - 162s^4t^5$

15) If $\dfrac{x-6}{12} = \dfrac{x+2}{8}$, then $x =$?
(a) −12   (b) −16   (c) −18   (d) 24   (e) 8

16) The ratio x to 10 is 2 to y. Find x.
(a) $\dfrac{y}{20}$ (b) $\dfrac{20}{y}$ (c) $\dfrac{y}{5}$ (d) $\dfrac{5}{y}$ (e) $20y$

17) If $x = 1$ and $y = -1$, what is the value of the expression $-x^2 + 3xy$?
(a) −1   (b) 2   (c) −2   (d) 4   (e) −4

18) If $x = -2$, what is the value of $\dfrac{x^3 - 2}{x^3 + 1}$?
(a) $1\dfrac{3}{7}$ (b) $\dfrac{7}{10}$ (c) 2   (d) $-1\dfrac{3}{7}$ (e) $1\dfrac{3}{5}$

19) If $2x^2 - 5x - 3 = 0$, then a solution to this equation is:
(a) $x = \dfrac{1}{3}$ (b) $x = 3$ (c) $x = \dfrac{2}{3}$ (d) $x = \dfrac{1}{2}$ (e) $x = 1$

20) Factor the following expression completely: $4x^3y^4 - 12x^6y^2 + 20x^7y^2$
(a) $4x^3y^2(y^2 - 3x^3 + 5x^4)$ (b) $2x^3y^2(y^2 - 3x^3 + 5x^4)$ (c) $2x^2y(y^2 - 3x^3 + 5x^4)$
(d) $4x^3y(y^2 + 3x^3 - 5xy^4)$ (e) $2x^2y(y^2 - 3x^3 + 5xy^4)$

21) What is a factor of the expression $9x^3 - 45x^2 + 54x$?
(a) $x - 1$ (b) $x - 6$ (c) $9x - 1$ (d) $x - 2$ (e) $x + 3$

22) Simplify the following expression: $\sqrt[3]{\dfrac{125}{216}}$

(a) $1\dfrac{2}{3}$ (b) $\dfrac{5}{8}$ (c) $\dfrac{5}{6}$ (d) $\dfrac{1}{6}$ (e) $1\dfrac{1}{5}$

23) Simplify the following expression: $17\sqrt{6} - 3\sqrt{24} + 6\sqrt{36}$
(a) $11\sqrt{6} + 36$ (b) $12\sqrt{6} + 36$ (c) $23\sqrt{6} + 36$ (d) $47\sqrt{6}$
(e) $11\sqrt{6} + 216$

24) Which of the following is a factor of $8x^2 - 30x - 27$?
(a) $2x - 3$ (b) $4x + 9$ (c) $4x + 1$ (d) $4x + 3$ (e) $8x - 3$

25) For all $x > 0$, $x \neq 1$, the radical expression $\dfrac{\sqrt{x} + 1}{\sqrt{x} - 1}$ is equivalent to:

(a) $\dfrac{x + 1}{x - 1}$ (b) $\dfrac{x + 2\sqrt{x} + 1}{x^2 - 1}$ (c) $\dfrac{1}{x - 1}$ (d) -1 (e) $\dfrac{x + 2\sqrt{x} + 1}{x - 1}$

26) For $x \neq \dfrac{1}{3}$, $\dfrac{9x^2 - 9x + 2}{3x - 1} = ?$
(a) $3x - 2$ (b) $3x + 1$ (c) $3x - 4$ (d) $3x + 2$ (e) $x - 3$

27) For $x \neq -3$, $\dfrac{x^2 + kx - 24}{x + 3} = x - 8$. Find k.
(a) 5 (b) -8 (c) -5 (d) 3 (e) 6

28) If $x^{-4} = 81$, then what is x?
(a) 3 (b) $\dfrac{1}{3}$ (c) -3 (d) 9 (e) $\dfrac{1}{9}$

29) $\left(\dfrac{1}{4}\right)^{-2} + 8^{\frac{1}{3}} = ?$
(a) 14 (b) 16 (c) 18 (d) 10 (e) 6

30) If $\dfrac{4}{\sqrt{x+1}} = 2$, then $x = ?$

(a) –3   (b) 3   (c) –1   (d) 2   (e) 1

31) What are (x, y) coordinates of the point where the line determined by the equation $y = x - 5$ intersects the line $y = -3x + 1$?

(a) (1.5, 3.5)   (b) (3, –2)   (c) (–1, –6)   (d) (1.5, –3.5)   (e) (2.25, –2.75)

32) The slope of the line with the equation $12x + 3y = -10$ is:

(a) –4   (b) 4   (c) 12   (d) $\dfrac{1}{4}$ (e) 3

33) An equation of the line that contains the points with (x, y) coordinates $(-5, 2)$ and $(3, -14)$ is:

(a) $y = 2x - 8$ (b) $y = \dfrac{1}{2}x - \dfrac{1}{2}$ (c) $y = 2x + 12$ (d) $y = -2x + 8$

(e) $y = -2x - 8$

34) The distance between the two points $(\sqrt{3}, 4)$ and $(0, -1)$ is:

(a) $7\sqrt{2}$ (b) $5 + \sqrt{3}$ (c) $3\sqrt{3}$ (d) $2\sqrt{3}$ (e) $2\sqrt{7}$

35) An equation of the straight line that passes through the point $(7, -1)$ and which is parallel to the line $y = -x + 4$ is:

(a) $y = -x - 8$ (b) $y = x - 8$ (c) $y = -x + 6$ (d) $y = x - 6$ (e) $y = -x - 4$

36) The equation of the straight line that passes through the point $(2, 0)$ and which is perpendicular to the line $y = -\dfrac{1}{4}x + 1$ is:

(a) $y = 4x - 8$ (b) $y = 4x$ (c) $y = -\dfrac{1}{4}x + \dfrac{1}{2}$ (d) $y = -4x + 8$ (e) $y = 4x - 2$

37) Simplify the following expression: $\sqrt[3]{72a^3b^7}$

(a) $2a^3b^7\sqrt[3]{9}$ (b) $2ab^2\sqrt[3]{9b}$ (c) $9ab^2\sqrt[3]{2b}$ (d) $2ab^3\sqrt[3]{9b^2}$ (e) $a^3b^2\sqrt[3]{72b}$

38) If $4.3(x + 2) = 8.6x - (2.15x - 4.3)$, then $x = ?$

(a) –2   (b) 0.2   (c) 3   (d) 1.2   (e) 2

Answers to Exercises and Practice Tests

Chapter1, Section A

1. 1,365	2. 1,234	3. 997	4. 9,149	5. 11,121
6. 11,768	7. 757,554	8. 80,074	9. 642,187	10. d
11. b	12. 376	13. 73	14. 599	15. 669
16. 112	17. 91	18. 25,966	19. 100,942	20. 2,068
21. c	22. e	23. 270	24. 2,232	25. 2,040
26. 138,446	27. 335,258	28. 262,075	29. 12,239,682	30. 5,331,558
31. 56,069,424	32. c	33. a	34. 14	35. 273
36. 409	37. 301	38. 7,003	39. 30,004	40. 87,001 R 39
41. 1,256 R 328	42. 1,067 R 40	43. d	44. a	

Chapter 1, Section B

1. $4 < 7$ 2. $4 > -4$ 3. $9 = 4 + 5$ 4. $-12 < 11$ 5. $-6 < -5$

6. $-32 > -32$ 7. $-45 < 14$ 8. $-156 > -303$ 9. c   10. a

11. $-5, -3, 0, 4, 5, 7$ 12. $-9, -2, 0, 3, 5, 6, 9$ 13. $-3, -2, -1, 1, 2, 3, 8$

14. -45 15. 34   16. 12   17. -59 18. 94

19. 1   20. 31   21. $|-3| = |3|$ 22. $|-3| < |-4|$ 23. $|10| > |-9|$

24. $|-13| > |-11|$ 25. $-|10| < |-9|$ 26. $|14| < |-22|$

Chapter 1, Section C

1. 145   2. -134 3. $-1,033$ 4. 1,019   5. 32

6. −78   7. 150   8. 122   9. − 89   10. e

11. b   12. −11   13. 13   14. −331   15. 331

16. 570   17. −149   18. −4,556   19. −1,224   20. −3,872

21. c   22. d   23. 272   24. −225   25. −84

26. 186   27. −1,298   28. − 2,325   29. − 6,762   30. −4,498

31. 1,396,224   32. a   33. b   34. 13   35. −173

36. 14   37. −152   38. −250   39. −65   40. −103

41. 125   42. 1,092 R 410   43. d   44. c

Chapter1, Section D

1. 64   2. 32   3. −216   4. −125   5. −1

6. 1   7. −512   8. 77   9. −33   10. −6

11. 2   12. 170   13. −127   14. −129   15. 81

16. −45   17. −1,730   18. 8,262   19. 95   20. −177

21. 0   22. 8   23. 1,996   24. 667   25. d

26. a   27. a   28. e

Chapter 1, Section E

1. 1, 2, 23, 46   2. 1, 2, 5, 10, 25, 50   3. 1, 2, 3, 6, 17, 34, 51, 106

4. 1, 23   5. 1, 2, 6, 9, 185. 1, 2, 6, 9, 18   6. 1, 2, 3, 6, 23, 46, 69, 138

7. 1, 67   8. 1, 2, 4, 10, 20, 25, 50, 100   9. 1, 7, 19, 133

10. 1, 2, 3, 4, 6, 8, 12, 24   11. 1, 3, 9, 11, 33, 99   12. 1, 3, 9, 37, 111, 333

13. $2^2 \times 3 \times 5$ 14. $2 \times 3^2 \times 5$ 15. $2 \times 3 \times 13$ 16. $2^2 \times 5 \times 37$

17. $2^3 \times 37$ 18. $2^4 \times 3 \times 13$ 19. 2   20. 5   21. 5

22. 36   23. 25   24. 5   25. 60   26. 600

27. 300   28. 72   29. 150   30. 840

Chapter 1, Section F

1. $940   2. 8   3. 29   4. 58 mi.   5. 84

6. $30   7. $170   8. c   9. a   10. b

11. c   12. e   13. d   14. b   15. b

16. a   17. e   18. c   19. d   20. d

21. b   22. d   23. b   24. c   25. c

26. e   27. d   28. a

Chapter 2, Section A

1. 8   2. 1   3. 0   4. 22   5. undefined

6. 0   7. undefined   8. 1   9. proper fraction   10. proper fraction

11. improper fraction   12. mixed number   13. improper fraction

13. improper fraction   14. improper fraction   15. mixed number

16. proper fraction   17. a   18. b   19. d   20. a

Chapter 2, Section B

1. $1\frac{22}{23}$ 2. $6\frac{7}{10}$ 3. $4\frac{11}{12}$ 4. $11\frac{1}{7}$ 5. $4\frac{1}{12}$

6. $7\frac{24}{27}$ 7. $3\frac{7}{8}$ 8. $31\frac{1}{3}$ 9. $13\frac{11}{17}$ 10. $\frac{33}{5}$

11. $\frac{39}{4}$ 12. $\frac{163}{12}$ 13. $\frac{74}{3}$ 14. $\frac{179}{9}$ 15. $\frac{232}{17}$

16. $\frac{796}{31}$ 17. $\frac{1,123}{36}$

Chapter 2, Section C

1. $\frac{24}{30}$ 2. $\frac{20}{30}$ 3. $\frac{14}{30}$ 4. $\frac{2}{24}$ 5. $\frac{21}{24}$ 6. $\frac{18}{24}$

7. $\frac{20}{24}$ 8. $\frac{11}{15}$ 9. $\frac{4}{7}$ 10. $\frac{2}{5}$ 11. $\frac{3}{5}$ 12. $\frac{2}{3}$

13. $\frac{1}{3}$ 14. $\frac{25}{56}$ 15. $\frac{1}{3}$ 16. $\frac{3}{22}$ 17. $\frac{26}{33}$ 18. $\frac{3}{10}$

19. $\frac{111}{331}$ 20. $\frac{14}{27}$ 21. $\frac{11}{210}$.   22. $\frac{1}{80}$ 23. $\frac{17}{201}$

Chapter 2, Section D

1. $2\frac{2}{9}$ 2. $1\frac{1}{2}$ 3. $\frac{20}{99}$ 4. $2\frac{2}{9}$ 5. 10   6. $3\frac{3}{4}$

7. $\frac{5}{72}$ 8. 2   9. $\frac{5}{72}$ 10. $\frac{7}{10}$ 11. $3\frac{6}{7}$ 12. $2\frac{50}{59}$

13. $1\frac{1}{27}$ 14. 198   15. $49\frac{1}{2}$ 16. $10\frac{10}{27}$ 17. $32\frac{1}{7}$ 18. $21\frac{1}{12}$

19. $1\frac{1}{3}$ 20. $5\frac{2}{5}$ 21. $102\frac{6}{7}$ 22. $\frac{1}{12}$ 23. $\frac{2}{5}$ 24. 12

25. 72   26. $\frac{17}{4,992}$ 27. $1\frac{1}{8}$ 28. 6   29. 2,550   30. $\frac{17}{1,400}$

31. $\frac{13}{20}$ 32. $\frac{28}{35}$ 33. $58\frac{2}{7}$ 34. $\frac{17}{666}$ 35. $\frac{7}{12}$ 36. $2\frac{16}{67}$

37. $\frac{25}{33}$ 38. $\frac{2}{629}$ 39. $\frac{81}{472}$ 40. $5\frac{33}{41}$ 41. $3\frac{259}{273}$

Chapter 2, Section E

1. $3\frac{7}{18}$ 2. $2\frac{9}{20}$ 3. $\frac{89}{99}$ 4. $3\frac{5}{6}$ 5. $12\frac{5}{6}$ 6. $21\frac{5}{28}$

7. $\frac{7}{12}$ 8. $18\frac{1}{9}$ 9. $\frac{23}{60}$ 10. $1\frac{5}{26}$ 11. $18\frac{3}{14}$ 12. $4\frac{42}{59}$

13. $4\frac{8}{9}$ 14. $46\frac{5}{7}$ 15. $20\frac{3}{4}$ 16. $6\frac{8}{9}$ 17. $12\frac{4}{21}$ 18. $9\frac{5}{12}$

19. b   20. a   21. c   22. b   23. d   24 c

25. a   26. b   27. $\frac{7}{36}$ 28. $\frac{11}{15}$ 29. $59\frac{5}{12}$ 30. $97\frac{10}{13}$

31. $\frac{12}{25}$ 32. $4\frac{1}{8}$ 33. $5\frac{11}{12}$ 34. $127\frac{22}{39}$ 35. $\frac{5}{48}$ 36. 0

37. $67\frac{11}{15}$ 38. $\frac{31}{75}$ 39. $\frac{1}{2}$ 40. $\frac{3}{11}$ 41. $25\frac{5}{12}$ 42. $\frac{17}{37}$

43. $2\frac{29}{102}$ 44. $8\frac{3}{10}$ 45. $1\frac{2}{3}$ 46. $1\frac{2}{37}$ 47. $5\frac{41}{72}$ 48. $11\frac{10}{17}$

49. $6\frac{13}{132}$ 50. d   51. c   52. b   53. a   54. e

55. e   56. a   57. b

Chapter 2, Section F

1. $\frac{8}{9}$ 2. $\frac{1}{10}$ 3. $\frac{4}{9}$ 4. $\frac{3}{10}$ 5. $\frac{5}{6}$ 6. $\frac{5}{28}$ 7. $\frac{1}{6}$

8. $\frac{7}{63}$ 9. $\frac{5}{12}$ 10. $\frac{23}{25}$ 11. $\frac{2}{3}$ 12. $\frac{63}{41}$ 13. c   14. a

15. e   16. d   17. a   18. $6\frac{5}{36}$ 19. $1\frac{197}{208}$ 20. $1\frac{7}{30}$ 21. $\frac{5}{39}$

22. $\frac{243}{328}$ 23. $6\frac{39}{67}$ 24. $2\frac{61}{84}$ 25. $3\frac{67}{72}$ 26. e

27. b   28. c   29. b   30. d   31. a   32. e

33. a   34. a   35. b   36. c   37. b

Chapter 2, Section G

1. 225   2. $\frac{8}{9}$ 3. 275   4. $2,000   5. c   6. d   7. e

8. c   9. a   10. b   11. b   12. e   13. a   14. c

Chapter 3, Section A

1. 0.9   2. 0.02   3. 0.00013   4. 5.007   5. 25.0313

6. 31.5   7. 4.56   8. 0.02345   9. 10.489   10. 0.7143

11. c   12. d   13. $\frac{39}{100}$ 14. $\frac{9,003}{1,000}$ 15. $\frac{9,931}{10,000}$

16. $\frac{20,001}{100,000}$ 17. $\frac{206}{10,000}$ 18. $\frac{4,580,081}{10,000}$ 19. $\frac{3}{10,000}$

20. $\frac{474}{1,000}$ 21. b   22. a   23. 0.431   24. 395.003

25. 9.305   26. 45   27. 1.37   28. 5.203   29. 0.3052

30. 5.02   31. Thirty-one hundredths   32. Three hundred ninety-five and two tenths

33. Nine and two hundred eighty-five thousandths

34. Four and forty-five thousand ninety-two hundred thousandths

35. Seven hundredths   36. One and two ten thousandths

37. Three hundred sixty-six thousandths   38. Two tenths

Chapter 3, Section B

1. 0.1 < 0.6   2. 21.13 < 22.13   3. 0.375 > 0.325   4. 3.63 < 4.52

5. 1.112781 > 1.11201   6. 0.6110 < 0.61101

7. 12.209, 12.0999, 12.099, 12.098   8. 112.12, 112.099, 109.9, 109.099

9. 45.9, 45.65, 45.56, 45.056   10. 2.94   11. 3.76   12. 10.19

13. 23.99   14. 0.01   15. 3.241   16. 24.608   17. 60.102

18. 7.906   19. 9.223   20. 0.150

Chapter 3, Section C

1. 27.2209	2. 12.447	3. 1.284	4. 240.5609	5. 136.861
6. 7.03033	7. 2,086.419	8. 19.09	9. 19.89	10. 16.76
11. 8.992	12. 5.9881	13. 185.047	14. 1.889	15. 105.291
16. 13.099	17. a	18. c		

Chapter 3, Section D

1. 74.0982	2. 0.0864	3. 0.340875	4. 123.5247	5. 3,612.69717
6. 0.05616	7. 1.84869	8. 0.900009	9. 34.86	10. 53.12
11. 12,170	12. 0.711	13. 2,230	14. 1.2	15. 1,070
16. 3,470,000	17. d	18. 22.98	19. 21.85	20. 12.005
21. 36	22. 2.5	23. 877.5	24. 23.1	25. 9.25
26. 0.3486	27. 5.312	28. 0.01217	29. 0.00711	30. 0.00002
31. 0.092	32. 0.107	33. 5.614347	34. d	35. 153.05
36. 4.20	37. 10.61	38. 6.31	39. 14.22	40. 6.49
41. 0.72	42. 0.27	43. 1.124	44. 5.032	45. 5.759
46. 1.610	47. 57.341	48. 155.875	49. 9.906	50. 0.953

Chapter 3, Section E

1. 1.6	2. $0.2\overline{27}$	3. $0.\overline{6}$	4. 0.8	5. $0.\overline{81}$
6. 0.25	7. $0.\overline{2}$	8. $0.41\overline{6}$	9. 0.4375	10. 0.32
11. c	12. d	13. 0.2	14. 0.96	15. 25.89

16. 0.38   17. 13.28   18. b   19. 0.385   20. 0.171

21. 30.118   22. 0.214   23. 13.672   24. e

Chapter 3, Section F

1. e   2. c   3. a   4. b   5. e   6. d

7. c   8. a   9. a   10. d

Chapter 3, Section G

1. 3×10^{-1} 2. 7.34×10^{-3} 3. 7.229×10^{-4} 4. 1.000101×10^{-2}

5. 8×10^{0} 6. 7.612×10^{0} 7. 5×10^{1} 8. 2.3×10^{1}

9. 9.416×10^{1} 10. 4.52935×10^{2} 11. 1.726×10^{3}

12. b   13. c   14. d   15. b   16. 40.0   17. 910.0

18. 75.6   19. 1,105.3   20. 56,209.3   21. 400,000

22. 200,000,000   23. 26,169,400   24. 60.195   25. 0.8

26. 0.0073615   27. 0.0004112   28. 6×10^{3} 29. 1.25×10^{8}

30. 1.23×10^{9} 31. 2×10^{-6} 32. 7.2×10^{2} 33. 6.3×10^{-3}

34. d   35. c   36. c   37. b   38. 2×10^{2}

39. 3×10^{-6} 40. 3.6×10^{-7} 41. 6×10^{12} 42. 9×10^{-9}

43. 1.3×10^{5} 44. e   45. c   46. a   47. 4.02×10^{1}

48. 3.36×10^{-1} 49. 6×10^{-3} 50. b   51. 4×10^{4}

52. 2.875×10^{4} 53. 5×10^{5} 54. a

Chapter 4, Section A

1. natural, integer, rational   2. rational   3. natural, integer, rational

4. integer, rational   5. rational   6. irrational   7. rational

8. rational   9. irrational   10. rational   11. integer

12. natural, integer, rational   13. 0.25   14. 0.4   15. 1.5

16. 0.75   17. 0.125   18. 0.875   19. –0.1   20. –0.9

21. $5.\overline{6}$ 22. $7.\overline{3}$ 23. $-0.\overline{1}$ 24. $-0.\overline{5}$ 25. 3.6

26. 3.2   27. $0.\overline{16}$

Chapter 4, Section B

1. 9   2. –9   3. doesn't exist   4. 4   5. –4

6. doesn't exiast   7. $\frac{1}{3}$ 8. $\frac{5}{9}$ 9. $-\frac{8}{5}$ 10. doesn't exist

11. $\frac{10}{11}$ 12. doesn't exist   13. 0.2   14. 1.2   15. –0.5

16. 0.13   17. irrational   18. rational   19. rational   20. irrational

21. rational   22. irrational   23. irrational   24. rational   25. c

26. c   27. b   28. a   29. b   30. d   31. c

Chapter 4, Section C

1. a   2. c   3. b   4. e   5. b   6. d

7. e   8. b   9. d   10. b   11. d   12. e

13. c   14. b   15. c   16. e   17. b   18. b

19. c   20. b   21. a   22. a   23. d   24. b

25. c   26. e   27. b   28. a   29. b

Chapter 4, Section D

1. $11\sqrt{5}$ 2. $16\sqrt{6}$ 3. $-7\sqrt{10}$ 4. $\sqrt{5}$ 5. $-10\sqrt{2}$ 6. $-5\sqrt{15}$

7. c   8. e   9. a   10. b   11. e   12. d

13. e   14. b   15. a   16. d

Chapter 5, Section A

1. $\frac{1}{3}$ 2. $\frac{1}{2}$ 3. $\frac{7}{2}$ 4. $\frac{5}{2}$ 5. $\frac{1}{1}$ 6. $\frac{34}{71}$

7. $\frac{2}{15}$ 8. $\frac{9}{4}$ 9. $\frac{1}{8}$ 10. $\frac{1}{9}$ 11. $\frac{1}{6}$ 12. $\frac{15}{2}$

13. $\frac{12}{1}$ 14. $\frac{30}{1}$ 15. $\frac{60}{1}$ 16. b   17. a   18. a

19. c   20. e

Chapter 5, Section B

1. 6 feet per second   2. $5 per hour   3. 12 kilowatts per hour   4. 25 miles per hour

5. $5 per gallon   6. $5.50 per square feet   7. 12 miles per hour   8. 50¢ per orange

9. John   10. c   11. d   12. c   13. e   14. a

15. c   16. d   17. a   18. c   19. d   20. e

Chapter 5, Section C

1. true   2. true   3. false   4. true   5. true   6. false

7. true   8. false   9. false   10. false   11. false   12. false

13. false   14. true   15. d   16. c

Chapter 5, Section D

1. $x = 12$ 2. $x = 5$ 3. $x = -22\frac{1}{3}$ 4. $x = -8$ 5. $x = 8$

6. $p = 5\frac{1}{2}$ 7. $y = -29$ 8. $a = -2\frac{21}{34}$ 9. $x = -\frac{16}{39}$ 10. $y = -2$

11. $x = -11$ 12. $x = 4.$ 13. c   14. b   15. c

Chapter 5, Section E

1. $x = 5$ 2. $y = 72$ 3. $x = 42$ 4. $z = 3$ 5. $x = 3$
6. $x = 1$ 7. $x = 6$ 8. $x = 25$ 9. $x = 22$ 10. $x = 11$

11. $x = 160$ 12. $x = 3$ 13. $x = \frac{1}{2}$ 14. $x = 4$ 15. $x = 1\frac{11}{13}$

16. $x = 242$ 17. $x = 12\frac{4}{9}$ 18. $x = 3$ 19. $x = 49$ 20. $x = 7$

21. $x = 45\frac{10}{11}$ 22. $x = 0$

Chapter 5, Section F

1. 72   2. 1,200   3. $203   4. 1 hour 49 minutes 12 seconds

5. $x = \frac{km}{l}$ 6. $251.10   7. 145   8. 9   9. 16,000

10. 770   11. c   12. d   13. a   14. d

15. b   16. c   17. e   18. a   19. b   20. c

Chapter 6, Section A

1. 30% of cars made are red.   2. 41% of students scored a *B* on their test.

3. 7% of games played are won.   4. 84% of students handed in their quiz.

5. 21% of stocks decreased in value yesterday.   6. This year's enrollment is 90% of last year's enrollment.

7. 0.7%   8. 9.3%   9. 11%   10. 31%   11. 3%

12. 23%   13. 45%   14. 35%   15. b   16. c   17. c

Chapter 6, Section B

1. 0.035   2. 1.22   3. 0.01   4. 0.0022   5. 0.002

6. 0.3   7. d   8. 98%   9. 20%   10. 1,298%

11. 0.8%   12. 110%   13. 309%   14. b   15. d

16. $\frac{23}{100}$ 17. $\frac{6}{5}$ 18. $\frac{1}{50}$ 19. $\frac{3}{5}$ 20. $\frac{3}{800}$

21. $\frac{7}{500}$ 22. c   23. 20%   24. 90%   25. 70%

26. 25%   27. 66.67%   28. 54.55%   29. e   30. 0.02

31. 0.01   32. 0.4   33. 0.75   34. 0.53   35. a

36. $\frac{17}{50}$ 37. $\frac{37}{25}$ 38. $\frac{1}{25}$ 39. $\frac{41}{200}$ 40. $\frac{11}{100}$

41. $\frac{99}{1,000}$ 42. a

Chapter 6, Section C

1. 20%   2. 28.   3. 280%   4. 60   5. 100

6. 94.7%   7. 20   8. 0.032   9. 2.75   10. 1.2

11. 2.5   12. 437.5   13. a   14. b

Chapter 7, Section A

1. 26.2	2. 24.5	3. 49	4. 55	5. c
6. d	7. a	8. d	9. 23	10. 19
11. 38	12. 49	13. c	14. a	15. b
16. e	17. 3	18. 2 and 4	19. There is no mode	
20. 43	21. b	22. c	23. e	24. c

Chapter 7, Section B

1. d	2. c	3. e	4. d	5. a	6. b
7. c	8. a	9. e	10. b	11. c	12. a
13. d	14. a	15. b	16. d	17. e	18. b
19. b	20. c	21. e	22. a	23. b	24. c

Chapter 8, Section A

1. 27	2. 45	3. 10	4. 36	5. −544	6. −19
7. −23	8. 60	9. 18	10. −19	11. 29	12. 23
13. −36	14. 12	15. 16	16. 30	17. 18	18. 14
19. 1	20. −37	21. b	22. a	23. d	24. d
25. e	26. c	27. b	28. d	29. d	30. b
31. d	32. d	33. e	34. b	35. c	36. d

Chapter 8, Section B

1. $-12x^2$ 2. $84st$ 3. $-20m^5$ 4. $-12y^4$ 5. $120x$

6. $247a^3b^2$ 7. t^2 8. $-69j^3k^2$ 9. d   10. b

11. c   12. a   13. a   14. c   15. a

16. d   17. c   18. e   19. c   20. b

21. d   22. e   23. c   24. a

Chapter 8, Section C

1. b   2. d   3. a   4. c   5. e

6. b   7. d   8. b   9. a   10. d

11. c   12. b   13. a   14. e   15. c

16. a   17. c   18. e   19. b   20. b

21. b   22. c   23. a   24. d   25. b

26. e   27. b   28. c   29. d   30. c

Chapter 8, Section D

1. d   2. b   3. c   4. b   5. e

6. d   7. a   8. c   9. c   10. a

11. a   12. b   13. b   14. a   15. a

16. b   17. a   18. c   19. e   20. a

1. 25

2. $\dfrac{27}{64}$

3. $\dfrac{729}{343}$

4. $\dfrac{4}{121}$

5. 36

6. −36

7. $-\dfrac{1}{125}$

8. $-\dfrac{1}{243}$

9. −64

10. −64

11. 81

12. 7

13. b

14. a

15. d

16. c

17. c

18. a

19. 5

20. 4

21. −27

22. 4

23. $\dfrac{1}{16}$

24. $-\dfrac{1}{5}$

25. $\dfrac{1}{49}$

26. 1

27. 1

28. −1

29. e

30. d

31. d

32. b

33. b

34. c

35. a

36. $\dfrac{1}{6}$

37. $\dfrac{1}{81}$

38. $-\dfrac{1}{343}$

39. $-\dfrac{1}{343}$

40. $\dfrac{1}{64}$

41. $-\dfrac{1}{64}$

42. $-\dfrac{1}{15}$

43. 64

44. 81

45. $\dfrac{1}{25}$

46. $\dfrac{1}{4,096}$

47. 125

48. 1

49. −1

50. $\dfrac{1}{x^2}$

51. $\dfrac{1}{y^3}$

52. $-\dfrac{1}{y^6}$

53. $\dfrac{1}{a^3}$

54. t

55. x^4

56. $\dfrac{x^5}{y}$

57. $\dfrac{5y^6}{x^5}$

58. $\dfrac{1}{y^{12}}$

59. $\dfrac{1}{t^{16}}$

60. b

61. a

62. c

63. e

64. b

65. e

66. b

67. a

68. $\dfrac{a^4}{b^4}$

69. $\dfrac{x^8}{y^8}$

70. $\dfrac{81}{x^6}$

71. $\dfrac{25}{a^{16}}$

72. $\dfrac{x^3}{216y^6}$

73. $\dfrac{10,000x^{16}}{y^{12}}$

74. $\dfrac{1}{m^4t^8}$

75. $-\dfrac{512s^6}{u^{12}}$

76. b

77. a

78. d

79. c

80. b

81. a

82. a

83. e

84. b

85. c

86. b

87. d

88. b

89. a

Chapter 9, Section B

1. 3　　2. $\dfrac{9}{64}$　　3. $\dfrac{343}{64}$　　4. $\dfrac{9}{5}$　　5. 180

6. 36　　7. $\dfrac{1}{128}$　　8. $\dfrac{1}{196}$　　9. $-\dfrac{1}{162}$　　10. $-\dfrac{1}{392}$

11. $\dfrac{81}{25}$　　12. $\dfrac{729}{64}$　　13. $-\dfrac{64}{81}$　　14. $\dfrac{243}{4}$　　15. $\dfrac{49}{81}$

16. $\dfrac{1}{30}$　　17. $\dfrac{8}{3}$　　18. $-\dfrac{2}{5}$　　19. 11　　20. $\dfrac{9}{4}$

21. $\dfrac{52}{27}$　　22. $\dfrac{8}{3}$　　23. $\dfrac{16}{25}$　　24. $\dfrac{1}{21}$　　25. b

26. e　　27. a　　28. d　　29. a　　30. d

31. a　　32. c　　33. b　　34. e　　35. a

36. b　　37. a　　38. c　　39. c

Chapter 10, Section A

1. coefficient is 4, degree is 0　　2. coefficient is −5, degree is 1

3. coefficient is 8, degree is 1　　4. coefficient is 7, degree is 3

5. coefficient is −8, degree is 7　　6. coefficient is $-\dfrac{10}{11}$, degree is 6

7. $3x^2$ has coefficient 3, $5x$ has coefficient 5, −6 has coefficient −6

8. $\dfrac{1}{4}a^3$ has coefficient $\dfrac{1}{4}$, $-a^2$ has coefficient −1

9. $\dfrac{y^2}{9}$ has coefficient $\dfrac{1}{9}$, $-\dfrac{7y}{3}$ has coefficient $-\dfrac{7}{3}$, 8 has coefficient 8

10. $\dfrac{3x}{13}$ has coefficient $\dfrac{3}{13}$, $\dfrac{x^2}{12}$ has coefficient $\dfrac{1}{12}$, $-\dfrac{1}{2}$ has coefficient $-\dfrac{1}{2}$

11. degree 1, linear　　12. degree 2, quadratic　　13. degree 2, quadratic　　14. degree 1, linear

15. 2   16. 3   17. 6   18. 8   19. $7x + 15y$

20. $-x^2 - 9xy + 10$ 21. $-8a^2 + 8ab$ 22. $-11st^2 + 4s^2t - st$ 23. $-7 - 3m^2 - 9m^2n$

24. $2x^2 - x - 7$

Chapter 10, Section B

1. $6a + 8$ 2. $7b + 5$ 3. $5a^2 + a$ 4. $x^2 - 2x + 3$ 5. $-2x^2 + 14y^2 + 2y$

6. $6mn^2 - 2mn + 7nm^2$ 7. $6m^2 + 14m + 2$ 8. $4a + 7b + 2 - 6ab$

9. $10p + 3q + 2 + 4pq$ 10. $7t^2 - t + 5$ 11. $6x - 3$ 12. $5a + 5b$

13. $s + 7t$ 14. $-9p + 3q$ 15. $x^2 - 5x + 3$ 16. $9uv + 14v - 13u$

17. $-4x^2 + 12x + 4$ 18. $5a^2 - 5a$ 19. $8a^2 - 7ab - 8b^2$ 20. $-2s^2 - 2st + 8t^2$

21. a   22. a   23. c   24. c   25. d

26. a   27. c   28. d   29. e   30. e

31. d   32. d   33. b   34. a

Chapter 10, Section C

1. $12x^4$ 2. $54a^6$ 3. $-60s^3t^{11}$ 4. $48a + 12$ 5. $72x^7 - 16x^4$

6. $56t^5 - 42t^4$ 7. $24p^4 - 16p^6$ 8. $-21x^3y^{11} + 28x^7y^{10}$ 9. $15a^2 + 30a - 10$

10. $-15x^6y^3 + 21x^6y^5 - 27x^4y^5$ 11. $x^2 + 5x + 4$ 12. $t^2 + 5t - 24$

13. $6y^2 + 17y + 15$ 14. $10x^2 + 11x + 3$ 15. $12x^2 + 4x - 21$

16. $6y^3 + 19y^2 - 7y$ 17. $x^2 - 49$ 18. $64 - 16p^2$

19. $4x^4 - 100y^2$ 20. $x^2 + 8x + 16$ 21. $25y^2 - 30y + 9$

22. $x^3 + x^2 - 2x + 12$ 23. $-10a^3 + 39a^2 - 19a + 2$

24. a   25. a   26. b   27. d   28. d

29. e   30. a   31. c   32. b   33. b

34. e   35. a   36. d   37. d   38. b

39. $16x - 2$ 40. $11a^3 + 41a^2$ 41. $-2p^4 - 17p^3 + 5p^2$

42. $8y^3 + 37y^2 - 30y - 21$ 43. $2x^3 + 6x^2 + 11x^2y - 12y$ 44. $2x^2 + 13x + 15$

45. $-4a + 1$ 46. $2y^2 - 74$ 47. $2x^2 + 4x + 20$ 48. $-r^2 - 13r - 52$

49. $2y^2 + 20y + 132$ 50. $2a^2 - 12a + 36$ 51. $3x^5$ 52. $10b^4$

53. $-4y^4$ 54. $\dfrac{4a^2c}{7}$ 55. $3x + 9$ 56. $-8y^2 + 9y$ 57. $-7x + 3x^8$

58. $a^3 + 13a^2$ 59. $-5b^7 + 7b^4 - b$ 60. $-3x^3y^5 - 2xy^4 + \dfrac{4x^9y^6}{3}$

61. c   62. a   63. e   64. c   65. d

66. a   67. d

Chapter 11, Section A

1. $5(y + 7)$ 2. $7(2b^2 - 1)$ 3. $5(x^2 + 2x - 4)$ 4. $4(t^2 + 3t - 7)$

5. $3x^2(x - 8)$ 6. $p^2(11p + 5)$ 7. $4q^2(2q + 3)$ 8. $9x^2(2x^2 + 3x - 1)$

9. $8y^2(4y^2 - 2y + 1)$ 10. $2ab^2(10a + 11b)$ 11. $s^2t(6s - 5st + t)$

12. $3p^4q(9pq^2 + q^5 - 2p^2)$ 13. $5xy^3z^3(3x - 2y + 7z)$

14. d   15. a   16. e   17. c   18. d

19. a   20. e   21. c   22. c   23. d

Chapter 11, Section B

1. $(x + 2)(x - 2)$ 2. $(a + 4)(a - 4)$ 3. $(3 + y)(3 - y)$ 4. $(11t + 1)(11t - 1)$

5. $(8t + 3)(8t - 3)$ 6. $(5p + 6)(5p - 6)$ 7. $(2q + 11)(2q - 11)$ 8. $(x + 8y)(x - 8y)$

9. $(9a + b)(9a - b)$ 10. $(12m^2 + n^8)(12m^2 - n^8)$ 11. $(6u^3 + 13v^7)(6u^3 - 13v^7)$

12. $(7x^8y + 10z^6)(7x^8y - 10z^6)$ 13. a   14. c   15. b   16. e

17. a   18. b   19. a   20. $5(x + 2)(x - 2)$ 21. $7(y + 3)(y - 3)$

22. $3m^3(m + 4)(m - 4)$ 23. $2n^2(n + 6)(n - 6)$ 24. $4(a + 2)(a - 2)$

25. $9(b + 1)(b - 1)$ 26. $16(x + 2y)(x - 2y)$ 27. $4(4x + y)(4x - y)$

28. $x^2y^2(x + 10)(x - 10)$ 29. $11t(t + 5x^4)(t - 5x^4)$ 30. $2ab^2(3a^2b^5 + 7)(3a^2b^5 - 7)$

31. d   32. e   33. b   34. d   35. e

Chapter 11, Section C

1. $(x + 2)(x + 5)$ 2. $(y - 10)(y - 3)$ 3. $(a + 8)(a - 7)$ 4. $(p + 3)(p - 14)$

5. $(m + 12)^2$ 6. $(y + 8)(y + 3)$ 7. $(b - 9)^2$ 8. $(x + 9)(x - 2)$

9. $(b - 9)(b - 4)$ 10. $(p - 7)(p + 3)$ 11. $(x + 11)(x + 5)$ 12. $(q - 9)(q - 6)$

13. $(2x + 1)(x + 1)$ 14. $(3y - 2)(y + 1)$ 15. $(2y + 3)(y - 1)$ 16. $(5a + 4)(a - 1)$

17. $(7x + 2)(2x + 1)$ 18. $(4y + 3)(2y + 3)$ 19. $(2x - 7)(2x - 3)$ 20. $(3y + 4)(2y + 3)$

21. e   22. b   23. a   24. b   25. c

26. e   27. b   28. e   29. $2(x + 2)(x + 1)$ 30. $3(x + 3)(x + 2)$

31. $4a(a - 5)(a + 3)$ 32. $5u^3(u - 6)(u - 5)$ 33. $8v^2(v - 3)(v - 2)$

34. $2x^2y(y - 7)(y + 4)$ 35. $4mn(m + 2)(m - 5)$ 36. $9(3x + 1)(x + 2)$

37. $4s(5t + 3)(t + 1)$ 38. $6x(2y + 1)(2y - 3)$ 39. $7(4y + 3)(2y - 1)$

40. d   41. a   42. c   43. a   44. b

Chapter 11, Section D

1. $(t + 4)(t^2 + 2)$ 2. $(2a + 3)(9a^3 + 2)$ 3. $(x + 7)(x^3 - 3)$ 4. $(y - 5)(2y^2 - 14)$

5. $(x + a)(2x + 3)$ 6. $(6n - 11p)(7m + 2)$ 7. $(b^2 - t)(a^2 - s)$ 8. $(2p^2 - 1)(p + 3q)$

9. $(8s^2 - 5)(10s^2 - 3y)$ 10. b   11. b   12. a   13. e

14. b   15. c

Chapter 11, Section E

1. $x = 3, x = 4$ 2. $x = -1, x = -6$ 3. $y = 2, y = 7$ 4. $y = 4, y = 8$

5. $t = -9, t = 4$ 6. $t = -11, t = 3$ 7. $x = -\frac{3}{2}, x = 7$ 8. $x = -\frac{2}{3}, x = 9$

9. $m = \frac{15}{4}, m = 2$ 10. $m = \frac{7}{6}, m = 2$ 11. $x = -5, x = 0$ 12. $x = -16, x = 0$

13. $y = 0, y = 8$ 14. $b = \pm 5$ 15. $t = \pm\frac{7}{2}$ 16. $p = 0, p = 5$

17. $q = 0, q = 8$ 18. $k = -12, k = -3$ 19. $l = -8, l = -2$ 20. $x = -1, x = \frac{2}{5}$

21. $y = -\frac{2}{9}, y = \frac{3}{2}$ 22. $x = 3, x = 7$ 23. $a = -6, a = 8$ 24. $x = -9, x = 2$

25. $x = -3, x = 7$ 26. $x = 0, x = 14$ 27. $x = 0, x = 3, x = 6$ 28. $x = 0, x = \pm\frac{10}{11}$

29. $x = -2, x = 0$ 30. 5   31. -6 32. 0   33. -6

Chapter 11, Section F

1. $\frac{7}{5}$ 2. $-\frac{1}{63}$ 3. $\frac{9}{92}$ 4. undefined   5. 1

6. $-\frac{64}{43}$ 7. undefined   8. $\frac{11}{7}$ 9. $x = 12$ 10. $x = -3, x = -9$

11. $x = \pm\frac{1}{2}$ 12. $x = -\frac{5}{2}, x = -\frac{3}{2}$ 13. $\frac{2}{3}$ 14. $\frac{1}{3}$ 15. $\frac{4}{3}$

16. 3   17. $\frac{3p + 8}{2p - 1}$ 18. $\frac{2q - 7}{4q + 1}$ 19. $\frac{2x - 3}{2(1 - x)}$ 20. $\frac{3y - 4}{2(2y - 1)}$

21. $\frac{x + 1}{3}$ 22. $\frac{x + 3}{4}$ 23. $\frac{2}{3(x + 4)}$ 24. $\frac{7(x + 3)}{2x}$ 25. $\frac{2t - 7}{2t + 3}$

26. $\frac{3t - 5}{2t + 1}$ 27. $-\frac{a + 2}{4}$ 28. $-\frac{8x^2}{1 + 2x}$ 29. b   30. d

31. d   32. a   33. b   34. c

Chapter 11, Section G

1. b	2. d	3. c	4. c	5. b
6. b	7. a	8. c		

Chapter 12, Section A

1. 9	2. 17	3. −5	4. −12	5. 2
6. −6	7. −4	8. 9	9. 2	10. 3
11. −1	12. −4	13. −3	14. 2	15. −3
16. 10	17. 6	18. 5	19. does not exist	20. −2

21. does not exist   22. −3   23. 0   24. does not exist

25. rational   26. irrational   27. irrational   28. rational

29. rational   30. irrational   31. irrational   32. irrational

Chapter 12, Section B

1. c	2. c	3. c	4. b	5. d
6. d	7. c	8. c	9. d	10. b

Chapter 12, Section C

1. a	2. c	3. b	4. b	5. d
6. e	7. b	8. a	9. c	10. b
11. d	12. b	13. c	14. a	15. b

16. d   17. e   18. e   19. c   20. a

21. $4\sqrt{2}$ 22. $-6\sqrt{2}$ 23. $5\sqrt[3]{4}$ 24. $y^2\sqrt{y}$

25. $x^2\sqrt[3]{y^3}$ 26. $3x^3\sqrt{2}$ 27. $3y\sqrt[3]{2y^2}$ 28. $2ab^4\sqrt{2b}$

29. $3m^2n\sqrt[3]{m^2}$ 30. $-2a\sqrt[3]{8ab^2}$ 31. $\dfrac{3x\sqrt{6x}}{y^2}$ 32. $\dfrac{a^3}{5b^2\sqrt[3]{b}}$

33. $5\sqrt{2}$ 34. $\sqrt[3]{84}$ 35. $10x^2$ 36. $5x^4$

37. $18x^2$ 38. $36\sqrt[3]{6x^2}$ 39. $56b$ 40. $\sqrt{2x}$

41. $\dfrac{1}{2x^2}$ 42. $\dfrac{2y^4}{x^3}\sqrt{\dfrac{3}{11}}$ or $\dfrac{2y^4\sqrt{3}}{x^3\sqrt{11}}$

Chapter 12, Section D

1. $17\sqrt{10}$ 2. $-12\sqrt[3]{9}$ 3. $9\sqrt[3]{7}$ 4. $5\sqrt{3}$ 5. $8\sqrt[3]{2}$

6. $41\sqrt[3]{2}$ 7. $7\sqrt{6x}$ 8. $-5y\sqrt{3y}$ 9. $5\sqrt{3}$ 10. $5a$

11. $8x\sqrt[3]{5x}$ 12. $-\sqrt[3]{2}$ 13. $-45x\sqrt{2x}$ 14. a   15. a

16. e   17. d   18. b   19. c   20. b

21. d   22. d   23. a   24. d   25. e

Chapter 12, Section E

1. 15   2. $84x$ 3. $12\sqrt[3]{18}$ 4. $-12a$ 5. $6+4\sqrt{2}$

6. $42-10\sqrt{3}$ 7. -210 8. 171   9. $\sqrt[3]{6}+6\sqrt[3]{2}$

10. $\sqrt[3]{30}-2\sqrt[3]{5}$ 11. $2\sqrt[3]{4}+10\sqrt[3]{6}$ 12. $3\sqrt[3]{36}-2\sqrt[3]{9}$ 13. $11+4\sqrt{6}$

14. $11-3\sqrt{15}$ 15. $9+57\sqrt{2}$ 16. $x+3\sqrt{x}-28$ 17. $48+2\sqrt{y}-y$

18. $15-\sqrt{t}-2t$ 19. $\sqrt[3]{4}-5\sqrt[3]{2}-14$ 20. $\sqrt[3]{9}-2\sqrt[3]{3}-8$ 21. $\sqrt[3]{x^2}-12\sqrt[3]{x}+35$

22. 3   23. -44 24. -4 25. $x-64$ 26. $a-9b^2$

27. $144y - 1$ 28. $8 + 4\sqrt{3}$ 29. $26 - 8\sqrt{10}$ 30. $119 - 12\sqrt{33}$

31. a   32. d   33. d   34. d   35. a

36. b   37. b   38. a   39. e   40. 10

41. 10   42. $\dfrac{4\sqrt[3]{3}}{3}$ 43. $\dfrac{2}{9}$ 44. $2\sqrt{7}$ 45. $\dfrac{\sqrt{2}}{2}$

46. -1 47. 3   48. $5 + 2\sqrt{2}$ 49. $2\sqrt{3} - 3\sqrt{2}$

50. $3\sqrt{5} + 4\sqrt{7}$ 51. $2 - 5\sqrt{2}$ 52. $\dfrac{4 + \sqrt{2}}{2}$

Chapter 12, Section F

1. $\dfrac{3\sqrt{2}}{2}$ 2. $\dfrac{\sqrt{26}}{2}$ 3. $\dfrac{5\sqrt{2}}{2}$ 4. $\dfrac{4\sqrt{5}}{25}$ 5. $-\dfrac{\sqrt{6}}{5}$

6. $\dfrac{\sqrt{5}}{5}$ 7. $\dfrac{\sqrt{42}}{4}$ 8. $\dfrac{\sqrt{33}}{6}$ 9. $\dfrac{3\sqrt{x}}{x}$ 10. $\dfrac{\sqrt{2y}}{3y}$

11. $\dfrac{\sqrt{10}}{8x}$ 12. $\dfrac{2\sqrt{2x}}{3x}$ 13. $\dfrac{4\sqrt{21t}}{21}$ 14. $\sqrt{2} - 1$ 15. $-2 - \sqrt{5}$

16. $\dfrac{8\sqrt{3} + 12}{3}$ 17. $\dfrac{4 + 3\sqrt{2}}{2}$ 18. $\dfrac{17 - 2\sqrt{70}}{-3}$ 19. $\dfrac{8 + 6\sqrt{x} + x}{4 - x}$

20. $\dfrac{x - \sqrt{5xy} - \sqrt{7xy} + y\sqrt{35}}{x - 5y}$ 21. a   22. c   23. a   24. a

25. e   26. c

Chapter 12, Section G

1. $x = \pm 2$ 2. $t = \pm 6$ 3. $y = \pm 2\sqrt{10}$ 4. $x = -8, x = -6$

5. $a = 1$ 6. $t = -15, t = -7$ 7. $x = 23$ 8. $x = 17\dfrac{3}{5}$

9. no solution   10. $x = 25$ 11. $m = 6$ 12. $t = \pm\sqrt{19}$

13. b   14. a   15. e   16. a   17. d

18. a   19. a   20. d   21. b   22. d

23. e   24. c   25. d

Chapter 12, Section H

1. 7   2. 5   3. 27   4. 216   5. 4

6. –4   7. –243   8. –243   9. $\frac{1}{4}$ 10. $\frac{1}{343}$

11. $\frac{1}{16}$ 12. $\frac{1}{5}$ 13. $\frac{1}{9}$ 14. $-\frac{1}{9}$ 15. $\frac{7}{2}$

16. $-\frac{3}{10}$ 17. a   18. d   19. d   20. d

19. d   20. d   21. c   22. a   23. a

24. c   25. e   26. b   27. d   28. c

29. b   30. c   31. e   32. d   33. e

31. e   32. d   33. e   34. c   35. a   36. b

Chapter 13, Section A

(See the next page.)

1 - 8.

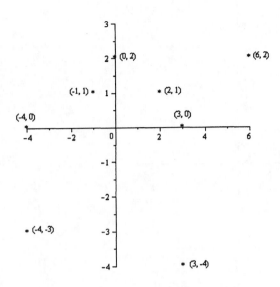

9. c   10. a   11. d   12. b   13. e

14. b   15. e   16. a   17. c   18. e

Chapter 13, Section B

1. c   2. d   3. a   4. b   5. e

6. a   7. e   8. c   9. $2\sqrt{17}$ 10. $2\sqrt{10}$

11. $2\sqrt{13}$ 12. no   13. $\sqrt{17}$ 14. 10   15. a

16. c   17. b   18. e

Chapter 13, Section C

1. Yes   2. Yes   3. Yes   4. Yes   5. No

6. No   7. Yes   8. No

9.

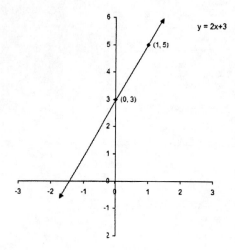

10.

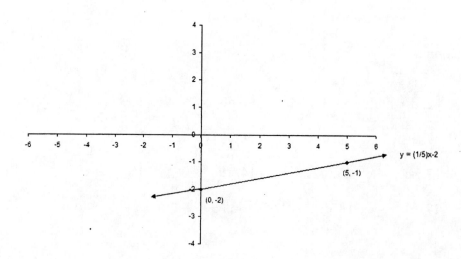

11.

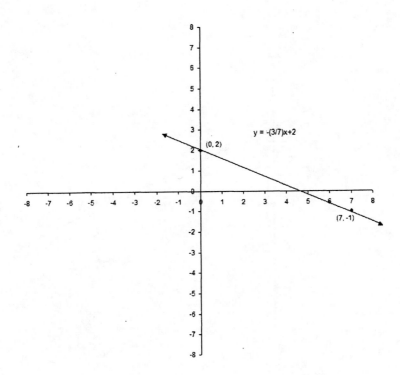

$y = -(3/7)x+2$

$(0, 2)$

$(7, -1)$

12.

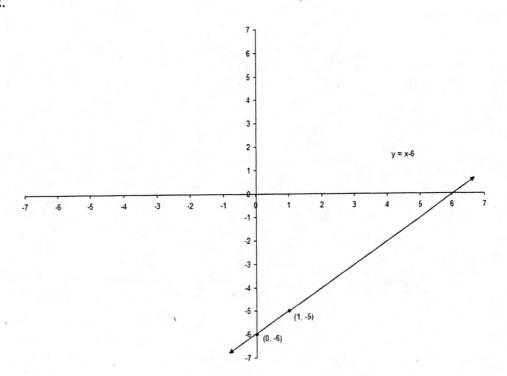

$y = x-6$

$(1, -5)$

$(0, -6)$

13.

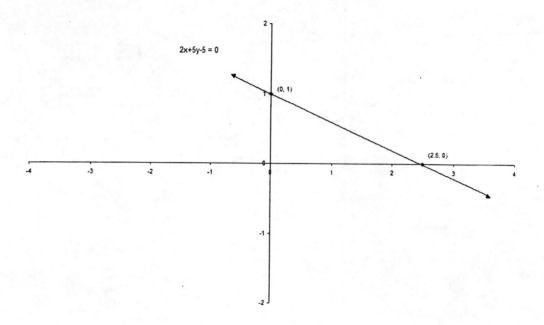

14.

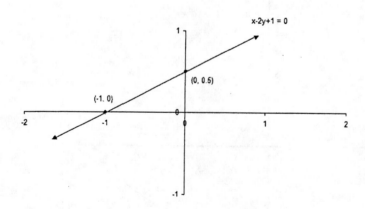

15. Yes   16. No   17. Yes   18. No   19. c

20. a   21. b   22. d   23. c   24. a

Chapter 13, Section D

1. -2 2. $-\dfrac{15}{2}$ 3. 2 4. $-\dfrac{14}{11}$ 5. 0

6. $\dfrac{3}{2}$ 7. d   8. b   9. a   10. b

11. c   12. e   13. c   14. d   15. c

16. d   17. a   18. c   19. d   20. slope $= 3$, y - intercept is $(0, 6)$

21. slope $= \dfrac{4}{11}$, y - intercept is $\left(0, -\dfrac{3}{11}\right)$ 22. slope $= -8$, y - intercept is $(0, -1)$

23. slope $= -\dfrac{1}{3}$, y - intercept is $(0, 2)$ 24. slope $= \dfrac{8}{3}$, y - intercept is $(0, 8)$

25. slope $= -\dfrac{5}{3}$, y - intercept is $\left(0, \dfrac{2}{3}\right)$ 26. slope $= 4$, y - intercept is $(0, 6)$

27. slope $= 0$, y - intercept is $(0, -1)$ 28. undefined slope, no y - intercept

29. undefined slope, no y - intercept   30. slope $= 0$, y - intercept is $(0, 3)$

31. b   32. a   33. a   34. e   35. c   36. c

37. b   38. e   39. b   40. d   41. a

Chapter 13, Section E

1. parallel   2. parallel   3. perpendicular   4. perpendicular   5. neither

6. neither   7. parallel   8. parallel   9. neither   10. perpendicular

11. neither   12. parallel   13. d   14. b   15. c

16. d   17. c   18. a   19. d   20. a   21. e

22. c   23. d   24. b

Chapter 13, Section F

1. yes   2. yes   3. no   4. no   5. yes

6. yes   7. no   8. no   9. $(1, 8)$ 10. $(1, -2)$

11. $\left(5\frac{2}{7}, -\frac{3}{7}\right)$ 12. $\left(3\frac{2}{3}, -34\right)$ 13. $(2, 4)$ 14. $(5, -3)$

15. $(5, -2)$ 16. $(-13, -9)$ 17. a   18. c

19. d   20. c   21. e   22. d   23. a

24. b   25. e

Chapter 13, Section G

1. c   2. b   3. e   4. a   5. b

6. c   7. e   8. a   9. c   10. a

11. a   12. d   13. b   14. c   15. a

Answers to Practice Prealgebra Tests

Practice Prealgebra Test A

1) e	2) a	3) b	4) c	5) a
6) d	7) e	8) d	9) b	10) c
11) a	12) b	13) d	14) c	15) e
16) b	17) d	18) b	19) a	20) c
21) b	22) c	23) a	24) d	25) e
26) c	27) d	28) b	29) a	30) e
31) d	32) c	33) c	34) a	35) e
36) b	37) c	38) a		

Practice Prealgebra Test B

1) b	2) b	3) e	4) c	5) d
6) a	7) e	8) a	9) b	10) d
11) a	12) c	13) b	14) e	15) d
16) d	17) c	18) b	19) a	20) e
21) d	22) b	23) c	24) e	25) e
26) b	27) c	28) a	29) d	30) e
31) c	32) b	33) d	34) a	35) d
36) a	37) c	38) b		

Practice Prealgebra Test C

1) c	2) a	3) b	4) e	5) d

6) c	7) b	8) a	9) c	10) d
11) e	12) b	13) b	14) d	15) a
16) c	17) e	18) d	19) b	20) b
21) a	22) e	23) c	24) d	25) e
26) b	27) a	28) b	29) c	30) d
31) c	32) b	33) e	34) e	35) e
36) b	37) a	38) d		

Answers to Practice Algebra Tests

Practice Algebra Test A

1) c	2) b	3) b	4) b	5) b
6) d	7) a	8) b	9) e	10) c
11) e	12) c	13) b	14) a	15) e
16) c	17) b	18) d	19) e	20) c
21) d	22) c	23) d	24) b	25) d
26) c	27) e	28) d	29) c	30) a
31) b	32) c	33) a	34) b	35) e
36) a	37) c	38) d		

Practice Algebra Test B

1) b	2) b	3) c	4) a	5) e
6) a	7) d	8) b	9) d	10) a
11) c	12) e	13) b	14) d	15) d
16) e	17) a	18) c	19) b	20) a
21) b	22) e	23) d	24) c	25) c
26) d	27) b	28) a	29) c	30) c
31) b	32) d	33) e	34) d	35) a
36) b	37) e	38) c		

Practice Algebra Test C

1) a	2) d	3) b	4) e	5) b

6) c	7) a	8) c	9) d	10) e
11) b	12) a	13) a	14) d	15) c
16) b	17) e	18) a	19) b	20) a
21) d	22) c	23) a	24) d	25) e
26) a	27) c	28) b	29) c	30) b
31) d	32) a	33) e	34) e	35) c
36) a	37) b	38) e		